the group RETREAT BOOK

the group RETREAT BOOK

By Arlo Reichter
& dozens of contributors

group BOOKS

P.O. Box 481
Loveland, CO 80539

THE GROUP RETREAT BOOK

Copyright © 1983 by Thom Schultz Publications, Inc.

Library of Congress Catalog No. 82-062532

Fourth printing

ISBN 0936-664-08-8

CREDITS

Edited by Gary Richardson
Designed by Jean Bruns

Art

Rick Bundshuh—76
Laurel Watson—cover design, 47, 48, 49, 50, 51, 52, 53

Photography

Tracy Borland—cover (top)
Jerry Bushey—16
Paul Conklin—79
Michael Goldberg—16, 17
Rick Kotter—18
Roger W. Neal—18
Thom Schultz—323
David Strickler—16, 17, 18, 132
Jim Whitmer—cover (bottom), 16, 17, 107

DEDICATION

The Group Retreat Book is dedicated to . . .

. . . the members and friends of First Baptist Church, Los Angeles, California

. . . and the thousands of professional and volunteer youth leaders and pastors who risk themselves to plan and lead life-changing retreats for young people.

ABOUT THE AUTHOR...

Dr. Arlo R. Reichter is the program director of the American Baptist Assembly (Green Lake, Wisconsin), the national conference center of the American Baptist Church. He was recently co-pastor of First Baptist Church of Los Angeles, California, where he served for more than a decade. During those years he directed the church's youth program and led several regional, national and worldwide youth events. He's led scores of retreats for youth groups, children, adults and families.

Dr. Reichter was raised in rural Iowa. He earned his bachelor's degree from Sioux Falls College, his master of divinity from American Baptist Seminary of the West, an additional master's degree from the University of Southern California and a doctor of ministry from the Jesuit School of Theology.

He has contributed to the **Respond** series, the **Retreat Handbook: A-Way to Meaning** and the **Vision for Leadership** series (all published by Judson Press).

Dr. Reichter is married to Dianne. They have two daughters, Kristi and Kari.

CONTENTS

Foreword

By Dennis C. Benson

I led the first retreat I ever attended! In fact, I had only been a youth advisor for three weeks. Fear filled me as I loaded the kids into the cars. As a freshman at the University of Michigan, I only knew that God had, for some reason, called me to spend my weekends with a wild bunch of high school young people in a small-town church. Suddenly, I was about to lead them into this strange thing called a retreat. My home youth group experience had never included such an event. Somehow we had missed the experience of a weekend away from home with just youth advisors and youth.

I didn't know how to plan the two-and-a-half days. Little preparation had been made. At the last minute, the two couples who were to aid me cancelled. One woman agreed to accompany us. No one had ever seen the retreat area, which turned out to be a small island on a deserted lake! Surely, there could be no problems if the youth stayed on the island. The single rowboat slowly made its way back and forth between the mainland and our secluded haven. It took an eternity of rowing to make our exodus from the world. Twenty-five folks finally took control of our new wilderness.

We found an amazing environment. There were yellow beds, spider webs, broken windows and a kitchen which would have been rejected even by the hardy wagon-train cooks of another age. Before I could find an answer for the problem raised by the fact that there was only one sleeping area for both males and females, the kids discovered the creative possibilities in throwing fully dressed members of the group into the brisk fall lake water. Just as I solved the problem of instant baptism, our volunteer cooks came to me in tears. The hot dog buns had somehow become a giant fishing lure behind the boat. We had been trolling with the basic ingredient of my planned weekend menu! How do you make sandwiches without bread?

Screams filled my ears as I was fighting the sense of fear which was about to overwhelm me. Twelve teenaged girls came pouring into the door. Everyone was talking at once. They were angry and excited about an unfolding drama. It seemed that the boys had stolen the toilet tissue from the women's bathroom. They wanted revenge. Before I

13

could sort out this crisis, the boys came streaming into my command post. They were carrying Bill. He had stepped on a nail. My adult advisor overlapped this scene with the announcement that there was no running water.

I wish that I could report a smashing and inspiring tale of how I pulled all of these problems into the world's most efficient retreat. I didn't. However, some wondrous things happened to all of us during those 72 hours apart from Brighton, Michigan. We cried, fought, laughed and fell in love with how God could work through all of us. A fusion of energies and gifts formed a community. Yes, we slept in one room, endured a strange menu, found the key to the water pump, reclaimed the toilet tissue, got Bill to a doctor, sang a lot and worshiped in such a way that God claimed our lives in a special way. It was this group of young people that helped me affirm the call of God in my life.

I am not suggesting that you base your youth ministry and the retreat event on ignorance. I suffered a great deal of guilt and pain that weekend. I owed the youth much more than I gave them. I was fortunate that God pulled us out of our confusion. What I needed—and what every person called to ministry with youth needs—was the support of other Christians. We are a historical people. It is vital that our faithful ministry rest upon the legacy of the saints who have preceded us and who are contemporary with us. Their witness and experience make our risks of ministry possible.

This book provides such a texture and context for your ministry. You may have done numerous retreats. Yet, even the most experienced leader will find the host of witnesses represented in this text helpful to his or her creative ministry with youth. We need the help of others to be the authentic representative of the Christian family. There is no place for the Lone Ranger as we lead others into the wilderness to walk with God.

The retreat is one of the most demanding and potent experiences available to both adults and youth. When we covenant to be an intentional people of God for a few hours or days, we join hands with sisters and brothers who have taken such journeys of growth over the past 4,000 years. Our fathers and mothers in the faith (Abraham and Sarah, Moses, Esther, Jesus and Paul) all followed God into a focused time apart.

This text shares many solid clues for the building of exciting retreat experiences. Yet, the forging of a faith community is based on authenticity. Even the most inexperienced youth advisor can enable a meaningful spiritual event for young people. The stories of these pages call you to bring together your own authenticity with the seasoned experience of other sojourners. You are the major ingredient in the whole process of creating a meaningful retreat.

Trust God's nudges and risk for your folks. The companionship of this book will provide you with the support you need for this movable feast: the retreat.

Dennis C. Benson
Pittsburgh, Pennsylvania

Retreats are . . .

. . . a special kind of tired

. . . lots of singing

. . . forgiveness & reconciliation

. . . lugging gear

... learning & encountering

... games &
fun stuff

... friendships

... prayers

"And Jesus took with him Peter and James and John, and led them up a high mountain apart by themselves; and he was transfigured before them . . ."

...growing
spiritually

Today's young disciples also search for the living Christ. You can help them find him at that powerful mountaintop experience: the retreat . . .

...a new
start

PART 1

The Retreat Planning Guide

An exhaustive "how-to" approach for your step-by-step retreat planning, execution and follow-up.

CHAPTER 1:

Get Started Right: Writing Retreat Purposes & Goals

"**W**e want to go swimming. That's what we came here for." My friend, the retreat director, had a nasty insurrection on his hands. He'd planned the entire retreat by himself (and he was proud of it) for the purpose of helping young people and their sponsors grow in the faith.

He assumed everyone else had the same purpose in mind, even though no one actually discussed purposes and goals with each other.

Fortunately, everything worked out okay. After some on-the-spot planning and some humorous logistical hangups, the young people went swimming. And many of the retreat participants grew in the faith.

My friend could have saved himself, and everyone else, unneeded tense moments by answering one very important question.

WHY DO WE DO RETREATS?

"Why do we do retreats?" is a question that's well worth your time as you consider your church's overall youth program. Reflect for a moment and then jot down your responses to that question. Your youth, their parents and the congregation's leadership should also ask themselves that question.

Worthy goals for retreats include fun, fellowship, recreation, Bible study, issues study, discipleship and faith-growth. Any one retreat may include several of these goals or others which you find important. Whatever the goals, it is important for everyone who attends a specific retreat to have the same goals in mind.

A general purpose statement for all retreats might be: "The purpose of a retreat is to set apart a time and place from the ordinary events of life during which a specific group of people can relate to one another

"Why do we do retreats?" is a question you, your sponsors and your young people should answer. This chapter helps you write a general purpose retreat statement that sets the basis for specific planning.

through a variety of modes centered around a common theme."

Well in advance of any specific retreat, meet with the appropriate board or committee of your church and develop a general purpose statement for retreats. Alter the previous suggested purpose statement so that it becomes a general retreat statement for your church. After agreeing on a multipurpose retreat statement, discuss it with the youth group or a youth group representative.

After accepting the purpose statement, it's time to list specific goals such as:

•Build closer relationships
•Develop better understandings of God's Word
•In-depth study of issues faced by youth
•Study of a current social issue

Brainstorm a list of goals which your church's retreats might have. Involve youth and adults in this step. Everyone who agreed to the purpose statement should also be involved in the listing of possible goals.

SPECIFIC RETREAT GOALS

Once a purpose statement and a variety of goal statements are agreed upon and a retreat experience seems appropriate, the planning group for a specific event can determine which of the goals apply for that particular event. The planning group should also, of course, review the general purpose statement. The purpose statement and the various goals are guidelines and shouldn't be seen as unchangeable. Consider annual goal-setting sessions.

Goals for a specific retreat should be based on the particular needs of the youth group and the individual members of the group who will be a part of the retreat they are planning.

It is helpful to project the general flow of retreat experiences one year at a time. A possible retreat flow:

Fall Retreat (October, November, December)
Winter Retreat (January, February, March)
Spring Retreat (April, May, June)
Summer Retreat (July, August September)

If this is the general flow of retreats, then a planning group might want to project tentative goals for each event. This is not to say that specific goals aren't important. But the year-long plan helps to cover a variety of needs during the year. It also adds variety to the events for the participants. General goals might be:

Fall Retreat	Building of relationships
	Getting to know new group members
Winter Retreat	Developing a better understanding of God's Word, in-depth Bible study
Spring Retreat	Understanding missions and other world issues
Summer Retreat	Personal issues, in-depth

This suggested flow of general goals is based upon a constant growing and maturing of relationships between the retreat participants which allows them to share deeper and deeper personal issues and a more mature understanding of faith.

When considering the purpose and goals of retreats, an excellent book to use as a study book with an adult group or the leaders of the youth fellowship is **Faith Shaping** by Stephen D. Jones (Judson Press, 1980).

YOUTH PROGRAM COMPONENTS

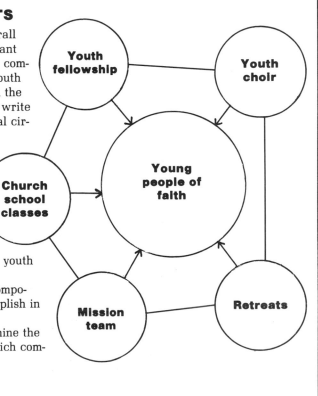

Retreats are only one component of your overall youth program. Even though they are an important part, retreats are only one of several important components. To illustrate the components of your youth program try a simple diagram: Draw a circle in the center of a sheet of paper (see illustration) and write in it "Young people of faith." Then draw several circles on the rest of the paper with arrows pointing toward this central circle. In these circles write the various components of your youth program and draw lines connecting these component circles. This illustration of your youth program should accomplish three things:

1. Illustrate the various components of your youth program,

2. Help you to realize that any one of the components cannot accomplish all you want to accomplish in your youth program, and

3. Begin a process by which you can determine the compatible goals of the various components which combine to make an effective ministry with youth.

BE REALISTIC ABOUT RETREATS

A word of caution before we move on to the planning process for a specific retreat. **Be realistic with the goals you set.** Any one retreat is limited in what it can accomplish. Focus on a few goals for a retreat and meet some of them. Focus on a large number of goals and end up frustrated for not having accomplished any.

The Holiday Inn Camper

I'll never forget the day I got my nickname—the Holiday Inn Camper. I was chaperoning my first youth retreat, and I was beginning to wonder why. Already, I had been installed into the Order of the Fork. (A group of obviously crazed retreaters, during the breakfast hour, apply a fork to an unmentionable spot on the backside of one's body.) And I had also spent the night being serenaded by a variety of very bad bird calls and a unison rendition of 12½ cuckoos (delivered precisely at 12:30 a.m.). But the nickname didn't really catch on until one of the teenagers saw me wandering around mumbling, "Where's the outlet for the curling iron?"

After that, there were young people sweeping out my tent (no floor) every hour and hanging No-pest Strips all around me. Then, when someone noticed I had brought along a blouse with a "dry clean only" label, I began to see that I was never going to hear the end of it. "Why me?" I started groaning to myself, but I didn't expect to get my answer so soon.

"I never before realized how much I love the Lord," one of the teenagers smiled as we gazed into our crackling fire that night.

"I know," replied another, "and I never knew anyone cared enough about me to take me camping anywhere."

Holiday Inn Camper though I may be, I guess I can live without shag carpeting and air conditioning for a weekend every so often after all.

Denise Turner

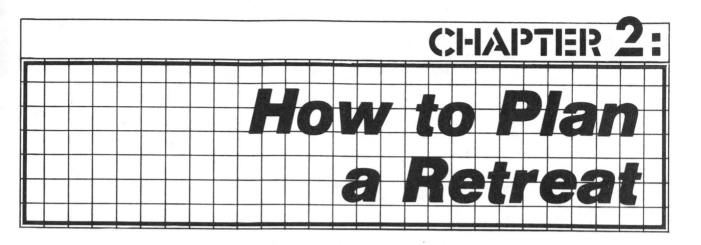

CHAPTER 2:

How to Plan a Retreat

PLANNING PROCESS CHECKLIST:

_____*Establish Purpose and Goals*
_____*Select Planning Group*
_____*Program Content and Style*
_____*Leadership Recruitment*
_____*Budgeting*
_____*Publicity and Promotion*
_____*Coordination with Church Program*
_____*Parental Involvement*

Planning is a process that takes time and teamwork. This chapter gets you headed toward planning a smooth-running and life-changing retreat.

This chapter will deal in general with the eight steps of the planning process. Subsequent chapters will deal in more depth with a number of the areas.

Planning is a "process" that takes time and the involvement of many persons. The first thing to keep in mind regarding any specific retreat is that you must begin well in advance of the actual event so that each step of the planning process will have adequate time to be accomplished.

ESTABLISH PURPOSE AND GOALS

The first step in the planning process relates to the subject of the previous chapter—purposes and goals. You shouldn't begin the planning process for a specific retreat until you've written a general purpose statement and brainstormed a list of retreat goals. If that purpose statement and the various goals are in place, then the planning for a specific retreat can begin.

The planning process should begin at least six months in advance of the event. That may very well mean you have started the planning process for a future retreat before you have completed some prior retreat. But it is important to begin early. Facilities may not be available if your planning begins too late; the leadership you want may not be available at a short notice; the finances you need may not be available without some prior fund raising efforts.

Recently I received a call from a member of the college-age group in another church who had attended a retreat I had led. She was looking for a facility for a retreat scheduled for a month from that day. While I gave her several referrals, I told her that I seriously doubted she would find any vacancy that near to the time of need. (She didn't find space and the retreat had to be postponed six weeks.)

Each year in July, I request the campsite for our January retreat, and usually by the last of August, the camp is filled for the winter schedule.

What are the reasons for a youth group to travel, retreat or have work projects?

1. Getting acquainted in a "neutral" setting. Many of us work with youth who are unchurched and "getting away from it all" (church, family, school, the city, suburbia, etc.) provides a setting in which youth can become better acquainted with other youth and with their counselors.

2. We all need a break from the rush of life wherever we are and just being away provides an opportunity for personal renewal.

3. Roles such as "son of Deacon Brown" or "Associate Minister" do not get in the way of building relationships.

4. Time restrictions—such as youth programs must end by 7:30 p.m. for the evening service—are not as much a problem at a retreat.

5. It gives a chance to really deal with some of life's questions over a concentrated period of time. Bible study and discussions have a chance to settle in the minds overnight with more discussion the next day.

6. Youth on trips are able to meet new friends in other churches, cities, countries and there is rich sharing.

7. Youth and leaders may get new ideas about their "back home" youth group by sharing with other groups.

8. Education through experience is real on a youth trip. "Reconciliation," "separation," "community," "trust," etc., become real as they become a part of a group's experience.

9. Youth have a chance to work and serve others.

SELECT A PLANNING GROUP

After setting general purposes and goals, your first step is to select a planning group. Include youth and adults in this group and don't make it so large that it can't function—five or six members is adequate. If necessary, have the group approved by the appropriate church board or committee.

The planning group should first look at the overall purpose statement and the list of goals, then select realistic goals based on their young people's needs. The planning group might begin by answering these questions: "What is a current concern of the persons who will be attending this retreat?" "What does the group need?" "Who will be attending?"

PLANNING GROUP QUESTIONS

- *Who will be attending the retreat?*
- *What are the interests of those who will attend?*
- *What are the interpersonal needs of those who will attend?*
- *What are the faith needs of those who will attend?*
- *What are the social issues of concern to those who will attend?*
- *What should be the focus of this retreat?*
- *What goals are realistic for this retreat?*

After working through the appropriate questions, set specific goals for the retreat. You may want to test these out with more youth and adults in the church before making a final decision.

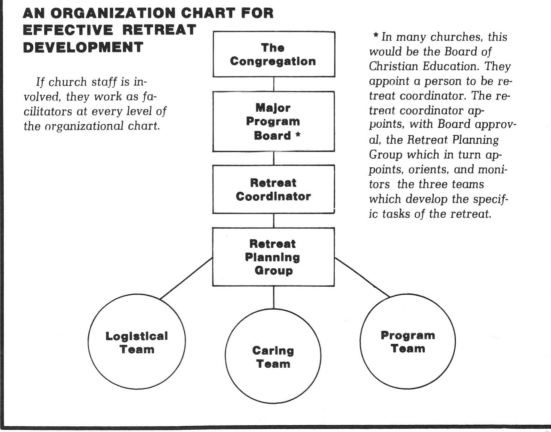

AN ORGANIZATION CHART FOR EFFECTIVE RETREAT DEVELOPMENT

If church staff is involved, they work as facilitators at every level of the organizational chart.

The Congregation

Major Program Board *

Retreat Coordinator

Retreat Planning Group

Logistical Team

Caring Team

Program Team

* In many churches, this would be the Board of Christian Education. They appoint a person to be retreat coordinator. The retreat coordinator appoints, with Board approval, the Retreat Planning Group which in turn appoints, orients, and monitors the three teams which develop the specific tasks of the retreat.

PROGRAM CONTENT AND STYLE

Once the purpose and goals are clarified and affirmed, consider the retreat program content and style. Is the content personal issue oriented? Bible study oriented? social issue oriented? The content will, of course, be directed toward accomplishing the goals you've chosen for the retreat.

The "style" is another important issue to discuss. Will the style be:

- Small group interaction
- Speaker
- Audio-visual input
- Individual study
- A combination of two or more of these styles

As you consider the retreat's style, remember that the best learning happens when persons are taking part in the learning process.

PLANNING AND PRAYER

Inviting the presence of God into the planning team work and into the life of the retreat is necessary to the planning process.

As you begin to consider the resources suggested in this book, and as you review the retreat designs, allow yourself to be open to the rich possibilities which retreats will have for you and your group.

LEADERSHIP RECRUITMENT

After the planning group members agree on the retreat's content and style, they will be ready to consider the retreat's leadership needs. Basically three teams of leaders are needed for any retreat.

RESPONSIBILITIES:

Logistical Team facilities, transportation, cooking, sleeping, etc.
Caring Team individual emotional needs, discipline, etc.
Program Team input and interaction sessions and "free-time" activities. (You may want a separate "free-time" team, but they should work closely with the program team to coordinate efforts.)

For some retreats the same people must manage all three areas of need; for others, you'll have different people working in the three areas. It's a good idea to have one youth and one adult on your planning team be responsible for working with each leadership team. See chapter 8 for ideas on recruiting leaders.

BUDGETING

Each of the teams should begin early to consider its budget needs. The teams should present their financial needs to the planning group, which coordinates the finances and ultimately determines the retreat budget. Budgeting the retreat is treated in detail in chapter five. A general observation: having good leadership costs money. Perhaps the expense is providing the transportation, lodging and food for the leaders. Perhaps the cost includes an honorarium for a major speaker or facilitator for the event. Whatever the leadership needs, they must be remembered when it comes to the budget step.

PUBLICITY AND PROMOTION

Publicity and promotion are essential procedures which must not be overlooked. Your plans may be the best ever made, your speaker or facilitator might be a great person, the camp might offer wonderful facilities, but if you don't get that word out, it won't make any difference. Publicity and promotion are covered in detail in chapter seven. As a general rule, early publicity never hurts a retreat—late publicity can kill it.

PERSONAL GOAL-SETTING

In the column below, have each person list all of his or her goals (make new friends, meet some girls, grow closer to God, etc.) for an upcoming retreat. Share these in pairs. Each evening, give your group time to fill in their charts, using the symbols presented in the LEGEND. At the end of the week, have everyone share goals once again with partners.

GOALS	DAY 1	DAY 2	DAY 3	DAY 4	DAY 5

--- LEGEND ---

Mountaintop Experience: Surmounted most expectations; GREAT! Very moving.

Hilltop Experience: A little less than a Mountaintop. Fulfilled most expectations.

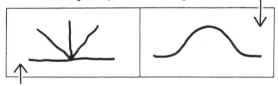

Flatlands: Average, run-of-the-mill experience. No real highs or lows.

Swamp: The pits; far below expectations. I need to climb out of this.

Ben Sharpton

COORDINATION WITH CHURCH PROGRAM

Coordination of the retreat with overall church programming is important so that it is compatible both in program and in timing with other major church events. One year, our church planned a major youth retreat for the same weekend as an annual parents' group retreat in the church to which the youth were invited. Result: a cancelled youth retreat. Another important factor in coordinating the retreat with the overall church programming is the "report back" to be given by the retreat participants to a group within the church or to the entire congregation. Coordination is important!

You're Special

An all-church retreat is a perfect setting to give special recognition to an outstanding church member! We recognized our church organist for 25 years of voluntary service. It was a complete surprise for her! We gave her a chime clock with a "Thank You" engraved on an attached plaque. She'll never forget the experience. Neither will we.

Ruby Becher

PARENTAL INVOLVEMENT

The final step in the planning process relates to how the parents are involved. While some parents might be on the planning group, all parents should be kept informed regarding the retreat plans. This may take the form of a pre-retreat meeting for parents (or for parents and youth). Parental involvement might take the form of a special newsletter to the parents explaining retreat policies, goals, etc. It is also important to report back to the parents as a part of the follow-up to a retreat. The parents should know what goals were accomplished, what needs which surfaced should be discussed at home, etc. There are many possibilities and this also needs to be a part of the planning process.

A code phrase with many Christian educators is "trust the process." The planning of any retreat is a very important process which takes time, but you'll find the payoff when the retreat runs smoothly and the established goals are met.

CHAPTER 3:
Choosing the Best Location

One of the first retreats I planned was for a group of 30 youth. My plans called for the entire group to be together some of the time and for them to share ideas and feelings in small groups in the same room at other times. Since I hadn't seen the retreat setting (a major mistake), I didn't realize the only room available for the program was small and had a large, round stone fireplace in the middle. Needless to say, it was nearly impossible for everyone to see the speaker. The small groups were jammed uncomfortably together. The discussions competed with noise from the other groups. I learned about facilities the hard way!

WHERE TO BEGIN

The planning process becomes very practical as you start thinking about a specific retreat. You may be fortunate enough to have to decide between the mountains or the seashore for a retreat location. On the other hand, you may have no choice at all. Whatever your situation, begin considering potential locations by having the planning group review the retreat's purpose and style. For instance, needing many separate locations for small groups will determine the kind of facility you need. Or, if you have a group of 10 to 12 participants, you'll not want a retreat center that seats 100.

COSTS

Retreat centers vary greatly in accommodations and in fees they charge. Developing and maintaining a file of available retreat centers gives you a variety of locations to consider.

Geographical proximity is also important in scheduling and planning a retreat. Transportation costs must be considered. (Chapter four will deal with this in detail.) Also consider the amount of time necessary to get to and return from the retreat location. Travel time determines the amount of time during which program content can be shared. The prox-

The mountains? Seashore? Primitive camping? Church basement? Where you choose to hold your retreat contributes greatly to whether or not you meet your goals. This chapter helps you decide on the retreat location that's just right for you.

imity of the retreat center to other facilities which may be required is also important, i.e., ski lifts, lake, ocean, etc.

To assemble such a file, get information from sources such as other local churches who may own or know of retreat centers, denominational offices, Boy Scouts, YMCA, YWCA (and other community groups), city and county governments, departments of recreation, etc. Also check with national and state parks for available facilities. You might want to develop a retreat location file with a number of other churches in your community as a cooperative effort.

A LOCATION CHECKLIST

You can develop a checklist which will help you determine the appropriateness of a particular retreat center for any specific retreat. Here's a checklist I've used successfully:

RETREAT CENTER CHECKLIST

CENTER	Oakdale	1000 Pines	Boy Scout Camp	St. Francis
Capacity:				
Location:				
Costs:				
Flexibility:				
Dorms:				
Facilities:				
Climate:				
Insurance:				
Safety/Medical:				
Other:				
Contact & Address:				

Once you've selected a center, use the same type of checklist to get details your young people will ask you about: "How long will it take to get there?" "Can my four friends and I stay in the same room?" "What kind of clothing and bedding do I need to take?" You probably know the questions!

RETREAT CENTER EXPECTATIONS

Camp managers have a difficult task in maintaining camp policies and facilities. Knowing their expectations in advance will help in your work with them.

Tensions and frustrations grow quickly if you're not sensitive to their expectations. For instance, I once directed a retreat where I thought the camp manager understood that my young people were planning to prepare the food. But it became apparent quite early that the camp manager's wife didn't share this understanding. She quoted camp regulations regarding youth not being allowed in the kitchen as she shooed my teenage cooks away. I spent quite a bit of time clarifying expectations necessary with the camp manager and his wife. Clarifying expectations with everyone in camp positions saves time, effort and frustration.

The retreat center will have specific expectations of you and your group before, during and after the retreat. It is good to clarify these expectations early in the negotiations so that you don't overlook any of them. Develop a "Retreat Center Expectations" worksheet such as the example provided (see next page). Time limits and responsibility assignments for each expectation help you and your group be accountable.

Camp facilities exist for the service of many different groups. As you utilize these facilities, you need to be considerate of the staff and the facilities. A goal my groups keep in mind is to leave a retreat facility in better condition than we found it. This is good stewardship and communicates appreciation to the camp staff more than anything else.

Putting Up the Tent

The first night of our traveling retreat, we had no problem putting up the big green monster eight-man tent. But the second night was a different story. We had traveled about 200 miles in 90° weather to reach Mesa Verde National Monument in Southwest Colorado. We started to put up the big green tent but none of the aluminum poles would go together. We tried everything: grease, water, prayer, gentle persuasion, hammer persuasion. Girls tried and guys tried. Nothing we could do worked.

We gave up and took some long hot and cold showers. We returned to the camp after dark and tried the poles once more. The poles fit together. Apparently, the heat had affected the poles, and after they had cooled they fit together nicely.

Bruce Nichols

RETREAT CENTER EXPECTATIONS

	Who's Responsible?	When does it need to be completed?
Before the Retreat:		
During the Retreat:		
After the Retreat:		

CHAPTER 4

Getting There: Tips for Transporting Your Group

Funny things happen when you take 25 kids from a little town in Kansas to the mountains. And, funny things happen when you take 25 kids from inner Detroit to the uninhabited wilderness of northern Michigan.

Funny things happen, all right, but beautiful things happen too. Some kids find themselves. Some kids find new, close friends within their group. And some kids find God.

Lots of things happen when a Christian youth group travels to retreat centers.

Transportation is one of the most important aspects of the trip that requires careful decisions.

The purpose and goals of your retreat and the size of your group will affect your transportation needs. Consider the interaction that takes place between young people as you travel to and from a retreat site. This interaction can be an important part of the retreat experience, even an effective aspect of the program. The planning group should discuss how the transportation experience might be designed to contribute to the goals for the retreat.

Here are some strategies which might make the idea of transportation as "program" understandable:

1. If your retreat plan uses small groups and you are traveling to the retreat center in cars, assign each group or half of each group (depending on the size of the groups) to a car. They can begin interacting with each other on their way to the retreat center. You may want to guide their discussions as they travel, such as having them discover some family history, special interests, etc.

The retreat experience starts when your young people step onto a bus or wiggle into the back seat of a subcompact. Getting to a retreat location can be a memorable experience. This chapter gives you notes on insurance, permission forms, safety and different methods of "getting there."

2. If you have some retreat interaction planned in pairs, assign car or bus seats so the young people are paired with their retreat partner.

3. If you are traveling in a large bus, direct some low-key interaction which will not distract the driver.

4. Perhaps you'll take an unusual mode of transportation. We have traveled to a weekend retreat by train—one of those unforgettable experiences which contribute to our group's history and life. How about other modes: bicycles, horses, boats, etc. Again, the retreat's purpose and goals should be well served by the way you travel together.

It is important that the planning group understands your church's transportation policies. If you are not aware of any policies, ask the pastor or the board responsible for the operation of the church. If there is no policy, suggest to the board that it develop such a statement. Some items for a policy might be:

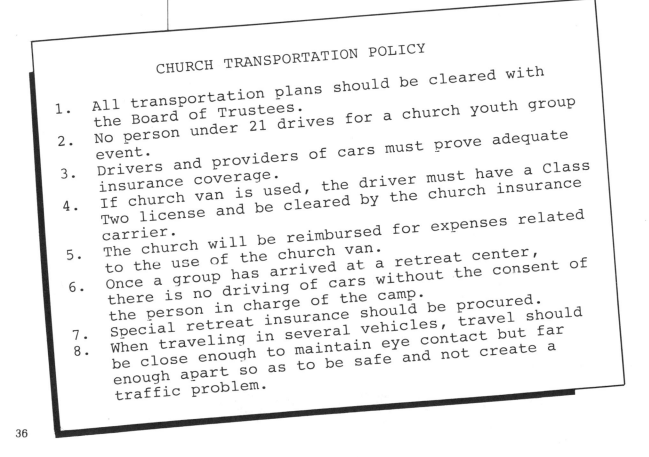

CHURCH TRANSPORTATION POLICY

1. All transportation plans should be cleared with the Board of Trustees.
2. No person under 21 drives for a church youth group event.
3. Drivers and providers of cars must prove adequate insurance coverage.
4. If church van is used, the driver must have a Class Two license and be cleared by the church insurance carrier.
5. The church will be reimbursed for expenses related to the use of the church van.
6. Once a group has arrived at a retreat center, there is no driving of cars without the consent of the person in charge of the camp.
7. Special retreat insurance should be procured.
8. When traveling in several vehicles, travel should be close enough to maintain eye contact but far enough apart so as to be safe and not create a traffic problem.

INSURANCE

Insurance is a necessary part of a retreat experience. Determine what coverage is needed for the entire retreat experience. Do this early in your planning process. Many insurance companies offer low-cost inclusive coverage for weekend retreats and other youth events. While none of us expects an accident, accidents do happen. The young people and their families deserve adequate insurance protection.

Church vans and buses are becoming more and more popular forms of retreat transportation. A church-owned vehicle can keep the cost of transportation at a reasonable level. If you plan on using a church-owned vehicle, notify the person or group responsible for the vehicle several weeks before you plan to use it so the van or bus can be safety checked and prepared for the trip. Also be certain that your drivers have the proper license and are experienced in driving the vehicle to be used. If the route is complicated (most retreat centers are located in hard to find places), give maps and specific directions to each driver. Make sure you have adequate space for the young people to stow their belongings and any program materials you need at the retreat site. Overcrowding and overloading a vehicle contributes to unsafe conditions, not to mention nasty attitudes. Enlist drivers well in advance of the retreat so last-minute decisions regarding who will drive won't tempt you to ask anyone who's available.

Schedule commercial vehicles (Greyhound, Trailways, etc.) with professional drivers well in advance. Some carriers require a cash deposit. Clarify those charges before scheduling as well as specific times the bus is needed. Ask the carrier for a list of general passenger regulations. Also determine what insurance coverage the carrier has for your group and decide the type of additional coverage you need. Most commercial carriers will send a bill or present a bill in writing. Paying promptly will insure you of receiving good service in the future.

> ## Lost
>
> Whenever retreat time rolls around, we sponsors are always very careful about making sure that all our drivers are over the age of 18. Once, however, we booked a retreat site less than 15 miles from home and we decided to allow a couple of 16-year-olds to drive there. One of those teenagers, a much honored Boy Scout, left the church in a car loaded with compasses. Three hours later, we called the State Police.
>
> Soon, the authorities brought us a carload of kids accompanied by a very red-faced driver (who had gotten lost before he had even made it to the highway).
>
> Soon the episode was apparently forgotten and we had a successful retreat (on the topic of forgiveness, no less). And today our group still kids about its Boy Scout who got lost.
>
> Denise Turner

SAFETY

Whether using a church bus, vans, cars or a commercial bus, everyone should understand the need for safety. You may want to review the following "Ten Commandments for Passengers" with the planning group, adapting or changing it for your situation. Give each person in your group a copy and discuss each point before leaving.

TEN COMMANDMENTS FOR PASSENGERS

1. Thou shalt not litter inside or outside the bus.
2. Thou shalt not use flashlights or other lights in the bus.
3. Thou shalt not play loud music or sports events.
4. Thou shalt not be a back seat driver.
5. Thou shalt not stick anything (arm, leg, friend) out the window.
6. Thou shalt sit on the seat facing forward.
7. Thou shalt keep thy conversation at a reasonable level.
8. Thou shalt assist the driver in loading and unloading the luggage.
9. Thou shalt help to make thy trip a safe one.
10. Thou shalt express appreciation to the driver for a safe trip.

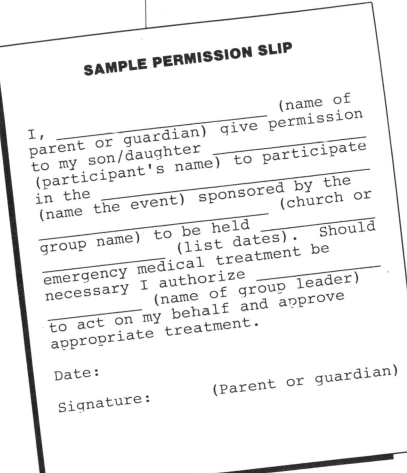

SAMPLE PERMISSION SLIP

I, _____ (name of parent or guardian) give permission to my son/daughter _____ (participant's name) to participate in the _____ (name the event) sponsored by the _____ (church or group name) to be held _____ (list dates). Should emergency medical treatment be necessary I authorize _____ (name of group leader) to act on my behalf and approve appropriate treatment.

Date:

Signature: _____ (Parent or guardian)

PERMISSION SLIPS

Each person in your group should give you signed permission slips and release of liability statements. The permission slip is a simple statement which assures you that the young person's parents or guardian have given permission for the young people to attend the event. This slip should also authorize some adult on the trip to approve emergency medical treatment should that be necessary. The release of liability statement, while not being legally binding in most states, at least "puts in writing" the intention of the parent or guardian in the event that some incident does take place. Your church board should set a policy regarding the use of a permission slip and a release of liability statement and review the wording to determine what is appropriate. The board may wish to consult an attorney or their insurance carrier. These statements are important, not only regarding the transportation but the smooth functioning of the entire experience. Take the permission slips with you on the trip. Leave the release of liability forms at the church.

Psychologists consider traveling as a major life event—something that startles and alters our normal day-to-day living. Changes often come about from such experiences. The opportunity is here for your group to make lasting positive changes in your members—through the experience of a group trip.

SAMPLE RELEASE OF LIABILITY STATEMENT

We the parents or legal guardian of _____ (participant's name) do hereby release from any liability _____ (list the church name) and any and all adult sponsors or church staff in the event of any accident enroute, during and returning from _____ (name the event). We further express our appreciation for the church organization of the event and the adults who are giving their time for the event to happen.

Date:

Signature: _____ (Parent or guardian)

INVOLVE EVERYONE

Make sure everyone has a specific responsibility during the trip to and from the retreat. Examples: An oil and water team (checks oil and water every time the group stops); a window-washing team; a clean-out-the-vehicle team; a nose-counting team to make sure everyone's present before moving on; a luggage-loading team; a pop break team (ices down your soda pop supply and rations it to the passengers).

The youth group at Thief River Falls, Minnesota, really gets involved in creating the travel magic. At the beginning of each planning year, the group selects a committee to help plan the different trips. Each high school year gets two representatives (two freshmen, two sophomores and so on). The leaders do most of the footwork, but nothing is definite until the youth planning team makes the final decision.

This group also gets people involved with each other by having daily seat assignments during the travel periods. "That way, everyone has a chance to get to know everyone else in the group," says Jim Mattson, the group's leader. "And it works just great. Now, everyone in the group looks forward to sitting with someone new each day."

Here are some options for group transportation:

Church bus

This is doubtless the easiest and most economical form of group transportation. Even if your church bus is not fancy, it will serve well for cross-country treks. Many church youth groups take their buses (school bus type) on 5,000- to 10,000-mile trips every year. If your church does not own a bus, you should be able to actually buy one for much less than it would cost you to charter a Greyhound for a couple of weeks. Check with local used bus sales firms.

Rented school bus

Many local bus companies rent buses to groups. You supply the driver. Check the yellow pages or your school district.

Charter bus (Greyhound type)

You may charter a fine bus, complete with air conditioning and bathroom. The prices and packages vary. Shop around for the trip package that best suits your group. These buses hold from 38 to 46 passengers, depending upon the bus style. For more information, you may call Greyhound toll-free at 800-528-0447.

Cars

For a small group, this is okay. Be sure to plan for relief drivers. Larger groups have a tendency to become separated in a number of ways if your members are spread out over several vehicles.

Bus Fun

Whether you're lounging in a high-back seat on a chartered Greyhound or bouncing along in your church's recycled school bus, those traveling hours can become long.

Here are a few suggestions to help make the time spent on the bus fly by faster.

Foreign Tourists

Pick up a hitchhiker after you've conspired with your group to change your identities for the visitor. As your bus driver opens the door for the hitchhiker, he says in a thick British accent, "I say, climb aboard, old chap." Everybody on the bus then commences to converse with the hitchhiker in a British accent. He will no doubt question you about your home country. Keep up the gag until just before your visitor disembarks, then start talking in your normal way. If your group can keep up the British routine for a long period without laughing, consider yourselves experts. You can use any accent you wish; Oklahoman, Brooklyn, German are other favorites.

Seat Cram

See how many people you can stuff into one seat. Then, if you're really ambitious, try to fall asleep that way.

Talent Show

Give everybody 30 minutes to come up with an act to be presented to everyone else. Encourage solo or group acts. These hasty talent shows often turn out to be very hilarious.

Sightseeing Tours

One of your members gets up in front of the bus and narrates a "tour." (Example: "Ladies and gentlemen, if you'll now turn your attention to the right-hand side of the bus, you'll see this city's gravest danger to its citizens—the city water supply." If you've got a crazy, creative kid with a good sense of humor, this tour bit can really be funny.

Shoe Thief

At night, if people are asleep, take everybody's shoes and your own and stuff them into the minister's or sponsor's seat with him. Then accuse him of stealing everyone's shoes in his sleep. Ask him if he's ever had his dreams analyzed.

Charades

This is an old favorite that adapts nicely to bus travel.

The Wave

Select an oncoming car or hitchhiker and have everyone gather on that side of the bus.

And as you pass the car or pedestrian, have everyone slowly wave in unison in a broad, sweeping motion. The looks on the faces of the strangers are priceless.

Abandoned Sponsor

While one of your sponsors is in the rest room at the gas station, have another sponsor move the bus out of sight. Then watch the look on your sponsor's face as he sees that he was left behind.

Cuddly Teddy

Find a married sponsor or minister on your bus. When he is asleep, give him a teddy bear or other stuffed toy. Watch him cuddle up to it.

I'm All Tied Up

Select a person who sleeps soundly. Once your victim is asleep, tie him up with rope, yarn, tape or whatever is handy. Tie him securely to the seat. Then wake him up and go to dinner.

WORSHIP ON TRIPS

If your trip to a retreat or camp site takes more than one day, be sure to set aside time for worship. This type of worship could be one of the most touching experiences of the entire retreat.

Some groups prefer a first-thing-in-the-morning worship. Others prefer a last-thing-in-the-evening worship. Some do both. Some place the worship at a different time each day. Beware of the last-thing-in-the-evening time. Usually everybody is really pooped by this time of the day, and many kids may drift off to sleep during a prayer.

It's a good idea to form a worship committee before departure. This group of kids and leaders is then responsible for each day's worship. Some plans and worship outlines should be set before the trip. But, the worship committee should also meet to specifically design each worship, taking into consideration the day's happenings, experiences and feelings.

Trips offer a beautiful opportunity to "watch God work." Some groups include a "God-watching" session in each worship, where the members relate experiences from the previous 24 hours where they've seen God at work. A typical response might be, "When we made that wrong turn yesterday, we were able to stop and help those newlyweds get their car unstuck from the mud. If we wouldn't have made the wrong turn, who knows how long they would have been stranded. I think God had something to do with that."

Music is a central part of worship too. Be sure those with musical talent bring along their instruments—unless, of course, they happen to play something like a piano. Also be sure to pack some songbooks.

Members with a talent for writing should be enlisted to write a trip journal.

Floating Candles

We held a retreat candlelight service that made a lasting impression on everyone. We went to the lakeside, each sat a small candle on a waxed paper plate and sealed it fast with hot wax. Then we floated our lighted candles out onto the lake as we sang "How Great Thou Art."

We then discussed how much the candles were like our lives: Some traveling together, some apart, some sinking, etc. The discussion took no urging. Some candles stayed alight far into the night and some plates were still floating the next morning. Several people got up in the middle of the night to see what the candles were doing.

Ruby Becher
Defiance, Ohio

42

CHAPTER 5:

Setting a Budget That Works

itting down to add up retreat costs of transportation, food, lodging and conference fees can be a deflating experience.

Take heart. It's really not as bad as it looks.

First, you have the assurance that retreats are done all the time, all over, by groups of all sizes.

And, your members certainly do not need to be independently wealthy to participate in your retreat.

You can add to the retreat's effectiveness by cutting down on financial headaches. This chapter provides a simple budget worksheet which will help you balance retreat costs with retreat income.

As you consider the budget, realize once again that the retreat's purpose and goals have an impact on the financial support required. The retreat may be for a very small number (a youth officers' retreat, for example) which requires some outside leadership. Or, the retreat may include 100 teenagers using your church's leader. Or, the goal might be to include some young people on scholarships who cannot afford to pay their own way. Or, a goal might be to provide each young person with a copy of a book being used as the focus of the retreat study.

Obvious costs involve transportation, the retreat center, food, etc. The tendency is to budget first for those logistical needs and then use whatever money remains for the program costs. Yet, while it's important that logistical expenses are met, program expenses should have priority. Otherwise, you will be "short changing" the retreat's goals.

OTHER COSTS

There may be costs related to pre-retreat planning. It is a nice gesture to take the planning team to lunch or give them a book or some item that says "Thank you" for the work they do for the retreat. A follow-up evaluation meeting, including refreshments, may be planned following the retreat. All such expenses should be included in the cost of the retreat.

Retreats can be shockingly expensive. This chapter helps you set a realistic budget that allows you enough money to insure a quality retreat.

Leadership is a cost item. Perhaps your leaders don't receive an honorarium, but aren't required to pay as much or anything for the weekend. At the very least, you are partially subsidizing their participation as leaders. Include this "cost" in the pricing of the retreat so that you develop a responsible budget.

Guest speakers or guest musical leaders or groups may add significantly to the retreat's cost. Don't assume you need outside speakers and groups, but don't forget to thank them financially if you involve them. Clarify in advance the speaker's or group's financial expectations. If "all" they require is a "love" offering, be certain that the young people are prepared to give an offering. Also be certain to find out if there is a minimum expectation for such an offering. Whenever possible avoid the "love" offering approach in the retreat setting. Most leaders are disappointed with how much their young people give retreat offerings.

A BUDGET WORKSHEET

This sample budget worksheet will help you develop a budget that's appropriate for your retreat. Have the planning group review this sample worksheet and add/subtract categories as necessary.

The Budget Worksheet has two separate but equally important categories: Expenses and Income. Under the "Expense" column as well as the "Income" column, it's necessary to estimate the number of young people you expect. Your estimate must be realistic so you can reasonably expect the amount of money available for the re-

---

SAMPLE BUDGET WORKSHEET

For: _____ (List event and date)

Projected Expenses

Program needs	_____
Leadership material needs	_____
Recreation supplies	_____
Audio-visuals	_____
Planning team expenses	_____

Retreat Center
Basic fee	_____	(Based on estimate of
Per person fee	_____	_____ participants)
Other	_____	

Transportation
Church van/bus	_____
Gas for cars	_____
Commercial bus	_____
Other	_____

Food (if not included in retreat center charges)
   # participants _____   _____ |

Insurance (if not included in retreat center charges)
   # participants   _____ |

TOTAL ESTIMATED EXPENSES   _____

Projected Income

Fees from participants	_____	(Based on estimate of
Budget from church	_____	_____ participants)
Fund-raising event	_____	
Special scholarship gifts	_____	
Other sources	_____	

TOTAL ESTIMATED INCOME   _____

treat. Also find out if the retreat center has certain minimal charges which must be paid regardless of how many people attend.

Here are four ways to keep retreat costs down:

1. Use retreat center space efficiently by filling the dorms/cabins/rooms to capacity.

2. Locate a retreat center where you can do your own cooking using volunteers.

3. Find a retreat center reasonably close so that the transportation costs are lower.

4. Ask participants to bring items such as paper, pencils, Bibles, etc., so that they do not need to be furnished.

If the budget is tight, have the planning group brainstorm ideas for saving money. Once you've developed a budget, the planning group must monitor it to be certain everyone stays within the budget limits.

The budget worksheet also projects a variety of income areas. It is important that the young people pay the bulk of the expenses. Paying their own way helps young people to "buy in" emotionally to the experience. If they've "invested" money in the experience they will want to get their money's worth out of the event.

For many years our youth group had an annual fruitcake sale which helped to underwrite the expenses for our annual youth snow camp. The adults of the congregation and the community knew they were helping to send young people to a retreat when they purchased a fruitcake. We also have "work scholarships." When someone asks for financial assistance or when we are aware of a financially limited family, we let the young person earn his or her way to the retreat by working around the church. Adults often give money when they know the young people will be working for it. Having young people work for the money helps them feel good about their ability to make money. It also helps them to appreciate the value of the retreat experience.

Keep accurate records of everyone's registration. Here's a sample registration form:

Christmas in September

The theme of our weekend family retreat was CHRIST'mas all year, with emphasis on Christ. We took the Christmas season to camp with us in September. We decorated the lodge with a Christmas tree, outside Christmas lights, and all the season's trimmings. What a thrill for the little ones! We posted a huge chart on the wall with everyone's name on it. We had to say CHRIST'mas instead of Christmas, and people who slipped got a sad face sticker placed behind their name.

As we held our Saturday evening Christmas program, a neighboring youth group came over to share ice cream, cake and punch with us. We all joined in singing Christmas carols.

Ruby Becher

SAMPLE RETREAT REGISTRATION SHEET

NAME	Amount of Fee	Paid	Present	Group	Cabin	Forms	Other

Explanation of Registration Sheet

Amount of Fee — List here the appropriate amount to be paid. This may vary if you offer a discount for early registration or a discount if more than two from one family attend, etc.

Paid — This is to be checked when the payment is made in total.

Present — Mark ▨ when person arrives for departure and is on the bus. Mark ▨ when person is back on the bus after snack stop, etc. Mark ✳ when present at an input session, etc. Use different colored pens for continued multiple use of this space.

Group — If persons are assigned to small groups, number the small group and note the group number in this space.

Cabin — Code the living space so that you have a record of where each person is to sleep.

Forms — Check this when you have received the permission slip and the release of liability form.

Other — You can use this space for whatever other use you may determine necessary.

This form can be used for a variety of needs throughout the retreat. Requiring full payment for the retreat *before* the retreat is a good policy. This will keep you from playing "bill collector" after the event. It may also avoid embarrassing situations for young people who later discover they can't afford the event.

As we conclude this chapter on budgeting, it is appropriate to look ahead to the chapter on publicity and promotion. Proper budgeting depends on reaching the projected registration number. Getting people to attend the retreat depends on good advance publicity.

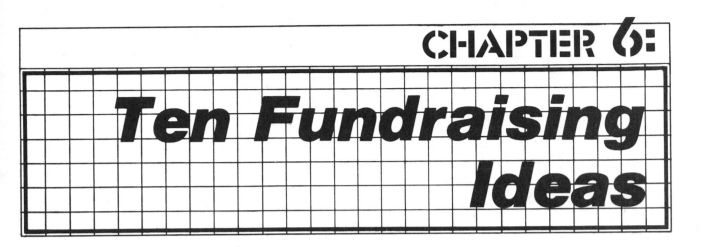

CHAPTER 6

Ten Fundraising Ideas

1. "ALL-CHURCH BAKE-OFF"

This delicious fund raiser can involve everyone in your congregation. We've used the Annual All-Church Bake-Off here the last two years. And we've raised $2,500 and $4,000.

Church members are all encouraged to enter the Bake-Off by submitting baked goods in any of five categories—cakes, pies, cookies, candies and breads. First-place winners in each category receive trophies. Other top winners receive ribbons.

After the judging, the baked goods are auctioned. By this time, the Bake-Off has attracted so much attention that auction attendance is great and bids are high.

Here are our rules for the Bake-Off: 1) No age limit. 2) Enter as many items as you wish in any or all of the five categories. 3) Entries must be in noon on the Sunday of the Bake-Off. 4) Entries become the property of the youth group so that they may be sold at auction. 5) Anything goes—your entry may even be store bought if you wish, but we feel home-baked entries will have a better chance of winning.

Our judges are selected from outside the church. We try to find caterers, bakers and other professionals. We find at least one judge for each category.

On Bake-Off Sunday all judges are asked to meet in our fellowship hall at 2 p.m. All baked items are numbered. Judges are asked to score each entry—giving first consideration to taste. Appearance is secondary.

After a top winner in each category is established, all judges taste these and vote on a grand prize winner.

After the evening service that night, everyone converges on the fellowship hall for the announcement of winners and the giant auction. We don't have a professional auctioneer in our congregation, so we use a good public relations person to do the auctioneering.

Raising money for a retreat isn't as hard as you may think. Here are 10 successful fundraising ideas for you to use.

We encourage everyone to enter. It's not just the grandmas who have kitchen talents. Matter of fact, this year our grand prize winner was a 15-year-old male athlete.

To help promote the Bake-Off we encourage entrants to publicly challenge other people in the congregation. We publish about 25 persons' challenges in the church bulletin—"Mary Guest challenges Bob Galley," etc. Those challenged do not have to accept, but their names in the bulletin put them on the spot and they usually participate.

We're also planning to gather the prize-winning recipes and sell a special cookbook.

Charles Stewart

2. "CONGREGATIONAL CHRISTMAS CARD"

Writing and mailing stacks of Christmas cards can be tedious. Well, our group came up with an energy-saving idea. We made a huge Christmas card, using poster board, felt, glitter and paint. We patterned it off a regular card. We placed our supercard near the front door of the church.

A sign near the card instructed church members to send Christmas tidings to their church friends by simply jotting their greetings on the big card. They were urged to then donate the cost of cards and postage to the youth group.

Publicity was generated in our Sunday bulletin, church newsletter and during Sunday announcements.

The cost for materials was less than $5. We profited $200 on the project.

Renee Lofgren

3. "CHRISTIAN SKATE"

Every sixth Wednesday we sponsor an evening of Christian roller skating. And we net more than $100 profit each time.

We rent a local rink from 8:30 to 11 p.m. We use our own DJs and contemporary Christian music. Admission is $2. Attendance averages 200.

We draw kids from all kinds of churches. And we hardly have to advertise anymore—just a few posters here and there.

David Wiebe

4. *"ICE CREAM SOCIAL"*

The old-fashioned ice cream social has to be one of the classics of youth group fund raisers. A few new twists can add a freshness that may make this summer's ice cream social the big event of the year.

Establish a theme for your social. It might be turn-of-the-century, western, or greasy 50s. But come up with a theme and design your social around it. Gather appropriate costumes for your members, prepare theme decorations, and plan special added attractions.

Then get your publicity committee rolling. Build interest in your church and community.

When the big day arrives, set up the goodies buffet-style. Offer two or three flavors of homemade ice cream. And offer a table of home-made baked goods—cookies, pieces of pie and cake, brownies, etc. Also include a table of drinks—punch and coffee. Reserve the last table for your cashier. Charge for each item selected by your customers.

Provide entertainment for your customers. Make the entertainment fit your theme. You may choose ragtime piano music, strolling musicians, magic shows or even comedy acts. The entertainment will delight your customers—and they'll likely return for next year's social. Also, live entertainment tends to make people stay longer. And the longer they stay, the hungrier they get and the more ice cream they buy.

Also plan added attractions, such as some simple games. If it fits your theme, you may want to include that old summertime favorite—the sponge throw. It's simple to put together. Hang a heavy plastic drop cloth from the eave of your roof or from a frame of 2 × 4s or, if your social is inside, from the ceiling. Cut a hole big enough for a head to fit through. Supply your contestants with a bucket of soggy sponges. The object: to hurl the sponge from about a 20-foot distance and hit the "victim," whose head is protruding from the hole.

You'll find the sponge throwers lining up dozens deep for a chance to splat the minister in the face—or perhaps the mayor or the police chief.

The sponge throw and other activities may be offered free to your patrons or you may ask an additional charge.

Thom Schultz

5. "BAKE AUCTION"

■ Our group sponsors a bake auction.

First we set a theme for the auction. Then our members go to work baking the goodies according to the theme. *Only* the kids are allowed to enter goods. No mom-baked goodies allowed.

Then we set the time for the auction—right after church on Sunday when everyone is hungry. We select an auctioneer who calls the bids just like at a regular auction.

Our most recent auction was held by our baseball team. One player baked a cake that looked like a bat and ball. Another baked one that resembled an open Bible. It sold for $40.

Our bake auctions easily raise $200 each time.

Foch Fuller

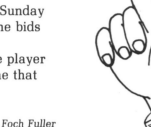

6. "GARAGE SALE"

Your group can turn unwanted items into cash. A garage sale can be a most successful fund raiser.

My group has always called them "garbage" sales. I guess we've called them that because the stuff always looks amazingly like garbage. But—even more amazing—people pay good money for that stuff!

My youth group has made anywhere from $200 to $900 on each garage sale. Some groups have made as much as $2,000 on a single sale.

The key to a successful sale is good planning. If you'd like to have a garage sale this summer, now's the time to start planning. Summer is usually the ideal season for a sale. Warm temperatures will generally bring flocks of bargain-hunters to your sale. Colder winter weather may force a sale to the basement or other indoor location. And it seems the garage sale shoppers feel less hesitant about browsing in someone's yard or garage than they do about venturing into a person's basement.

Selecting the site for your sale will be one of your first considerations. Your church may be a logical selection. But we've always found members' homes to be better sales headquarters. The ardent garage sale shoppers seem more attracted to a home address than to a church location.

In choosing a member's house to host the sale, you've got a couple of things to consider. First, is it okay with the family to clutter the yard or garage with a jungle of second-hand goodies for a day or two? And second, is the member's house in the right location for a sale? A house on a well-traveled city thoroughfare is, of course, a natural selection. Or, you may find that a house in one of the prestige areas of town may be

50

ideal. Sometimes the mere "classy sound" of an address will bring out many more shoppers to your sale.

I might point out here that you may want to warn the people in your hosting house that they're bound to get a few questions from neighbors. It never fails—at least one little old lady from down the street will survey all the stuff in the front yard, saunter over, and say, "I didn't know you were moving out." Then—when you tell her you're not—she takes another look at the new neighborhood "junk yard" and says, "Oh, that's too bad," and waddles home, scowling.

As soon as you can, you should begin notifying all of your friends and everybody in your church about your upcoming garage sale. Make sure people all over town start going through their attics, basements and garages looking for items they no longer use or need. Put announcements in the local paper and the church bulletin urging "garbage" contributors to call one of your members. When they call, pick up the goods and take them to a central storage place.

What kinds of articles should you seek to sell at your sale? Just about everything.

Gather all of your old Mad magazines. The little neighborhood kids will snatch them up in a moment. Your collection of National Geographics will be easily sold to older shoppers at your sale.

Anything that might be considered antique will be very popular. A word of advice: if you believe that you've got a truly valuable antique, visit an antique dealer first. You may be able to sell it to him for a lot more than you'd get at your garage sale.

Thom Schultz

"Gather all of your old Mad magazines. The little neighborhood kids will snatch them up."

7. "CAFE TAKE-OVER"

We "take over" local restaurants.

We make arrangements with local restaurants to work there on a given Saturday as busboys, waiters and waitresses, cashiers, and hosts and hostesses. The management agrees to pay a percentage of the profits for the day to the group.

Our members participate in a day of training and orientation prior to the workday.

We also do extensive publicity with posters, fliers and announcements in the church paper to encourage people to eat at the restaurant during the day. This is great free publicity for the restaurant.

We have no cost involved. And in addition to making big money, it's a great experience for our group.

For added income, we're planning a car wash simultaneously in the restaurant's parking lot.

Jan Hancock

8. "SINGING VALENTINES"

Here's a musical fund raiser that'll bring cheer to people all over town.

Just before Valentine's Day our group offered "singing valentines." Customers would pay us to call their sweethearts and sing them a love song.

Here's how it worked. A few weeks before Valentine's Day we spread the word about our "singing valentine" service. We put notices in the church newletter, and we put posters up in the high school. We kept our "singing valentine" fee small so that anyone could order at least one. We charged 50 cents per call. When taking orders, we asked for the sweetheart's name and phone number and the name of a song to be sung to the sweetheart. (We offered a list of possible songs, such as "You Arc My Sunshine" and "Happy Valentine's" sung to the tune of "Happy Birthday.")

Then, on the night before Valentine's Day, our group split up into teams of six or seven and went to different homes for the calling. (An office building with several phones would have worked better.) Our teams then made the calls, explaining first to the sweethearts that these special "singing valentines" were sent by so-and-so.

We made 110 calls, earning $55. And we received requests to continue the service for birthdays and anniversaries.

Susan E. Norman

52

9. "WINDSHIELD WASH"

A group of Texas high school students recently raised funds for a local project with a "windshield-wiper brigade."

Enthusiastic students, armed with clean rags and window cleaners, worked one Saturday afternoon at the parking lot of a large shopping mall. Offering to clean car windows for a 25-cent donation, they found a surprising response from car owners arriving and departing from the lot. The cleaning process took an average of one minute, and generous tips were offered to workers to clean the chrome or dashboard. A steady clientele was ensured by shoppers arriving in large numbers throughout the day.

Colorful posters placed at the entrance of the parking lot told of the 25-cent charge, and the project for which the students were raising the funds.

With the decline and expense of full-service gas stations, shoppers were pleased at this low-cost convenience provided by the students.

At the end of an extremely busy day, the group found they had earned twice as much money as anticipated and made plans to work at other large parking lots across the city for future projects.

With little preparation and a small investment in spray window cleaners, this innovative idea turned into a profitable success.

10. "BUY A MILE"

This project is a take-off on the old "rising thermometer" idea. We took a large colored sheet of poster board and sketched a map of the travel route to and from our destination. We added up all of our travel expenses and divided by the total number of miles we'd be traveling. After coming up with our cost per mile, we began drawing a red line over our route, showing how far we'd get on the money received thus far.

Church members were given the opportunity over the next few months to help advance us around the route by showing a number of miles. As money was received each week, the line was extended.

This plan had two primary benefits in addition to the money raised. First, it really unified the church family in supporting our youth trip. The whole project was one of cooperation because church contributions were combined with our funds that we raised in other ways. Second, the chart provided a great visual picture of how we all were doing. It became a focal point each Sunday as our members and the congregation came to church.

Brian Newcombe

ADDRESSES OF FUND RAISING ORGANIZATIONS

Here is a list of companies that supply products for youth group fund raising drives.

America's Best
P.O. Box 121
Mobile, AL 36601

Angeles Studio
P.O. Box 400
Chambersburg, PA 17201

Kathryn Beich Candies
Bloomington, IL 61701

C. C. Marketing Service
70-25 Parsons Blvd.
Flushing, NY 11365

Christian Art in Action
P.O. Box 3426
Granada Hills, CA 91344

Collegiate Candies
1000 N. Market St.
Champaign, IL 61820

Verne Collier
900 N. 19th St.
Birmingham, AL 35203

Collingwood Fund Raising Co.
50 Warren St.
Providence, RI 02901

Fund Raiser Associates
391 Third Ave.
Troy, NY 12180

Heavy Thinking Publishing
Box 1792
Sioux Falls, SD 57101

Abigail Martin
1113 Washington
St. Louis, MO 63101

Mascot Pecan Co.
Glennville, GA 32047

Mary Mayfair Fund-Raising
4411 W. Cermak Rd.
Chicago, IL 60623

Ole Virginny Plantations
100 W. Putnam Ave.
Greenwich, CT 06830

Fund Raising Division
Standard Brands
365 W. Passaic St.
Rochelle Park, NJ 07662

Revere Company
Scranton, PA 18504

J. H. Schuler
1649 Broadway
Hanover, PA 17331

U.S. Pen Company
21 Henderson Dr.
W. Caldwell, NJ 07006

Uni-Print, Inc.
2-9th St.
Des Moines, IA 50309

Anna Elizabeth Wade
Lynchburg, VA 24505

Zokan International
474 W. Wrightwood
Elmhurst, IL 60126

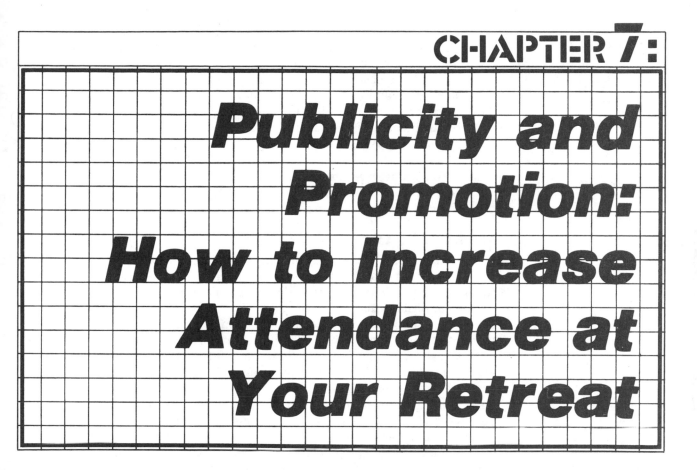

Publicity and Promotion: How to Increase Attendance at Your Retreat

O n her way home from school, Linda stops at the mailbox and browses through the day's mail. She flips quickly through the bills and handful of plain-looking letters addressed to her parents.

Her eyes open wide when she gets to the piece of mail that looks like a hamburger, complete with artsy sesame seeds and a small bug sitting near her name and address.

"My youth group's at it again," she says, chuckling to herself.

Once inside the house, Linda dumps her books and the rest of the mail on a corner of the kitchen table and takes a closer look at the paper hamburger.

As she opens this piece of youth group "junk mail," the first thing she reads is a large headline. "Attack a Big Mac." She reads on.

The flier introduces an upcoming youth group starve-a-thon retreat to raise money for a world hunger organization.

That weekend at church, strategically placed posters, attractive reminders of the retreat, caught her attention. Not only did the posters

A creative promotion and publicity campaign can increase interest and attendance at your next retreat. This chapter helps you develop your own effective promotion and publicity plan.

55

give information, but they helped everyone in the group get excited about the upcoming starve-a-thon.

In the weeks to come, Linda would receive two more creative mailings, be telephoned by a friend telling her about the event, read about it in the church bulletin and hear announcements in church and her youth group meetings. Her parents would even receive an informative letter and an invitation to a special "parents-of-potential-starve-a-thon-people" meeting.

Linda was impressed. In the past, she never quite knew much about upcoming retreats. This time, though, she felt as though she were a part of the retreat already. And she couldn't wait to take part.

PUBLICITY PAYS

A planning team's work will be wasted if it isn't communicated adequately to the group. The best planned retreat will never "make it" if the advance publicity and promotion isn't complete, attractive and motivational. Besides just listing the date, time, place, cost, etc., a good publicity poster or mailing piece should communicate the retreat's theme and general objective. Good promotion motivates.

Timing is an extremely important factor in the planning of any promotional effort. The planning group should arrive at their decisions early enough so that the first announcement of the retreat appears at least two and one-half months before the event. The planning group can even list in a church newsletter or on a bulletin board in the youth room the calendar of the events for the year even before detailed, specific planning has taken place. As soon as you know the date for your retreat, work backward—developing your own promotion time line. A promotion time line looks something like this:

SUGGESTED PROMOTION TIME LINE

2½ Months Before . . . Initial announcement: verbal and brief written notice in newsletter, bulletin, posters, etc.

2 Months Before . . . . . Detailed flier distributed to potential participants. (See the Publicity Checklist on the next page for things which should be included.)

1½ Months Before . . . Telephone contacts. (Could organize a phone-a-thon to all potential participants.)

1 Month Before . . . . . . Deadline for "early bird" special which may include a special price or a special incentive.

3 Weeks Before . . . . . . Another flier perhaps listing "early bird" sign ups. Give more details as available. (See Publicity Checklist for things to be included.)

2 Weeks Before . . . . . . Personal contact follow-up.

1 Week Before . . . . Registration deadline.

The planning group should also determine the target group for the specific retreat. What age is the retreat designed to serve? What persons within that age is it designed to serve? Also consider such questions as "How can we assemble all the names of potential participants, especially if it is open to more than just our church youth group?" "If there is a capacity which restricts how many can attend, and on what basis is the selection made? First come, first served? Priority to church members? Priority to a certain age?"

PUBLICITY CHECKLIST

Whether you design a promotional flier, an article for the church newsletter, a poster or a press release for your local newspaper, the following checklist will help you include the necessary information.

Publicity Checklist	**Publicity Checklist**
(For fliers and posters two months before the event)	*(For fliers and posters three weeks before the event)*
☐Theme, purpose, goals	☐Same information as initial checklist
☐Who should attend	PLUS
☐What is it?	☐Who has signed up already?
☐Where is it to be held?	☐Telephone number at retreat center
☐When is it being held?	☐Name of movie, musical group, etc.
☐What is the cost?	☐What to bring: sleeping bag, flashlight,
☐When is the registration due?	toothbrush, deodorant, etc.
☐How do I register and refund policy?	☐Registration deadline
☐Permission slip for registration	
☐Address and telephone of sponsoring group	

There is almost never a danger of providing too much publicity. Too often the lack, lateness or incompleteness of communication causes retreats to be poorly attended. Even though a member of your planning group should coordinate publicity and promotion, each member of the planning group should take an active part in the promotion effort.

MORE IDEAS

Posters placed in the church and community where youth will see them can increase interest and participation. Perhaps you will want to launch a poster contest early in the promotion schedule and award a free trip to the retreat to the winning design. Perhaps you can offer a discount to each person who enters the poster contest. Maybe a business person in your church would donate a prize for the contest winner.

Another promotion technique, used often in the airline industry, is to give a special discount or prize to each member of your group who signs up five other participants. Or, you could even give a discount to each of a group of five who sign up together.

Pay attention to special promotional techniques used in successful businesses in you area. Don't be afraid to use those special ideas in your own retreat promotions.

WORD OF MOUTH IS BEST

Publicity and promotion is an extremely important component in any retreat's success formula. Even though fliers and posters are crucial, the best promotion is still one-to-one personal communication. The best "recruiters" are your young people themselves as they become excited about the retreat and spread the news to their friends. The planning group begins this communication process as they themselves get excited about the event. Fliers and posters provide potential participants with the information they need to consider their own involvement in the retreat. But the dimension of personal one-to-one communication is the key to promotional success. Printed publicity usually can't carry the entire promotional load.

Other ways to encourage one-to-one communication:

1. Give each person who registers a button or sticker to wear which says something like "YES." or "I'M GOING," etc.

2. Make a display on a bulletin board where the youth will see it, that lists the number of youth who are attending and/or their names.

History Book

We made home movies during our retreat to be shown at our future weekly meetings. We also took a lot of snapshots. As youth leader, I always take a lot of pictures of our activities and keep a scrapbook. The scrapbook has grown quite large and we take it with us each time we go on a weekend retreat. The kids really enjoy looking through it over and over. There are always the new photos to see.

Peggy Frey

The aim of promotion and publicity is to build interest and anticipation of the retreat. Remember, effective promotion and publicity take time and careful planning. Effort is the key.

RETREAT JOURNAL

Your members will probably experience some of the best times of their lives on your retreat. These times will be too good to forget. So, get a volunteer or two from the group to write a trip journal.

At the end of each day, the journal writer should sit down and write out everything that happened that day. Include good and bad things, laughs and miseries, fun and boring times. Be sure to include lots of the kids' names. Matter of fact, it's best if you can mention

KISS!

NOW THAT WE HAVE YOUR ATTENTION, take this brief survey and see if you need to come to our retreat. Do any of these situations fit you?

—you needed a club on your last date
—your girl likes to date in groups—like 25!
—on your first date, you went to kiss her and missed
—you get turned on holding hands
—your date seems to have 12 hands

Whether or not you fit into these categories, you'll not want to miss this retreat on

♥ THE DATING GAME ♥
April 28-30
Camp Sweetwater

See attached facts/registration sheet for all the info.
Registration deadline: April 18

each member for each day of the retreat. Write the journal like a diary—a separate entry for each day. Don't let anyone else see your journal entries.

When you return from the retreat, type out the journal and have it mimeographed. You may want to add some artwork on the cover. Then, set aside a part of one of your regular meetings to pass out the journals. Everybody will look forward to them with as much (or more) anticipation than your school yearbooks.

Your retreat journal will become one of your prized possessions, read and reread year after year.

RETREAT PHOTOGRAPHY

Be sure to have at least one retreat photographer who'll take plenty of pictures. The photographer should remember to capture all the different facets of the trip. Don't get so wrapped up taking pictures of buildings and scenery that little things such as sleeping on the bus or eating in a tiny restaurant go unrecorded. Sometimes it's those little experiences that are really treasured and should be preserved on film.

Upon your return, share the retreat experience with the church, family and friends. A good way to accomplish this is through a simple multimedia presentation.

RETREAT MULTIMEDIA SHOW

Your retreat can be shared, preserved and recycled through the use of multimedia.

A simple multimedia program can be extremely effective to communicate your group's activities to others. It's also great to show the program one year later to your own group to generate enthusiasm for your next retreat.

All you'll need are slides from your retreat and a couple of tape recorders. All put together, these will let your audience experience sights and actual comments from your members.

Be sure one of your members always takes plenty of slides on your retreat. Include all phases of group life in the photography. Don't ignore simple things like meals and people sitting around. Sometimes those simple times are the most memorable.

Then, after you return from your retreat, set up a time when all the members can talk individually with an interviewer. The interviewer can be either the leader or a member, but should have some skill at interviewing. The interview time can be scheduled during, before or after your regular group meeting time, or you may wish to plan a special get-together for the taping.

Your interviewer should have a number of questions prepared to ask each member. The questions should be geared to the slides you have from the trip. Some sample questions might be: "How did you like the closing worship service?" and "What did you think of the small group experiences?" and "What was it like eating food your friends cooked?" and "How did you like the hike we took Friday night?"

Also ask some general questions about the value of the trip or camp. Examples: "What did you get out of the retreat?" and "How did you see God working in our group and in the retreat?" Your interviewer should also feel free to ad lib some questions.

Avoid questions that could be answered with a "yes" or "no."

Take each member separately to a quiet spot for the taping session. Use a good tape recorder and microphone. Try not to spend more than four or five minutes with each member. This will make editing easier.

Now, play the tape, and make note of good quotes from members. This job will be easier if you use a recorder with a footage counter. With that gadget, you just need to mark down the footage numbers of the good quotes and they're simple to find later.

In editing, be sure to include at least one quote from each member. Don't leave anyone out.

After you've selected the best comments, arrange on paper the quotes and the slides. You needn't follow chronological order. For longer comments, you may plan to use four or five slides. Or, sometimes you may wish to stay on the same slide for one or two or three comments. But, as a general rule, plan to leave one slide on the screen for only a few seconds.

When you've placed your selected comments in their best order, you may want to write some additional narration. But hold this narration to a minimum. Use it to tie thoughts together, etc. Your audience is much more interested in the voices and comments of all your members.

Next, record your narrator's introduction. Or, you may want to begin with one of the actual comments from a member.

Then, proceed to put all the comments and other narration in the proper order on your master tape. You'll need two tape recorders. Cue up the selected quote on one machine. Set the other machine on record, put a mike to the speaker of the first recorder, and start both machines. If you have a member with talent in electronics, he can do a better job by using patch cords between machines.

Continue to master-record every comment and bit of narration in proper order. You may want to end the program with a little music.

Then, turn the master tape and slides over to one member who will spend the necessary time familiarizing himself with the proper spots on the tape to change the slides on the screen. This must be well rehearsed.

Use a good tape player for your actual presentation. If it is not powerful enough, you may need to run it through an auxiliary PA system to get necessary volume.

This project takes some work, but is tremendously effective with audiences. Plus, it provides a permanent record of your group's experiences together.

USING THE MEDIA

Ever sent some information about your retreat to your local newspaper, then watched the news appear as an obscure sentence or two on the last page? Or maybe never appear at all?

Knowing and heeding a few simple ground rules will enable your group to prepare publicity material that the media will use.

Your goal should be to produce retreat publicity material that the media will use without excessive editing. The less rewriting the media have to do, the better. But don't feel badly if your news release that you labored over for hours doesn't appear exactly as you prepared it. Many in the media rewrite everything that crosses their desks.

When preparing a news release, remember always to include the "who, what, where, when, why and how" at the beginning. Never wait until the end of your release to "spring the surprise" of important information. News should be delivered in the fashion of an "inverted triangle," to use journalists' jargon. That is, the most important informa-

SAMPLE LETTER TO PARENTS

January 13, 198-

Dear Parents and Pray-ers:

WANTED: The Teenager!!
        Who wants him?

Disc jockeys and record companies do. Rock singers find bending the teenager's ear a profitable business. Hair spray and cosmetic companies. So do soft drink and jeans manufacturers. Uncle Sam, too. TV commercials and McDonald's hamburgers gobble these attractive "clients."

All these interests seek to influence and entice him to try what they offer. Each of the five senses becomes a gateway of approach to the young high school student of today. These groups want the teenage market, or the teenage mind and the teenager himself and they go after him.

Who else wants the teenager? WE DO!

There is a chorus many kids are singing today..."We are one in the Spirit, we are one in the Lord...and they'll know we are Christians by our love." If the world needs anything demonstrated more graphically today, it is this concept. Because of our oneness with Christ, we are one with each other. Our high school retreat offers a unique position to extend helping, loving hands to each other.

The retreat takes place February 12-14. The theme is "Christian Love." The key verse from 1 Corinthians 13:4: "Love is patient, love is kind, and is not jealous; love does not brag and is not arrogant."

WANTED: Adults who care enough to invest in our labors through prayer.
        Would your love for Jesus Christ impel you to spend time in prayer
        for us from now through Feb. 15th? Attached is a prayer reminder
        for you to place in a strategic spot in your home. Thank you for
        your part as prayer warriors.

                                                        Bob Good

SIGNED: High School Youth Group and Youth Leaders.

WHAT TO BRING/FACT SHEET

This is an outline of a "Fact Sheet" many churches give to their young people and sponsors one week or so before the retreat.

Here are different parts of the "Fact Sheet" you could include in your own special letter.

What to Bring

Ideas: clothing items, swim suit, rain gear, personal toilet articles, Bible, camera and film, insect repellent, plastic for wet or soiled clothing, jacket, handkerchiefs, Chapstick, tennis racquet, sunglasses, suntan lotion, pen or pencil, towels, washcloth.

Money

What are extra costs, if any? How much spending money is needed?

Accommodations

Does the housing have any special requirements people need to know about? Do the accommodations have electricity? Should the retreat people bring pillows and bed clothing?

Conduct

What are the retreat rules and consequences of breaking those rules?

Free Time

Any "free time"? If so, what are the optional structured activities?

Retreat Location Information

Mailing address?
Emergency phone numbers.

---

tion appears at the beginning and least important details are found at the end. This allows the editor to use as much of the story as he has room for—knowing that wherever he's chosen to cut your story, he's hacked the less important material.

Use short paragraphs. Two or three sentences are usually plenty.

Do not editorialize. Do not write, "The M.Y.F. is planning a great retreat with lots of fun activities and neat sessions." The editor will cringe and your news release may wind up in the trash.

That same information should be written more like this: "The M.Y.F. has scheduled a retreat featuring John Johnson, well-known retreat leader. This retreat is to be held . . .''

Always type your releases. Editors hate hand-writing—even when it's legible. Double-space your material, and type only on one side of the paper.

Begin typing halfway down on your first sheet. This allows space above for the editor to write a headline. Always number consecutive pages.

Never deliver a carbon copy or a photocopy to the newspaper. It's an insult to any editor to believe that the *other* newspaper got the original copy. When an original typed release reaches the editor, he's impressed that you prepared the material especially for him. A photocopy signals to the editor that all the other media in town have the same release. And he may have no interest in your mass-produced ''news.''

If you plan to use more than one newspaper or broadcast station, type a different release for each of them. It's a lot of work, but you'll have a much better chance of having your releases used.

Your stories for large metropolitan daily papers should usually be shorter and more concise than the stories you'd write for the smaller newspapers.

For most events, the best time to submit your releases is one week beforehand. Smaller auxiliary stories could precede and follow the mail story, if the local media are prone to use such material.

Studies have shown that readers give much more attention to photographs than to printed words. So, whenever you can, submit photos with your stories. Use black and white prints—not slides, color snapshots or negatives.

Always include caption information with the photo. It's best to attach a slip of paper to the back of the photo that has the typed information about who or what appears in the picture.

You'll find that you will get better results from many of the newspapers and stations if you deliver your releases and photos to the editors in person. Many times that personal touch will be enough to make the editors want to help you.

Always put your name and phone number on your releases in case an editor has a question.

Give the newspaper or radio station a call if you have any questions about submitting a news release. They'd be happy to help you.

CHAPTER 8:

Leaders

"**S**ponsors"—those adults without whom youth events would fizzle—are a vital part of the retreat process. These volunteers give their time and energy to make things happen in a church youth group.

Carefully consider and plan their role in the retreat experience. In my early years of retreat planning and directing I suffered through several uncomfortable experiences with sponsors. I encountered sponsors who wanted to run the retreat like an army camp. Other sponsors who weren't youth oriented saw the experience as a burden rather than an opportunity to learn and grow with the youth. Yet many sponsors through the years have found new friendships with young people which have led to long-term supportive relationships.

Perhaps the greatest downfall of the use of sponsors is that we take them for granted. We tend to "use" sponsors without giving them the same careful attention we give the retreat participants. This chapter will help you make the adult volunteers, the sponsors, an integral part of the event. The retreat can be a growth-producing event for them too.

FINDING GOOD SPONSORS

Who should the sponsors be? Perhaps you have ongoing sponsors who work with the youth group who will be involved in the retreat you are planning. Or maybe you are the youth sponsors and you're reading this book to hone your retreat planning skills. People who become retreat sponsors should meet several basic requirements. Retreat sponsors should:

- respect youth
- be willing to grow in their understanding of youth
- be growing in their own faith experience

If you are responsible for recruiting retreat sponsors, begin the process in the planning team by listing the qualities the team feels are im-

Getting good sponsors isn't easy. Yet, those adults are key to your retreat's effectiveness. Here's a plan for finding and training the right people for your retreat.

65

portant for youth sponsors. Then brainstorm a list of potential sponsors from your church.

SAMPLE #1—Brainstorming

Qualities important for sponsors of youth retreats:

Open	Like the out-of-doors
Fun to be with	Know the youth
Knowledge of Bible	

Persons in our church who have these qualities:

Jim Atkinson	Jackie Johnson
Sally Rush	Ben Millard
Lee Fuller	Ralph Martinez
James Johnson	Sue George
Nan Joo Lee	William Turner

At this point, don't eliminate any names. You may find new persons never considered; you may also find someone you thought didn't like retreats will say "Yes."
It is essential that the planning team have ownership of those who are invited to be sponsors.

After you have listed potential sponsors based upon the list of qualities, begin to list the expectations you have of the sponsors for this specific retreat.

SAMPLE #2—Expectations of Leaders:

✔ Drive car
✔ Supervise food preparation
✔ Supervise dorm
✔ Lead small group Bible study
✔ Lead recreation
✔ Organize hike
✔ Lead singing

This list will help you meet the specific needs of the retreat with specific abilities. After listing the expectations, prepare a "Leadership Need Statement" which includes the specific needs which you will be asking a person to fulfill. This "job description" will be helpful as you approach specific individuals.

LEADERSHIP NEED STATEMENT

In order for our November 3-5 Youth Retreat to be successful, we need an adult leader who will:

1. Provide transportation
2. Supervise the kitchen
3. Be a dorm supervisor

We will appreciate your consideration of this invitation to serve. If you accept this invitation, you will be invited to an orientation and training session in October so that you can understand more fully the retreat and your responsibilities. We appreciate your consideration.

WE NEED YOU!

(A different Leadership Need Statement would be prepared for each separate job description. The recruitment is to be done face to face and this statement will be given to the potential sponsor at that time.)

WHO MAKES A GOOD SPONSOR?

Parents may be good sponsors. Parents may be terrible sponsors. People over 65 years of age may be good sponsors. People over 65 years of age may be terrible sponsors. People between 28 and 35 may be good sponsors. People between 28 and 35 may be terrible sponsors. Get the picture?

"Who" the sponsors "are" is important as it relates to the initial qualities listed on page 66. Don't eliminate any potential sponsors because they are "parents" or are too "old." Don't automatically assume "young adults" will be the best sponsors. Think deeply in your consideration of potential sponsors!

HOW MANY SPONSORS?

There is no simple formula for determining how may leaders are needed. A rule of thumb might be to consider a basic ratio of six participants to every one sponsor. That ratio allows for enough sponsors to adequately monitor a retreat experience. This 6:1 ratio is arbitrary and should be reviewed by the planning team. Basically, of course, the ratio for junior highs will allow for more sponsors than for senior highs. As a planning group, determine the basic ratio for your retreat.

Before actually recruiting sponsors, the planning team should discuss "how many" sponsors you'll need. The number of sponsors will relate to the needs of the logistical team, the caring team and the program team. How many sponsors to recruit also relates to the group: will this particular group need a great deal of adult "presence"? Is this group "close" enough and able to provide the necessary leadership needs—cooking, program leadership, etc., without much "adult" presence?

RECRUITING SPONSORS

Recruit sponsors face to face—no telephone calls, no letters, no appeals from the pulpit. After the planning group has done its homework of developing job descriptions, determining how many leaders will be needed and selecting those to be asked, the actual "asking" may be done by any member of the planning team. But the asking must be face to face.

Ask only those persons whom the planning team has targeted for recruitment. Give each person being asked a copy of the leadership need/job description. Allow the potential sponsors time to think about the decision if they are not prepared to respond immediately. Encourage them to talk with other members of the planning team. Tell them how and why they were selected. Explain to them that they will be orientated, trained and supported in their responsibility. Report responses back to the coordinator of the planning team.

If you have sponsors who are automatically a part of the leadership team, discuss with them the leadership needs, and naturally, the purpose and goals of this particular retreat. Permanent sponsors should be involved in the planning process.

Once the leadership is recruited, there are tasks for you to complete before, during and after the retreat to ensure a positive experience.

Embarrassing Moments

Retreats can bring out the "funniest" in people and situations. Students are always interested in the latest jokes or "off color" stories. On one such occasion, Linda was unraveling a steamy story to a group of gals in the girls' dorm. When she reached the punch line no one laughed; their faces drew somber looks. Someone nodded and Linda turned around to discover that G. J., one of the adult leaders, entered the room while she was talking and heard the whole crude mess. There was a moment of silent, serious embarrassment as Linda's ears turned red. Then G. J. smiled and broke out in a hilarious roar. Everyone followed suit, laughing not so much at the punch line, but at the situation itself.
Frank Zolvinski

Before the Retreat:

☐ Recruit sponsors face to face.
☐ Provide them with written leadership need/job descriptions.
☐ Orient them to the retreat. (Gather all the adult leadership at which time the planning team should share their planning process, the retreat goals, the role of the leaders, the "rules" of the retreat, etc.)
☐ Train them. (If they are to have "program" responsibilities, lead them through all or part of the curriculum which they will be expected to coordinate.)
☐ Review "behavior expectations" for participants and how leaders are to communicate those expectations.
☐ Review logistical needs for which they are responsible.
☐ Worship together through Bible study and prayer.

During the Retreat:

☐ Schedule a regular leadership time to review the retreat's progress.
☐ Support the leaders informally.
☐ Encourage leaders to be mutually supportive.
☐ Provide room and board at no cost to the sponsors. Transportation too, if possible.
☐ Publicly thank them at the conclusion of the retreat while still at the retreat.
☐ Seek their evaluation of the retreat.

After the Retreat:

☐ Thank them with a written note.
☐ Thank them publicly—by listing names in the church newsletter and recognizing them in a worship service.
☐ Have a follow-up evaluation session perhaps with the planning team.
☐ Solicit written recommendations to be used as input for future retreats.

SPONSORS ARE SPECIAL

Retreat experiences will be valuable faith-shaping events only if the adults who work with the youth are growing in their own faith experience. It is vital that the adults who work with youth have ample opportunities to grow separate from their sponsor responsibilities as well as during their sponsor responsibilities. Sponsors should not be the "leftover" leadership of the church—they should be the strongest leaders in the church. Sponsors should not be recruited by every other group in the church at the same time—they need to devote quality time and energy to their own faith growth and their sponsoring opportunity. Protect your sponsors from "overkill" in trying to do too many things in the church.

In summary, keep the following things in mind when considering your retreat adult volunteers: Recruit them carefully and personally. Orient and train them, support them in their role, learn from them, appreciate them and protect them. Sponsors are one of your most valuable resources!

CHAPTER 9

Retreat Rules

Have you ever been to a youth event where you felt the youths' primary goal was to break the rules? The adult-written rules were a challenge to the youth which said, "We dare you to break these." Rules should never be the focal point of a youth group or youth event. Good rules remain in the background to provide structure and reasonable limits so members of the group can live positively together in a Christian atmosphere. Here are some guidelines for setting effective rules for youth fellowships and events.

by Dr. Larry Keefauver

How to develop retreat rules your young people will respect.

BE POSITIVE

Start with a positive attitude by setting rules in an atmosphere which expects the best of youth and adults. Too often we expect the worst and try to legislate against it. A large number of negatively stated rules says to youth, "We expect the worst from you. We don't believe you can be responsible, so we're listing these restrictions because we expect a terrible outcome." Sure enough, the youth meet their leaders' expectations.

Even the act of discipline can be a positive experience when it's used to teach instead of punish or put down. What happens when a rule is broken? If the young rule-breaker is singled out, embarrassed and put down, both the group and the individual youth suffer tremendous damage. In the biblical context, to discipline means to correct or teach. It does not mean to punish, put down or destroy a young person's self-esteem. Proverbs 18:14 reads, "A man's spirit will endure sickness; but a broken spirit who can bear?" When a rule is broken, sit down with the youth, person to person, outside of the group and discuss both the problem and the appropriate consequences.

Another aspect of being positive in rule setting is to ask, "What is the loving thing to do?" Recall Paul's saying that love is the fulfillment of the law. The end result of every rule should be, "What is loving?" Granted, love should not be sentimental or vacillating. Following through on prescribed consequences to breaking a rule is love.

BE PRECISE

Say what you mean; be brief; be precise. When rules are set by *both youth and adults,* be clear about what is expected. Keep your list of rules brief. State the essentials and the consequences if the rules are broken.

Have adults and the youth set rules at a parents meeting. Go over the rules and consequences for special events and lock-ins as well as Sunday evening fellowships.

If parents feel certain rules need to be added or modified, take their suggestions to a special council comprised of responsible youth and adults who work with youth. Let those recommendations be considered and appropriately implemented.

BE PREPARED

Rule preparation takes many stages. First, be sure that the rules are set by responsible *youth and adult leaders.* Next, help the entire group "own" the rules by allowing everyone to say "yes" to them.

Prepare both parents and youth before a trip or retreat by publishing the rules in the information about the event. Before our youth group heads off on a trip retreat, parents and youth gather with the youth

---

A team of youth and adults made the following set of rules for a weekend retreat. The rules were so popular that they've been used for many years.

I. Thy car shall not be used during the retreat.

II. Thy body shall not leave the retreat grounds.

III. Thy body shall not be with the body of the opposite sex in the opposite sex's room.

IV. Thou shalt not puff a weed of any kind nor space out on any pills or drink during the retreat.

V. Thou shalt report any injury immediately to the sponsor.

VI. No fireworks shalt thy burn.

VII. Thou shalt not trespass on thy neighbor's body or self-esteem.

VIII. Thou shalt be at events on time.

IX. Thou shalt observe all camp rules.

X. Thou shalt be okay.

Anyone caught breaking these rules will be talked with. Considering the seriousness of transgression, the youth council has the option of asking that person's parents to come and take him or her home.

workers immediately prior to leaving. The leaders explain the trip's details and rules. Everyone, including the parents, sponsors and young people hear the rules and the consequences for breaking the rules. Everyone is prepared, so that no one can say, "I did not know." The rules are also printed on the program booklet for the retreat or trip or convention so that everyone knows what to expect.

The most major consequence we have used (beyond a sponsor personally confronting someone about breaking a rule and working it through with him or her) is sending a rule breaker home. We explain to the parents that they will be responsible for providing their young person's transportation home. In over 12 years, I have had to exercise that consequence only twice. Both times were learning and growing experiences for the youth.

MORE POINTERS FOR SETTING RULES

● **Have enough adult supervision.** Our practice is to have one adult of the same sex for every 10 youth. This rule is particularly important when planning trips, conventions or outings with other church youth groups. When other groups are involved, the youth need to understand that they come under the supervision of adults from their own congregation. It is very difficult to have adults supervise youth from other churches without adults from those churches being present.

● **Pass off supervision to responsible young people.** There comes a point after positive adult modeling where the most effective group discipline is handing it off to the youth themselves. We have our youth officers enforce the rules. The objective is to get to a stage where the youth maintain discipline and the adults give support.

● **A controlled environment limits temptation.** If there are large portions of unscheduled, unsupervised, unplanned time during a youth event, you can count on problems arising. When we plan a lock-in, every minute of it is structured. That doesn't mean we structure heavy stuff all of the time, but it does mean that we know what is going on at every moment. When we go on a trip, we don't turn unsupervised youth loose on the town. There are planned and scheduled activities at each

Worried

I've directed and worked on youth retreats for the past seven years. I'm always worried about the possibility of accidents or injury to our retreaters. I can state that out of all the retreats I've directed, we have never had a serious student accident. However, on one occasion we did have a broken ankle, not from one of the students, but a staff member. Here's what happened: It had been a long day of talks, discussion and sharing. We took a break on Saturday evening for refreshments. Joan, our 40-year-old grandmother type, but really 16 at heart, decided to show off her gymnastic agility. She gathered a small crowd around her and proceeded to do a flip. Joan's only problem was she had forgotten to take off her high-heeled boots. Needless to say, she landed on her ankle and was in quite a bit of pain. The next time I saw Joan, she was in a cast with crutches, but glad to be alive.

I sometimes wonder who needs more supervision, teenagers or adults?

Frank Zolvinski

point in the schedule. During lock-ins, it is clear for those who are sleeping during the lock-in where the girls sleep and where the guys sleep and those sleeping areas are off limits to people of the opposite sex.

● **Decide who owns the problem.** On one youth retreat, one of the parent sponsors saw his child holding hands with another youth. The parent lost his temper and berated his son in front of the entire group. It was a devastating thing for the parent/youth relationship as well as for the group itself. Much of the problem in this particular incident was with the parent. Adults need to ask themselves two questions when they see misbehavior: "Is this something I personally disapprove of, but which is within the limits of the rules?" and "Is this behavior a clear violation of group rules?" Times when adults come down too hard on youth can be avoided initially by determining immediately who owns the problem.

● **Always get the facts directly from those involved.** On one of our trips, I found out that some of the guys had marijuana with them. No one had smoked anything, but its presence was well known to many of the youth. Instead of asking, "Is this true?" or "Can you tell me

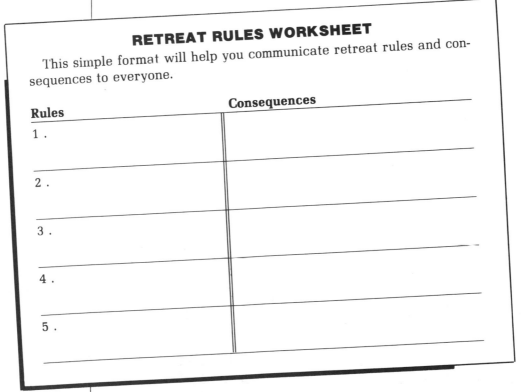

RETREAT RULES WORKSHEET

This simple format will help you communicate retreat rules and consequences to everyone.

Rules	Consequences
1 .	
2 .	
3 .	
4 .	
5 .	

more?'' I asked them to give me the facts of the situation. (I also explained that the trip could not go on until the situation was resolved.)

In one-to-one conversation, I got the facts of the situation. The marijuana was disposed of, appropriate disciplinary action was taken and the trip went on without incident. Getting the facts directly from the people involved was indispensable in being able to work out fair discipline.

LOVE RULES ALL

The ultimate question to ask yourself in setting solid rules is ''What is the loving thing to do?'' as Paul emphasizes in his letters. Rules point toward *agape*, the love that builds people's worth and self-esteem. It finds worth there even when the people themselves do not feel worthy. *Agape* is tough love that seeks to discipline, teach and correct within the biblical norms. There are times when the letter of the law gives way to the spirit which is love.

A final illustration. I was on a weekend youth retreat. One of the girls with us attended retreats but never came to youth fellowships, Sunday school or any other youth activities. Some parents and other youth were resentful that she came, particularly because she often brought drugs and immoral activity with her. Knowing these problems in advance, we still had a place for her. True to form, she broke the rules. We found her in bed with one of the guys. We caught her with a group of youth in the woods with some marijuana.

My initial reaction was to send her immediately home. Yet, something told me more was needed with this girl. We insisted that she stay in the sessions which stressed the loving care of Jesus Christ for each individual during the course of this retreat.

> ### The Night My Group Almost Slipped Out
>
> Getting young people to bed on retreats is an age-old problem. Another job is keeping them there. On one retreat several guys planned to sneak out of the cabin after everyone was asleep. (It was easy to tell something was brewing when they climbed into bed with their clothes on.) After things had quieted down at 1 a.m, I stepped out for a cup of coffee. When I returned an hour later, everything seemed quiet so I turned in.
>
> In the morning I discovered that the guys fell asleep waiting for me to return. We all got a good laugh when they got up wearing all their clothes, including shoes and socks.
>
> Frank Zolvinski

Near the end of the retreat, we had a ''warm fuzzy'' line. Clothespins attached to a clothesline had names of each youth on them. During the course of the event, youth would write positive affirmations of other youth in the group and clip them under the clothespins. People could read notes that built up their self-esteem throughout the event. At the end of the retreat I was taking down the clothespins when I ran across a note with my name on it. The note said, ''Larry, during this retreat I have felt God's love for me for the first time in my life. I have given my life to Jesus Christ. Please pray for me.'' It was from our problem girl.

I was skeptical as I read the note, but I started praying. I learned later that the next day this girl went to her school counselor, gave up drugs, and asked for help. She went to a Christian halfway house for drug abusers. Over the next four months her life changed and she became a new person in Jesus Christ.

Rules are important. People are more important. Act out of the depth of love—a tough love—as you work on rules with your youth group.

CHAPTER 10

When You Have a Problem with Someone

I found myself out in the subzero night before I knew where I was and what was happening. I hadn't even stopped to tie my shoelaces. "Jay's missing" were the two words that started me on my middle-of-the-night trek. The added phrase, "I think he's smoking dope," didn't help any.

This was Jay's first winter retreat with our group. From the start, I wasn't sure I liked his cocky, macho attitude.

I crunched across the frozen northern Wisconsin snow toward the lights in the recreation building. After what seemed like a frozen eternity, I reached the icicle-covered building. As I walked through the door I recognized one of the voices as that of the retreat speaker. He and his wife were murdering Jay and his girlfriend in a game of Rook. They were talking about one of the retreat's topics: dating relationships.

With still sweaty palms, I crunched back through the frozen snow toward my now cold sleeping bag. There had been no confrontation. No punishment. No action. I'd been reprieved—this time.

In the years since that experience, I've faced quite a few sticky problems. And I've seen other youth leaders react in a thousand different ways when they were confronted with a tense situation. Those reactions range from seeing a leader fling one of his rebellious kids against a wall to hearing a leader, in his one-of-the-gang voices, tell some of his group members to keep quiet about the beer drinking and promise not to do it again.

Retreat problems are universal. No one is immune. Just when you think things are going smoothly you get zapped. Someone is drinking

by Gary Richardson

What will you do if you catch a couple of young people with beer at your next retreat? This chapter gives you a practical problem-solving process.

beer. Or you stumble across passionate lovers. Or three of your macho types "light up" in front of other group members. There's no end to the creative hassles that happen when you're in charge.

AN ATTITUDE CHECK

Your attitude toward problem situations and the kids who get tangled up in them can often determine whether the end result is guilt, notoriety or spiritual growth.

Ask yourself these questions: What should the relationship be between a leader and young people who cause problems? How responsible do you feel for the behaviors of your young people? Do you feel that you can handle most problem situations yourself? Or do you feel comfortable letting other people help you deal with your problem kids? What's your pastor's attitude toward kids who cause problems? Your church's attitude? Your kids' parents' attitude?

"The mark of a spiritually mature youth leader is his or her ability to focus on the youth and not on himself when problems come," says Perry Downs, professor of youth ministry at Trinity College, Deerfield, Illinois. "Too many youth leaders put their feelings and their responsibility as leaders ahead of the youth with the problem. Many leaders are ruthless in dealing with a problem because they want everything to return to normal as quickly as possible. But they should be more concerned about talking with the young person and listening to why he did what he did. We need to look at those problems as a sign of pain; that something's not right."

While you can't handle any two problems or any two young people in exactly the same way, there are several principles that will apply to almost any situation you'll face. Here are a few:

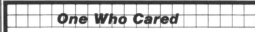
One Who Cared

As a recent graduate, I've attended several retreats with my youth group. Every retreat I've been on has had its ups and downs—from the joy of staying awake most of the night to the agony of facing the enthusiastic smiles of the well-rested staff. Each retreat has unforgettable memories. Good or bad, they're always beneficial.

The Friday evening and the following day of my first retreat in ninth grade were full of excitement, insight and plain ol' fun. On Saturday evening, one of the retreat staff members shared an experience of reconciliation. She finished her talk by passing out letters to us from our parents. We didn't know that our parents had written these. As the letters were distributed, I patiently waited for mine. I watched as the last letter was handed out and how my fellow retreaters cried as they read things most of their parents usually didn't say. When I told the staff that I didn't get one, they frantically

● The world's future doesn't depend on how powerfully and decisively you react in a problem situation. Stay calm, take a few deep breaths. Sometimes it's even helpful to put everything on "hold" for a couple of minutes while you think things through. If so, tell the problem person you need a little time—then let him or her do some thinking and evaluating too. Realize that your relationship with the problem person after the incident is more important to his future behavior and spiritual growth than the problem itself.

searched for it.

Eventually, they said I didn't have a letter. Not waiting for an explanation, I stormed out, crying. I thought I was alone and everyone else was wrapped up in their own letters. I was quite wrong. Within moments, my friends were yelling for me to come back. I, being stubborn, refused. It took a lot to persuade me back into the building. By then, I was embarrassed and cold. Entering the fireplace room, everyone had open arms and compassionate, understanding faces.

The most significant point of the evening was when one boy, who I thought was "cool," consoled me. I remember him because I least expected him to be concerned. After talking a while, he convinced me that my letter was just lost (which it was) and, most importantly, that he cared about me.

Paula Keeton

● If you're relatively new to youth work, you've probably noticed that "older" leaders seem to handle problems better than you. Of course, experience is a valuable asset. But more importantly, the people in the group have learned to trust and respect him or her. Caring enough to look beneath the surface of a problem to where a kid is hurting is a big chunk of the problem-solving process.

● It's better to deal with a problem while it's still fresh than to wait till later. Dealing with a problem as soon as you've gathered your thoughts can prevent a guilt reaction from building up in the problem person. In some cases, a prompt reaction can put the brakes on a publicity flood, where the problem kids gain notoriety from others who hear about whatever happened.

● Don't make threats or give ultimatums unless you can follow through with them. One leader at his church's district retreat threatened to send two guys and three girls home if they went swimming instead of attending one of the seminars. They went swimming. And when the leader tried to make good his threat, he found his pastor unwilling to remove the kids. Everyone lost something from that experience: the kids, the leader, even the pastor.

● Cut down on potential problems through careful planning. One group that spends several weeks on the road each summer in a singing ministry doesn't allow the girls to wear running shorts or halter tops. The guys aren't allowed to wear running shorts either. And shirts are required. "Those rules have almost eliminated the sexually-related hassles we used to have," the leader comments. "And the kids don't seem to mind the rules. In fact, I think most of the guys are relieved."

● Include other youth leaders in your problem-solving process. Talking about specific problems with other leaders can help you be more objective and keep your emotions and ego from getting too heavily involved. The added perspective can be a valuable asset in working with the young person to nurture his personal and spiritual growth.

WHEN YOU HAVE TO ACT

Even though each problem and each young person is different, there is a valuable person-oriented process you can follow.

John Shaw, veteran youth leader, former mental health worker and present director of GROUP Magazine's National Christian Youth Congress and annual workcamps, outlines a basic process which facilitates personal and spiritual growth on the part of the person involved in the problem.

This process includes the person or persons involved in the problem, the leader, and potentially the people affected by the problem. This problem-solving process is designed to get at the causes of the problem, its effects and consequences by using listening, feedback and clarifying skills. At each step in the process the young person is at the center of attention.

"Even though each problem and each young person is different, there is a valuable person-oriented process you can follow."

A FOUR-STEP PROBLEM-SOLVING PROCESS

Step 1: It's important to identify and clarify all aspects of the problem: its effects on the group, on individuals, on property and how it relates to the people who created it. For instance, it's important to know whether the problem arose because the kids were releasing anxiety, striving for attention, for notoriety, and so on.

Step 2: Identify what led to the problem. How did it come about? Did the events that led to the problem occur spontaneously? Or was the problem the result of prior planning and premeditation? Who else might have been involved that could have shaded the importance of the problem-causing action?

Step 3: Once you've identified the problem and what caused it, look at its consequences. Who is affected by the problem? (The whole group? The entire church, retreat or camp? Property?)

Ask questions so you know the problem people understand exactly the problem and its consequences. If you make assumptions about what the kids understand and feel, you may infer things that they don't intend.

Step 4: It's important to find out in their words what they see as potential solutions to the problem and its consequences. What things would they do to correct the problem?

WHO ELSE SHOULD YOU TELL?

As far as relating the problem to the rest of the youth group, you need to make a value judgment after talking with the person or persons involved in the problem. What will airing the problem do to relationships within the group? within the church community?

Whether or not you should include parents in the process depends on the nature of the problem. The most effective guideline is to involve the parents if the young person feels they can be constructive to the outcome. On the other hand, a parent may be quick to administer punishment that's far out of proportion to what happened.

However, if you see the problem as continuing or serious, like pot smoking, drinking or vandalism, you may have to bring the parents in as a resource in order to get something constructive done. If so, tell the young person, "I'm asking your parents to become involved because I feel you need their help to deal with this problem effectively."

Regardless of who you include in the process, it's your responsibility to inform the church leadership about the problem before they hear of it from secondary (and usually unreliable) sources. Explain what happened and how you handled the situation.

PRACTICE, PRACTICE, PRACTICE

Your problem-solving effectiveness will get pretty watered down if you wait till you have a crisis before working through this process with your young people. A practical way of preparing for potential problems is through using role plays. For example, choose a potential problem situation (slipping from a room at night on a retreat, drinking, disregarding group rules). Work through the "problem" with the entire group using the process outlined earlier.

Before you role play potential problems with your group, meet with other leaders and work on listening skills, feedback methods, question-asking skills and clarifying techniques. All are vital to getting at the root of what the young person feels, thinks and values.

Your careful consideration and planning for problem situations will pay off in the lives of your members. Seasoned youth workers have found that the greatest growth often arises not from smooth times but from those painful problem episodes.

CHAPTER 11:

Retreat Themes and Formats

The theme of a retreat is the main topic that will be explored (for example, death and dying). Everything done and studied during the retreat should somehow promote a better understanding of the theme (for example, visiting a center for terminally ill patients, listening to a Hospice trainer talk about living with the knowledge that death is imminent, visiting a mortuary, etc.).

Choose your theme carefully; ask your group members for suggestions. They may have a particular topic they want to learn more about.

Once you have chosen the theme, you will need to determine the format of the retreat. The format is the way the retreat is put together. It's the combination of studies, activities, discussions, role plays, etc., that make up the whole event.

Since the format determines how the theme will be experienced, consider all possibilities before making your final decisions. Sometimes a film is best (for dealing with subjects that may be awkward to discuss in detail). Sometimes a special leader is best (for learning about particular topics, such as cults). And sometimes experiential activities are best (for practicing self-improvement skills).

The retreat format also influences who will attend (for example, brothers and sisters may be at a retreat on siblings), where the retreat will be held (for example, a houseboat is a great place to study Paul's journeys) and when certain events will happen (for example, a sense of persecution may be more effective in the middle of the night). Generally, your theme will be the what and why of the retreat; your format will be the how, who, where and when.

Here are several ideas for retreat themes and formats. Imagine how they'd work in your group. Expand them or tear them apart and use the pieces. Let them prime your mind for further ideas.

by Cindy Parolini, Virgil Nelson and Lynn Nelson

Here are all sorts of creative ideas and suggestions for retreat themes and formats. Use your imagination to come up with dozens more.

Senior Special—Your church could honor its high school graduates by giving them a unique retreat experience—all about them! Stage a surprise "This Is Your Life" presentation for each senior. Have parents contribute memorabilia (particularly baby pictures, favorite stuffed animal, first-grade artwork and handwriting samples). Ask friends to share childhood memories. Collect as much information and material as possible and plan the programs. Parents, siblings and pets could make "unexpected" guest appearances.

Marriage Retreat—Pair guys and girls and have a mock wedding ceremony. Hand out marriage certificates (that expire at the close of the retreat). The couples must sit together at meetings, eat together and spend free time together (but not room together). Discuss managing budgets, assign "salaries" and instruct each couple to plan a budget; discuss problems with in-laws, give each couple a specific difficult situation and have them decide how to handle it; etc. At "inappropriate" times, inform couples that the husband has been laid off, or the wife's $150 eyeglasses broke or the dog needs an operation. Invite (real) couples to talk with your group about special joys and problems of different stages of marriage. Invite a marriage counselor to discuss "getting along" in marriage—or show a film on the subject. Study scripture verses about marriage.

Decision-Making Retreat—Take your group away to study and practice making decisions using biblical guidelines and principles. Pack the weekend with decisions that the youth need to make. You might provide food for meals but let them decide what combinations of food to eat when, who will prepare it, how, etc. Discuss biblical principles for determining what's right and what's wrong. Set up situations where kids must make decisions—outside the movie theater when friends suddenly decide to sneak in through the side door; in the classroom during a test when Sue's paper is in clear view. **Tension Getters** (Youth Specialties, Inc.) has many such situations and case studies.

Cult Awareness Retreat—Your youth will expect to learn about cults. Teach them by using some of the methods that cults use. **The Youth Group How-to Book** (Group Books) provides detailed instructions on sessions like this. Become familiar enough with the marks of the cults to simulate two cult groups. Determine beliefs and entice kids to join. Develop rituals and incantations, use peculiar dress, etc. "Deprogramming" (debriefing) is vital. Discuss how kids felt. Have them identify the marks of the cults and list what separates cults from Christianity. Discuss why so many youth are drawn into the cults and what can be done about it. This is an experience they'll remember.

Backpack Retreat—With a leader experienced in backpacking, your group could leave civilization behind and head into the mountains, forest or national park. Preparation is important; one helpful resource is **The Youth Group How-to Book** (Group Books). Study scripture passages like the Israelites wandering in the wilderness and Jesus' experience in the wilderness. Discuss the "wilderness" areas in group members' lives.

Current Events Retreat—Take your kids on an adventure in exploring the difficult issues that Christians face. Have plenty of newspapers on hand and have the group members identify articles that contain controversial or otherwise difficult issues. Discuss them. Find scripture verses that apply. Try to determine the responses your group would like to have (to hunger, prejudice, homosexuality, etc.). A good resource is GROUP Magazine's "World Times" section which contains actual newspaper articles accompanied by relevant scripture verses and discussion questions.

Get-Acquainted Retreat—Use this at the beginning of a new year with your youth group—or anytime during the year when there are new members. Set aside each hour during the weekend for getting to know a person. For instance, 9 to 10 Saturday morning could be "John Smith hour": John may tell about himself and show his rock collection or play the drums for you; his friends may add interesting details about childhood schemes; his parents may provide a letter about him for you to read to the group, as well as photographs to pass around, etc. Work with each individual ahead of time to plan his or her hour-long "presentation."

Solo Retreat—Take your group to a campsite in the great outdoors during warm weather. Friday evening study together the times Jesus was alone and discuss solitude. Saturday after breakfast send group members off with sack lunches to spend the whole day alone. They may take items with them—Bible, books, etc.—but encourage them to experience at least one hour doing nothing but sitting on a rock and thinking about life. When the group is back together, discuss reflections and discoveries. Then have a party to celebrate community!

Death-and-Dying Retreat—Visit a nursing home and talk with the residents; visit a center for terminally ill patients and talk with them. Return to the retreat site and study Jesus' and Paul's attitudes toward death. Discuss how they compare with the attitudes your group saw in the elderly and terminally ill people. Invite a Hospice trainer to talk about life before death. Visit a mortuary. Go back to your site and study scripture verses about death and what happens when people die. Have a church member who's had a relative die tell how he or she handled the loss. Perhaps a group member who's had a family member die would relate that experience. Have everyone write his or her obituary. Discuss what group members would like to be remembered for.

Explore Faiths Retreat—Saturday attend a Seventh-day Adventist service, a Jewish Synagogue and Catholic Mass; Sunday attend a Mormon service and some other churches in your city. Discuss why there are so many different faiths, how they are alike and how they are different, what was liked about each, etc. Kids may want to write their experiences in journals.

Retreat in the Future—The year is 2025. Everyone should wear clothes from "2025 Designers." Use food coloring to turn milk, mashed potatoes, etc., into weird foods of the future. Create a special language ("What-yips are-sug you-yips thinking-sug?"). Discuss future subjects: knowing God's will, choosing a career/college/job, living with the threat of nuclear war, etc. Have group members write their autobiographies (through the year 2025) and discuss them.

Happy Retreat—Leave problems at home and have a happy retreat! Pass out plenty of warm fuzzies (colored pompons) for giving to others when saying something nice about them. Decorate your meeting area with balloons and streamers. Study scripture passages like the Psalms and the beatitudes. Sing praises to God. Sing fun songs. Discuss the best things that have ever happened to group members. Close with everyone in a circle around one person; everyone says something nice about him or her. Each person has a turn in the middle.

How-to-Help Retreat—Have an instructor train your group in basic first-aid procedures. Take along **Friend to Friend** by J. David Stone and Larry Keefauver (Group Books) and have kids learn how to counsel their friends who have problems. Role play situations where group members help others. Study Jesus' ministry of healing people both physically and spiritually.

Persecution Retreat—Group members pretend they are first-century Christians who are experiencing persecution or 20th-century Christians who must worship secretly behind the Iron Curtain. Take everyone camping. The group must move secretively and quietly or risk being discovered. Study the actual persecutions of the early Christians and the present-day troubles of Russian Christians. Tell Corrie ten Boom's story. During the night have a couple of church members dramatically "discover" your group and threaten torture, yet allow everyone to safely "escape" to a predetermined hiding place. At dawn, return to the campsite for more rest. After breakfast, discuss how Christians now can prepare for possible times of persecution (for example, by memorizing scripture, developing good prayer habits, worshiping in homes as well as the church, etc.).

Career Retreat—Have church members from a variety of occupations give presentations to your group about their work—including what they like most and what they like least. Encourage the youth to ask questions. You may be able to get aptitude tests from school guidance counselors that can help determine what professions your group members are best suited for. A good general resource is John W. Zehring's **Preparing for W*O*R*K** (Victor Books). Provide materials on a variety of vocations and encourage kids to seriously consider which they will choose. Discuss strategies for achieving career goals.

Video Retreat—Take your video recording equipment and have some fun. Your group could role play and videotape situations that could serve as discussion starters for the church members or other youth groups. Brainstorm and produce commercials for God. Take your equipment to a street corner a couple of blocks away from your church, or downtown, and ask folks for directions to the church. Interview people on the street. Ask them what they think about God, nuclear weapons, prayer in the schools or some other topic of concern for your church. Have your group stage a full production and videotape it. The options are endless—and the learning is fun.

Drug Awareness Retreat—Invite a special leader to talk with your group about drug use and abuse. Have kids learn how to recognize when their friends are abusing drugs and need help. Discuss why people "do drugs" and what Christianity can offer them. Role play talking with such friends and offering them help. Discuss how kids can try to convince friends to stop abusing drugs. Play an album or show a film about a person who was once addicted to drugs but isn't anymore (for example, **Mike Warnke Alive**, Myrrh Records).

Fund-Raising Retreat—Devote a weekend to fund raising—planning and doing. Use a posterboard calendar of the upcoming year to help your group pinpoint the events for which they need to raise money. Brainstorm ideas for raising the money and choose the ones the group will do. Plan the projects as much as possible. For a half day of this retreat your group could run a car wash or other basic fund raiser.

Poverty Retreat—Take your group to the ghetto or a migrant workers camp or other poverty-stricken area. Everyone should dress in "rags" and eat the poverty-level food of the area. Separate kids into pairs to visit people and offer services to them (cleaning, repair work, etc.). Visit a local church, soup kitchen, community center or rescue mission. Discuss experiences; what did the kids "hear" when they listened to the folks they were with? Have an in-depth Bible study on Jesus' ministry to the poor and his instructions about caring for them. Resolve to serve your retreat site in the future by sending money or clothes or by doing work projects.

Parable Retreat—Explore the meaning of Jesus' parables with your group. Act them out. Discuss for each what Jesus was trying to say to his listeners then and what the parable can say to people now. Create a modern version of a parable, as though Jesus were telling it today, and act out that. Is the meaning easier to see in the new version? You might also talk with your group about some of the background information on the parables.

Film Festival—Get away with your group for a weekend of good movies. Don't limit yourself to films from Christian producers. Discuss the films' meanings and implications from a biblical perspective. Use resources like GROUP Magazine's "Inside the Movies" section to aid in finding relevant scripture verses and study questions.

Confirmation Retreat—For those youth about to be confirmed: a special weekend of fun and review. Their confirmation instructor leads an overview/capsule study of the lessons that led to their readiness for confirmation. Plenty of fun and games will help build unity and a sense of community as the youth prepare to be confirmed.

Leadership Development Retreat—Here's a chance to discover the leadership potential and abilities in your youth. Let the kids lead sessions on what they're good at. You may have a potpourri of topics— from how to start a stamp collection to how to say a few phrases in German. Some may prefer to lead discussions on familiar Bible passages. Work with each youth ahead of time to help him or her determine a topic. The experience of leadership is what's important. Invite a speaker on leadership. Give the group a project to do (for example, list reasons why parents should give teenagers more or less responsibility) and assign a leader. Give small groups projects to do (for example, build a campfire) and don't assign leaders; watch for natural leaders to emerge. Study the leaders God used in the Bible and point out that some (like Moses) did not consider themselves as having "outgoing" personalities, yet God accomplished great things through them.

Brothers-and-Sisters Retreat—Siblings of youth group members attend this retreat as well. Plan activities that require brothers and sisters to work together on tasks—and experience a mutual sense of accomplishment. For example have siblings describe or act out something unique about their family life for the rest of the group. Have the group discuss problems that arise in sibling relationships, suggest possible ways of handling the problems and role play the suggestions. Study siblings' conflicts in the Bible (for example, Cain and Abel, Mary and Martha) and determine whether they were properly resolved. Study scripture passages about the unity among Christians as the children of God. If the retreat group includes younger children, allow plenty of time for developing relationships by playing games.

Jail Retreat—Arrange ahead of time with your police department to let your youth group spend a night at the local jail (locked behind bars). Study the correctional system and have an officer from the police department talk with the group. You might stage an "arrest" during one of the preparatory sessions. When all the kids are "arrested" for overnight, let the police officers know they expect no special treatment. Frisking, "booking," fingerprinting and mug shots are all a part of the experience. Debriefing the next morning is important. Discuss what happened and how everyone felt about it. Study what the Bible says about justice.

Adventure Retreat—Take a risk! Have your group go rafting, rock climbing, rappelling or wilderness camping. Or challenge your kids to climb a 14-foot wall, walk balance beams, figure how to get all the group members onto a three-foot square platform—or over a five-foot high taut rope without touching it. Some resources for ideas like these are Adventure Works in S. Lynnfield, Massachusetts and the Institute for Creative Living in Cleveland, Ohio. Kids will enjoy the support from other group members and the sense of accomplishment. Study scripture verses about overcoming fear. Discuss building community and the importance of Christian community.

Gifts Retreat—Help your group members identify their spiritual gifts. Study the scripture passages about spiritual gifts and make a "master list" of them on newsprint. Discuss how to recognize each gift in others and how to know if you have it. Then—practice doing just that: Set up learning centers to help kids discover any hidden talents; encourage group members to think about whether they have ever noticed any of

---

A "Pilgrim" Service

We held a memorable "pilgrim's church service" at our camp retreat. Our theme was "Thanksliving Thanksgiving". We held the traditional pilgrims' silent walk to services. The minister led the group, wearing a large pilgrim hat the youth had made. The women wore pilgrim aprons and bonnets made from old drapery lining. The men wore white collars and silver shoe and belt buckles. The youth wore Indian headbands and necklaces. The only noise was the rustle of their clothes as they walked. At the services, the women sat on one side of the church and the men on the other side. The youth sat in front. It was quite an educational experience for the younger youth!

Ruby Becher

the gifts in other kids, and if so, to tell them. When each youth has identified at least one gift, he or she should spend time developing that gift. Close the retreat with a "gift show"; each youth acts out his or her gift.

A Weekend With the Shrink—Arrange with a Christian psychologist, psychiatrist or counselor to be with your group for the weekend and administer a variety of personality tests for individuals in the group, such as the Taylor Johnson Personality Inventory. There are a number of such tools which can help an individual better understand him/herself and the unique gifts God has given him/her.

The rest of the focus for the weekend could be Bible study and worship celebrating the uniqueness/similarities God has created in each of us. If appropriate, small groups could also generate development of trust and love in discussing/sharing what they learned about themselves through the tools that were used.

Media Retreat—Whether your group is only four or five members or 150 members, media can be an exciting way to celebrate your group life and to see Scripture and the world with new eyes.

Spend a whole weekend creating your media resource bank for use in slide-sound programs, creative Bible study, and reporting to your church on your group.

Let different individuals (or small groups) take different areas of focus. For example, one group might take "hands" as its focus and shoot a whole roll of slides just showing different hands: contrasting age, size, what the hands are doing, etc. Other groups might consider feet, faces or children. Emotions can be included as well as feelings—love, tension, anger, happiness.

Tools and techniques can vary with the equipment you have available. The simplest way to start is with slides: you can get slide film even for Instamatic cameras, or you can borrow a 35mm camera. Slides can be **made** without a camera, and some individuals or groups can do this while others are using the photo equipment.

If you have access to a Super 8 movie camera, one group or person can be shooting footage around the above themes or recording the whole process of the media retreat for later use in worship celebration of the life of the group, and God's gifts to it.

One of the best resources for those just starting out in the area is Ed McNulty's **Handbook of Gadgets, Gimmicks and Grace** (Abingdon, paperback). This volume includes hundreds of practical how-to-do-it suggestions and theological/scriptural bases for our use of media in the church.

Lock-In Retreat—Right after school, everyone comes to the church and is "locked-in" for the night until school time the next day. For how long? A week. (This may also be planned for a weekend.)

This gives a group a unique opportunity to live, study and play together. People agree not to leave the church once they have arrived, and there are no ingoing-outgoing phone calls once the week has begun.

The focus of the week can vary as widely as the needs of your group. The results can be fantastic in spiritual growth; people getting genuinely acquainted with each other, learning to work together, etc.

You can choose whether you want to let the group do its own cooking as part of the learning experience, or to find someone to handle that for you.

You might even consider a lock-in retreat at a special place, for example at a rest home, mental hospital or juvenile hall, where the group would be involved each evening in a special ministry with the folks who live there.

Lock-ins can also include special program features:

1. *No talking* for one whole evening through breakfast the next day. Here's a genuine opportunity to experience the frustrations of being handicapped, and the opportunities for nonverbal communication, the lack of pressure to "talk" or have "something to say."

2. Or a *no see* (or *no hear*) time dividing the group into partners, possibly one for one evening and switch for the next.

Planning Retreat—Do you get frustrated planning your programs for your group at the last minute? Is it a hassle getting people to look ahead and take responsibility for some aspect of your group's life and spiritual growth?

A planning retreat might just be what you need to help you determine your purpose, to clearly identify your focus for the next few months or a year.

Identify the persons you feel should be involved. Do you have elected officers or coordinators? If so, they would be a core. Others might be invited as well. Sometimes the whole group can be involved in planning ahead for the year.

Some possible questions for group focus during the retreat:
- The purposes of our group are . . .
- This next year I feel our group needs to . . .
- God seems to be telling us to . . .
- One of the prime opportunities we have is . . .

These open-ended questions can lead to input and goal statements that can then be specifically translated into program ideas and suggestions. The retreat can even include calendaring of events and the division of labor for implementing them.

Star Wars or Star Power Weekend—Encourage your group to create a simulation game that you would live/play for a whole day or weekend.

Dennis Benson's book **Gaming** (Abingdon Press) is a fantastic resource that will help you experience the fact that you can create your own exciting simulation games. It also contains eight complete simulation games.

One simulation that we have had good experiences with is **Star Power**, developed by Garry Shirts, Simile II, Box 1023, La Jolla, CA 92037. This game simulates a three-class society based on wealth. The wealthy gain advantages as the game progresses, which ensures their continued position.

Others:

Baldicer: simulates the problem of feeding the world's people (John Knox Press).

Credit and Debt: sets up the experience of being in debt and the frustrations that can come trying to meet the bills (Brethren Press).

Action Weekend—Does your church have special mission projects with which your group might organize to serve? Do you live near (within 200 miles) a large city that has community centers, or special programs for youth, adults, elderly citizens?

Do you have any special concentrations of people near you—a rest home, a juvenile placement facility, a halfway house, a treatment facility for alcoholics, a hospital, a child-care center, a seniors' center, a mental institution?

You have a unique opportunity for Christian action and involvement. Have your group make a list of such institutions and organizations. Do several Bible studies on some of the following scriptures: 1 John 2:5 and 4:16-21; John 13:34-35; Matthew 5:43-48 and 25:37-41; 2 Corinthians 5:17-18; Luke 4:16-17; and Ephesians 5:16.

Have someone contact several of the organizations to find out what kind of involvement they might appreciate. Encourage the group to select one.

You could contact them and arrange to work together for a day, a weekend or a week. Have the joy of learning to be Christ's reconcilers and healers!

Explore the possibility of going to another country for mission service. Select a group of two or four more. Go, return, and share.

Travel Retreat—Have a yearning to see the world? to go to new and distant places? There are lots of ways to travel.

Determine the cost you can afford for the weekend and then figure out how far you can go on that amount of money. The possibilities are endless, and the fun and creativity in stretching the dollars is fantastic.

Bike it. The bicycle has been determined to be the most efficient and ecologically sound means of transportation ever devised. (See May '79 GROUP Magazine for ideas on bike trips.)

Road show. Your group, large or small, can create a 20- or 30-minute program that you can share with other groups along the way. Write to other churches and arrange to sleep in their fellowship halls and to perform for them. Great fun, and a neat way to make new friends.

You don't have to be professional actors. One group started with the Peanuts theme "Happiness is . . ." and created 20-second scenes illustrating the different ideas, plus many that they created on their own. These were interspersed with appropriate short Scripture readings, poetry and other creations from the group.

Backpacking and foot-washing can make an exciting and meaningful activity of fellowship.

Discovering Your Community—A home retreat can give you new eyes to see your neighbors.

Send out several people with cameras to photograph parts of your community that few people ever see.

Call and arrange for 15-minute interviews with several community leaders—chief of police, a policeman, a barber or hairdresser, a business-person, a welfare worker, a lawyer, a psychologist/counselor, a labor-union leader, a farmer, the mayor, a school board member, a newspaper reporter, etc.

Ask them three questions and record their answers on a cassette tape recorder and take notes:

1. What do you see to be the genuine strengths/assets of our community?

2. What do you see to be the needs or problems, issues that face our community?

3. What can the Christian community do to be part of the solutions to our community's problems, from your perspective?

Map your community. Ask members of the group, using crayons, to draw your community as they see it— significant groups, structures, "dividing lines," etc.

Do a newspaper collage. Create collage from back issues of the paper showing strength and problem areas.

The above information can be the basis for continuing discussion and

Journey

One retreat we designed used the idea of "journey" for a theme. We are all on a journey, traveling through life toward God. A very good get-acquainted exercise included students tracing their footprints on a piece of construction paper. One footprint became the person's name tag for the weekend. Or, students could exchange a footprint with another person and interview that person. They could ask such questions as what school they attend, favorite food, favorite sport, what size shoe they wear. The other footprint was taped to the wall. On the other side of the room hung a wooden cross. This became a focal point for the retreat. Students were invited to move their footprint on the wall closer to the cross anytime throughout the weekend that they experienced a good feeling or change of heart.

By the end of the weekend all the footprints had been moved many times closer to the cross as the students drew closer to the Lord and one another. The sense of journey was visually expressed in this activity. The song "By My Side" from Godspell became a theme song for this retreat.

Frank Zolvinski

"*You* are the only ones who can determine what you need and what a particular retreat experience can do for you and your group. You have the opportunity to use your God-given creativity to adapt the ideas for your group."

reflection on your opportunities as Christians to influence the communities in which you live as ministers/servants of Jesus Christ.

The pain/problem areas can be listed during the report time. These could be ranked and one selected for possible group action.

The above information might be the focus for a special reporting session to the whole congregation regarding what you have learned and what opportunities you have to love the people God has created.

Multi-Cultural Extravaganza—Do people from another racial or ethnic background share your community? Possibly many different heritages? Even if it is only one, you can have a ball finding out more about each other and experiencing what it would be like to be part of that culture.

Plan the weekend to include the foods, the folkstories, the history, the dances, the games and the religious heritage of the cultures in your community. (Maybe the other cultures are non-Christian. This will give you an opportunity to share your faith with them.)

If there are ethnic churches nearby, be in touch and work together in joint planning.

You might have only 10 participants total, or you might have over 100, as did an event in the Philadelphia area that involved five different ethnic groups.

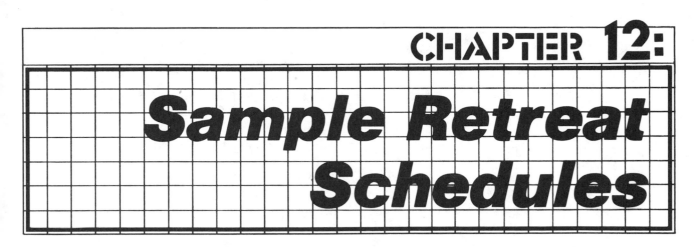

CHAPTER 12

Sample Retreat Schedules

The first retreat schedule is a somewhat typical format for a weekend retreat which allows for a balance between input sessions and optional times. The second retreat schedule is quite different. If you use it, be certain your adult leaders and sponsors have a restful week before the event. You may want to schedule the retreat on a three-day weekend when the Monday following the retreat is the holiday.

Both schedules work well. The first schedule always has the reluctance of the young people to "go to bed" the first night. The second retreat schedule does not have that problem.

Two sample schedules and a worksheet to help you get the most from your retreat.

A "TYPICAL" RETREAT SCHEDULE

Friday	6:00 p.m.	Depart from your church
	7:30 p.m.	Stop for a snack (assumes retreat center is 2½ to 3½ hours from your church)
	8:15 p.m.	Continue
	9:30 p.m.	Arrive at camp and move in
	10:00 p.m.	Input Session #1 (getting acquainted with one another, brief introductions to the theme, learning guidelines/expectations, finding facilities)
	11:00 p.m.	Optional time (conversation, move into sleeping quarters)
	12:00	Lights out
Saturday	8:00 a.m.	Breakfast
	9:00 a.m.	Input Session #2 (theme presentation and development; continue interaction—music, etc.)
	10:30 a.m.	Optional time (recreation, rest, etc.)

95

	12:00	Lunch
	1:00 p.m.	Input Session #3 (continued theme development)
	2:00 p.m.	Optional time (hikes, organized recreation, rest)
	5:30 p.m.	Dinner
	6:30 p.m.	Input Session #4 (continued theme development)
	7:30 p.m.	Celebration time (party games, skits, talent show)
	9:00 p.m.	Special event (movie, slides, musical group, etc.)
	10:30 p.m.	Refreshments and optional time
	12:00	Lights out
Sunday	**9:00 a.m.**	Breakfast
	10:00 a.m.	Input Session #5 (theme conclusion, worship, group closure)
	11:00 a.m.	Clean up camp site and dorms
	12:00	Lunch
	1:00 p.m.	Optional time
	2:00 p.m.	Depart for home
	3:00 p.m.	Snack stop
	3:45 p.m.	Resume trip home
	5:00 p.m.	Arrive back at the church

RETREAT SCHEDULE WORKSHEET

Write in sessions, activities, meals, games, free time, etc.

DAY:	Friday	Saturday	Sunday
6:00 a.m.			
7:00 a.m.			
8:00 a.m.			
↓	↓	↓	↓
1:00 a.m.			

A "DIFFERENT" RETREAT SCHEDULE

Friday	**6:00 p.m.**	Depart from your church
	7:30 p.m.	Stop for snack
	8:15 p.m.	Continue travel
	9:30 p.m.	Arrive at retreat center and move in
	10:00 p.m.	Input Session #1 (explain schedule, interaction to get acquainted with participants and the place, theme presentation)
	11:00 p.m.	Crazy recreation (rope hike, organized crazy indoor olympics, etc.)
	12:00	Input Session #2 (must be interaction oriented to keep attention)
Saturday	**1:00 a.m.**	Optional time (set the limits, such as quiet in the dorm, must stay indoors, etc. Provide table games, singing, etc. Food should also be available.)

Everything after 1:00 a.m. is optional

	2:00 a.m.	Creative worship (Make it candlelight, silent, have learning center to guide the worship. Be creative.)
	3:00 a.m.	Movie (Show an appropriate religious or secular film.)
	5:00 a.m.	All lights out. Everyone to bed!
	11:00 a.m.	Brunch (This needs to be a good, full meal.)
	12:00	Input Session #3 (continued theme development)
	1:00 p.m.	Optional time
	5:00 p.m.	Dinner
	6:00 p.m.	Input Session #4 (continued theme development)
	7:00 p.m.	Celebration time (party games, sing-a-long, talent show)
	8:30 p.m.	Refreshments and optional time
	10:00 p.m.	Lights out
Sunday	**9:00 a.m.**	Breakfast
	10:00 a.m.	Input Session #5 (theme conclusion, worship, group closure)
	11:00 a.m.	Clean up retreat center site and dorms
	12:00	Lunch

SAMPLE RETREAT SCHEDULES

1:00 p.m.	Optional time
2:00 p.m.	Leave retreat center for home
3:00 p.m.	Snack stop
3:45 p.m.	Resume trip home
5:15 p.m.	Arrive back at the church

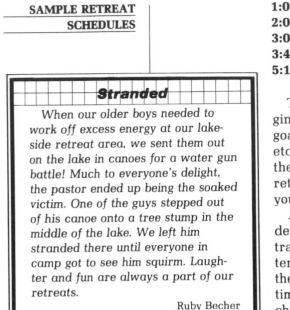

Stranded

When our older boys needed to work off excess energy at our lakeside retreat area, we sent them out on the lake in canoes for a water gun battle! Much to everyone's delight, the pastor ended up being the soaked victim. One of the guys stepped out of his canoe onto a tree stump in the middle of the lake. We left him stranded there until everyone in camp got to see him squirm. Laughter and fun are always a part of our retreats.

Ruby Becher

These schedules are presented as a place to begin. As your planning group considers the purpose, goals, program style, program content, leadership, etc. they must also consider the schedule. Introduce the schedule to your young people in advance of the retreat, especially if it is out of the ordinary for your group.

Another code phrase to remember after you've developed a schedule is *be flexible*. One year, as we traveled by bus to our retreat center, and encountered snow and ice. Our bus driver didn't stop at the lower elevations to put on the chains. By the time he stopped, it was so icy he couldn't get the chains on. We spent three hours with a busload of young people working to get the chains on. Needless to say, we arrived at the camp rather late—2:30 a.m. We had to reschedule all of our opening night plans and all of the first full day plans! That night was one of those unforgettable experiences which is now a part of our "oral retreat tradition."

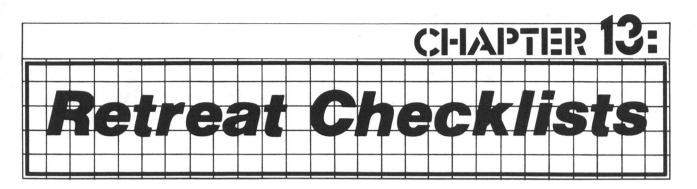

he following checklists are guides to help you in developing a checklist that's appropriate for your particular retreat. The checklist should be used by the retreat coordinator—the person selecting and working with the retreat planning group. The first checklist is consistent with the planning needs as represented in this book. Each task or need on the checklist will direct the planning group or the coordinator to more tasks which must be completed. As the planning group meets, you may want to reproduce the checklist on newsprint so the entire group can see the needs to be met and feel good when something is completed.

The checklist may also become a time line. After each general category or specific task, you may wish to write in the appropriate date to have the task completed and underway. Various chapters in this book will give suggestions as to when these tasks should be begun and completed.

Coordination and organization are keys to a retreat's success. This chapter helps you keep the different retreat planning teams running smoothly.

THE RETREAT CHECKLIST

───────── PURPOSE AND GOALS: ─────────

____Review chapter one
____Select planning group
____Establish purpose and goals
____Appoint and orient logistical team
____Appoint and orient caring team
____Appoint and orient program team

───────── LOCATION: ─────────

____Review chapter three
____Review available sites
____Select site
____Determine budget needs
____Visit site, if possible, with program team

Camera Caper

The young man had never fished before this retreat. But he shouldn't have admitted it to his fellow retreaters. Soon, the entire group was shoving a fishing pole into his hand and telling him all sorts of "fish stories."

Much to his surprise, however, the untrained fisherman felt a little tug at the end of his line. "The kids back home are never going to believe this," he started bellowing as everyone began to join in the act. And, although the new fisherman did refuse to remove his fish from the hook, he was clearly the one who had caught the 8" perch. Singlehandedly.

One of the teenagers agreed to hold the catch of the day so that the youth minister, a trained photographer, could snap a picture of the evidence.

Long after the fish had been returned to its clear blue home and the last sleeping bag had been packed away, a young fisherman tried to convince everyone back home of his great prowess.

"Sounds fishy to us," they all said.

"Just wait until we get the film back," he told them.

But no one was going to be able to wait that long. For, the youth minister had been too excited about his retreat program on that fateful day. Much too excited to think about putting film into his camera.

Denise Turner

TRANSPORTATION:

____Review chapter four
____Determine modes available
____Review church policy transportation
____Select appropriate mode
____Reserve leadership and orient
____Determine budget needs
____Check insurance
____Safety check if using church vehicles

BUDGET:

____Review chapter five
____Estimate expenses using suggested worksheet in chapter five
____Determine with planning group income sources
____Determine amount to charge participants
____Estimate income
____Determine the working budget
____Receive monies
____Disburse monies
____Provide a written summary after the retreat to the planning group

PUBLICITY AND PROMOTION:

____Review chapter seven
____Determine target group
____Prepare appropriate time line
____Design promotional materials
____Distribute promotional materials

RULES:

____Review chapter nine
____Review church policies
____Review retreat center policies
____Establish your guidelines with planning group
____Communicate guidelines to participants

PROGRAM DESIGN:

____Review chapter two
____Review chapter 11
____Research and develop needs to which the retreat should respond
____Select writer for retreat design

____Select retreat design from those presented in this book which fits your purpose and goals
____List materials and leadership needed
____Check design with appropriate staff and board of church
____Determine and communicate schedule

_____ **FOLLOW-UP:** _____

____Review chapter ten
____Orient caring team to follow-up needs
____Establish post-retreat processes
____Prepare written evaluation for use by future retreat planning groups

PLANNING GROUP AND TEAM CHECKLIST

If you use the planning group and the teams suggested in this book, the following checklist will help you. Remember, this checklist is only a guide. Develop your own checklist which is unique to your own retreat.

_____ **FOR THE COORDINATOR:** _____

____Select planning group in consultation with appropriate staff or committee
____Develop initial checklists
____Monitor the work of the entire retreat planning process
____Read this book—each chapter *before* beginning

_____ **FOR THE PLANNING GROUP:** _____

____Review planning group responsibilities (see chapter two)
____Develop purpose and goals (see chapter one)
____Determine appropriate program content and assign development to the program team
____Form the logistical team and orient
____Form the caring team and orient
____Form the program team and orient
____Discuss leadership needs
____Develop tentative budget (see chapter five)
____Develop publicity and promotion (see chapter seven)
____Organize registration (see chapters five and seven)
____Consider the role of parents (see chapter two)
____Review and establish retreat rules (see chapter nine)
____Establish follow-up process (see chapter 10)

A SANITY CHECK FOR RETREAT LEADERS

✔Are you completely satisfied that every detail of the retreat has been planned?

> Yes or No

✔Are you certain every leadership need is filled with highly capable people?

> Yes or No

✔Is the retreat site perfect in every way?

> Yes or No

✔Do you plan to get a full eight hours of rest each night of the retreat?

> Yes or No

✔Does this check make sense?
> Yes or No

(Evaluating your responses: If you had four or more "Yes" responses, you are probably out of touch with reality. If you had four or more "No" responses, you have a great deal in common with other retreat leaders. If you had an equal number of "Yes" and "No" responses, you cheated!)

_____FOR THE LOGISTICAL TEAM:_____

____Review purpose and goals
____Review the logistical team responsibilities (see chapter two)
____Consider possible sites (see chapter three)
____Visit those to be considered
____Study facilities and costs
____Recommend site to planning group
____Determine transportation needs (see chapter four)
____Check insurance needs (see chapters three and four)
____Study food needs
____Submit budget recommendation to the planning group

_____FOR THE CARING TEAM:_____

____Review purpose and goals
____Review purpose of caring team (see chapter two)
____Consider personal and group needs
____Develop strategies to be responsive
____Prepare for follow-up needs (see chapter 10)

_____ FOR THE PROGRAM TEAM:_____

____Review purpose and goals
____Review program team responsibilities (see chapter two)
____Review suggested program content as determined by planning group
____Discuss program leadership needs
____Have curriculum developed
____Recommend program budget to planning group
____Determine program segments of the retreat (see chapter eight)
____Plan evaluation of program (see chapter 14)

Follow-up

he value of any retreat is not limited to the new learnings and friendships gained during the actual experience. The real "pay off" comes in the days, weeks, months and years following the event as young people live out their learnings and turn new friendships into long-term understandings and commitments. It is for this reason that any retreat planning group should consider a deliberate follow-up process to the experience as a definite part of its responsibilities.

What you do after the retreat is just as important as the retreat itself. This chapter gives you guidelines on making a retreat's effects last longer.

EVALUATION

Evaluation is the term we often use when attempting to measure a retreat's success. Some evaluation should take place before you leave the retreat center as well as further evaluation some period of time after the retreat experience.

Evaluation immediately after the retreat gives you general reactions and feelings regarding the input and interaction. This immediate evaluation may target some persons who had a particularly traumatic experience—either positive or negative. The caring team should pay special attention to these persons following the retreat. The value of the later evaluation is to determine the ongoing impact of the retreat experience. Both evaluations should be aimed at determining if the purpose and goals established by the planning group have been met or to what degree they were met.

Evaluation also gives the planning team information which will help them plan the next retreat experience. Each planning team should have the evaluative input from previous retreat experiences. Don't just do things the same because they've always been successful. Be willing as a planning group to study and understand the evaluations from past retreats. Also be willing to venture out into new areas of retreating which might produce better results.

Following is a sample of one church's retreat evaluation form, completed by the young people just before the closing worship service on Sunday morning.

RETREAT EVALUATION

1. How would you rate your experience at this retreat?

      Very meaningful   10   9   8   7   6   5   4   3   2   1   **Not meaningful**

2. What is your reaction to these specific sessions:

Friday night:	Squirms (crowdbreaker)	**Good** 10 9 8 7 6 5 4 3 2 1	**No good**
	Who are you? (session 1)	10 9 8 7 6 5 4 3 2 1	
	Friday surprise	10 9 8 7 6 5 4 3 2 1	
Saturday:	Breakfast	10 9 8 7 6 5 4 3 2 1	
	Exercise showdown	10 9 8 7 6 5 4 3 2 1	
	Shoe mess (crowdbreaker)	10 9 8 7 6 5 4 3 2 1	
	I am special (session 2)	10 9 8 7 6 5 4 3 2 1	
	Lunch	10 9 8 7 6 5 4 3 2 1	

        The taming of the west
        (large group game)
          or
        Swimming   10 9 8 7 6 5 4 3 2 1
          or
        Hiking

Getting to know God better (session 3)	10 9 8 7 6 5 4 3 2 1	
Dinner	10 9 8 7 6 5 4 3 2 1	
Talent show	10 9 8 7 6 5 4 3 2 1	
Special devotions (session 4)	10 9 8 7 6 5 4 3 2 1	
Redeye, midnight theater	10 9 8 7 6 5 4 3 2 1	

Sunday:	Early morning quiet time	10 9 8 7 6 5 4 3 2 1
	Breakfast	10 9 8 7 6 5 4 3 2 1
	Exercise showdown	10 9 8 7 6 5 4 3 2 1
	Creative worship	10 9 8 7 6 5 4 3 2 1

3. What personal reactions or feelings do you have about this retreat?

4. What did you like best about this weekend?

5. What would you change?

6. What suggestions would you have?

_____
                     Name (optional)

FOLLOW-UP IS MORE THAN EVALUATION

Follow-up is not only evaluation. Follow-up is maintaining contact with the participants on a personal basis to help them along their faith journeys. A young person who discovered something painful in his life during the retreat experience may need to be referred to the pastor. Other young people may want you to set up a conference with their parents. Or, you may want to design your own follow-up with the individual.

If the follow-up warrants, help the young people clarify their experience and refer them to someone with the appropriate pastoral counseling training. Young people may also discover something quite exciting about their own future life direction at a retreat. Again, the follow-up should include referring them to people who can help them sort out their experience and aid them in taking appropriate steps.

A gathering of retreat participants a week or two (even a month) following the retreat may be a valuable learning experience as they reflect upon "life since the retreat." Have they acted upon decisions they made at the retreat? Have they found new meaningful experiences since the retreat? What you will expect to share together at the post-retreat experience will generally depend upon the purpose and goals of the particular retreat. You may want to share the goals and invite the group to comment on how these goals were or were not met. The post-retreat meeting might include the parents as well.

BACK HOME FOLLOW-UP

Follow-up may also include helping the group share their collective feelings with the congregation or community. For instance, a retreat on the topic of sharing concern for others could result in the youth group planning regular visits to a convalescent hospital to visit with and listen to the patients. Some retreats may result in new faith commitments which individuals and groups can share in an adult worship service.

Whatever the method or activity, the retreat experience should connect with the young people's "back home" life. Perhaps the critical question for the planning group is how to connect the retreat experience with the back home lives of the individuals and the life of the group.

BRIDGE IDEAS
to help you connect the retreat to back home

- An art display expressing the meaning of the retreat
- A worship service designed to share the impact of the retreat
- Participant statements in a regular worship service
- A display of pictures or a slide show of the retreat
- A parent/participant sharing meeting
- An article in the church newsletter
- A report to the appropriate board or committee

FOLLOW-UP

Just as the retreat experience began when you started the journey by car or bus, the evaluation and follow-up begin as you begin the trip home. You might want to design an evaluative sheet to be completed during the travel. Recording your own observations as you travel home will give you some feelings of the retreat's meaning and success. Be aware of what young people and their sponsors are talking about. Are their feelings positive or negative?

A great deal of the caring team's responsibility is helping young people to re-enter the back home setting. Some young people may want to remain at the retreat site and bask in the spiritual and emotional sunlight. The caring team should encourage these young people on the trip home.

The planning team may want to travel together and discuss their reactions to the experience. If you have the time, the planning team may remain an extra hour at the retreat center to begin their evaluative process and to do their own group closure and follow-up with one another.

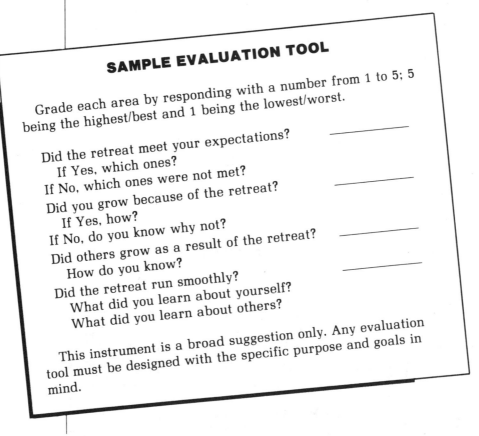

SAMPLE EVALUATION TOOL

Grade each area by responding with a number from 1 to 5; 5 being the highest/best and 1 being the lowest/worst.

Did the retreat meet your expectations?   _____
   If Yes, which ones?
If No, which ones were not met?
Did you grow because of the retreat?   _____
   If Yes, how?
If No, do you know why not?
Did others grow as a result of the retreat?   _____
   How do you know?
Did the retreat run smoothly?   _____
   What did you learn about yourself?
   What did you learn about others?

This instrument is a broad suggestion only. Any evaluation tool must be designed with the specific purpose and goals in mind.

MOUNTAINTOP TO PLAIN

Retreat "mountaintop" experiences are fantastic. However, it is important to work on "coming down" as one leaves the retreat and heads home. It seems that when we get into a peak experience of a retreat it is sometimes tough to re-enter the home situation. This state can sometimes bring on depression or bad feelings. But this doesn't have to happen.

You and your group can take the experiences at the special event and blend them into your home situation. There are some steps to facilitate this process.

First, each person should gather with other members of the retreat and spend some intentional time debriefing. Begin by focusing on a personal reflection of the warmest moment of the event. Ponder this question, for example: "What was the best thing about this retreat?" It might help to write down that memory. After everyone has recorded or focused on that one aspect of the event, each person shares it with the group. If the memory is too personal, go on to the next person.

The next step toward re-entry will be the group's brainstorming on how your group can use some of those retreat experiences in your youth program. This may be a small idea or memorable moment. You might remember something that another young person shared in a small brainstorming session. You might begin this step as individual reflection and then move into a group sharing and discussion. During the youth session, be sure to write every idea on a piece of newsprint or blackboard. You will be amazed how

continued

MOUNTAINTOP TO PLAIN
continued

the space will be filled with ideas. As one person remembers a useful idea, it will trigger a new idea in someone else.

The last step draws these highlights into your program. Have the group members develop the ideas for use in next week's meeting or in following weeks.

Mountaintop experiences need not stay on the mountain. This procedure I've described can make them beginning points in youth ministry long after returning from the mountain.

Thom Schultz

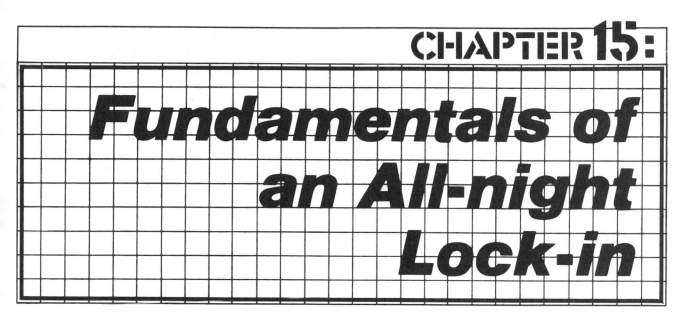

CHAPTER 15

Fundamentals of an All-night Lock-in

By Rickey Short

A lock-in is a one-night, jam-packed form of a retreat. If planned well, a lock-in can become a high point in your ministry.

For a great change of pace, why not try an all-night lock-in? Your young people will get to know each other in ways they never realized. This dusk-to-dawn extravaganza mixes games, foolishness, Bible study, discussion—well, almost anything you want to plan. If planned well, a lock-in can become a high point of your summer (or fall or winter or spring) youth program. Whether you schedule a mixture of serious and fun times or whether you plan to skate all night, several basic techniques can increase your lock-in's effectiveness.

The *purpose* of your all-night event, the *planning* and the *preparation* will all affect the lock-in's *performance*. An all-night lock-in involves the total person on the physical, mental, emotional, social and spiritual levels. Everything that happens affects someone on one of these levels.

Because the lock-in is a time of total involvement it becomes a time of high risk for failure by the youth group. Stress, fatigue and social factors affect activities that would be successful in a normal two-day retreat or a daytime mini-retreat. These different factors will not necessarily cause a good program to fail, but they may produce a lack of motivation to get involved in an activity which seems much less exciting at 5 a.m. than at midnight.

Why risk the failure? Because the chance for success is equally high. Fatigue does wonders in lowering a person's personality defenses (not to mention a clique's defense mechanisms). Youth who are just "speaking friends" will build a bond of friendship after 12 hours of shoulder-to-shoulder, eyeball-to-eyeball interaction.

There is an old saying that you should not marry a person until you have seen your prospective spouse with a bad cold or sick with the flu.

There is a "knowing" and "being known" that comes out of being bone tired. Discussions and openness take on new dimensions when the makeup begins to wear off and cute interpersonal techniques wear out.

The following tips can help you increase the potential for success.

TIPS FOR PLANNING

Begin planning well in advance of when it seems most likely that you could schedule a lock-in. Two or three months are usually required. You will need to meet with different committees three or four times to check up on how programs and preparations are progressing. The committees must have their different programs clearly in mind by the last planning session. There are no exceptions. Plan well and plan in detail if you want a successful lock-in.

DETERMINE THE PURPOSE FIRST

It may not be easy to get the entire youth group to discuss and determine why you want to have a lock-in. Some will want the overnighter because it was done before or because another group in town had one. The "Why are we doing this?" should be clear to everybody before any lock-in plans are made. The time you've spent in answering this question will bear fruit at the lock-in when someone asks, "What are we supposed to be doing here anyway?"

Drafting a statement of purpose may seem unnecessarily time consuming, but it will bring into focus much of what you plan to do and how it is to be done.

If one goal for your lock-in is to attract other teenagers to your youth group, you will want to advertise like crazy. If you want to experience

> "The 'Why are we doing this?' should be clear to everybody before any lock-in plans are made."

Zilch Night Prayer

Here is a night prayer that is very effective on retreats. Needed is a zilch, a pan of water, Bible, matches, record player and the song "Dust in the Wind" by Kansas.

To make a zilch, take any plastic holding device from a six pack of pop cans and cut the six rings into a straight strip of plastic. (It won't be perfectly straight, but just be sure it can hang from one end.) Then, hang this plastic strip (called a zilch) from the ceiling using a coat hanger or other non-burning device. Place a wide pan of water directly beneath the zilch. Light the bottom of the zilch with a match. As the zilch burns upward, pieces of melted plastic will drip into the pan of water and extinguish themselves. This is particularly effective as a focal point for meditation.

Before you light the zilch, calm the group down and say a few words about life and death and the meaning of both. Mention that ashes in the Bi-

and develop a small intimate fellowship, do no advertising except to let the parents and church leaders know your plans.

SEVEN IMPORTANT PLANNING AREAS

1. ■ Recreation

Energetic and fast-paced recreation times can provide a positive contribution to your lock-in. Determine who will be in charge of the recreation and sport times. Ask the planning team to develop a program the planning committee can discuss. The key is to have a well-prepared outline of games, skits and strenuous physical sports. Explanations of how to play new games should be thought out and any materials needed for the recreation time should be secured well in advance. Have all the things you need at the lock-in site a day early.

Balance recreation time with worship and spiritual programs. Balance new games with old favorites everybody knows how to play. Balance competitive games with non-competitive games. Balance skill games with non-skill games.

Use physical activity to stimulate and create energy in the early morning hours. Use table games, crafts and fun songs to fill free time or to make transition to other programs on the agenda.

How about free time? It is better not to fill up the final hours of your lock-in with free time. If the group is tired the free time may be seen as a signal that the lock-in is over. Getting a final wrap-up session started may be impossible if kids have been dozing for an hour or more.

"Balance recreation time with worship and spiritual programs."

ble have always been a symbol of the grave and our own mortality. God created woman/man out of the earth and to dust they shall return. Have students reflect on the quality of their own lives and the direction they are heading. Tell them to listen to the readings and the song you are about to play.

After this brief introduction, turn the lights out and light the zilch. Then read Matthew 6:31-34. Play "Dust in the Wind."

Have everyone listen to the lyrics and watch the zilch burn upward, extinguishing itself. Usually students are so fascinated by the zilch that they don't say a word. You may wish to conclude with a brief prayer. Timing is important in this prayer, so that things move smoothly. You may want to practice and rehearse this until you feel competent with it. We've always had excellent results with this technique.

Frank Zolvinski

2. ■ Food

Plan food times to follow recreation times or preceding, during and after any film you wish to show. Choose a food committee to prepare, serve and clean up after snack times. Be sure that whatever you plan to serve can be prepared in large quantities with the available facilities. A household oven will keep a lot of hamburgers or pancakes warm but it will not cook seven pizzas at once. Make arrangements so that you can serve everyone at one time.

3. ■ Devotions, spiritual growth and worship

Determine if the youth sponsors or members of the youth group will be in charge of these sessions. The atmosphere of the room sometimes plays a part in sensitive spiritual times. Setting the stage for a serious spiritual time is especially important if you have been running relays in the area you now plan to worship in.

Balance spiritual times with social and physical sports times.

Sunrise devotions seem like a natural but they may be hard to pull off effectively at the end of a lock-in. Physical fatigue becomes a competitive factor to spiritual sensitivity in the early morning hours. The peak spiritual time should come three or four hours into the lock-in while the mind is fresh and the emotions are still responsive.

Select music in advance. If you use a guitar be sure the guitarist can play the songs before the song leader teaches them to the group.

4. ■ Bible studies or training programs

If your lock-in has a theme and you plan three or four sessions around that theme, you can separate each serious session with recreation, food, free time or a film. If free time precedes a serious session, be sure everyone is clear about when and where they are to meet next.

It is difficult to do serious, concentrated thinking much after 3 a.m. Plan to meet your major objectives before that time. Be creative in your teaching method and use a variety of methods to stimulate interest. If small group discussions are planned, break down into small groups by age so that the older kids will not dominate their group's discussions. If your youth group is large enough and you have qualified leadership, you can offer optional activities during your lock-in and allow kids to choose a session that appeals to them the most.

Place a guest speaker on the program early and allow him or her to leave during a later session.

5. Discipline

It is impossible to come up with a set of rules that would cover every possible circumstance. It is best to keep the rules few and simple. Be specific in advertising and in prelock-in sessions about appropriate dress at the lock-in. Electronic games, radios, comic books and TVs are not a problem at a marathon rocking session, but strict controls should be placed on them at lock-ins where group and individual participation is crucial to the lock-in's success.

Telephone use should be restricted. Youth should expect to stay for the entire lock-in when they come. Check with parents if a teenager must leave early.

6. Finances

Mention the cost in every lock-in advertisement. Plan how and when to collect money so that no one fails to pay. It is a good idea to close registration two or three days before the lock-in so that final food plans and financial arrangements can be made. If possible, collect all monies before the lock-in. This gives them an added incentive to come to the lock-in even though some other optional activity came up at the last minute.

7. Starting with a bang

What happens at the lock-in during the first hour sets the tone for the entire lock-in. Plan the first hour to involve every person. Schedule surprises to excite them about the rest of the lock-in.

Four things need to happen at the beginning of the lock-in:

1. Reduce tension and nervousness while building community. This can be done many ways but usually involves doing strange and unusual things together such as crazy songs, unusual exercises or weird games. Acting silly reduces tension and is fun.

2. Get in touch with the overall group feelings, attitudes and expectations about the lock-in. Simple, non-threatening questions allow people to express something about their current emotional state. (Such as: "The color I most feel like . . ." or "The things I hope to get out of this lock-in are . . .")

3. Clarify rules, purpose and schedule. Answer questions about the rules and schedule.

4. Determine teams for relay and sports events to break down existing cliques and contribute to the overall unity of the youth group. Random drawings or fun exercises help the young person identify with and belong to his or her new team. Controlling the team formations reinforces the similarities among the members in the group and allows them to discover important things about other kids in the group.

With your purpose clearly in mind and a well-planned, well-prepared program your youth group can create lifetime memories—and short-term fatigue at your most successful lock-in.

CHAPTER 16

Food, Glorious Food

"Food, glorious food!" Oliver Twist and friends aren't the only ones who feel this way when they smell something cooking.

Any group at almost any retreat will be starving and beg for "food, glorious food." So make it good, make it plentiful and make it nutritious.

If you are going to do your own cooking, read through these menus, recipes and special "food fundamentals." A veteran retreat cook shared her menus, recipes and helpful hints to make your first tries at cooking for a crowd as easy as possible.

So read on. And Bon Appetit!

Menus to help you make it good, make it plentiful and make it nutritious.

FOOD FUNDAMENTALS

Balance—Balance easy and difficult meal plans so they don't all appear the same day. Three hard-to-prepare meals in one day will exhaust you.

Beverages—Orange drink—Check with your local McDonald's. Some branches will give you the use of the cooler and cups free, and you can buy the concentrate at a cheaper price than in the grocery store, too.

Milk—Try to use five-gallon containers and a dispenser. It's easy and neat!

Bottles of pop—In the long run a poor choice. Kids end up shaking the bottles and squirting each other.

Budget—A dirty word, but the sky isn't the limit. Every penny counts. Buy in large quantities and by the case if possible. See if you can return unopened cans for a refund.

—Figure on an average of $1 for each meal and snack per person.

—Try to get beef on the hoof and then butchered if you're cooking for a large group.

Bug Juice—A camp nick-name for any colored liquid that is drinkable. Much like Kool-aid only worse. Lime bug juice reminds everyone of squashed green bugs.

Clean up—Have one or two young people to help lift heavy pans and do clean up. Counselors or tables can take turns doing the dishes.

Cooks—For a large crowd have four cooks. (It takes time to make even celery sticks.) Cooks cook—they don't wash dishes.

Eggs—Buy eggs by the crate, if possible. Also, buy brown or cracked eggs—they're cheaper in most areas! When making scrambled eggs don't worry if any "bloods" show up—toss them in. They'll disappear and no one will ever know.

Elephant Stew—A delightful recipe that's economical and goes a long way once you find the special required cut!

Facilities—Take a good look. How may ovens? How many large pots? Do you have your own key? What are the breakage and damage costs? Test the ovens for proper temperature. Make sure all necessary equipment is there.

Food—The key word to every retreat. Everyone loves to eat so make it good and make it plentiful.

Grocery List—Don't forget to make a detailed one—down to the salt and pepper. Remember, you start from scratch.

Jam—That gooey stuff that you spread on bread, toast, and anything that doesn't look very edible. Buy it in large tins and only pick a small assortment.

Julia Child—A great cook whose recipes will break your budget.

Knife—Take along your electric knife from home. It makes cutting extra easy.

Know-how—The thing that every experienced chef has and every kitchen helper wishes he or she possessed.

Large Meals—Generally large meals like roasts with potatoes and vegetables are easier to prepare and serve than hot dogs or hamburgers—especially for a large crowd.

Leftovers—Those fabulous morsels that don't look so fabulous two days later. Use them wisely—

leftover ham from dinner is great in scrambled eggs;

leftover bread, pancakes, crusts, even coffeecake will disappear (with no side effects) into a large meatloaf.

Measuring—Most recipes are in gallon quantities or parts of a gallon. For easier measuring take a plastic gallon jug and mark it on the outside according to 1/2-1/4-3/8-etc.

Milk—The white- or chocolate-colored liquid that comes from a cow and kids can't get enough of. Buy it in five-gallon containers with a dispenser if possible. It's easier and cheaper that way.

Nutritious—Have GOOD food to make nutritious and balanced meals. Kids love to eat! Make it nutritious—the last thing you need is sick kids.

Pam—Use a spray shortening like PAM to coat pans. Use it generously. It saves on clean up.

Plan Ahead—Make as many sauces, salads, etc. as you can at home before the retreat. It saves time and headaches when you're busy.

Oven—Check your oven temperature with your own oven thermometer from home. Most institutional ovens are not accurate, so don't trust the setting without testing them out.

Salads/Salad Bar—Get your lettuce mixture from a local produce supplier. The mixture is sold by the pound (ask how much you'll need) and usually consists of a variety of lettuces, cabbage, carrots, etc. all cut, mixed and in large bags. Stays very fresh.

Buy dressing in large bottles and put it out in bowls. Roquefort, French and Thousand Island are favorites.

Sauce/Spaghetti—Although you can make your own sauce, it can be messy and time consuming. If you do want to make your own, make it ahead of time and bottle it before the retreat.

Better yet, buy canned sauce with meat. It's usually cheaper and very good (starving kids will never know the difference). Add some additional spices to the canned sauce to give it some pizzazz!

Snacks—Friday evening, have a big snack since the kids will probably be hungry after driving and may have skipped supper.

Spaghetti—Fixing spaghetti may sound like a nice, easy and inexpensive meal. But beware: Cooking pounds of noodles can be tricky especially if there aren't enough pots for both the sauce and the spaghetti, or it if takes ages for the water to boil and stay boiling.

One other trick is figuring out how many pounds of dry spaghetti is needed for your gang. (Most recipes only give the needed pounds of cooked noodles.)

So think before you choose spaghetti—make sure it's worth it.

Tongue—As in tongue-in-cheek—which is the way you should be reading some of this.

Warmth—To keep food warm, spread towels or lay tins over the pans. Leave the dish in a warm oven.

MENUS

SNACKS:
Pizza
Hot cider*
  or
Doughnuts
Hot cocoa*
  or
Hot dogs
Orange drink
Coffee
  or
Pie and Redi-whip
Orange drink

BREAKFASTS:
Pancakes/syrup
Whipped butter
Dry cereal
Juice, milk and coffee
  or
Scrambled eggs*
Coffee cake*
Peaches
Dry cereal
Milk and coffee

LUNCHES:
Sloppy joes*
Frosted fruit salad*
Carrot sticks
Milk and coffee
  or
Spaghetti with meat sauce*
Cole slaw*
French bread
Pears
Beverages
Rolls with butter
  or
Tuna casserole*
Salad bar* and jello*
Carrot sticks
Milk and coffee

SUPPERS:
Meat loaf*
Fruit salad
Vegetable (peas)
Au gratin potatoes
Rolls with butter

RECIPES

Baked Potatoes
Use #110 count, wash and oil and prick. Bake at 350 degrees for 1½ hours.

Easy Jello
4½ lb. pkgs. with 2 #10 cans of fruit cocktail serves 90 people.

Hot Cider (raw)
4 gallons cider
4 sticks cinnamon
1 cup brown sugar
2 large cans orange juice

Easy Cocoa
Use Swiss Miss. One 32 oz. box and 1½ gallons water times 3 serves 90 thirsty folks.

continued

   or
Roast beef
Whipped potatoes with gravy
Corn
Orange jello with fruit*
Relishes
Beverage
   or
Baked ham (Virginia style)*
Baked potatoes with butter & sour cream*
Green beans
Applesauce
Rolls
Milk and coffee
   or
Oven-fried chicken*
Whipped potatoes with butter
Corn
Salad bar
Carrot and raisin salad*
Beverages

*recipes given

CANNED VEGETABLE YIELDS

Carrots	#10	26 portions
Beans	#10	25 portions
Corn	#10	23 portions
Tomatoes	#10	25 portions

AMOUNTS AND EQUIVALENTS

7 #1 cans equal 1 #10 can
5 #2 cans equal 1 #10 can
4 #2½ cans equal 1 #10 can
3 #3 cans equal 1 #10 can
2 #5 cans equal 1 #10 can

119

Frosted Fruit Salad—serves 70

2 cups lemon jello
2 cups orange jello
3 qts. hot water
2¼ qts. cold water
12 bananas
1 #10 can crushed pineapple (drained)
3 cups miniature marshmallows

When set—add topping.

Topping

2 cups sugar
4 eggs (beaten)
½ cup flour
½ cup margarine
4 cups pineapple juice

Cook and cool above ingredients. Add 8 cups Cool Whip.

Cole Slaw—serves 125

4 large heads of cabbage
2 large cans of crushed pineapple
grated carrots
salt to taste
salad dressing until moist
add celery seed for "class"

Do ahead of time—put in 2 bread bags.

Meat Loaf—serves 50

14 lbs. ground beef
3 lbs. ground pork
12 cups bread crumbs (3 qts.—use leftover crust, pancakes, etc.)
9 cups milk
1½ cups finely chopped onion
1½ tsp. dry mustard
¾ tsp. sage
4 tbsp. salt
1½ tsp. pepper

Mix all ingredients together. Pack into greased pans. Bake 1½ hours in moderate oven (350 degrees).

Spaghetti Sauce—#10 institutional can with meat; add spices to taste.

Look under restaurant supply in the yellow pages.
It may not look it, but it saves time and money.
See if you can bring back unopened cans—buy by the case and return it. (See spaghetti under "Food Fundamentals.")

Salad Bar

Lettuce mixture from produce market.
Dressing in large bottles (Roquefort, French, Thousand Island).
Put out any leftover jello, carrot raisin salad, carrot sticks or applesauce. (See Salad under "Food Fundamentals.")

Tuna Casserole—serves 200

15 lbs. dry egg noodles (use 2 10-lb. boxes of noodles if necessary)
8 lbs tuna
8 51-oz. cans cream of mushroom soup
Frozen peas

Cook egg noodles until tender and drain and rinse thoroughly (can be done a night ahead). Mix tuna, soup and peas and add mixture to drained egg noodles.

Bake until top is golden brown. 350 degrees at least 1 hour.

Coffee Cake—serves 50

Can be baked the night before and reheated in the oven for 15 min.

1 gallon flour
1½ cups sugar
1¼ cups powdered milk
¾ cup baking powder
2¾ tablespoons salt
6 eggs

Topping for Coffee Cake

3/8 gallon brown sugar
3/8 gallon white sugar
3/8 cup cinnamon
1¼ cups flour
1¼ pounds butter

Mix base ingredients. Add water to desired consistency. DO NOT make batter runny. Spread out evenly into 2 16" × 26" pans. Crumble topping over base. Bake at 350 degrees for 35 minutes.

Oven-Fried Chicken—serves 50

30 pounds of fryers (or 12 fryers, approximately 2½ pounds each)
6 cups flour or biscuit mix
½ cup salt
2 tablespoons paprika
1½ teaspoons pepper
8 to 10 cups shortening

Mix all dry ingredients. Melt the shortening in shallow pans, allowing about ¼ cup per serving. Wash pieces of chicken and shake off excess water. Dip pieces in the flour or dry mix until well coated. Place them skin side down in the pans with the shortening. Place in a 400-degree oven for 20 minutes, then turn and sprinkle with additional paprika. Continue baking for 45 to 60 minutes at the same temperature or until the chicken is tender and golden brown.

Baked Virginia Ham

25 lbs. of ham serves 90 if it's sliced ¼" thick (slicer set on #15).

Scrambled Baked Eggs—serves 50—they're GREAT!

1 lb. butter
18 dozen eggs
1 gallon milk
½ lb. soda crackers

Take eggs out of cooler and crack the night before so they're room temperature. Spray heavy pan thoroughly with Pam. Melt butter in pan. Pour in milk and heat to scalding; add finely crushed crackers. Heat until mixture steams. Add eggs and salt and pepper to taste. After ½ hour turn eggs every 10 minutes or when sides begin to stick. Don't let mixture dry out. Bake 1 hour to 1¼ hour at 350 degrees.

Sweet-and-Sour Sauce for Chicken

Buy chicken already cut up—just legs and thighs. Two pieces per person.

7 qts. and 2 cups pineapple juice
15 cups brown sugar
3¾ cups corn starch
2½ tablespoons ginger
20 cups vinegar
1¾ cups soy sauce

Grease pans—place chicken in—pour sauce over. Bake at 325 degrees for 2 hours.

Sloppy Joes—serves 50

15 lbs. ground beef
1 cup chopped celery
½ cup onions—chopped
4 cans chicken gumbo soup (10¾ oz. size)
2 large cans tomato soup
½ cup brown sugar
½ cup Worcestershire sauce
2 tsp. dry mustard
2 tablespoons salt
½ cup vinegar
pepper—dash

Brown ground beef and add remaining ingredients and simmer.

Carrot and Raisin Salad—serves 50

4 pounds raisins
4 pounds carrots, grated or chopped fine
1 quart mayonnaise

Steam the raisins to plump, then cool. Combine them with the carrots and salad dressing and mix lightly. Serve on lettuce.

Reprinted from **Get Away From It All—Have a Retreat!** from Young Calvinist Federation, Box 7244, Grand Rapids, MI 49510. Used with permission.

HOW TO FIND A COOK FOR YOUR RETREAT
by Mark Lawrence

You've booked the camp site, you've planned a terrific program (you're sure the weather will be good!), there's a good number of kids coming along . . . whoops! . . . What about a cook for the retreat, someone to take care of the inner person?

Begin thinking about a cook for the retreat well before the actual date. Anybody who cooks for retreats is probably a busy person—start searching for your cook a couple of months before the date of the retreat.

What is required of the cook?

Before you actually think about who will cook, consider the responsibilities. Is the cook required to do all the preparation or to be a coordinator ensuring that the campers prepare the food properly? If yours is a study retreat, do you want some students to be called out of sessions to prepare the meal? If not, how can you program appropriately to have preparation and session times not conflicting? (In the case of a study retreat, it is usually a good idea to have cooks preparing the whole meal.) If it is an activity retreat it may be good to have campers being involved in preparing the food. In this case it would be helpful to have a cook who will be a coordinator.

Once you have decided what responsibilities the cook will have to undertake, approach a person to do the job.

How do you begin looking?

Before approaching a potential cook, it's beneficial to have a publicity program about your youth ministry. This publicity, apart from being good general public relations, will help to impress on your church members the importance of retreats in the total program of youth ministry. Below are some points that could be taken up in such a publicity handout:

● Inform the church of the general nature of your youth program: the regular activities, the innovations, the numbers involved, frequency of meetings, general aims of the youth group.

● Highlight the importance of retreats in the total youth ministry of the church.

● Make known that you are looking for a cook for the forthcoming retreat. Points to mention here are that (a.) cooking for a retreat is a valuable service opportunity to the young people and to the church as a whole, and (b.) help will be available for time-consuming tasks (peeling potatoes, for example). Stress the fun aspect of being a retreat cook!

continued

The publicity can be presented in the church notices or may be specially printed. Announcements can also be made at the appropriate time in worship and/or at a meeting of the congregation or parish.

Where do you look?

Most people will be reluctant to volunteer as a retreat cook but would be flattered to be approached. Listed below are some avenues to be explored in finding a suitable person to approach.

Fellowship groups in the church. Spend time with the president of the women's fellowship, young marrieds group or any other likely organization in your church. Explain your needs and ask this person for suggestions of anyone who might be willing to undertake the job.

The minister. He or she may have suggestions—or even be the person you are looking for! Cooking at a retreat is a great way to build relationships. It's likely that the minister will not be available for the whole weekend, but you may be able to work out some kind of part-time arrangement.

Older brothers and sisters of group members may be willing to cook for the retreat. Ask members to check with other members of their families. A parent is another possibility, of course.

When you approach potential cooks, be clear about what will be required of them. Don't try to make it sound easier (or harder) than it really is.

Support the cook!

Cooking for a new group of people can often have the cook feeling nervous and uncertain—both in terms of cooking for a large number and in being with a group of (almost) strangers. Prior to the retreat, work with the cook in developing menus and ordering the food, etc. Also, let the congregation know who has accepted the challenge of cooking for the retreat and thank the church members for their interest.

During the retreat, introduce the cook to the campers and vice versa. Where possible (and if desired by the cook) involve him/her in the regular retreat program. At the close of the retreat, thank the cook for his/her help and the terrific food and present him/her with a simple gift. Reinforce this action with a letter of thanks and appreciation from the group a week or so after the retreat.

Reprinted from **Youthleader**, Issue 21, 5th Floor, 177 Collins St., Melbourne, Australia. Used with permission.

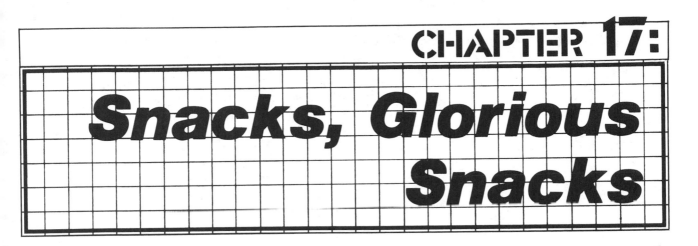

CHAPTER 17

Snacks, Glorious Snacks

ALTERNATIVE SNACKFOOD IDEAS

There is some good news and some bad news about snackfoods. The bad news is that many of the commercially produced snackfoods consist largely of fats and sugar. These include candy bars, soft drinks, potato chips and commercially-made cookies. This type of snackfood is calorie-rich but not nutrient-rich.

Not many people are ready to rid their diet of cookies and cakes. The good news is that this isn't necessary. Snacks, when thoughtfully chosen, can give you quick energy and supply the kind of nutrition which keeps your body looking fit, functioning properly, and resistant to annoying illnesses such as colds, sore throats and flu.

By making your own snackfoods, you can control the amount of fat and sugar they contain and include nutrient-rich ingredients such as oatmeal, whole wheat flour, fruits and nuts. The more snacks you learn to prepare yourself, the less dependent you will be on heavily processed, calorie-rich, nutrient-poor, convenience snackfoods.

The following recipes have been kept low or moderate in cost by using basic, nutritious ingredients that have been processed as little as possible, keeping sugar to a minimum; and by making use of foods that are home or locally grown in many communities.

By Catherine Mumaw and Marilyn Voran

Snackfoods don't have to be calorie-laden and bad for you. Here are seven nutritious snackfood recipes your retreaters will love.

Peanut Butter Popcorn

2 qts. popped corn

½ c. sugar
½ c. light corn syrup or honey
½ c. chunky peanut butter
½ t. vanilla

Cook sugar and syrup or honey together until they come to a rolling boil. Remove from heat and add peanut butter and vanilla. Pour over popcorn, stirring to coat.

Key to abbreviations in recipes:
   T. = tablespoon
   t. = teaspoon
   c. = cup

Barbecued Popcorn

4 c. popped corn
nuts (if desired)
½ c. grated Parmesan cheese
¼ c. butter
½ t. chili powder
½ t. garlic salt
½ t. onion salt

Melt butter, add cheese and seasonings; pour over corn and mix. Makes 4 cups.

Roasted Wheat Berries

Heat a small amount of oil in skillet. Add wheat berries (whole wheat) and pop like popcorn. They don't actually pop, but will puff up. Serve hot with salt.

Pizza

DOUGH:
1 c. warm (not hot) water
1 package or cake Fleischmann's
   yeast, active dry or compressed
1 t. sugar
1 t. salt
2 T. olive or salad oil
2 c. whole wheat flour
1½ c. sifted enriched flour

TOMATO MIXTURE:
6 oz. can tomato paste
½ c. water
1 t. salt
1 t. oregano, crushed
¼ t. basil
1 t. fennel seed, if available

Measure water and place in bowl. Sprinkle or crumble in the yeast. Stir until dissolved. Stir in sugar, salt and oil. Add 2 c. flour. Beat until smooth. Stir in about 1½ c. additional flour. Turn out on lightly floured board. Knead until smooth and elastic. Place in greased bowl; brush top with soft shortening. Cover and let rise in warm place, free from draft, until doubled in bulk (about 45 minutes).

Mix together ingredients for tomato mixture. Set aside.

When dough is doubled in bulk, punch down; divide in half. Form each half into ball; place on greased baking sheet. Press out with palms of hands into circle about 12″ in diameter, making edges slightly thick. On each circle of dough arrange and/or spread the following:

4 oz. mozzarella cheese, sliced about 1/8'' thick
½ of the tomato mixture
2 T. olive or salad oil
2 T. grated Parmesan cheese

Bake in hot oven at 400 degrees about 25 minutes. Serve hot. Makes two 12″ pies.

Pizzaburgers

1 lb. ground beef
⅓ c. Parmesan cheese, grated
¼ c. onion, finely chopped
¼ c. ripe olives, chopped
1 t. salt
dash pepper
1 t. oregano, crushed
6 oz. can tomato paste
6-8 slices mozzarella cheese
6-8 hamburger rolls

Combine all ingredients except mozzarella cheese and blend together. Spread on bottom half of rolls. Place in pan and broil 5" to 6" from heat for about 10 minutes until meat is cooked.

Add cheese slices and put back in oven until cheese begins to melt. Remove from oven and place other half of roll on the sandwich.

Serves six to eight.

Soft Pretzels

2 pkgs. dry yeast
1½ c. warm water
½ t. salt
4½ c. enriched flour
¼ c. baking soda in 1 c. water

Dissolve yeast in warm water. Sift flour into a large bowl. Add yeast and salt to flour. Mix well and let rise about 15 minutes.

Roll in long strips about 8" long and place in soda solution for 2 minutes.

Shape and place on greased cookie sheet. Sprinkle with salt.

Bake 20 minutes at 350 degrees. Makes 12 pretzels.

Homemade Vanilla Ice Cream

6 Junket rennet tablets
¼ c. cold water
2¼ c. sugar
2 qts. milk (not canned)
2⅔ c. heavy cream
8 t. vanilla

Dissolve rennet tablets in cold water. Combine remaining ingredients and heat to lukewarm (110 degrees). Quickly stir in dissolved rennet tablets and pour into freezing container. Let stand undisturbed for 10 minutes.

In a hand freezer, pack freezer can in crushed ice and allow to cool before freezing (30-40 minutes). This reduces freezing time and assures smooth-textured ice cream. Freeze in 4 parts ice to 1 part salt until dasher is hard to turn. Remove dasher and repack in ice and salt. Let stand about 2 hours before eating.

Makes 4 qts.

VARIATIONS

Omit vanilla in basic recipe. Add one of the following ingredients when thickened rennet ice cream mixture is cooled and ready to freeze (or stir in when dasher is removed).

Fruit: 2 c. mashed, sweetened strawberries, raspberries, peaches, or bananas, 2 t. lemon juice

Maple walnut: 2 t. maple extract, 2 c. chopped walnuts

Chocolate chip: 2 c. shaved sweet chocolate or semi-sweet chocolate bits (do not omit vanilla in recipe)

Chocolate: Follow recipe for vanilla ice cream, adding 1½ c. cocoa (not Dutch processed). Blend sugar and cocoa. Add liquid slowly, making a smooth paste. Continue according to directions.

Reprinted from **The Whole Thing**, edited by Catherine Mumaw and Marilyn Voran, © 1980 by Herald Press, Scottdale, PA 15683.

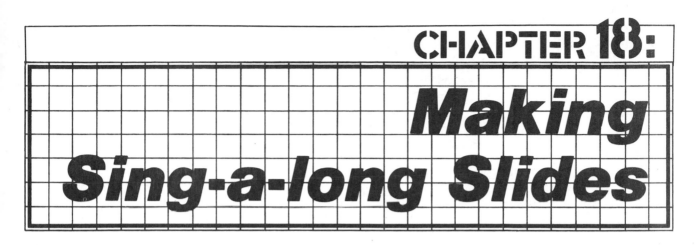

CHAPTER 18:
Making Sing-a-long Slides

According to many multimedia specialists the easiest, most accessible, and most effective audio-visual medium is the 35mm slide. Programs can be assembled and changed at the producer's discretion. The variety of possibilities are endless:

PHOTOGRAPHY

New or old slides can tell a story. Sometimes the effect is aided by the proximity of two slides being projected at the same time, sometimes the addition of sound effects, narration or music helps the slides to come alive, and at other times it is the rapid succession of different images that stirs an audience. Photography slides let you share the emotions and instances in the lives of real persons caught by the photography. There's nothing like seeing yourself on the screen, either in a picture made a decade ago or an hour ago.

CONTACT SLIDES

An easy method for making slides without a camera is to use clear Contact paper cut to the size of a slide frame. The back is peeled off and the sticky side is placed over a chosen illustration which has been printed on clay-based paper. (You can tell by wetting your finger, rubbing it over the paper and seeing if some of the paper comes off on your finger.) All of the air bubbles must be worked out by pressing your thumb or a stiff object over the Contact paper until the image can be seen very clearly. The section of the paper with the illustration or picture is cut from the magazine and dropped into clear, warm water. In a couple of minutes the paper falls away (peeling it along may be needed), and the ink remains in the Contact glue. The transparency can then be mounted and a slide has been created.

By Bill Wolfe

If you're planning a retreat for a large number of people, you may want to make sing-a-long slides. They're simple, easy to make and effective.

"Project lyrics on several screens while playing the record of a favorite, singable pop song over the PA system, and everyone can sing together."

SING-A-LONG SLIDES

For years contemporary music presented not only a threat to churches because of its unfamiliar phrases and often outspoken references, but also because it was profoundly difficult for organists, choirs and congregations to learn quickly. The result was that the most devoted fans of the music—the young—were disappointed with the amateurish representation of some of their favorite selections.

Things improved greatly when Garrett Short of Riverside, California, discovered that he could project lyrics on several screens while playing the record of a favorite, singable pop song over the PA system, and everyone could sing together. He used Ortho film to photograph art contributed by members of his congregation, and his son, John, added color to the slides to create a spectacular worship environment.

The copyright law makes unauthorized printed duplication of lyrics illegal (as in the familiar song sheets) while at the same time it permits the owner of a copy of a song "to display that copy publicly, either directly or by the projection of no more than one image at a time, to viewers present at the place where the copy is located" (S109 of Public Law 94-553). Illegal song sheets allow a member of the congregation to physically take home a copy of the song and thereby not need to purchase a copy. But the projection of the material allows the person to be introduced to the song but not have ownership of a copy. The "no more than one image at a time" clause permits short quotes at a time, else the projector with all the lyrics could be left on and anyone could copy the entire song.

The sing-a-long slide-making procedure can be a fun experience for groups and can involve numerous persons, particularly those with technical and photography skills. Artists, typists and even attentive lyric listeners are definitely needed. Often the process can be done on two successive Sunday evenings and serve as a combination mixer, program (lyric analysis), creative activity and Bible study.

Here are a few general tips for use with any of the previous three methods. Use at least two screens and two projectors for projection since even a brief pause for changing slides on just one screen makes group singing difficult. The sound source should be sufficiently strong to be heard so that when the group really gets involved, the accompaniment, especially the tempo, will not be lost. Place only a few phrases of lyrics on each slide, preferably in a way to represent pauses, loudness and feeling. Graphics should be added for use during instrumental portions of the song. Complete credits (song title, author, singer, record label and number, copyright date and publisher) should be printed on the first slide.

In addition to music, slides can also be made of liturgies, scripture, prayers, illustrations, announcements or whatever.

OFFSET SLIDES

This is a way to make slides without having to own a camera, buy film or develop it. You can utilize as much or as little artistic talent as is available. The process involves having an offset printer (usually located in every community) make a negative of your material. You can then color the negative and mount it as slides.

First, you will need a roll of butcher paper (or any other totally white paper—newsprint is not white enough). Draw a dark black line (magic marker) 16 inches across the top of where you are going to place your material. Then draw two 21-inch lines down from both ends of your first line. Connect at the bottom—you have a vertical rectangle 16 x 21 inches. Across the first line make markings at each 4-inch length and draw lines all the way to the bottom. On both sides, starting at the top, make markings at each 3½-inch length and draw lines across to the other side. At this point you should have 24 boxes, each 4 x 3½ inches. Each of these will eventually be a single slide. (See diagram.)

Now you will need to set margins on each of the 24 slides in order to know what will later appear on a screen and what will fit inside the slide mount. The margins on each of those 24 squares should be one-half inch on top and bottom. You can indicate this on your drawing by using a light blue (non-reproducing) pencil and actually drawing these margin lines across and down each line of slides. Or, you can make a pattern of these on another piece of paper with a dark pen to put under your drawing (which is faster in the long run because you can use that pattern over and over).

Inside the margins of each slide put any kind of print, type, or artwork you may choose, using a rather dark impression. You can fold the paper and put it into a typewriter. You can cut out art, preferably line drawings and high contrast graphics, and paste it within the margins. You can even paste corrections over mistakes. Make each frame as full as you wish.

When completed, take the entire sheet to your neighborhood offset printer. Tell that person that you want a negative made of the material. (Normally, the negative is the middle process prior to burning a metal plate that will be used in the printing.) Explain that you will need it to be reduced on a setting of 38 percent. Actually, this means that the reduction will really be almost two-thirds, so that

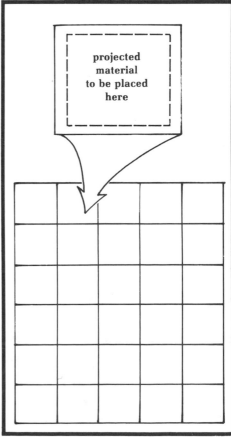

projected material to be placed here

you will wind up with a negative approximately one-third the size of the paper drawing you brought in. Or to say it another way, you will want the negative to be 38 percent the size of the original.

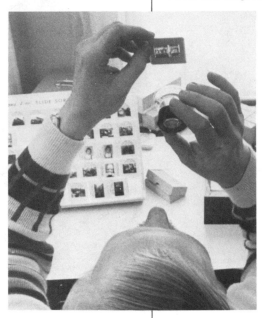

We have tested the price of this at various places in the nation: It ranges from $2 per sheet in one community, where the printer was a member of one of the churches, to $8 in another city, where I'm sure the clerk was reading the wrong scale. Normally, we have found that the price is four dollars per sheet almost everywhere, and that's not bad for 24 perfect slides with no other photography costs. And normally, the time involved is less than an hour. We have conducted workshops in which all the artwork of an entire week could be made into negatives during a lunch hour one day.

Speaking of costs, watch this next item. The coloring you will need in order to transform these stark negatives into radiant color positives for projection can be found at your neighborhood grocery at 69 cents per set of four containers of food coloring. Better pick up a small box of toothpicks and cotton. You now have enough supplies for several years!

Twist a tiny amount of cotton onto the end of a toothpick. A Q-tip of cotton contains too much cotton. Put a few drops of food coloring, full strength or diluted, on the cotton and begin coloring the lines of the soon-to-be-slides. The coloring works just like water colors and needs to be blotted occasionally before circles of residue form and two different colors mix. Most persons will use all of blue, let it dry, then use orange, etc. The more layers of coloring you apply, the darker will be the picture.

Felt-tip marking pens also work well for coloring the negatives.

A light table (opaque surface with light inside) is delightful to use for this, but if one is not readily available, a slide sorter tilted to one side works well.

Either side of the film can be colored. You will probably notice that some printers will blot out all little dots of extraneous matter that might appear on the film. The ink they use may run with your coloring, so it is usually a good idea to put the coloring on the side of the film opposite the black ink.

When you are ready to mount the slides, cut out each small square along the first bold lines that you drew. They can be mounted into cardboard mounts and lightly ironed together, or you can use any one of the variety of plastic mounts.

Most groups have a camera buff who could easily be the key to a process that involves a 35mm camera, a roll of Pantomic-X film (found at most photo supply stores), a few sheets of butcher paper, Magic Markers and a little time in a dark room, makeshift if necessary.

Lyrics are written with bold markers on the butcher paper in any size with a 2′ × 3′ proportion. For instance, if the camera to be used is a rather simple one with no close-up lenses, you might prefer to put the print within an area 14 inches in height and 11 inches in length. You can discover the exact margins for your camera by looking through the viewfinder (probably about three feet from the paper) and checking out the scope that can be clearly captured. You may wish to make a pattern using bold lines for the margins within which the lyrics can be placed, and put this pattern under the butcher paper to serve as a guide for where each section of the lyrics are being printed.

Load the camera with the Pantomic-X (used because of its non-grainy texture).

In order to avoid using a flash or special lighting, the entire sheet of paper containing the lyrics can be placed on the side of a building outside and photographed using available light, preferably a shady space or the light of a cloudy day in order that the glare not be too harsh.

Once all the pictures have been taken, develop the film (based on the instructions with the film) or have it done by a commercial photo shop. If you have the film processed by a commercial shop, just order the developing, no prints. In fact, the film should be left in rolls, so that later you can add color, cut the slides apart, and mount.

At this stage, the film will look like an X-ray or a negative with all the letters transparent and the background grayish black. Magic Markers can be used to give color, though they will give a slightly streaked effect; food coloring for the entire slide will add a solid tint throughout. More preferable: Thin, colored plastic sheets or color gels can be placed beside the film and put into the same slide mount. Various shapes and designs can be made with the colored plastic to give symbolism and variety.

GLASS SLIDES

Admittedly, this is not the best name for a very exciting method of creating slides. It may give the impression that we are talking about the old-fashioned mounts that were made of glass. Instead, this is a process of photographing images through glass, with wording printed on the glass and the final slide being a combination of the words and images. Any camera that makes 35mm slides is acceptable, and either Kodachrome or Ektachrome film can be used.

The process came about when we discovered that audiences seem to appreciate actual pictures of objects and scenes mixed in with line

"This is a process of photographing images through glass, with wording printed on the glass, the final slide being a combination of the words and images."

drawings and graphics. In order to get words written across the scene, we had the idea of holding up glass in front of the scene or object, with the words printed on the glass. After a little exploration, we realized that a large sheet of storm window, conveniently encased in an aluminum frame to make it more easily moved from place to place, could be held in front of large scenes, making a striking slide with amazing clarity.

The painting can be done with tempera paints available from any education supply store. The best size of strokes are made by a medium-sized brush. It is at this stage that your imagination can run wild. For instance, in making a slide of a children's song, finger paints could be used (it gives a neat hollow effect since the finger will usually touch the surface in the middle of each letter). Or a cake decorator can give unusual effects, in addition to adding a raised or textured feel to each letter (perhaps emphasized by a colored spotlight across the letters).

A variety of glass can also be used. We've used outside windows, windows between offices (some have stimulating frosted patterns), car windows, storm windows of all shapes and sizes and mirrors.

If a close-up lens is available, glass can be placed over pictures in magazines and books with the words written on the glass. Obviously, the glass need not be as large as in the prior examples, even an 8″ × 10″ piece of glass out of a picture on the wall can be used. As far as we can tell, the same copyright restrictions apply to pictures as to lyrics, and complete credits will need to be given somewhere in the presentations (sources, copyright date and publisher, and photographer, if known).

The background can give meaning and symbolism to the words. If the mood of the lyric is joyous, a suitable background can be chosen. Abstract concepts can also be supported with appropriate representations, causing a dialogue between the viewer and the presentation. A song about rain could be written with words that have started to run with a drop or two of water applied to them; some mud puddles and wet leaves could be used as background. A hymn such as "Blest Be the Tie That Binds" could have scenes of the church members leaving the sanctuary.

Though not necessary, various accessories could be helpful during this process. To further cut down on possible glare across the glass, the use of a polarizer on your camera is a little extra insurance. An automatic through-the-lens metering device will help to ensure that the right amount of light will be allowed to enter the camera.

Since these will be regular slides, development can be accomplished at any photo store or individuals can do their own.

"Abstract concepts can also be supported with appropriate representations, causing a dialogue between the viewer and the presentation."

Reprinted from **The Basic Encyclopedia for Youth Ministry** by Dennis C. Benson and Bill Wolfe, published by Group Books.

CHAPTER 19:

Resources

The following names and addresses are of companies that publish Bible studies, current issues studies and studies on numerous need-related topics.

The theological slant and educational methods and content of the studies published by these companies vary widely.

Drop postcards to the companies requesting their catalogs. Then purchase sample materials and evaluate the materials for yourself.

Where to find games, camps, creative materials and other resources.

Abingdon Press
201 Eighth Avenue South
Nashville, TN 37202

Argus Communications
P.O. Box 5000
Allen, TX 75002

Augsburg Publishing House
426 South Fifth Street
Minneapolis, MN 55440

Baker Book House
P.O. Box 6287
Grand Rapids, MI 49506

Bethany House Publishers
6820 Auto Club Road
Minneapolis, MN 55438

Broadman Press
127 Ninth Avenue North
Nashville, TN 37234

C-4 Resources
210 West Church Street
Champaign, IL 61820

Concordia Publishing House
2558 South Jefferson Avenue
St. Louis, MO 63128

David C. Cook Publishing House
850 North Grove Avenue
Elgin, IL 60120

Educational Products Division
Word, Inc.
7300 Imperial
Waco, TX 76796

Gospel Light Publications
2300 Knoll Drive
Ventura, CA 93006

Group Books
P.O. Box 481
Loveland, CO 80539

GROUP Magazine
P.O. Box 481
Loveland, CO 80539

Harold Shaw Publishers
388 Gundersen Drive
Wheaton, IL 60187

Harvest House Publishers
1075 Arrowsmith
Eugene, OR 97402

Here's Life Publishers
P.O. Box 1576
San Bernardino, CA 92402

InterVarsity Press
P.O. Box F
Downers Grove, IL 60515

John Knox Press
341 Ponce de Leon Avenue NE
Atlanta, GA 30308

Judson Press
Valley Forge, PA 19481

National Teacher Education Project
7214 East Granada Road
Scottsdale, AZ 85257

NavPress
P.O. Box 6000
Colorado Springs, CO 80934

Paulist Press
545 Island Road
Ramsey, NJ 07446

Peter Li/Pflaum Press
2451 East River Road
Dayton, OH 45439

Scripture Press
1825 College Avenue
Wheaton, IL 60187

Standard Publishing
8121 Hamilton Avenue
Cincinnati, OH 45231

The Learning Seed Company
145 Brentwood Drive
Palatine, IL 60067

Train Depot
982 El Monte Avenue
Mt. View, CA 94040

Winston Press 430 Oak Grove
Minneapolis, MN 55403

Zondervan Publishing House
1415 Lake Drive SE
Grand Rapids, MI 49506

RESOURCES FOR IDEAS/GAMES/CROWDBREAKERS

Try This One Series
Group Books
P.O. Box 481
Loveland, CO 80539

The Ideas Library/
Youth Specialties, Inc.
1224 Greenfield Drive
El Cajon, CA 92021

Recycle Catalog
Dennis Benson
Abingdon Press
201 Eighth Avenue South
Nashville, TN 37202

Way Out Ideas for Youth Groups &
Others
Wayne Rice and Mike Yaconelli
Zondervan Publishing
1415 Lake Drive SE
Grand Rapids, MI 49506

Perspectives
Ann Billups
Judson Press
Valley Forge, PA 19481

Y.E.A.R.
C-4 Resources
210 West Church Street
Champaign, IL 61820

Creating and Playing Games with
Students
Jack Schaupp
Abingdon Press
201 Eighth Avenue South
Nashville, TN 37202

"Do It" Series
Success with Youth Publications
P.O. Box 27028
Tempe, AZ 85282

Encyclopedia of Serendipity
Serendipity Foundation
P.O. Box 1012
Littleton, CO 80160

A Compact Encyclopedia of Games
Compiled by Mary Hohenstein
Bethany House
6820 Auto Club Road
Minneapolis, MN 55438

Fun N Games
Wayne Rice, Denny Rydberg, Mike
Yaconelli
Zondervan Publishing
1415 Lake Drive SE
Grand Rapids, MI 49506

Games For All Ages and How to Use
Them
Marjorie Wackerbarth and Lillian
Graham
Baker Book House
P.O. Box 6287
Grank Rapids, MI 49506

The Good Times Game Book
Baker Book House
P.O. Box 6287
Grand Rapids, MI 49506

Guide for Recreation Leaders
Glenn Bannerman and Robert Fak-
kema
John Knox Press
341 Ponce de Leon Avenue NE
Atlanta, GA 30308

More New Games
New Games Foundation
1236 Arguello
San Francisco, CA 94122

The New Games Book
Andrew Fluegelman
Dolphin Books/Doubleday and Co.
501 Franklin Avenue
Garden City, NY 11530

FILM AND VIDEO RESOURCES

Ken Anderson Films
P.O. Box 618
Winona Lake, IN 46590

Argus Communications
P.O. Box 5000
Allen, TX 75002

Augsburg Films
426 South 5th Street
Minneapolis, MN 55440

Blackhawk Films
Davenport, IA 52808

Carousel Films, Inc.
1501 Broadway
New York, NY 10036

Cathedral Films
P.O. Box 4029
Westlake Village, CA 91359

Cinema Associates, Inc.
P.O. Box 9237
Seattle, WA 98109

Concordia Film Service
3558 South Jefferson Avenue
St. Louis, MO 63118

Family Films
14622 Lanark Street
Panorama City, CA 91402

Films, Inc.
5625 Hollywood Blvd.
Hollywood, CA 90028

Franciscan Communications
(TeleKETICS)
1229 S. Santee Street
Los Angeles, CA 90015

Gateway Films
P.O. Box A
Lansdale, PA 19466

Gospel Films, Inc.
P.O. Box 455
Muskegon, MI 49443

Learning Corporation of America
1350 Avenue of the Americas
New York, NY 10019

Mark IV Pictures
5907 Meredith Drive
Des Moines, IA 50322

Mass Media Ministries
2116 North Charles Street
Baltimore, MD 21218

Omega Films
428 8th Street
Del Mar, CA 92014

Paramount Oxford Films
5451 Marathon Street
Hollywood, CA 90038

Phoenix Films
470 Park Avenue South
New York, NY 10016

Pyramid Film and Video
P.O. Box 1048
Santa Monica, CA 90406

Quadrus Communications
610 E. State Street
Rockford, IL 61104

ROA Films
1696 North Astor Street
Milwaukee, WI 53202

World Wide Pictures
1201 Hennepin Avenue South
Minneapolis, MN 55403

MUSIC RESOURCES

Avery & Marsh Songbooks
Proclamation Productions, Inc.
Orange Square
Port Jervis, NY 12771

Come Share the Spirit
Hope Publishing Company
380 South Main Place
Carol Stream, IL 60187

Arthur Meriwether Educational
Resources
P.O. Box 457
Downers Grove, IL 60515

Gather Round
Resource Publications
P.O. Box 444
Saratoga, CA 95071

The Song Book
Myrrh Music/Word Books
Box 1790
Waco, TX 76703

Songs and Creations
P.O. Box 559
San Anselmo, CA 94960

CAMPING RESOURCES

Each of these organizations is a clearinghouse for information, catalogs and books.

American Camping Association
Bradford Woods
Martinsville, IN 46151

Christian Camping International
P.O. Box 646
Wheaton, IL 60187

SIMULATION GAMES AND ROLE PLAYS

Bobbs-Merrill Educational
Publishers
P.O. Box 558 (4300 W. 62nd Street)
Indianapolis, IN 46206

Arthur Meriwether Educational
Resources
P.O. Box 457
Downers Grove, IL 60515

Friendship Press
475 Riverside Drive
New York, NY 10027

The Wright Group
7620 Miramar Road Suite 4100
San Diego, CA 92126

Interact
P.O. Box 11465
Lakeside, CA 92040

DRAMA, PUPPET, MIME, CLOWN RESOURCES

Christian Church Dramas
Augsburg Publishing House
3224 Beverly Blvd.
Los Angeles, CA 90057

341 Ponce de Leon Avenue NE
Atlanta, GA 30308

How the Word Became Flesh: Story
Dramas for Education and Worship
Michael Moynahan
Resource Publications
P.O. Box 444
Saratoga, CA 95071

Hesed Script Services
805 Hennepin Avenue
Minneapolis, MN 55403

Contemporary Drama Service
P.O. Box 457
Downers Grove, IL 60515

Jeremiah People Sketch Books
Compiled by Chuck Bolte, 5 Volumes
Continental Ministries
P.O. Box 1996
Thousand Oaks, CA 91360

Christmas Drama for Youth
Sarah Walton Miller
Broadman Press
127 Ninth Avenue North
Nashville, TN 37234

Time to Act
Paul Brubridge and Murray Watts
InterVarsity Press
P.O. Box F
Downers Grove, IL 60515

Happy Tales, Fables and Plays
Gordon C. Bennet
John Knox Press

139

20 Ways to Use Drama in
Teaching the Bible
Judy Gattis Smith
Abingdon Press
201 Eighth Avenue South
Nashville, TN 37202

The Complete Floyd Shaffer Clown
Ministry Workshop Kit
P.O. Box 12811
Pittsburgh, PA 15241

The Dan Kamin Mime Kit
Recycle
P.O. Box 12811
Pittsburgh, PA 15241

Puppet Scripts for Use at Church
Everett Robertson
Broadman Press
127 Ninth Avenue North
Nashville, TN 37234

To Walk in the Way (Dramatic Inter-
pretations from the Gospel of Mark)
Urie A. Bender
Herald Press
610 Walnut Avenue
Scottdale, PA 15683

Puppets From One Way Street
P.O. Box 2398
Littleton, CO 80161

OTHER SPECIAL RESOURCES

World Wide Games, Inc.
P.O. Box 450
Delaware, OH 43015

The New Games Resource Catalog
New Games Foundation
1236 Arguello
San Francisco, CA 94122

Med-Tek Corporation (kazoos and
other trinkets)
401 East Elmwood Avenue
Troy, MI 48084

Edmund Scientific (balloons,
parachutes)
101 E. Gloucester Pike
Barrington, NJ 08007

Stuff (surplus items and junk)
Jerryco, Inc.
5700 Northwest Highway
Chicago, IL 60646

PART 2

Retreat Designs for Youth Groups

Thirty-four helpful, detailed and "field-tested" retreat designs to help you meet your young persons' diverse needs, interests and concerns.

RETREAT OUTLINE 1:

"We Are

By Arlo R. Reichter

This retreat design builds community and awareness of your members' various "families."

The theme of "family" includes all persons, especially as it's used in this outline. This retreat touches on three types of "family": natural family, peer family (family of friends) and family of God. (If orphans are a part of your retreat group, they should use the grouping in which they grew up as their natural family. Be sensitive to how they feel during this part of the retreat. You may wish to explain this emphasis to them ahead of time.)

This retreat is outlined for a weekend setting with four major program segments and plenty of time for fun and games. This outline may be used with family units or with just youth attending. I have used this retreat with senior highs and their parents with positive results in helping them to communicate better.

Since the retreat uses small groups throughout, you may want to recruit and orient small group leaders before the event. Or, you can give instructions which each small group can carry out on its own.

A WORD ABOUT ATMOSPHERE

If you are using a retreat center you can decorate, have the youth bring the following items:

- ✔ pictures of themselves at various ages (especially pictures of them in family groupings)
- ✔ pictures of various family members
- ✔ pictures of good friends (past and present)
- ✔ pictures of importance to their "family of God" relationships: church school class, baptismal group, past youth retreats
- ✔ poems or other writings about "family"
- ✔ records with the theme of family

Encourage the adult sponsors to bring the same items too.

If the retreat center does not lend itself to be decorated, use large pieces of cardboard or posterboard and tape so people can develop their own "portable family display." Building a family display could even be a pre-retreat project completed in a youth meeting.

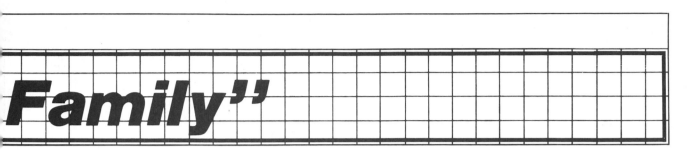

Family"

A WORD ABOUT THE BIBLE

The Bible is an important resource for this weekend. Each person should bring a Bible or be provided with one.

A WORD ABOUT GAMES AND ACTIVITIES

Games and zany activities are crucial for this retreat's success. They'll help young people get to know each other better, set the tone for the program sections and help people burn off excess energy.

You know how your young people will react to different types of activities and games. Here's how to develop a good mix of games and learning sessions: First, read through the following "possible retreat schedule" and the actual retreat outline, taking notes where activities and games would add to the retreat's effectiveness.

Then thumb through various ideas and games books with your specific needs in mind. Look for ideas you can use or adapt. Often the most effective ideas are ones you've customized and redesigned to meet your group's unique personality.

There are plenty of resources to help you come up with great ideas. A few you might consider:

- **Try This One; More . . . Try This One;** and **Try This One . . . Too,** available from Group Books, Box 481, Loveland, CO 80539.
- **The New Games Book** and **More New Games!**, available from Doubleday and Company, Inc., 245 Park Avenue, New York, NY 10017.
- **Ideas Books** (30 different volumes of ideas), available from Youth Specialties, Inc., 1224 Greenfield Drive, El Cajon, CA 92021.

POSSIBLE RETREAT SCHEDULE			
FRIDAY EVENING		8:30 p.m.	Games
5 p.m.	Meet at church to load and pack; final payments due	9-10 p.m.	Session 1: "We Are Family"
		10 p.m.-Midnight	Night hike or free time
8 p.m.	Arrive at retreat center and get settled	Midnight	Sack time continued

SATURDAY

8-8:30 a.m.	Breakfast
9-11 a.m.	Session 2: "Your Natural Family"
11-Noon	Organized fun 'n games
Noon	Lunch
1:30-5 p.m.	Fun 'n games, hiking, plan a special event at your retreat center
5:30 p.m.	Dinner
7-9:30 p.m.	Session 3: "Family of Friends"

9:30-11 p.m.	Fun 'n games
11 p.m.	Options: devotions, singing and films
Midnight	Sack time

SUNDAY

8-8:30 a.m.	Breakfast
9-11 a.m.	Session 4: "Celebrate Our Families"
11-11:15 a.m.	Evaluation
11:15-Noon	Clean up, pack up, get ready to leave
Noon	Lunch and depart

FRIDAY EVENING SESSION:
"Getting to Know You"

THE WELCOME

Ask everyone to repeat the following phrases after you:
We have arrived!
We have come from different families!
We have come with different experiences!
We have come for different reasons!
Let's rejoice and be glad!
For we are with each other!
And God is with us!

GROUP SINGING

Sing your group's favorite songs. If you have new songs to learn, begin to learn one new song—save other new songs until later in the retreat. Singing familiar songs helps establish a festive atmosphere and bring unity to the group.

INTRODUCE THE THEME: "WE ARE FAMILY"

Say something like: "Our theme this weekend takes us on an exploration of our natural families (families we were born into), our families of friends and our family of God. I'd like you to share your family with the rest of us during this retreat. One goal of this retreat is that all of us here become a family.

"As all families have experiences and feelings, so will our weekend have experiences and feelings. Let us bring ourselves together for the retreat by praying together."

The group prayer begins as several of the participants complete the following sentences:

"I thank God for my natural family because . . ." (Have three to five people complete this sentence prayerfully.) When the volunteers have prayed, have the entire group repeat after you: "We thank God for our natural family."

A second group of young people completes the following sentence: "I thank God for my family of friends because . . ." (Have three to five complete the sentence prayerfully.) When the volunteers have prayed, have the entire group repeat after you: "We thank God for our family of friends."

A third group of young people completes the following sentence: "I thank God for the family of God because . . ." (Have three to five complete the sentence prayerfully.) When the volunteers have prayed, have the entire group repeat after you: "We all thank God for the family of God."

End the prayer with an "Amen" or close with your own prayer. (Orient several group members ahead of time about the prayers before this part of the session. Encourage them to be prepared with their part of the prayer.)

Continue with something like: "We all live in families. Some of these families are the groups in which we were born: our natural families. Some of these families we have chosen: families of friends. Both of these families are a part of the family of God: his creation under his control.

"Within each of these families is a variety of agreements which help to regulate our relationships. Every family has times which may be gloomy and every family has times which may be happy. This retreat will help us understand how to cope with life in the middle of these relationships."

THE THEME SCRIPTURE

Read Genesis 9:8-17. "The importance of this scripture to us is in the relationships which exist in the story. Noah is a part of a family which is coping with God's presence in their life in the middle of a tense situation. The 'covenant' establishes a relationship between God and Noah's family and, of course, in fact with everyone who's born afterward (even you and me).

"The concept of promises (the covenant) made to each other is an important dimension of family life. Many family problems (even those in our family of friends and family of God) are the result of unkept or misunderstood promises."

A large rainbow with the theme ("We Are Family") written on it is a fitting focal point for the weekend. Use the rainbow symbol for all your retreat promotion and publicity. You might also want to use rainbow buttons or specially made rainbow T-shirts for this retreat.

GETTING ACQUAINTED

Pair everyone randomly. If you have a variety of ages, either mix them up or pair similar-aged persons together.

Ask persons to tell any special meaning associated with their names: Are they named after a family member or a friend of their family? a famous person? a biblical character? Does their name have a symbolic meaning? What national background does their name represent? Our names, of course, are one of the ways we are identified with our natural families.

Next, ask the pairs (dyads) to answer the following question: "What group of which you are a member do you like the best?" Allow three to five minutes for quick sharing.

Now ask the pairs to share their relationship with the church. If they are members of your church, have them share date of membership, history of family involvement, how they're feeling about their spiritual lives, and so on. If your group includes unchurched young people, also include a question such as: "What group of church people or what church do you know the most about?"

SMALL GROUPS

Each pair should now quickly choose another pair. If you want the same ages together, have the groups choose another group with people their age. If you want the ages mixed, make that a requirement. If you want to have both boys and girls in groups, require that the groups of four include both sexes. This group of four will stay together throughout the rest of the retreat when groups of four meet.

Once the groups are formed, ask group members to tell something they learned about their partner. (Allow five to seven minutes.)

Each group of four now joins another group of four to form the groups of eight, which will be together later on in the retreat. In the group of eight have each person say his or her name and tell something which is "special" about him- or herself. (Allow eight to 10 minutes.)

Ask everyone to come up with a name for their group which in some way represents the various members' interests, families, talents. (Allow five to seven minutes.) Have each group share its name with the entire group. After each group shares, lead the entire group in saying with enthusiasm, "That's great!"

Have everyone share family pictures with the group of eight, describing the circumstances of the picture: Christmas card, birthday party, family outing, etc.

Ask the participants to post their pictures, poems, etc., which they brought. If you use a rainbow, consider placing the pictures under the rainbow where everyone can see them.

FAMILY CONCERNS

As a retreat family there are rules, expectations and arrangements to be announced and explained. Use this time to do so.

CLOSING THE SESSION

Ask the newly formed groups to close with a prayer in their "retreat family." The groups may want to close by forming a "huddle," where they stand and place their arms around each other's shoulders. You may also want to close with a song.

DEBRIEF

Check with several key youth or adults about how they feel thus far.

SATURDAY MORNING SESSION: "Your Natural Family"

Welcome the group back and encourage everyone to find their groups of eight. (This is also a quick way to find out who is missing.) Begin with several loud and active songs or a crazy game. This is a good time to learn new songs. Take 15-20 minutes for the gathering and opening.

GROUP SHARING

Ask everyone to answer this question: "When was the last time you were out of our town/city?" Depending upon the location and mobility of your group members, you may want to phrase the question: "When was the last time you spent a night away from home?" If necessary, ask the participants to restate their names before they answer the question.

After the groups have shared, ask six to 10 individuals to answer the question in front of the entire group.

CHOOSING A GROUP LEADER

If you chose and oriented group leaders before the retreat, announce who these persons are. (Make sure there's a leader in each group.) If not, ask each group to identify someone who will serve as the leader in keeping the group on the subject and moving. Note that families have leaders, some of whom we have no choice about (parents) and some of whom are chosen by the group (as in a peer group). You may wish to refer back to the theme scripture and the Noah story when God chose Noah to be the leader.

Also note that family problems sometimes are created when no one serves as the leader or when more than one person assumes leadership when it is not appropriate.

147

INPUT FROM SCRIPTURE

Have the groups reread Genesis 9:8-17. Ask them to focus on the relationship agreements between God and Noah. Have participants write on a piece of paper agreements which exist in their natural families. Some are unspoken, such as who makes certain kinds of decisions and how decisions are made, agreements such as how late you can stay out, who takes out the garbage, who prays at meals, which parent's family has the Christmas Day dinner, etc. Push them to list as many agreements as they can think of. They will be able to add to their list as others share and more agreements come to mind. Another way to think of agreements is as promises made within the natural family: Brothers and sisters won't tell parents certain things; father and daughter make certain promises to spend time together on the father's day off, etc. (Allow 10-12 minutes for this personal reflection and recording.) Then ask the group members to share with their group two agreements or promises which exist within their family of birth. (Allow 10 minutes.)

Next, invite the participants to a time of personal reflection. Ask: "Are there agreements or promises which you *should* make to members of your natural family which you haven't made?" Allow five minutes for this personal reflection.

MORE SHARING ABOUT NATURAL FAMILIES

Ask the participants to take a piece of paper and trace their family tree back two generations, if they are able. Demonstrate by sharing your own family tree on a chalkboard or newsprint. (Allow five to seven minutes.)

After these are drawn, have the participants show their trees and tell interesting facts about their families, such as national background, who is living, who has died, how many children. Divorce and remarriage may make some trees more complicated, but assure people it's okay to tell about their families. Ask each person to tell which of the following terms best describes his or her role in the family: leader, follower, complainer, partier, organizer, etc.

Finally, ask each person to describe the best family experience he or she remembers. (Allow eight to ten minutes for sharing.)

This is the time to share those important announcements.

CLOSING

Ask everyone to repeat the following statement after you:

In our family
Some times are happy,
Some times are sad,
Some times we're apart,
Some times we're together,
We thank God for the happy, the sad.
We thank God for the apart, the together.
Because we are family!
Amen.

SATURDAY EVENING SESSION:
"Family of Friends"

Have people find their groups of eight. Introduce this session: "Look at your group members and realize they too are family. You know them to some extent and you are now going to spend some more time sharing your life with them. They are one of your families of friends."

PERSONAL REFLECTION

Have the participants take a piece of paper and write the names of people their own age with whom they spend a significant amount of time. (Allow two to four minutes.) Next, have them draw five concentric circles on a sheet of paper. Put the name of their best friend closest to the center and the names of other friends on the remaining circles. This will help them realize who their most important friends are. Emphasize that no one will have to reveal names they wrote.

GROUP SHARING

In the groups of eight, have everyone pair with another person and respond to the following questions about their family of friends:

---

1. How did you choose your family of friends? Or, did they choose you?

2. What kind of a person are you when you are with your family of friends?

3. What good things happen to you when you are with your family of friends?

4. What bad things happen to you when you are with your family of friends?

(Allow 15-20 minutes for sharing.)

In the family of eight, have each person answer the following questions: "What do your parents think of your family of friends? Why? Are they correct in their thinking? Why or why not?"

SCRIPTURE

Read Mark 3:13-19. Discuss in the smaller groups how the various disciples responded to Jesus. (Use these passages: James—John 21:2 and Acts 12:2; Peter—Matthew 26:31-35, 69-75; Judas—Matthew 26:47-50, 27:3-10; Thomas—John 20:25-29.) Include especially Judas, who betrayed Jesus; Peter, who denied him; and Thomas, who doubted him. Discuss how those experiences are present in our family of friends.

Now is a good time to discuss parental reactions to our family of friends. Every peer family is not a good influence and this is a common concern of parents. This discussion can last as long as the group's energy and interest are apparent.

CONCLUDING THE SESSION

Say something like: "Enjoy your retreat family. Take time this weekend to get to know each other better. While we represent a variety of personalities and interests, we are a family. Let's make this family influence good as we enjoy the retreat together!"

A closing prayer, some singing, etc., are appropriate.

Oh yes, don't forget the announcements as needed.

SUNDAY MORNING SESSION: "Celebrating Our Family"

This experience is to celebrate the learnings and to highlight the joy of being a part of God's family. This is the final session and contains processes that are important to the successful re-entry experience as participants return to their homes and schools.

Group singing provides a fitting beginning to the session. Include songs that have been a part of the retreat—especially the joyful ones.

Following the singing, ask the young people to review what they've discussed during the session. Ask them to recall the positive influences of their natural families and their various families of friends. We should be grateful for these families because they make our lives livable! To conclude the guided reflection, ask everyone to list the positive influences from family.

SCRIPTURE

Read Ephesians 4:1-16 to the entire group. The "unity of the body" might be restated or reread as the "unity of the family," because the "family body" functions as "family body" members share their gifts.

Ask the entire group to list the positive influences they found during their reflection time on a large sheet of paper (at least 10 feet long). Have markers, crayons, pencils, pens available so the mural is colorful. Title the mural "We Are Family." You might want to have volunteers sketch a colorful rainbow ahead of time. Ask each person to sign the mural after writing the positive influences. Allow group members to express their positive influences and feelings through symbols, drawings, poems. Be certain everyone shares in the mural.

Take this mural to your church and display it so retreat participants will be reminded of what they've learned. You may want to store the mural for a month and then bring it back out for a discussion on its content. Use the mural in the manner you feel appropriate. But use it.

GROUP SHARING

Ask the participants to assemble in their groups of eight. Have everyone discuss the following questions. (You may want to make copies of these questions to distribute to the group leaders so that you do not interrupt this final small group time.)

1. Read Ephesians 4:4-16. Do you feel as though you are a part of God's family? Why or why not?

2. Is your experience with church friends a "family" of God experience? Yes or no. If yes, how do you know? If no, what do you need to do to make it more of a family experience?

These are not easy questions and may take some time to respond to. Allow the time. If helpful, have the small groups form dyads (pairs) for the sharing on these first two questions.

When discussion on the first two questions is complete, move to the next questions:

3. Share something you are thankful for from this retreat.

4. Share something new you have learned about "family" during this retreat.

Divide into the groups of four which were formed during the first session and answer the following question:

5. How do you know others better because of this weekend?

Next, have everyone divide into the original pair from the first session. Say something like: "Look at this person and realize he or she is probably now a part of your family of friends 'back home.' You two will have many future experiences together—they can be positive; they can be negative. Express to each other your appreciation for the friendship and your willingness to continue to be a friend in the days ahead."

THE CLOSING

Ask every to form a large circle. Say: "We are all a part of God's creation and are very special people. My challenge to you is to go from this place with a new appreciation of your natural family, your family of friends and a new commitment to being a part of the family of God. Be willing to re-examine how you can affect these families for better or for worse. Ask God to give you the guidance and strength to help your family grow and be whole."

Invite people to share sentence prayers. After a person shares, lead the group in responding: "Hear our prayer, O Lord." Close after several have shared.

Sing a closing song in the circle if there is one you can do from memory.

Invite the members of the group to hug each other.

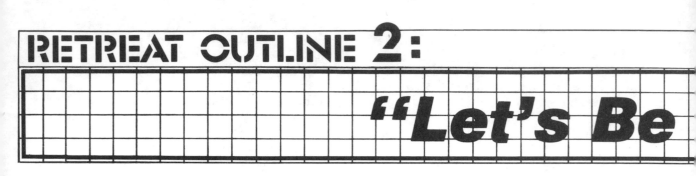

RETREAT OUTLINE 2:

"Let's Be

By Arlo R. Reichter

A retreat to encourage acceptance among young people.

One of the more frightening concerns on young people's minds is: "What will people I don't know well think of me; will I be accepted?" I invite you to consider a retreat dealing with friendship.

PREPARATION

A 1½-hour pre-retreat session may be used to gain interest in the retreat or it may be used as an experience for those who have signed up for the retreat. It may be helpful in arriving at some of the themes which will be considered during the retreat.

PLANNING THE PRE-RETREAT MEETING

To make this session a success, bring together two parents and two youth to help you. Explain to them the purposes of the pre-retreat session and retreat. Here is a brief format for the planning session:

● Ask one parent and one youth to act together as a team. Have them write as many responses as they can to complete the sentence, "A friend is. . ." After three minutes have the two teams share their lists.

● Read together Ephesians 4. This scripture refers to the life of faith and it is from this basis that we should consider friendship. List the things found in scripture which are important not only in maintaining the unity of the church but also in maintaining a friendship. (Be always gentle; show your love by being tolerant; everyone must tell the truth.)

● Ask the parents to respond to the question, "Why are parents so concerned about their children's friends?" At the same time ask the young people present to respond to the question, "Why should parents not be so concerned about their children's friends?" Allow ample time for the parents and youth to develop and share their responses.

● Ask the four persons to assist you in developing the following components for the pre-retreat meeting:

Atmosphere. Determine where the pre-retreat meeting should be held. Ask two of the persons to make banners and/or posters which can be used at the pre-retreat meeting. You will also want to take these items to the actual retreat.

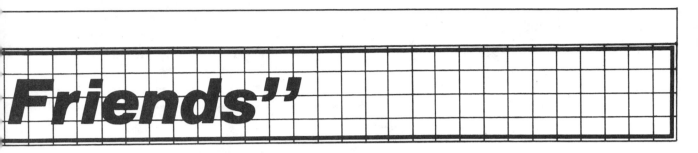

Friends"

Refreshments. A part of the pre-retreat session should be a social time following the meeting. This will give time for the youth and parents to interact.

The Role Play. The skit consists of a mother, a father, a son and a daughter. The son and daughter are both high school age. The parents are raising serious questions about their son's new friends. The daughter defends her brother's right and capability of choosing his own friends. The parents are not satisfied.

You are now ready for the pre-retreat meeting. This meeting should occur well in advance of the retreat date if it is a recruitment meeting. If it is to prepare those who will be attending, it can happen a week before the retreat. Invite the parents to attend the meeting to find out more about the retreat.

THE PRE-RETREAT SESSION

1. Explain the purpose of the session.
2. Introduce the theme by presenting the role play.
3. Following the role play, ask the persons present to divide into groups of four with at least one parent in each group. Ask the groups to list four issues relating to friendship which they saw in the role play. After three to five minutes, have the groups share their responses.
4. Have individuals reflect on their four best friends and explain why these people are their best friends.
5. Have everyone read Colossians 3:5-15. The scripture gives us some ideas of what we like in other people and what they like in us. Instruct each small group to make a list of characteristics of friends which they find in this passage. Have them write these on newsprint so they can be shared with the entire group. After five to seven minutes, ask the groups to share their lists.
6. Ask the people to notice the banners and/or posters which were made by the parent/youth committee to highlight the theme. Ask those who are going to the retreat to make a banner and/or a poster which expresses their ideas on friendship. Suggest that two or three work together on a poster or banner to bring to the retreat.

THE RETREAT

The special weekend has arrived! Depart with the youth and parents asking God to bless you with a safe journey and a meaningful and fun weekend.

NEEDS FOR THE RETREAT

☐ Newsprint, pencils, paper, Bibles, a movie for Saturday night, name tags.

☐ Duplicate the Friendship Survey Sheet and the Recycling Sheet so each participant can have one.

☐ Plan the games and activities for Saturday free time and fun time Saturday evening.

FRIDAY EVENING (1½ hours)

Even though you may have to travel some distance to the retreat site, it's important to set a focus for the weekend by conducting the following brief session:

1. *Welcome everyone.* Begin with 15 minutes of singing or with a crazy crowdbreaker. See the resource list at the end of this outline for helpful ideas. State the guidelines for the weekend as necessary. Ask individuals to make a name tag which includes their name and on which they complete the phrase, "Friendship is . . ."

2. Dyads. Have everyone place their name tags in a large box. Form the dyads by drawing two name tags at a time. Emphasize that this retreat is the place to make new friends. In the dyads have each person answer the question, "Why am I at this retreat?"

3. *Friendship Symphony.* Begin the symphony by saying "Friendship is . . ." and point to one of the participants who says one response written on his or her name tag. Next, the leader and the participant say "Friendship is . . ." and the initial participant points to someone else who says his or her response. Now all three say "Friendship is . . ." and the last to respond points to another participant. This process continues until all have responded.

4. *Sharing of banners/posters.* Have volunteers place their banners and posters on the wall as they explain them.

5. Instruct each dyad to choose another dyad to form a group of four. Have the groups read Galatians 6:1-10 and develop a body sculpture. Working together, all four group members "sculpt" themselves into a scene, situation or thought—humorous or serious—found in the passage. After 15 minutes, ask each group to share their sculpture with the entire group.

6. Distribute the Friendship Survey Sheet and ask each person to

complete it. Point out that no one has to share answers unless he or she wants to.

7. Ask the groups of four to share how they answered question seven on the Friendship Survey Sheet. Remember, a person has the right not to share anything.

8. To conclude, have the groups of four stand and hold hands. Read each line and have the participants repeat it as a closing prayer:

> We thank God we're here.
> *(Participants repeat it)*
> We thank God for friends.
> *(Response)*
> Help us to make new friends.
> *(Response)*
> Help us to be better friends.
> *(Response)*
> Bless us this weekend.
> *(Response)*
> Amen.
> *(Response)*

FRIENDSHIP SURVEY SHEET

1. How many friends do you have?
2. Do you have friends of both sexes?
3. Do you have friends who are five years younger than you?
4. Do you have friends who are five years older than you?
5. What's the craziest thing you've done with friends?
6. Who would consider you one of their friends?
7. What qualities do you have that make you a friend to others? List three.
8. What qualities does your best friend have?
9. Are your parents your friends? Why or why not?
10. Do you have any really close friends?
11. Do you have more or fewer friends than you had one year ago?
12. Are you a good friend? Why?

SATURDAY MORNING (1½ hours)

1. *Waking up exercises.* Form one large circle, turn and massage the shoulders of the person on your left, now the person on your right. Stretch and reach as high as you can. Touch your toes. Or try a crazy crowdbreaker activity.

2. *Music.* (15 minutes of group singing)

3. Find and get with your group of four from last evening. Have each person in the group tell about his or her most embarrassing experience.

4. *Group definition.* Take 10 minutes and define the term *friend.* In your definition include a scripture verse which helps you to understand who a friend is. Write the definition on a piece of newsprint so it can be displayed. After the definitions are completed, have each small group share its definition with the larger group.

5. *Jesus' friends.* Each group of four will need a New Testament for this exercise. Have each group select one of the four Gospels and skim through it, looking for the people they would call Jesus' friends. Have

the groups find the answers to the following questions:

> a. Who were Jesus' friends?
> b. How did Jesus treat his friends?
> c. What qualities did Jesus' friends have?
> d. What qualities did Jesus have that made him a good friend?

Allow 30 minutes for this exercise.

6. Encourage everyone to write answers to the following questions (not to be shared but for their own reflection).

> a. Who are your friends?
> b. How do you treat your friends?
> c. What qualities do your friends have? (They can compare their thoughts now with the answers they gave to the Friendship Survey Sheet last evening—question eight.)
> d. What qualities do you have that make you a good friend? (They can compare these thoughts as well with their thoughts last evening when they responded on the Friendship Survey Sheet to question seven.)

7. In their small groups, ask the participants to share what they have learned about friendships and about themselves as a result of this morning's exercise.

8. Solicit individuals who are willing to share their responses with the entire group.

SATURDAY AFTERNOON (1½ hours)

1. This session needs to be active because the young people will be eager for more free time. Ask them to find their groups of four. The assignment is to develop a role play about friendship. Some possible settings for this would be school, church, home. Encourage the groups to develop role plays based upon actual experiences in their own lives. Everyone must have a part—perhaps not a speaking part, however. Allow and encourage humor and creativity. Give only 20-30 minutes for the development of the role plays as this will force the group to work quickly.

2. *The role plays.* After each group presents its role play, ask the rest of the participants to share: 1.) The good aspects of friendship which the play brought out; and 2.) Problems raised by the play which perhaps illustrated a need for more friendship. List these responses on newsprint or a chalkboard.

3. Read to the entire group Colossians 3:5-15. Remind them this scripture was read at the pre-retreat meeting. Have them recall the list of characteristics of friends which were found in the scripture and shared at the pre-retreat meeting. Ask individuals to choose one of the

characteristics which they feel they need to work on. Have them write ways in which they can develop this characteristic. This is not to be shared. This part should take 20 minutes.

SATURDAY EVENING (1 hour plus fun time of 2 hours)

The evening begins with a session dealing with the theme of friendship and then a fun time concludes the evening. Before the retreat, form a committee of youth and an adult who will plan appropriate games and activities. You might also want to get a film for later in the evening.

1. Welcome back the group following dinner: "Tonight's session will help us to deal with some of the problems we may face concerning friendship." Ask the group to be silent and thoughtful as you suggest areas of their lives in which they might find a particular concern related to friendship. Use the following guide in this reflection time:

> a. Think of a time when you have experienced something unpleasant related to friendship. *(Allow quiet time—reflecting time—before going on to the next statement.)*
> b. Where did this happen? *(Quiet time)*
> c. Who was involved? *(Quiet time)*
> d. How did you feel? *(Quiet time)*
> e. How do you think the other persons involved felt? *(Quiet time)*

Remind the group that while this may bring back some unpleasant memories, it will help them to cope with similar happenings should they occur again in the future.

2. Ask everyone to find their group of four. Have each small group develop a situation (have each group pick a secretary to take notes) where there is obvious friction between friends. The groups can either act out the situation or write it up in the form of a brief case study.

3. *Recycling an experience sheet.* Draw on newsprint or a chalkboard or have duplicated before the retreat the Recycling Sheet form on which the participants will do some individual work relating to the event they have just acted out or written about.

RECYCLING SHEET

_____ The Experience _____
Note briefly the experience.

_____ Your Concerns _____
Briefly list your concerns about the experience—the problem.

_____ Alternative Actions _____
What are alternative actions you could have taken to make the experience turn out better?

_____ Examples _____
When have you used the alternative idea or when have you observed someone using this alternative idea?

Allow 15 to 20 minutes for everyone to work on the Recycling Sheet. You may need to give some individual help to interpret the form. The best way to understand the Recycling Sheet is to complete one yourself before the retreat to get a feel for the concept and how it works.

4. *Debriefing.* Ask the groups of four to share their responses to the following questions:

> a. What did you learn about yourself in this exercise?
> b. How did the exercise prepare you to cope better in a future situation?

5. Conclude with music which will help set the mood for the fun and fellowship which is to follow.

SUNDAY MORNING (1½ to 2 hours)

1. Begin with 15 minutes of singing and/or crazy crowdbreakers.

2. Read the following call to worship: "God has been with us this weekend and allowed us to enjoy one another and this place. God has helped us to consider the issues of friendship. Now in a spirit of friendship and fellowship, let us celebrate the best of ourselves and the best of our experiences in the presence of God."

3. Ask the groups of four to sit together and reread Ephesians 4. Each group, after reading the scripture, is to write their own scripture. It should be in the form of a letter and begin something like Ephesians begins. (Example: From Joe, Mary, Sally and Jim who by the grace of God have enjoyed together a weekend retreat. To our friends who have accompanied us. We have found and want to share with you some special meanings regarding friendship. Friendship is . . . , etc., etc. A good friend is one who . . . When a friend lets you down you are to . . .) Encourage creativity. Allow 20 minutes for the writing of these contemporary scriptures.

4. Have each group read their scriptures to the entire group.

5. *Closing statement.* Say the line and have the participants repeat after you:

We have come together and shared. *(Response)*	. . . because we have shared together here. *(Response)*
Now we must leave. *(Response)*	We ask God to give us courage and strength . . . *(Response)*
We are thankful for our friends. *(Response)*	. . . as we go from this place. *(Response)*
We'll be better friends in the future . . . *(Response)*	Amen! *(Response)*

RESOURCES

1. Game ideas for group recreation time: **Best of Try This One, More . . . Try This One, Try This One . . . Too,** Group Books.

2. Songbooks: **Songs,** Songs and Creations, Box 559, San Anselmo, CA 94960.

3. Retreat planning, philosophy and program ideas: **The Retreat Handbook: A-Way to Meaning,** by Virgil and Lynn Nelson, Judson Press.

"Unify Yo

By Virgil Nelson

A retreat designed for simple and effective group building

Anytime is a great time to give special focus to helping your group members get to know each other as persons and to develop a common sense of purpose and commitment to God, each other and the goals of the group for the year.

In retreat planning, some basic decisions need to be made in light of the "givens" in your group at the moment, and your goals for your group and the weekend.

THE PLACE

You may have a regular place you go for retreats and all you need to do is check schedules and make reservations. Or, someone in the group may have a home that could accommodate the group. You may have a friend in a distant church and your group could arrange to stay in that church building for its retreat. Or you may have state or county parks that would be ideal. Make your choice, and make your reservations.

STRUCTURE

If a primary goal is helping your group members know and love each other, consider determining room assignments before the retreat so that persons who do not know one another well will be together.

If you choose to structure group contact tightly in other parts of the program, then you may want to give participants free choice regarding rooming arrangements and let natural friendships be honored. For example: If people are together in small groups during group sessions, and are assigned to work together in food preparation, then somewhere in the weekend they need to have a "no pressure" choice.

Theme scripture: Colossians 3:12-17

IN TRAVEL

The process of travel can be a conscious part of building and developing friendships and group process. Try this game entitled "Chicken Roulette."

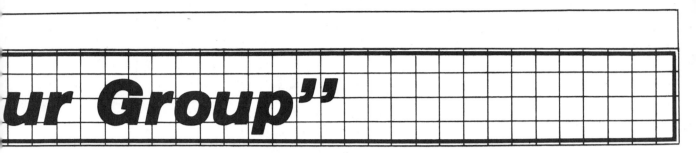

Step #1

Each car is given a number. Slips of paper with that number are put into a hat. If you plan five passengers in car #1, then put five #1 slips of paper in the hat. Each participant draws a number which assigns him/her to a car.

Step #2

Once in the assigned car, each person writes his/her name on a piece of paper, which again goes into a hat. The hat goes around and each person draws a name.

Step #3

One at a time, each person reveals the name drawn. The people in the car then try to guess the answers to the following questions about the person whose name was drawn. Each passenger gets one guess for each question. Go one question at a time. After hearing all guesses, the named person can give the real answer. If there is further discussion/-sharing, let it continue.

Questions:
1. Guess how this person likes his/her chicken prepared (barbecued, crispy, old-fashioned, boiled , broiled, etc.).
2. Guess birthdate.
3. Guess favorite TV program.
4. Guess color of eyes (without looking).
5. Guess favorite hobby.

POSSIBLE SCHEDULE

FRIDAY EVENING

3:30 p.m. Register at the church; final payments; cabin room assignments here or later at the camp

4:30 p.m. Departure for the retreat (actual time depends on the driving distance to the center)

6 p.m. Dinner on the road: individual cars on their own, or agree on a specific location and all meet there

8 p.m. Arrival at center: unload and move in

9 p.m. Opening session: "God's Chosen People: Who's Here?"

10:30 p.m. Free time: snacks, games

Midnight In the sack; lights out (This and other ground rules need to be agreed upon in advance of the weekend. Rules depend on the age/maturity of the group, rules of camp, program goals, morning schedule, etc.)

SATURDAY

7 a.m. Up and at 'em

7:30 a.m. Personal devotions

8 a.m. Breakfast

9:30-11:30 a.m. Morning session (with break): "God's People: Clothed With Compassion"

Noon Lunch

Afternoon Free time, with some structured optional choices: group games (see references); tournaments; swimming; outings, etc.

5:30 p.m. Dinner

7-9 p.m. Evening session: "God's People: Macramed (or Woven Together) in His Love," including film "The Nail"

9:30 p.m. Free time

SUNDAY

9:30 a.m.-Noon Morning sessions including break and worship: "God's People: Thankforgivefulness"

12:30 Lunch and evaluation: most/least valuable activity for me; most/least valuable activity for our group in its spiritual development; changes I would suggest; other comments

WEDNESDAY

Leaders' meeting to look over evaluations and reflect upon the strengths and weaknesses of the weekend.

Step #4.

The second and fourth persons whose names are drawn get to answer the "Chicken Roulette question of the day." Each person guesses a question that #2 or #4 might be "chicken" to ask. Persons #2 and #4 are free to acknowledge if each question is truly one they'd be afraid to ask or not. If not, they may respond with another question that they really would be afraid to ask someone. If a genuine question is asked, you shouldn't feel any compulsion to answer it. Move on; it can come up again later as appropriate.

If the trip is over two hours, plan to change cars in the middle, using the same process twice.

FRIDAY EVENING SESSION (1½ hours)

1. Group singing (10-15 minutes).

2. Put all the participants' names into a hat. Each person draws a name, and becomes a "secret friend" to that individual during the retreat, without the other person guessing that he/she is in fact a "secret friend." During the worship service on Sunday there will be an opportunity for revelation of who the secret friends have been during the weekend.

3. Find your identity: Number the group by counting around to end up with groups of eight persons. Each number is assigned a song tune to hum in finding the other seven persons in the group. This should be done with eyes closed, on your knees, on the floor. (Possible songs: "Old MacDonald," "Clementine," "Home on the Range," etc.) When all the group is found, stand and sing the song out loud at the top of your voice. (10 minutes.) Stay in this group.

4. Names Are No Game: Ask the groups to subdivide into groups of two persons. Share around the following questions:

a. How do you feel about your name? Anything unusual about it? How did you get it?

b. If you could change it, would you? To what? (5-7 minutes.)

5. Names—What's the Fame? Have the groups of eight reassemble.

a. Share briefly about the person you met and his/her name. (5-7 minutes.)

b. Individually share with the entire group: If you could be famous for something, go down in the Guinness Book of Records, be written up in the annals of history, end up in future editions of the Bible, what would you like it to be for? Allow two minutes of reflection before starting. Begin with the person whose eyes are bluest. (15 minutes.)

6. Mini-presentation (5-7 minutes) on the theme passage. Or, simply read the passage aloud to the entire group from two different translations without comment.

7. Prayer by leader for the total group, or within small groups using sentence prayers.

8. Announcements and overview-reminder of ground rules/assumptions for the weekend. Tell people to remember which persons are in their group.

SATURDAY MORNING SESSION (2 hours)

1. Group singing (10-15 minutes).

2. Form same groups as Friday evening. Read aloud to the entire group the theme scripture Colossians 3:12-17.

3. Reflection sheet on key theme words: Print 8½ × 11 sheet with the following words listed down the left side (distribute over entire length of page):

COMPASSION/KINDNESS, HUMILITY, GENTLENESS, PATIENCE, FORGIVENESS, LOVE, and THANKSGIVING.

Vertically divide the page into three columns with these headings at the top, from left to right:

WHEN I HAVE EXPERIENCED THIS, WHEN I GAVE THIS, A TIME WHEN I NEEDED THIS.

a. Have each person reflect and make notes in silence. (5 minutes.)
b. Divide into pairs and share feelings and responses. (7-10 minutes.)

4. Bible study based on Colossians 3:12-17. (30-45 minutes.) Print Bible study instruction sheet as follows (or read instructions to the group):

a. Reread the scripture to your group of eight. Focus on what the Holy Spirit is saying to *you* about the meaning of the passage in *your* life. Reflect on the meaning of this passage in the life of your group. Share. (10 minutes.)

b. Then create a way to share or demonstrate the meaning of the passage using the vehicles/tools suggested below. Groups must pick different categories until they are all taken and then there can be repeats. Creations will be shared during the Sunday morning session with the entire group.

Pick one word from the list of theme words in the passage listed above and:

a) **Letter writing:** Pretend you are Paul writing a letter to your group on the meaning of this word and this passage in the life of your group.

Now read this letter as though it were the year 2,180. You may want to write individual letters and then compile a "group letter."

b) **Poetry:** Pick one word and use the French poetry form "cinquain" (sin-kane) to express the meaning of this passage. It is difficult for more than two people to work on one verse, so work as individuals and in pairs so your group can create several.

Members of the group may want to use other poetry forms also.

c) **Crafts:** Using the craft materials available, make something that symbolizes, represents or demonstrates the truths of the scriptural theme passage. (Have available an assortment of colored paper, string, glue, wire, rubber bands, paper clips, straws, crayons, Play Dough, sticks, toothpicks and the like.)

d) **Slides and/or music:** Select slides (bring a bunch from family trips, etc.) to express the meaning of this passage. Or select one song from a record and pick slides to go with it. Or you may choose your own music and sing it live along with the slides.

e) **Song creation:** Use the tune of a popular song or TV ad and create new words to express the meaning of this scripture in your life as an individual or as a group. (Several may want to work with one tune, others with another. Or you may want to work in pairs writing different verses for the same tune.)

f) **Commercials:** Think up ad lines from radio, TV or magazines. Take the line and convert it to convey meanings around the theme and the truths of this scripture.

g) **Soap opera:** Create a skit, pantomime or role play that illustrates or demonstrates the meaning of the passage in a real-life situation.

5. Closing prayer by leader with the total group, or within small groups (sentence prayers).

6. Announcements; include a request for crazy skits for tonight, talent to sing, dance, etc., as a part of the evening session.

SATURDAY EVENING SESSION (2 hours)

1. Game: Divide group in half, on either side of an imaginary line, or use a line of chairs or a rope. Play balloon volleyball or Nerf volleyball,

using two balloons or Nerfs at once. Play to 7 points.

2. Singing as a group.

3. Fun 'n dumb skits, plus musical and other talent. You'll need one coordinator and an emcee for this event. Watch your time limit.

4. One or two songs as transition to the film.

5. Show film "The Nail." (20 minutes.) In pairs (does not have be someone from your base group of eight) share:

● feelings about the film

● if you were a person in the film, which person would you most likely be?

● what does this film tell you about being God's people bound together in love?

6. Prayer and close.

7. Announcements; reminders, etc.

SUNDAY MORNING SESSION (2½ hours)

At breakfast announce that each person is to bring something to the morning session from outside the building—for example, an object from the world of nature.

1. Group singing.

2. Small groups of eight meet to review or prepare their creations from the Saturday morning session. (15-20 minutes.)

3. Come back together in groups of eight all in the same room. In pairs share the object you brought and how this object reminds you of God. Then share how this object reminds you of your group as it has been in the past.

Then, share one final question: "How does this object reflect how I want our youth group to be in the future?" (20 minutes.)

4. Self-rating scale: On a scale of 1-10 rate yourself in the following:

I feel loved:	I am patient:	I am loving toward:	I am thankful for:	I express my thanks to:
____by self	____with self	____self	____self	____self
____by parents	____with parents	____parents	____parents	____parents
____by peers	____with peers	____peers	____peers	____peers
____by God	____with God	____God	____God	____God

Share responses to these with one other person in your group of eight. (10 minutes.)

5. Each group shares its creation from the Saturday morning session. Affirm each in a way appropriate—applause, etc. (15-45 minutes.)

6. In groups of eight, share: Who in our school, our community and

our church needs to have our love (and God's love) given to them?
Make a list of specific groups and even individuals. What are we going
to do about it? List possible actions. (10-20 minutes.)

7. Revealing of secret friends—go to your secret friend and share
with him.

8. Close in song and prayer.

9. Provide evaluation forms at lunch.

RESOURCES

1. Games: **The Best of Try This One; More . . . Try This One;** and **Try
This One . . . Too,** Schultz, Group Books.

2. Songbooks: **Songs,** Songs and Creations, Box 559, San Anselmo, CA
94960.

3. Film: "The Nail," available from Family Films, 14622 Lanark St.,
Panorama City, CA 91402.

RETREAT OUTLINE 4:
"A Youth Ministry

By Mike Eastman

A basic outline that helps youth and their adult leaders develop a 12-month youth group activity calendar.

INTRODUCTION

The purpose of this retreat is to lay the basic plans for youth ministry in the local church for a given year. This intergenerational approach to planning with elected past and present representatives is most helpful. It breaks the monotony and problems centering around the month-to-month or week-to-week approach to planning youth ministry.

POSSIBLE SCHEDULE

FRIDAY

9 p.m. — Opening session
Get acquainted—people and program

9:30 p.m. — Brainstorming, evaluation of last year and goal setting

SATURDAY

8-9 a.m. — Breakfast
9-9:15 a.m. — Devotions
9:15 a.m.-Noon — Outline job assignments; begin planning; a job for everyone

Noon-1:15 p.m. — Lunch
1:15-3 p.m. — If necessary, additional planning time

3-4:15 p.m. — Swimming, water-balloon bash, volleyball (free time)

5:30 p.m. — Dinner
7-7:30 p.m. — Total group planning: How are we doing?

8:30 p.m. — Campfire, skits, singing and eating. Bring a skit or talent.

SUNDAY

8:30-10 a.m. — Full council reporting and calendaring

10-10:15 a.m. — Break
10:15-10:45 a.m. — Closing worship
11:30 a.m. — Pitch-in lunch

PREPARATION

Preparation for this retreat requires a small group of young people, perhaps elected or appointed from your youth group. They lay out the basic plans and schedule for an annual youth planning retreat.

Several items are needed in advance to make the actual planning for the coming year flow smoothly. These items include: a church calendar

Planning Retreat"

from September to September or January to January, depending on how your youth group would like to calendar their activities. This calendar should include church school promotion, national youth week, state youth conventions, public school vacations, special advent and lenten dates, all-church experiences such as vacation church school or revivals, and other dates that would be appropriate to your individual church. In addition to your church calendar you will need copies of various public school calendars to avoid planning youth activities on highly scheduled dates of athletic, drama and musical events at your area high schools. Also in advance you will need a 12-month calendar (with space for writing on each date) for each committee.

MATERIALS, EQUIPMENT AND FACILITIES

Materials that will be useful include: pencils, markers, newsprint, Bibles, balloons, volleyball, nets, softball equipment, kickball and other recreational materials. Also necessary are aids for worship and devotions. Each young person or family should be prepared with his or her own copy of the Bible.

FRIDAY EVENING

Friday evening should be used as a get-acquainted session for all those who are present and should also be a time for evaluation of what you have done during the last 12 months in youth ministry in your local church setting. There should be time provided for brainstorming about what you would like to see happen in the future. An icebreaker or crowdbreaker could be used if people are not well acquainted with one another. Idea books published by Youth Specialties, Group Books and others are possible sources for locating icebreakers and crowdbreakers, etc. The discussion centering around this get-acquainted time could include such questions as: What did we do last year that was most effective? What did we do last year that was least effective? What would you like to see repeated in the future? What would you not like to see us ever try again? How did you feel about our most recent youth experience? How can our youth group be stronger? In what areas would you like to see us become more effective?

It is important to keep your program objectives in mind during this opening session. These include:

1. Evangelism . . . that youth come to experience a personal relationship with Jesus Christ to the end that they might be able to share their witness with others.

2. Study . . . that youth might explore the biblical, historical, philosophical, and experiential basis for their Christian faith to the end that they might mature in the faith and be able to interpret it to others.

3. Worship . . . that youth become involved in experience of private and public worship to the end that they might find meaningful ways to respond to God, submit themselves to God's will and praise the living Lord.

4. Outreach . . . that youth come to the knowledge that God is at work in the world confronting all people, calling them to live in relationship with him and work with him to the end that service might be characterized by redemptive, self-giving love, lived out in all areas of life, including the most commonplace.

5. Personal Relationships . . . that youth explore who they are, what their human situation means, life mate concerns, finding meaningful personal relationships, and how to relate to others in meaningful ways.

6. Recreation . . . that youth become physically equipped for ministry in God's world and that they experience wholesome fun and the joy of being together.

SATURDAY

On Saturday parents and youths attending the retreat are divided into committees of their own choosing. Possible committees include: church school, Sunday evening youth fellowship, youth service corps, conventions, and fund-raising projects, junior high, and senior high. In advance of the retreat it is the responsibility of the youth workers or youth minister to recruit for each of these committees a coordinator who is willing to serve in this capacity for one year. During a major block of time on Saturday these individual committees will work on specific plans for the coming year. These plans include dates on which these events will be carried out and any extra information that will be necessary once the retreat is over and more specific event planning is begun. The sample youth planning retreat minutes (on the next page) illustrates what was planned by the various committees for a given year.

The rest of Saturday is devoted to free time, the evening meal, skits, worship and time around the campfire. Some of the special activities our group enjoyed included volleyball and the greased watermelon race.

For the greased watermelon race the group is divided into two teams. Each team is required to retrieve its greased watermelon from the lake and return it to shore. One team has Crisco or grease applied to the end of their noses to distinguish themselves from the other team.

It is also during this free time that the young people are divided into groups to work on skits. These skits are then presented before the entire retreat group later in the evening.

The Saturday evening worship is usually directed and led by the youth leader or the youth minister. You can be as creative in this type of outdoor worship as you would like.

SUNDAY

On Sunday morning everyone who has been working on the retreat gathers together to report as a whole to the total group what they had in mind and what they have been working on. It is during this time that all the events and activities are listed on newsprint for the coordinating of dates, calendaring and people. After this process is finished we have our closing worship.

Graduating high school seniors attending the retreat are given additional leadership experience by having them conduct the closing worship experience. One option is for the seniors to share personal experiences of their years of involvement in youth ministry and how God has been actively involved in their lives during this period.

Once the retreat is over the work has just begun. A youth directory containing all the information that has been obtained from the annual youth planning retreat is printed following the retreat. This directory is distributed to each member of the youth group. They then have a listing of all the youth activities for a given 12-month period and the dates in which they will occur. It also gives them other helpful information about the youth ministry of our local church.

We have found this to be a very effective way of planning our program and are beginning our sixth year of planning our youth ministry in this fashion.

MINUTES FOR YOUTH PLANNING RETREAT

April 12 - Bike Hike (Aqua Gardens) and Cookout
Joe and Anita Womack - Chairpersons
Duane and Joyce Hoak
Mike Hoak
Paul Womack

May 3 - McCormick's Creek - Hiking, etc.
Charles and Naomi Whitmill - Chairpersons
Eldon and Glenda Flaming
Rich and Cheryl Willowby
Kim Grubbs
Christa Sherwood
Laurie Mathis

June 9,10- Cedar Point
Jack and Caroline Smith - Chairpersons
Paul and Barbara Gray
Bernice Edwards

July 19 - Swim Party
Gordon and Sandy Reitz
Ron and Jan Moore
*Girls - bring desserts
*Boys - bring drinks

August - Canoe Trip
Don Brandon - Chairperson
Jim Tinsley
Treva Gressman

Brookfield, Indiana

Sandy Reitz is the chairperson for the Special Events Youth II.

A discussion of problems concerning the meals on Sunday evening resulted in the decision that no one would be asked to serve more than two times a year. Approximately once a month, the group would go out or have alternate plans for the meal.

September 16   Burger Chef
October 14   Brown Bag   February 17
November 25

MINUTES FOR YOUTH PLANNING RETREAT

FUND RAISING PROJECT COMMITTEE

1. Goal
   (a) To choose the least number of projects with the highest profit.
   (b) No more than three (3) big projects.

2. Projects
   (a) Hoagies: Some additions
       1. Use van to transport Hoagies (and sell from van) at football games.
       2. Maybe supply drinks.
       3. We have presale but we need better on the spot sales.
       4. Tent on campground
       5. Date for Homecoming, October 6, 1979.

   (b) Christmas Card Delivery
       1. Start early! (November 1 or 1st Sunday after Thanksgiving)
       2. Let people know by Inspirer, news on Sunday
       3. Box at church office (bring cards mostly on Sunday)
       4. Same day delivery
       5. People save and we make money - 10c per card - goes to Youth

   (c) Tower Restaurant (organize better)
       1. Start sooner - June 18-30 is World Conference and Camp Meeting
       2. Be ready for peak selling items
       3. Use microwave oven for heating sandwiches
       4. Less junk foods
       5. Salads, maybe
       6. Good prices (by buying better wholesale prices)

3. Possible projects
   Wash: airplanes, trains, cars, windows

   A-thons: Skate, Rock, Trash, Starve

   Egg Sale   Spook Insurance for Halloween

   Skating

MINUTES FOR YOUTH PLANNING RETREAT

MINUTES FROM SUNDAY EVENING FELLOWSHIP COMMITTEE

Proposed New Time Schedule for Youth

3:30 - 4:00   Youth Swing Choir
4:00 - 5:15   Interest Centers and Rec Room Romp
5:15 - 5:45   Happy Munger Hunchie Munchie Bunch Lunch Time
5:45 - 7:00   Group Grope -- Grade 7

Group Grope   Grade 8
                                     Grades 9 - 12   Each names their own
                                                      Group Grope
News More Direction
Develop Study Sessions
Develop Philosophy

Possible Interest Centers

Volleyball Tourneys
Macramé   Group Games - More
Tennis   Creative Writing
Bowling   Yoga
Man Hunt   Marshall Arts
Destination Unknown   T.M.
Book of Records - World's Largest Popsicle   Cooking
                  Pennies   Ceramics
                  Banana Split   Treasure Hunts
Record Night   Snow Fest
Miniture Golf   Clearing at A.C.
Mime   Swimming at A.C.
Frog and Turtle Races   Frisbee Tourney
Car Scavenger Hunt   Body and Fat Painting
Water Balloon Fight   Oil Painting
                                     Hand Writing Analysis
Suggested New Equipment

Good Ping Pong Tables   Possible Periodic Leaders
Volleyball net
Park Place Gym   Duncans
Quiet Room   Shoemaker
Youth House   Grubbs - Jan and Jerry
Piano in Room 200 for Youth   Grubbs - Dwight
Fix Stereo
                                     FOOD
                                     1 night a month -- Burger Chef
                                                         Left Overs from Home
                                                         Bag Night
              Suggestions for Possible Special Events by Youth Fellowship
Almost Anything Goes
Christmas Party   Lock-In   Kidnapping (man hunt)
Easter Sunrise   Backwards Night   Youth Nativity
New Years Eve Party Youth Reunion (6 yrs.back) Parents Appreciation Eve.
Linger Longer   Mortuary Night   Walk In My Moccasins Night
                     Pumpkin Caroling   Christmas Light Surveillance
                     Starvathon

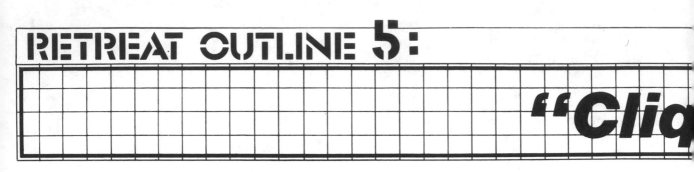

"Cliq

By Kent Hummel

An opportunity for your group to learn about, experience and design strategies for dealing with cliques.

One of the most potentially destructive forces in youth work is the clique. Cliques offer a teenager a place to belong and a sense of security. However, they also cause the exclusion of a great number of youth, hinder interaction and stifle outreach.

This retreat provides a group an opportunity to see how cliques develop, what it's like to be on the wrong side of a clique, how God feels about cliques, and what we can do about them.

> **Scripture theme:** John 13:34-35

BEFORE THE RETREAT

1. Prepare a list of things the youth will need to bring. Don't forget to include Bible, notebook and pen.

2. Collect permission slips and any monies owed before you leave to avoid confusion when you arrive.

3. Assign people to pray specifically for each youth while on the retreat. In the past we have enlisted people to pray and write a note of encouragement that we passed out at our Sunday morning meeting to their assigned youth.

4. Read through the sessions to familiarize yourself with the topics and the materials needed to be printed or assembled.

The materials needed are:
- Songs for Friday evening
- Chairs arranged for Saturday morning's first meeting
- Props for "Go Away" for Saturday afternoon's second meeting
- Copies of "English Test" for Saturday afternoon's second meeting—one per person
- Props for "Foto Match" for Saturday evening's third meeting
- Copies of "Human Bingo" for Sunday morning's fourth meeting—one per person
- Copies of "Back Rubs" for Sunday morning's fourth meeting—one per person
- Props for "Tie That Binds" for Sunday afternoon's fifth meeting.

5. Other items needed: projector, screen, movie (see Friday evening notes), snack foods.

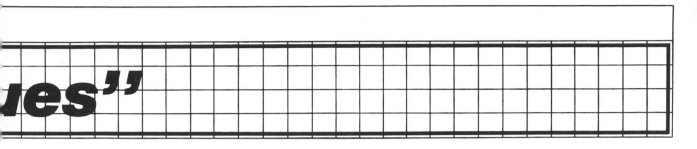
WHILE ON THE WAY

If possible plan interaction games or events to get the youth better acquainted and comfortably talking and sharing together while traveling to the retreat site.

Either while traveling or as soon as you arrive (can't be done ahead because of no-shows or last-minute attenders) get a core of your adult leaders together to divide the youth into small groups for the weekend. The groups will be used in your meetings, for free time, team games, cleanup, eating order, etc. These groups are essential in building unity and have a great bearing on the weekend's success. Try to get a good balance in each group between popular kids, shy ones, talkers, disrupters, the spiritually mature, and athletes (for team games). You should also separate as much as possible any existing or potential cliques you might already have. These groups should consist of six to 10 people. Seven to nine is ideal.

Once this is done, place your leaders in these groups to be responsible for facilitating sharing, group identity and spirit. Discuss with your leaders who would work best with which group.

WEEKEND DEVOTIONS

SATURDAY

Get the entire group together to give them their assigned reading, questions to think about and directed prayer. If the weather permits, let them find a place outside alone to do their devotions.

Reading—John 13:34-35

Question—What does this say to you

POSSIBLE SCHEDULE

Times may vary. Choose free time activities to fit your group.

FRIDAY

7 p.m.	Leave for retreat
8 p.m.	Arrive at retreat site
8-9 p.m.	Settle in
9:15 p.m.	Movie
11 p.m.	Lights out

SATURDAY

7 a.m.	Rise and shine
7:30 a.m.	Devotions
8 a.m.	Breakfast
8:30 a.m.	Cleanup
9 a.m.	Meeting 1
10:30 a.m.- Noon	Free time (Leaders pick youth for "Go Away" session #2)
Noon	Lunch
12:30 p.m.	Cleanup
2 p.m.	Meeting #2
3:30-5 p.m.	Free time
5 p.m.	Supper
5:30 p.m.	Cleanup
6-7 p.m.	Free time
7 p.m.	Meeting #3
8-10:30 p.m.	Free time
10:30—	Singing
	Lights out

(continued)

POSSIBLE SCHEDULE

continued

SUNDAY

7 a.m.	Rise and shine
7:30 a.m.	Devotions
8 a.m.	Breakfast
8:30 a.m.	Clean up
9 a.m.	Meeting #4
10:30 a.m.-noon	Free time
Noon	Lunch
12:30 p.m.	Clean up
12:30-1:30 p.m.	Free time
1:30 p.m.	Meeting #5
3:30 p.m.	Pack and leave
5 p.m.	Arrive home

about love?

 Reading—James 2:1-9

 Question—What does this say to you about love? Do you ever find yourself doing this?

 Prayer Time—Pray for yourself—to be open this weekend to God and to each other. Pray the same way for the others in your group.

SUNDAY

 Same directions as for Saturday.

 Reading—Colossians 3:12-14

 Question—How well do you exhibit these qualities?

 Reading—Matthew 13:1-8

 Question—What kind of people do these seeds represent?

 Prayer Time—Again pray for yourself, to be open and to take home and put into practice what you have learned. Pray the same for the others in your group.

FRIDAY EVENING

 After unpacking get everyone together for Friday evening's activities.

 1. It is important that you go over your own particular ground rules with the young people right away.

 2. Go over the schedule and purpose of the retreat. Put copies in the eating areas and other key places.

 3. After dividing the young people into teams for the weekend, do a song search in the dark. Directions: On a slip of paper, give each youth on a given team the title of the same familiar song. Do the same thing for each team using different songs for each team. Instruct them not to let anyone else see their paper. When the lights go out they are to start humming their song and finding the others with the same song. Tell them how many others there will be. The first team to finish gets a reward—to eat breakfast first, etc.

 4. Show a movie—perhaps a Walt Disney film or a Christian film that fits the theme.

 5. Group singing or lights out, depending on the time.

FIRST MEETING

Saturday Morning (1½ hours)
What is a Clique?

 1. Open with prayer.

 2. Play "Untangle." Organize everyone into their groups and have them stand in a circle. Everyone grabs hands with others not next to them and without letting go, gets himself back into a circle all untangled and still joining hands. Mention that the first group done gets a prize—first to eat lunch, etc.

 3. Read John 13:34-35.

4. Announce the weekend topic schedule—cliques—what causes them, how God feels about them, what you can do about them.

5. Ask everyone to define and discuss the meaning of a clique, then read the following definition: "A clique is a small exclusive circle of people who have common interests. Once formed, there is an unwillingness by members of the group to admit others into their circle of friendship."

6. Form groups and have each group (a) do a play or skit, (b) write a song, (c) write a poem or story about a clique—real or imagined, but typical of cliques. Vote on the best.

7. Explain and discuss the following types of cliques:

"Cool ones"—big-man-on-campus type, very popular with popular people. They feel others are socially inferior. Very judgmental.

"Rowdies"—love to cause trouble and pick on and make fun of others. Spend a lot of time telling others how rowdy they are.

"Super Straights" (Super Spirituals)—proud of being straight (not doing certain things, knowing Bible, etc.). Talk about how good they are and how bad others are. Look down on those who are less straight.

"Just Averages"—held together by need for survival. They are usually bitter and resentful, or awestruck by the other cliques.

"We sing or play in the band together"—talented people whose whole life is built around singing or playing music. They are so busy they don't have time for anyone else.

"Me and my girlfriend and my friend and his girlfriend"—they are easy to spot, they look welded together! All conversation revolves around Saturday's date (past, present, and future). Always looking at each other. No time for anyone else.

"The Athletes"—small but powerful group. They hang together because of athletic "greatness" which makes them feel above others. They love to talk about sports and have macho contests.

Ask the young people to come up with any others if they can.

8. Another way to illustrate cliques is to have the group play "Cliques and Loners" from **Ideas Book 25**, page 30. It is an effective way of getting kids talking about the effects of cliques on a youth group.

Ahead of time, arrange the chairs and tell the kids as they come in that the chairs are not to be moved. Following is how the chairs should be set up, and the people they represent:

a. A group of chairs in a circle all hooked together: the group of regular teens who attend the youth group.

b. A chair in the middle of the circle: the person who wants to be the center of attention.

c. A few chairs outside the group: visitors to the youth group who can't seem to break through and be a part of the group in the circle.

d. A chair next to the door: a new person who has just entered the group.

e. A chair outside the door, looking in: someone wanting to enter the youth group but who is afraid to come in.

f. A chair on top of the table: a person who criticizes and looks down on everyone else.

g. A broken chair or a chair that's different from all the others: a person in the group who may be a little different from the rest because of a handicap, a foreign accent, etc.

h. A small cluster of three or four chairs off from the large circle: that group of people who sticks together and won't let anyone into their group.

You can probably think of some other ways to represent various groupings within a group, and you should try to arrange it so that everyone has a chair, and there are no chairs left over. As the group arrives, give each person a number at random and instruct him/her to sit in the chair that has the same number. During the meeting have a discussion on cliques using the following questions. Everyone must stay in the seats that they have been assigned during the entire meeting.

9. Questions for discussion:
    a. How can cliques be helpful?
    b. How can cliques be harmful?
    c. Why are some people not included in a clique?

10. Some closing comments: Point out that your youth group doesn't have a clique problem and is trying to follow John 13:34 but we all have cliquish tendencies. This topic is being considered because:
    a. Cliquish tendencies can lead to some bad things if not nipped in the bud.
    b. This will help everyone deal better with cliques at school.

Ask the following questions to be answered silently. (A "yes" answer to any of these means the retreat will be helpful.)
    a. Do you ever catch yourself feeling that you and your friends are more "with it" than others in the youth group?
    b. Do you ever try to discourage someone from being involved with you and your friends because they wouldn't fit the mold of what's acceptable to your group?
    c. If you are talking to someone and one of your close friends comes into the room do you immediately leave that person and go to talk to your friend?
    d. Do you make it a point to get to know new students at our youth meetings?

11. Close in prayer.

SECOND MEETING

Saturday Afternoon (1½ hours)
What Causes Cliques?

1. Open with prayer.

2. Play "Squat." Have each team form a circle facing the same direction. On the count of three everyone sits down on the knees of the person behind him. Then do it as a total group, combining all the teams into one big circle. (Needs a large area.)

3. Play "Go Away," a clique simulation game. The following materials are needed: toothpicks, glue, old magazines, clay and poster board for each team.

Divide into groups. Explain that each team uses the supplies and works together to construct a symbol of what "community" or "togetherness" means to them. Tell each group to be prepared to explain its completed symbol and set a time limit.

The "sting": Before this session, for each team pick one person who is to argue, refuse to cooperate, hinder progress and otherwise be a headache. Caution the "plants" not to make their misbehavior too obvious. Explain to the "plants" that their purpose is to test the teams' reactions to negative behavior. Locate the teams far enough apart so they can't see each other.

After the teams have worked on the project long enough for the "plant" to cause some problems, stop the activity temporarily.

Explain that you're also trying an experiment to see if a new team can catch up with the existing teams. Explain that you'll form the new team by taking one person from each existing team. Tell each team to send one person from their membership to the new team. Normally, each team will send the troublemaker, but even if someone else is sent, it doesn't change the experience.

Under the guise of giving the new team "catch-up" instructions, explain that in a minute or two each person is to return to his original team and ask to be readmitted, saying he doesn't like the new group.

When each team has had enough time to react, either by accepting the person or by refusing readmittance, stop the activity and call all the groups back together. It's a good idea to confess that each group had a "plant."

Use some or all of the following questions:

    a. How did you feel about the "plant" on your team?

    b. How did you feel about having to tell one person to leave?

    c. Why did you reject the person you did?

    d. How did you feel when he returned and asked to be readmitted?

    e. If you didn't accept him, what were your reasons?

    f. If you accepted him again, why? Did you place any conditions for rejoining the group?

    g. How did you show him you really accepted him again?

    h. Ask the "plants" how they felt about the whole process.

    i. In what ways was this experience similar to the way groups treat some people at school or church?

    j. How do most "real" groups deal with someone who's different?

You could end this experience by having everyone help plan a session where the emphasis is on learning how to accept people who are new to the group.

If "Go Away" is too long and involved an alternate activity is "Misfit" taken from **Ideas Book 23**, page 30. It helps young people learn how to handle the misfit or newcomer to their group.

During one of your meetings send one of the young people on a short errand. While he is gone, lead the rest of the group in a game that requires total participation of all members so that a latecomer couldn't possibly play. Also, instruct the kids to ignore the "errand person" when he returns. After the game, discuss with the "misfit" his feelings about being left out. As a group, have the kids reflect on a time when they were a newcomer and have each share a one-word description of what it felt like. You might then read John 8:1-11 about the woman caught in adultery, and discuss Jesus' gentle attitude. Role play what might have happened the next day as the adulterous woman runs into two friends. Conclude with the following role play: A visitor walks into one of your weekly youth meetings. Repeat the role play several times until the kids have a handle on how to treat visitors.

4. Discuss the reasons for cliques:

a. *Prideful status seeking.* As human beings we have a sin nature, a big part of which is pride.

Pride tells us that we must be the center of attention, so we deceive ourselves into thinking that climbing into a higher status group will make us happier. We tend to use people.

Jesus was not a status seeker! He was more concerned with what God wanted him to do than with who accepted him.

Read Romans 12:16 and Matthew 9:9-13. Discuss why Jesus was not a status seeker. What can we learn from him?

b. *Fear and insecurity.* We all have a desire to be and feel needed and wanted.

The problem is that we look too much to our friends to meet that need. The last thing we want to lose is our importance and favor with our friends.

Because we don't usually love ourselves and have low self-esteem and aren't secure in our specialness to God and others, we tend to shut out newcomers because they might threaten our position in the group.

We put our security in people and not in God.

Read Isaiah 31:1 and 3 (Living Bible), Proverbs 3:5-6 and 1 John 4:18,19.

c. *Selfishness and laziness.* Have the group do this English Test (taken from **Ideas Book 17**, page 25).

Read the following instructions and pass out the test.

"Mark this paragraph into sentences using capitals at the beginning, periods at the end of sentences, and commas, etc. where needed. Once begun, *do not go back and try to correct.*"

ENGLISH TEST

He is a young man yet experienced in vickedness he is never found in opposing the works of iniquity he takes delight in the downfall of his neighbors he never rejoices in the prosperity of his fellow-creatures he is always ready to assist in destroying the peace of society he takes no pleasure in serving the Lord he is uncommonly diligent in sowing discord among his friends and acquaintants he takes no pride in laboring to promote the cause of Christianity he has not been negligent in endeavoring to tear down the church he makes no effort to subdue his evil passions he strives hard to build up Satan's kingdom he lends no aid to the support of the gospel among heathen he contributes largely to the devil he will never go to heaven he must go where he will receive his just reward.

Here is the way it should be corrected:

He is a young man, yet experienced. In vice and wickedness, he is never found. In opposing the works of iniquity, he takes delight. In the downfall of his neighbors, he never rejoices. In the prosperity of his fellow-creatures, he is always ready to assist. In destroying the peace of society, he takes no pleasure. In serving the Lord, he is uncommonly diligent. In sowing discord among his friends and acquaintances, he takes no pride. In laboring to promote the cause of Christianity, he has not been negligent. In endeavoring to tear down the church, he makes no effort. To subdue his evil passions, he strives hard. To build up Satan's kingdom, he lends no aid. To the support of the gospel among heathen, he contributes largely. To the devil he will never go. To heaven he must go, where he will receive his just reward.

As with the "English test" we judge too many things from our own perspective and are too lazy to check things out first. We do the same with people. We have prejudices and form opinions too soon and too easily without getting to know them. This is where we struggle most usually.

Once we reach a place where we have a close-knit group of friends it is easy to become indifferent to others. We feel we no longer need to reach out to someone who needs us as a friend. We are very content where we are. We all know how much easier it is to just be with our close friends. Making new friends is work. This is selfish and lazy.

God has something to say about this. Read Matthew 5:46, 47 (Living Bible).

Just loving our friends is no great deed of love. We need to go beyond that.

5. Close with prayer.

THIRD MEETING

Saturday Evening (1 hour)
Why God Opposes Cliques

1. Open with prayer.

2. In their groups have the youth team up with a partner. Have them play "Mimic." Each one sees how well he can mirror or copy the other's actions, speech, expressions. Each group picks their best pair to mimic before the whole group to see which pair is best.

3. Why God opposes cliques (discussion):

a. Cliques go against the fairness of God. Read Ephesians 5:1-2 (Living Bible).

As with the game "Mimic" we are to imitate or mirror our heavenly Father. Like a child we can't imitate our father perfectly in all things, but we can mimic our Father enough so that others should be able to tell whose children we are.

Following are some things about God we should mimic.

● *God's Impartiality*

Read Deuteronomy 10:16-19 (Living Bible). Looks, wealth, fame, heritage, get no special treatment from God. We should treat all people the same.

● *God's Love*

God is not only impartial, he loves all men too. Not just in words or ideas but with action!

Read Philippians 2:5-8 (Living Bible). God had every right to disassociate himself totally from us. But Jesus left his rightful status and came to earth for us. We should do the same. Read 1 John 3:16. This is love with action!

b. Do "Foto Match" first to illustrate reason #2 before giving it (taken from **Ideas Book 19**, page 25).

Cliques cause us to show favoritism to others on faulty, shallow standards.

Doing "Foto Match" shows us how we form strong opinions on appearance alone. Our first impression was exaggerated yet we all do it to a degree. Read James 2:1-9 (Liv-

---

FOTO MATCH

Hang up 20 or oo photos of people (all kinds . . . old, young, black, white, attractive, ugly, fat, slim, wealthy, poor, etc.). Have the kids write descriptions of each person based on what they see in the picture. Collect them all verbally and combine all the individual descriptions into a concise list which accurately reflects the group consensus. Attach the descriptions to each photo. Then answer the following questions:

● Choose five you'd like to get to know. Why did you choose these five?

● Is there any one person you would not want anything to do with? Why?

● Who, if any, would you be willing to marry?

● If only five people and yourself were allowed to live and the others executed, which five would stay with you? Why?

ing Bible). God is fair. He shows no favoritism.

Read Luke 10:30-37.

No doubt each of us knows people who are not naturally attractive to us. However, many of these people have emotional and spiritual needs and pains. God does not want us to further hurt these people through a spirit of excluding them. But he wants us to reach out to them and express compassion in meeting their needs.

No one can be rejected by a group for very long before they begin to realize that they are being rejected. This often results in a negative response from the person being "put-off." Not only is this divisive to the Body of Christ, but it may seriously hinder that person's growth in Christ. Paul warned the Galatian Christians: Read Galatians 5:14-15 (NAS).

Such backbiting and "devouring" is just what Satan wants to happen. Nothing could please him more. But God wants us to build one another up, to encourage each other. As Romans 13:10 (NAS) states: "Love does no wrong to a neighbor: Love therefore is the fulfillment of the law."

Jesus taught that one of the most powerful ways that a non-Christian is influenced to come to Christ is the love that he sees between Christians. In John 13:34, 35 (NAS) he said, "A new Commandment I give to you, that you love one another, even as I have loved you, that you also love one another. By this all men will know that you are my disciples, if you have love for one another."

It is sad when non-Christians come to our group seeking love, and find that because of our disobedience, fear, insecurity, laziness, selfishness and pride, we act just like the very people who have hurt them. These people look at our actions to see if there is living proof that Christ is real. If on the one hand, we say that Christ gives us love and on the other hand, we do not practice love, but rather are cliquish and cruel, we are living a lie.

4. Wrap up comments. Watch for little ways we might do any of these things we've discussed. It's very easy to forget and get lazy and comfortable with our close friends. It's normal to be afraid to reach out. We all do these things. If you do:

a. Confess your faults.

b. As an act of faith, show love to those outside your group. When you do, it will get easier and more fulfilling.

c. Be the initiator in reaching out and in telling your friends to reach out.

If you have been shut out by a clique, this can be a time of growth and understanding. Being left out of a group can draw you closer to God if you let it. Don't be bitter, angry or feel sorry for yourself. That's really more important.

5. Close in prayer.

FOURTH MEETING

Sunday Morning (1½ hours)
How to Be a Clique Breaker/What Can We Do?

1. Open with prayer.

2. Play "Human Bingo" (taken from **Ideas Book 8** page 11). The first person to get the necessary signatures wins.

HUMAN BINGO				
Someone who uses mouth-wash regularly	Someone with 2 brothers	Someone with blond hair at least 12 in. long	Someone who plays football	Someone who has been out of the U.S.
Someone who owns a dog	Someone who is wearing contact lenses	Someone who plays chess a lot	Someone who can touch his palms to the floor	Someone who owns a motor-cycle
Someone with red hair	Someone who watches soap operas	Sign your own name	Someone who got an A in English	Someone who has touched a snake
Someone who has been in Canada	Someone who weighs over 200 pounds	Someone who reads comic books	Someone who has played spin-the-bottle or post office	Someone who ate at McDon-ald's this week
Someone who never changed a diaper	Someone who weighs under 110 pounds	Someone who owns a horse	Someone wear-ing blue socks	Someone who can say all the books of the Bible

3. Discussion: Being a clique breaker also involves a "put on."

Read Colossians 3:12-14. It involves changing from what's natural! (See verse 10.) Have the youth come up with what these words mean in relation to breaking cliques: compassion, kindness, appreciation, humility, gentleness, patience, bearing with, forgiving.

All these are very similar to the fruit of the Spirit (Galatians 5:24-26). They are all also very important in being a servant—the key to friendship.

Read Colossians 3:14 concerning love.

4. Do "Back Rubs" (from **Idea Book 16**, pages 24, 25)

5. Close with prayer.

FIFTH MEETING

Sunday Afternoon (1½-2 hours)
Above All Love

1. Open with prayer.

BACK RUBS

RULES:

a. You may receive a back rub only after you have given one (after first round).

b. The giver will be scored by the receiver on a scale of one to 10 with 10 being best.

c. On your sheet, the score is automatically five points for any back rub received by you.

d. You will receive a score from one to 10 only on back rubs which you give. The receiver will judge your back rub.

e. No score is valid without the initials of the other person (giver or receiver).

f. You may not refuse to give or receive a back rub if someone asks you.

g. The same person may be used only twice, once giving and once receiving.

h. The highest score at the end of the time limit wins.

i. Next to each item completed have score and person's initials.

continued

BACK RUBS, continued

THE BACK RUBS:

a. Give to someone taller.

b. Receive from someone shorter.

c. Give to someone older.

d. Receive from someone younger.

e. Give to someone of the opposite sex.

f. Receive from someone of the same sex.

g. Give to someone with shoes on.

h. Receive from someone without shoes on—with boots on.

i. Give to someone with blue eyes.

j. Receive from someone with brown eyes.

k. Give to someone wearing red.

l. Receive from someone wearing green.

m. Give to someone who lives less than one mile from you.

n. Receive from someone who lives more than one mile from you.

o. Give to someone who wears glasses or contacts.

p. Receive from someone who doesn't wear glasses or contacts.

q. Give to someone with an even-numbered address.

r. Receive from someone with an even-numbered address.

s. Give to someone whose last initial is before yours in the alphabet.

t. Receive from someone whose last initial is after yours in the alphabet.

QUESTIONS ABOUT BACK RUBS:

a. What were your feelings? Were you embarrassed?

b. Was it harder to give or receive back rubs? If harder to give, what does that say about reaching out? If harder to receive, what does that say about your self-esteem?

c. Has this changed your feelings about your group at all?

d. Why did we do this? Are there any insights you gained from this about Christian love? Read 1 John 3:18. Our love must be active too.

2. Read Colossians 3:12-14. Explain that "put on" equals action. We are not to just talk about or think about being compassionate, kind, gentle, patient and loving. We are to act these ways.

3. Read John 13:34, 35. Discuss how "all men will know." What are some ways?

4. Read 1 John 3:18. Directions: Have your groups form a circle and put one person in the middle of the circle. Starting with the adult group leader go around the circle, each person non-verbally expressing his love and care for that person. When you've gone all the way around, put the next person in the middle and repeat this process until everyone has been in the center. Examples of non-verbal expression are a hug, a touch, a look, giving a gift. Be creative! Be genuine!

5. Get back in one large group and share how this went. Was it hard to do? Would it have been easier to do verbally? How did you feel receiving? Giving? Which was harder?

6. Give the youth the following challenge: "How will each of you and as a group reach outside this youth group to share with others in need of Christ and fellowship and friendship?"

7. Get them back in their groups and have them brainstorm about the following. Pick one target person that their group will reach out to.

Who will it be? A person from the church but not very involved or a person from school they all know? (If your situation involves many youth from many different schools and they can't come up with one person, adopt this and have the youth divide up into minigroups within the groups; do the best they can at picking several target people. You may want to initially divide up the groups so this problem can be avoided.)

What will you do? Examples: Invite to church or youth group; eat lunch with at school; say "hi" to them every day as a starter; call them on the phone; invite them to do something with you or your friends. Be creative! Develop a plan.

As a group pray for this person. The more you pray for someone the more you'll care and be concerned for them. This really requires you to be a servant, just as Jesus was.

8. Get them back into one large group and share together their results group by group.

9. In closing do "The Tie That Binds." Have all the kids stand in a circle. Any group of up to 50 will work. Take a long, thick piece of rope or cord and loop it around each person as in the illustration. Be sure there is no slack between people and have them move close together. With no explanation of the purpose or point, have each kid take a large step backward one at a time. Go all the way around the circle. (Normally, someone about halfway around will get the bright idea to give a good squeeze to the ones next to him; allow this.) When everyone has stepped back, have them drop the rope and sit down.

Discuss the following things: What happened when you stepped back (to you and the ones around you), and what happened when the persons next to you stepped back, and what part did the rope play in this experience? What is the rope? (It's our Christian love in action.) It's not just talk that holds us together but something concrete. If and when someone tries to fall away or is pulled away our Christian love should hold them in and pull them back.

The rope is also elastic. It has a gentle pull to it and it is big enough to include more people. As we strive not to be cliquish and to reach out to others our group should easily be able to expand.

10. Close with prayer.

RESOURCES

Ideas, Wayne Rice & Mike Yaconelli, Youth Specialties.

Discussion Manual for Student Relationships, Volume 3, Dawson McAllister, Shepherd Productions.

John from **I'm Out to Change My World**, by Ann Kiemel, Impact Books.

By Jerry Christensen

An overnight lock-in to help youth groups set ministry goals

The following retreat is for those new groups that want to evaluate where they're headed.

Choose a facility with a large conference room, small meeting areas and an area that can be used for snacks and recreation.

Materials needed for the lock-in are:

Name tags	Blindfolds
Scratch paper	Candle
Pins	Multi-colored pipe cleaners
Pencils	Movie: "Rocky"
Nerf balls	

Movie Projector and screen (or video-tape, video-recorder and TV).

"Rocky" is available from MGM Film Rental. Phone: 1-800-223-0933. (Bargain for a lower rental fee.)

Insight Film: "The Jesus Song" available from Insight Films, Paulist Productions, P.O. Box 1057, Pacific Palisades, CA 90272.

FRIDAY

8 p.m.

Greet the kids at the door and distribute name tags. The name tags are made in four different colors, four different shapes, and are numbered from one to four to facilitate breaking up into small discussion groups. Each participant writes his or her name on a small piece of paper.

8:30 p.m.

Warm-up activities: Use any activities to "loosen up" the kids and help them get acquainted with each other.

8:45 p.m.

Everyone pairs off and introduces himself to his partner. Each couple then takes turns introducing his partner to the entire group.

POSSIBLE SCHEDULE

FRIDAY EVENING

8 p.m.	Meet at lock-in location
8:30 p.m.	Warm-up activities
8:45 p.m.	Introductions
9 p.m.	Film: "Rocky"
11 p.m.	Group discussion
11:45 p.m.	Snack time

SATURDAY

12:45 a.m.	Talking about the youth group
1:15 a.m.	What a youth group should be
2 a.m.	Break
2:30 a.m.	Small group skits
3:30 a.m.	Film: "The Jesus Song"
4 a.m.	Discussion: "Friendship"
5 a.m.	Blindfold encouragement
5:30 a.m.	Candle-light celebration
7 a.m.	Closing worship service

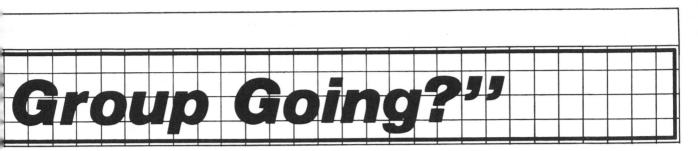

Group Going?"

Ask each person to write a response to this question: ''What do I think the lock-in is going to be and what do I want to get out of it?''

The pieces of paper with the names on them are handed out randomly. During the course of the night the participants should secretly get to know that person better.

9 p.m.
Show ''Rocky.''

11 p.m.
Small group discussions: (Groups are determined by colors with members of the retreat team as discussion leaders). The purpose of the discussion is to talk about developing friendships based on the movie.

Discussion Guide For ''Rocky''

1. What did you think of Rocky as a person?
2. Why do you think he never ''made it'' before? Motivation?
3. How do you feel about Rocky's relationship with:
- Pauly?
- Adreanne?
- his manager?
- his boss (the ''juice'' man)?

4. How important were his relationships with all those people?
5. Discuss his relationships with all those people. For instance:
- He and Pauly always fought but Rocky still tried to help him
- Do you think his boss really tried to help Rocky?
- Could he have gotten where he did without his manager?
- Why did he let his manager help him?
- Why did he try to help the girl on the corner? The other guys on the corner?
- Could he have gotten where he did without Adreanne?

6. How important are friendships to you?
7. What sacrifices did Rocky make for his friends? What sacrifices do you make for your friends?

continued

8. What sacrifices do you make for yourself? What sacrifices did Rocky make for himself?

9. How would you describe Rocky's character?

10. Do you see anything in Rocky that you'd like to see in yourself?

11. How did you feel at the end of the movie? about Rocky? about Adreanne?

11:30 p.m.

Sharing with the whole group: One member from each small group shares the ideas that were discussed with the entire group.

11:45 p.m.

Break time for refreshments and recreation. If facilities are limited we have developed a volleyball game using a Nerf ball and long lunch tables. The players must sit in chairs on either side of the "net" (table) using regular volleyball rules. They may not leave their chairs except to rotate after the serve changes hands.

12:45 a.m.

"What our youth group has meant to me": Members share positive experiences about the importance of the youth group.

1:15 p.m.

Small group discussion "What a youth group should be": (This time the groups are divided by name tag shapes.) The purpose of this discussion is to learn what the kids feel is important for a youth group.

Discussion Outline For
"WHAT A YOUTH GROUP SHOULD BE"

1. What should you expect from a youth group?
   - Social?
   - Religious education?
   - Christian action?
     Within church district?
     Outside church district?
   - Other
2. What should you contribute to a youth group?
   - Be open
   - Physical
   - Emotional
   - Other
3. Should you look to the group for developing friendships?
   - What about cliques?
   - Open to all?
   - Other

continued

4. Should members of the group reach out to help others?
   - Within the group?
   - Outside the group?
   - How?
5. Do you feel welcome? Why or why not?
6. How can you make others feel welcome?
7. How can you make the group more attractive to outsiders?

1:45 a.m.
Sharing with the whole groups: (See 11:30 p.m. above).

2 a.m.
Break. Try an active game. Or have someone lead the group in exercises.

2:30 a.m.
In small groups (determined by name tag shapes) plan commercials about "What a youth group should be." These commercials can use any resources available; humor should be encouraged.

3 a.m.
Each group presents its commercial. After all commercials have been presented the group judges the commercials by applause (a four-way tie is encouraged).

3:30 a.m.
Show "The Jesus Song."

Discussion Outline For
"THE JESUS SONG"

1. Why was Randy King having trouble writing songs?
   - No meaning in his life
   - He had nothing real or good in his life to draw from
2. Have you ever met anyone like Chris?
   - Willing to help and doesn't want anything in return
3. How do you feel about the "stories" in the Bible? Can you draw on them to help? Have you ever drawn on them for help? Give an example.
4. Do you ever feel you need someone the way Randy needed Chris?
5. Randy felt like everything was "falling apart." Have you ever felt like that? Where can you turn?
6. What was Randy really missing in his life? What kind of friendship did he get from the "groupies"?

continued

7. Mary wanted to be a true friend. Why wouldn't he accept her?

8. Where do real friendships come from?
- You have to know yourself and know Jesus
- Jesus will always be there when you need him—the way Chris was
- Put Jesus first, others second, and yourself last
- Real friendships come through Jesus

9. Do you think Randy really changed? Why or why not?

10. How do you think Randy's new songs were accepted? Is it important how they were accepted? Explain.

4 a.m.

Small group discussion (determined by name tag "numbers") on friendship. Have everyone read 1 Corinthians 13:4-7 and Colossians 3:18—4:1 and list qualities that make people good friends. Then ask each person to compare himself or herself to the list.

4:30 a.m.

Sharing with whole group (same as previous whole group sharings).

5 a.m.

Three-fourths of the group are blindfolded and sit on the floor. *Slowly* read off a list of positive attributes (e.g. sense of humor, courage, etc.). As these are read off, the remaining one-fourth should tap the head of any person they feel has that attribute. (Make sure that everyone gets tapped at least once.) After three or four attributes have been called, the group not wearing blindfolds takes a blindfold from one-fourth of the blindfolded group. This new "one-fourth" now become the "tappers" as *new* attributes are called out. This rotation of groups continues until each "fourth" has been both blindfolded and without blindfolds.

5:30 a.m.

The entire group sits in a circle around a lighted candle. (All other lights are out.) Members of the group are encouraged to express how they felt during the "head-tapping." Members are encouraged to share something positive about their secret pals.

6:30 a.m.

Large group discussion:
1. What are your feelings about this particular lock-in?
2. How do you feel about the future of this youth group?

7 a.m.

Worship service: Before this service each person is given a straight pipe cleaner and one bent in the shape of a circle. During the service everyone is asked to come forward and form their straight pipe cleaners into a "Unity Chain." This chain can be kept as a remembrance of the lock-in. Each person may keep their "circle" pipe cleaner as his or her own personal remembrance.

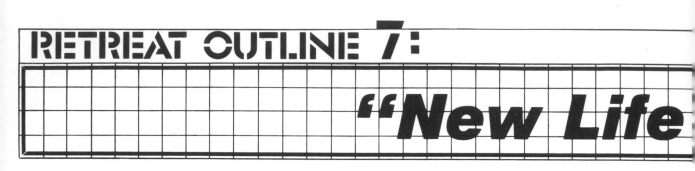

RETREAT OUTLINE 7:

"New Life

By David Olshine

An evangelistic retreat that includes a retreat speaker and emphasizes making a decision to become a Christian.

GOALS

Our goal was to have a holistic approach toward the retreat: spiritual, emotional, social, physical and intellectual. Our primary aim was directed at the spiritual aspect. We wanted to reach non-Christians. We also wanted to encourage Christians to renew their lives. Our secondary goal was to build group unity.

POSSIBLE SCHEDULE

FRIDAY EVENING

6:45 p.m.	Arrive, unpack, unwind
8 p.m.	Meet in lounge for crowd-breakers
9 p.m.	Speaker introduced Talk:"To Know Life and To Make It Known"
9:30 p.m.	A silence call: Letter to God
10 p.m.	Munchies
10:30 p.m.	Life-Wire Experience
11:30 p.m.	Hang loose
12:30 p.m.	Lights out!

SATURDAY

8-9:30 a.m.	Breakfast and devotions
9:30 a.m.	Group discussions
10:15 a.m.	Crowdbreakers, singing
10:30 a.m.	Talk: "Light Equals Life"
11:15 a.m.	Break time
Noon	Lunch
1-3 p.m.	Recreation and/or relaxation
3-4 p.m.	Talk: "Thinking About Sex"

4-4:30 p.m.	Reflection time
4:30-5 p.m.	Free time
5:30 p.m.	Dinner
7 p.m.	Meet together
8 p.m.	Talk: "The Test of Intimacy: Walking Your Talk"
9 p.m.	Time of commitment—peace candle
10 p.m.	Break time
10:30 p.m.	Movie time
12:30 p.m.	Lights out!

SUNDAY

8-9 a.m.	Breakfast
9-10 a.m.	Devotions and discussions
10-10:30 a.m.	Speaker shares on "Daring to be Different"
10:30-Noon	Communion, commitment, love-gift
Noon	Lunch
1-2 p.m.	Pack and leave

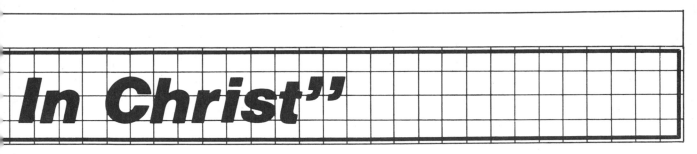

In Christ"

PREPARATION: KNOWING YOUR GOAL

1. Meet with counselors and youth. Each age group must decide what their goal will be. Is it for fun, group unity, planning the year's program, conversion, growth, leadership skills?

2. Delegate functions . . . Each youth and counselor can and should be involved. Draw the youth out for leadership.

3. Select a spiritual direction for your retreat. You could use topical studies such as witnessing, growth, vision or knowing God. Or you might do a book of the Bible study such as Ephesians or the First Epistle of John.

MATERIALS

I always give everyone attending the retreat a booklet which has the complete schedule for the retreat, crowdbreakers, devotions for each morning and additional space for note-taking. I bring pencils and paper for certain events, **Ideas Books**, published by Youth Specialties, and the necessary "tools" for games. Bring a movie projector if you want to show a movie, and name tags.

FRIDAY EVENING

We traveled in cars, vans or motor homes. After arriving we had time to unpack, unwind and goof around. At 8:00 we met to sing. Some of the youth played guitars for the group singing. We sang from books our youth ministry had put together.

After the singing I explained some crowdbreakers to get everyone laughing and feeling comfortable with each other. We had fun trying the "hat-drop" game: Each person drops his or her name in a hat. Then each person picks a name out of the hat. For the rest of the weekend they serve anonymously the person whose name they've drawn. On Sunday, before we left, there was a touching ceremony based on this activity (explained later in this article).

I introduced our speaker and gave his background. His lesson on "Discovering Life" from 1 John took 20 minutes. We then distributed paper and envelopes and asked the youth to "write a letter to God." They were to explain to God what they thought he wanted to do in them this weekend. They put their own address on the envelopes. The letters were sent to them three to four weeks following the retreat. The returned letter helped them see what had happened to them since the retreat.

Following a half-hour snack break we had the "Life-Wire Experience." Each person was given a pipe cleaner and directed to a small group. The groups took the pipe cleaner, and shaped it to describe their life (it could look up, down, startled, straight, etc.). This exercise helped them share intimacies about themselves. This can become very exciting and can build relationships.

SATURDAY

The second day was full of activity. The speaker gave three more talks on 1 John. There was time for crowdbreakers, singing, reflection, devotions and a "big guys" football game.

We used these questions as the basis for a small group discussion.

1. I am proud of . . .
2. I wish I were . . .
3. I wish I were not . . .
4. The funniest thing that ever happened to me . . .
5. The thing(s) I fear most . . .
6. My favorite place . . .
7. I wish my parents would . . .
8. If I had $100, I would . . .
9. If I were God, I would . . .
10. God doesn't seem like he is there when . . .

SATURDAY MORNING DEVOTIONS:
"Treasure and the Pearl"

Read Matthew 13:44-46 (the parable of the hidden treasure and the pearl of great price).

Complete individually, then in small groups:

1. Of all the things that I value in my life right now, the most important one is: _____
2. How is finding the life that Jesus wants to give you similar to finding the treasure in the field? _____
3. Why is Jesus telling us that the man sold all he had so he could go back and buy the field? _____
4. If the pearl represents people today looking for something in life that gives meaning and purpose, what are some of the different kinds of imitation pearls people are trying out today?
_____
_____
_____

continued

5. If Jesus Christ is the real pearl we can find in our lives, what does it mean when he says the man sold all he had and bought the pearl? _____

_____

6. If Jesus Christ is the treasure and the pearl, where would you see your own life right now? (Choose one.)

a. I'm really looking for the treasure and the pearl, but I haven't found it yet.

b. I have found the treasure in the field, but I don't know if I want to go sell all I have in order to buy the field.

c. I have found the treasure in the field and decided that I wanted to go out and buy the field, but on the way I got sidetracked by someone telling me the field wasn't worth it.

d. I have decided that the treasure in the field is the most important thing in my life, I have gone out and bought the field, but now I'm not sure what to do with it. I get embarrassed around friends who think I made a poor investment.

e. The field with the treasure in it is mine, and every day I'm finding out more and more just how valuable a possession I have. The cost of the field sure was worth it.

7. Right now the pearl of great price in my life is:

a. my girlfriend/boyfriend

b. sports

c. fun

d. grades

e. popularity

f. a degree

g. kicks

h. Christ

i. me

j. success

k. church

l. other

At lunch, we tied people's right and left wrists together. The object was to serve the other person. At dinner they had to eat one bite, then put the fork or spoon down until all was swallowed. The purpose was to teach that we are too fast-paced and need to slow down.

After the evening talk on "Walking Your Talk" we had a "peace candle." A candle was passed from person to person and no one could talk unless they had the candle. Once the candle was passed, the next person could talk. There was no pressure to talk, but usually they did. They could pray, tell what they learned, give thanks for certain people, etc. It was serious, as well as fun. No one talked while the candleholder was speaking. After the candle had made it around the room, people had expressed some deep feelings: tears, laughter, soberness. I then asked everyone to stand and hug one another. They went crazy! And what love.

We had snacks, then showed a movie.

We used this Serendipity exercise for one small group discussion period.

WARM-UP

What phone numbers do you use the most right now? List the numbers you call most frequently. (If you cannot remember a number, jot down the person or location. Include your home and church phone numbers.)

_____   _____
_____   _____
_____   _____

GOING DEEPER

Who would you call when? (Read Luke 10:30-37 and think about the phone numbers you listed. Place the following symbols next to the numbers you would call for the various situations. You may use a symbol more than once and more than one symbol next to a number if it is appropriate.)

 if you had a spiritual problem and needed someone to listen and understand

 if you had a serious personal problem and needed someone to talk to—one who would keep his mouth shut

 if you were at a crossroads in your life and needed some good counsel

 if you were really down and needed a good laugh and a good time

$ if you needed money but could not explain why

 if you received a "Dear John" letter and needed a shoulder to cry on

OVERTIME CHALLENGE

1. When it comes to friends, I tend to (circle one in each category):
   - a. make friends   quickly . . . . slowly
   - b. change friends   constantly . . . . never
   - c. break off friendships   easily . . . . with great pain
   - d. when I'm in trouble   call on my friends . . . . keep to myself

2. In times of trouble, I tend to rely on (rank top three):
   _____my partner   _____my family   _____myself alone   _____God
   _____my friends   _____my teachers/coach   _____one friend

3. When one of my friends is in trouble, I am best at (circle two):
   - a. listening
   - b. going to bat for him
   - c. praying
   - d. cheering him up
   - e. sticking by him
   - f. bringing him home
   - g. getting others to help
   - h. keeping my mouth shut
   - i. sharing my struggles with him

Reprinted from the **Encyclopedia of Serendipity**, copyright ©1980, Serendipity House.

SUNDAY MORNING

The final day. Devotions were held after breakfast:

SUNDAY MORNING DEVOTIONS:
"Counting the Cost"

Read Luke 9:23; 9:57-62; 14:27-33.

1. Everything in life costs something! What Jesus did for us cost him his life. We know that to accept Christ is free. But to follow him and live for him involves a cost. Luke 9:23 tells us to follow Jesus. What must we do? _____

   _____

2. What does this mean to you? _____

   _____

3. Read Luke 9:57-62. Here Jesus lays out some examples of the demands of following him. Read and think carefully over each of these situations. Ask yourself, "What do I need to leave behind?"

   _____

   _____

4. Read Luke 14:27-33. Jesus taught there is a cost required in living out the Christian life. Why is it important to count the cost?

   _____

   _____

5. Is it common to begin a project and not finish? Many people begin the Christian life. Why do some give up and never finish?_____

   _____

6. What might Christianity cost you? _____

   _____

7. Conclusion: Have you begun to count the cost? _____ If yes, explain how you are counting the cost. _____

   _____

RETREAT REVIEW

1. Did you enjoy the retreat and why?
2. What did you like *best* about the weekend?
3. In what ways could the retreat have been improved?
4. Did any event stand above all the others this past weekend? Why?
5. List some things that helped you grow closer to the Lord.

The kids were sleepy so we sang the song "Father Abraham" to wake them up. After a few crowdbreakers some of the kids shared thoughts and sang solos. We sent them outside to do a "trust walk." One person was blindfolded while his partner led him around. The purpose: learning to trust!

We had each person find a gift from nature. This was to be given publicly to the person they had been serving during the weekend. After they found a gift, everyone gathered for the final talk. The speaker closed with 1 John 2:15-17, calling it "Daring to Be Different." It is a challenge to be different for God . . . and from the world system.

RETREAT OUTLINE 8:
"Feeling

By John D. Cooke

A creative experience in learning how to deal with loneliness.

Lonely feelings strike everyone at one time or another. This retreat helps young people learn what to do when loneliness hits them and how to help others through loneliness.

MATERIALS YOU WILL NEED

a. Modeling clay—enough for each person to have a one-inch square.

b. Poster board or butcher paper.

c. Colored markers.

d. A ball of red yarn. (Rolling it into a ball before you get to the retreat will save you time.)

POSSIBLE SCHEDULE

FRIDAY
7:30 p.m.   Arrive at retreat center and get settled
8 p.m.   Get-acquainted session
8:30 p.m.   Session 1: "What Does It Mean To Be Lonely?"
10 p.m.   Refreshments
11 p.m.   Quiet time
11:30 p.m.   Sack time

SATURDAY
7:30 a.m.   Quiet time
8 a.m.   Breakfast
9 a.m.   Session 2: "Why Am I Lonely?"
Noon   Lunch
1:30 p.m.   Session 3: "Those Lonely Bible People"

3:30 p.m.   Fun 'n games
5:30 p.m.   Dinner
7 p.m.   Session 4: "Don't Let Me Be Lonely, But Let Me Be Alone"
9:30 p.m.   More games, films, etc.
11 p.m.   Singing and quiet time

SUNDAY
8 a.m.   Quiet time
8:30 a.m.   Breakfast
9 a.m.   Session 5: "Dealing With Loneliness"
11 a.m.   "A Yarn Ending"
11:30 a.m.   Clean up and pack up
Noon   Lunch and depart

FRIDAY

Begin with crowdbreakers and games.

Lonely"

Session 1: "What Does It Mean To Be Lonely?"

Here's a fun way to divide 16 or more young people into groups: On small slips of paper write the names of animals that make distinct noises, such as a pig, a cow, a horse, or a duck. Put four of each animal in a bowl and have youth draw one out, keeping their animal secret. After all have drawn a name, explain that you are going to turn out the lights. Then each must get down on his or her hand and knees and find the other three in their group by making only the animal sound.

After the group is divided into fours, have two groups of four get together. Instruct the two groups to form concentric circles, one on the inside facing out and one on the outside facing in. The inside groups should be sitting with their backs to each other.

A member of the outside circle should sit directly in front of a member of the inside circle, creating four pairs directly facing each other.

Introduce this exercise as a way to get to know people better. Ask the following questions while each young person answers to the person he or she faces.

The questions:
  1. Introduce yourself to the other person.
  2. What is your favorite color?
  3. What is your grandmother's name and give one reason why you like or dislike going to her house?
  4. Where did you live when you were six years old?

At this time have the outside circle move one person to the right with the inside circle remaining still. Proceed with the questions.

Introduce yourself to the other person.
  1. What kind of pet do you have?
  2. If you could be any animal, what would you be? Why?
  3. What kind of car do you wish you had?
  4. Why did you come to this retreat?

The outside circle moves again. Resume the questions.
  1. Introduce yourself to the other person.
  2. What is your favorite subject in school? Why?
  3. What kind of profession would you like to enter?
  4. What about the church is most meaningful to you?

5. If all of a sudden there was a major catastrophe in your family and you were the only one left, what would be most important to you? Why?

Move one more time, in the same manner as before. Allow more time with this series of questions.
1. Introduce yourself to the other person.
2. How would you define the word "lonely"?
3. Describe a time when you felt lonely.
4. What do you do when you feel lonely?
5. How do you feel about God when you're lonely?

Ask each group to share interesting responses to the last four questions with the entire group. Write these responses on a flip chart or a large piece of butcher paper so all can see the responses. Tape the sheet to a wall and leave it there for the remainder of the retreat. (It is important for you as a retreat leader to know how your youth respond to these last four questions. This knowledge will help you know what direction the rest of the retreat should take.)

Quiet Time

Explain the study on loneliness began tonight with the small groups sharing on what loneliness is and how it feels. During the rest of the retreat, explain that everyone will study the causes of loneliness and how to develop a personal strategy for dealing with it.

For a closing devotion, have the group sing songs. End with a few short thoughts on loneliness. You might want to consider using 1 Kings 19:4 and Romans 11:2-4.

SATURDAY

One of the greatest gifts you can give your young people is to teach them to develop a meaningful devotional life. Provide a quiet time for everyone on Saturday and Sunday mornings. Be sure to announce the location of the devotional guides the evening before to avoid confusion in the morning.

At the beginning of the devotional period, ask your young people to find a place to be by themselves, with no distractions. Provide a devotional guide to help them with their thinking and praying. A guide could look something like this:

Quiet Time

Do you ever have that lonely feeling when you wonder if anyone cares whether you exist? You even begin to wonder if God knows or cares about your existence, for there is no one who understands or listens. Do you ever feel desperately alone?

Read Psalm 139:1-6.

What has happened to you recently to show that God knows and understands you?

List things others have misunderstood about you. Write a note to God thanking him for not only knowing how you feel, but also why you feel that way.

Session 2: "Why Am I Lonely?"

Ask the group to meet in the same groups of four as the night before. Using modeling clay, have the youth sculpt anything that suggests how they feel when they're lonely. Give them time to share within the small group what they made and why. Save the sculptures for later use.

Hand out copies of the following observations of loneliness.

Observations about loneliness

- Loneliness is a companion that comes at birth and leaves at death. It is a fact of life.
- To be human is to experience the pain of loneliness.
- Faith in God will not insulate us from loneliness.
- The roots of loneliness come from unfulfilled promises, broken relationships, career disappointments, heated arguments with God, feelings of rejection and the uncertainty of tomorrow.
- Loneliness can be a challenge.
- Loneliness is not an idea but a voyage.
- Loneliness is a process that spans the seasons of life.
- No persons or age groups are free of the symptoms of loneliness. Only the causes and the responses vary.

Reasons for loneliness:

- Mobility
- Specialization
- Profit and production
- Television
- Urbanization

Definitions of loneliness:

- Loneliness is not having meaningful relationships.
- Loneliness means being afraid.
- Loneliness means feeling abandoned.
- Loneliness means failure and rejection.
- Loneliness is grief.
- Loneliness is the meaningless moment tucked into a routine schedule.
- Loneliness is being in a leadership position.

Divide the lists among the small groups, with approximately four items for each group to consider. Ask each small group to make a collage that illustrates one of the observations. Be sure plenty of materials are available, such as old magazines, newspapers, yarn, glue, wire, marking pens and other miscellaneous items.

Session 3: "Those Lonely Bible People"

Begin with a crazy game or activity.

Then divide into groups of four or five and have each group complete the following Bible study.

LONELINESS IS . . .

Read the following passages and complete the two columns on the right.

Bible Reference	Person	Lonely Situation
1 Kings 19:1-4	Elijah	Afraid of Jezebel + ran for his life; was alone + frightened
Jonah 2:1-6		
Job 16:20—17:4		
Jeremiah 38:6		
Matthew 26:36-46		
Luke 15:14-17		
Matthew 27:3-5		

Just as Bible people experienced loneliness, explain to your young people that they too will experience loneliness and encounter friends who are overcome by loneliness. It's important for them to be able to overcome loneliness themselves and aid their friends in overcoming loneliness.

Divide into small groups and distribute the following case studies. Ask your youth to read their case studies and react to them.

1.

Empty. That's how it feels to be lonely, a sense of being in a deep, dark pit with nothing in sight and no way out. It feels like a dark rainy day, just sitting there lonely. It's like a blue, dark blue, almost a black. But then it's also a light blue, washed out and dingy. It's a deep empty pit in your stomach. When I feel lonely I feel tired, not wanting to talk to anyone, not wanting to do anything.

2.

When loneliness strikes I feel thoroughly abandoned. It seems as though a large transparent garbage bag has separated me from my friends. Loneliness holds me captive until it chooses to release me.

Loneliness has torture methods of its own. Sometimes it convinces me that false truths are right, or it can let me see my friends having fun without me. And that can hurt.

3.

When I was in the sixth grade I was in a small group of girls, a clique. We had parties every weekend with the same girls, never letting anyone else in. But we did let some out or shall I say kick them out.

We took one girl and made life rough for her until she finally dropped out of our group. When the group tried to kick another person out I was against it and I guess it showed. Gradually the girls shoved me out too. Naturally I was hurt and lonely but I couldn't do much about it. Through this experience I have experienced the horrible feeling of loneliness.

4.

I walked up and down the room slowly. The house was empty. I felt small and alone. The shadow of the willow tree coated the ground in black.

Loneliness seemed to come like a shadow with the setting sun. It was not a new feeling. The scene made me want to be with someone, anyone. Time seemed suspended. No sound broke the silence of the evening. I was completely shut off from the world.

Questions to discuss:
- Have you ever felt this way?
- What reasons could this person have for feeling like this?
- How could each person overcome his or her loneliness?
- How do you overcome your loneliness?

When do you usually feel lonely? How does loneliness make you feel? When and why do lonely feelings usually go away? What do you do to keep from feeling lonely? Why is it that we can be in a crowd and still feel lonely? Should a Christian ever feel lonely? What part should your faith play in helping you deal with loneliness?

After discussing, bring youth back to large group and have them discuss their case and solutions with everyone. Look back to the scriptural examples and read beyond the assigned passages to determine how each Bible character resolved his loneliness.

Session 4: "Don't Let Me Be Lonely, But Let Me Be Alone"

Begin this session with a game or group activity.

Divide into teams of three or four and have the teams come up with short skits on things that cause loneliness or things that other people do to cause their friends to be lonely. Don't put on the skits yet. You'll use them later in this session.

Introduce this session by asking volunteers to explain the difference between being lonely and being alone. (Help them to understand that "being lonely" is a negative experience while being alone can be positive.)

Have the teams rehearse and perform their mini-dramas before the entire group. Ask the following questions about each skit:
- How does this demonstrate loneliness? aloneness?

● What are the negatives of loneliness? What could eventually be the outcome if the situations continue?

● What are the positives of the alone time? What benefits come from it?

On a poster or butcher paper have youth list the reasons for developing an alone time. Outline the ways they may implement it in their lives.

Examples:

● Decide on a good time of the day or week.

● Place?

● What to do in their alone time.

> Read?
>
> Study Bible?
>
> Pray?
>
> Reflect?

● Keep a log of alone time and what God does through it?

You may want to ask your youth to make a pledge with their youth group to begin an alone time.

SUNDAY

Quiet time: Ask youth to reflect on the weekend and write a prayer to God expressing the things they need God to help them with in dealing with their own loneliness and the loneliness of others.

Session 5: "Dealing With Loneliness"

Begin by restating that all of us at some time or another feel lonely, and we are surrounded by lonely people. God doesn't want us to be lonely nor does he want our friend to be lonely.

Here are some things we can do to develop an attitude for personal happiness.

● Develop strong, healthy self-love. Here are some scriptures dealing with this: Jeremiah 18; Phillippians 1:6; Ephesians 2:10. What promises does God give us regarding his work in our lives?

● Developing and using your spiritual gifts will aid you in dispelling loneliness and making you feel okay about yourself. What are your gifts and how are you using them?

● Your relationship to God will affect your confidence and security and dispel your loneliness. What are you doing to aid your spiritual growth?

● The answer to our loneliness and those around us is to be concerned about others and their needs.

● Have the youth look at the clay sculptures they made Friday night. In their small groups have them again explain how they saw loneliness. After all have shared individually, ask them to combine their separate sculptures with the others in their group. Explain how they may alleviate the loneliness in others, especially in each other.

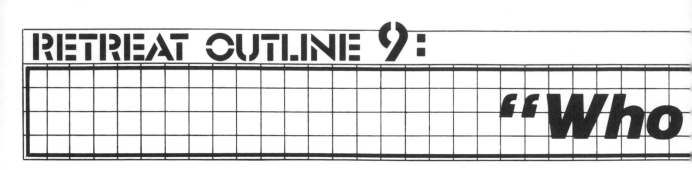

By Virgil Nelson

A self-discovery retreat.

The question "Who am I?" becomes a crucial issue for each of us at various times in our lives. The way we answer that question determines much of our openness and response to God, our feelings and actions toward others, our decisions about a career and a life partner—and even our sense of meaning in life.

While the focus in this retreat is self-discovery, the process of answering the question "Who am I?" from a biblical perspective demands that we hear from "God's people"—Christian friends—about our unique talents and abilites.

This retreat design assumes the need for group interaction and sharing as a necessary basis for helping individuals answer the question of "Who am I?" for themselves.

Before we can end up with personal answers to the "Who am I?" question, we also need to take a general look at some of God's answers. Without his perspective, we risk ending up with a distorted picture of who we are and what gives our lives meaning.

> **Theme scripture:** 2 Corinthians 5:17-18

BEFORE THE RETREAT

In planning for your group's retreat, consider a number of items: budget, the place, food preparation, adult leadership, youth leadership and the balance between the structured and unstructured interaction.

You'll also need to complete the following:

1. Before the retreat, encourage individuals in the group to try something they've never tried before. New experiences might include playing different games, variations of familiar games, trying out a new talent in a talent show, reading something in front of the group, praying aloud, creating a retreat menu and purchasing the food, registering campers, handling money, and so on. All of these are valuable opportunities for self-discovery.

2. Ask at least three people to do specific planning for the Sunday morning "Needs Reporting" session. For additional details see the program ideas for that time period later on in this article.

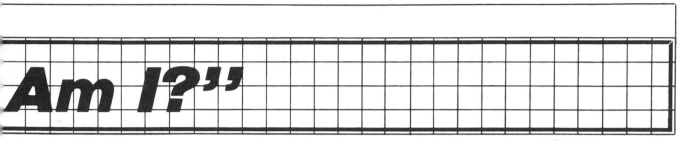
3. Prepare the "Journal Reflection Sheets." See the Saturday morning session for ideas in designing these worksheets.

4. Encourage each person who comes to the retreat to bring a favorite thing as a vehicle for letting the group know something about him or her. The item can be anything; a song from a tape or record album, a photo, a poem, a book, a sample of a hobby, a rotten tennis shoe—anything.

5. If most people in your group don't know each other well, you may want to spend time building a solid basis for trust by helping the kids get to know each other better.

GETTING THERE

Traveling to the retreat area can be an important part of the self-discovery process. To help your group get to know each other better, try the following "Traveling Scramble" game.

1. First, pick names out of a hat to scramble the riders in the different cars and vans. If you're traveling by bus, divide into groups of eight.

2. Create a "Scramble Puzzle Sheet"—a crossword puzzle you've copied from a newspaper will work nicely. Beside the puzzle, print the headings "ACROSS" and "DOWN." Leave quite a bit of blank space beneath each heading.

When riding, the group is to try to
- get every person's first name to fit somewhere;
- get at least one descriptive adverb or adjective for each person in the group;
- get at least one favorite activity listed for each person.

At the end of the trip, each team should have its puzzle completed and clues to the puzzle written out. For instance, the "Across" clues could read: "Jane's hobby;" "Name of a girl who is very friendly;" "Bob's favorite sport" and so on.

Have each team score its own puzzle. Each team that fits all the names of its members into the puzzle gets 300 points. Award 100 points to the teams that get adverbs or adjectives for each member and 200 points for including at least one favorite activity for each person. Allow

WHO AM I? 10 bonus points for each additional adjective, adverb or favorite activity the team includes.

Award a crazy prize to the winning team during the Friday evening program.

POSSIBLE RETREAT SCHEDULE

FRIDAY
3:30 p.m.	Register at the church; final payments; cabin room assignments here or later at the camp
4:30 p.m.	Departure for the retreat (actual time depends on the driving distance to the center)
6 p.m.	Dinner on the road: individual cars on their own, or agree on a specific location and all meet there
8 p.m.	Arrival at center: unload and move in
9 p.m.	Evening session
10:30 p.m.	Free time; snacks; games
Midnight	In the sack; lights out

(This and other ground rules need to be agreed upon in advance of the weekend. Rules depend on the age/maturity of the group, rules of camp, program goals, morning schedule, etc.)

1 a.m.	Absolute quiet

SATURDAY
7 a.m.	Up and at 'em
7:30 a.m.	Personal devotions
8 a.m.	Breakfast
9:30-11:30 a.m.	Morning session (with break): "Who Am I? God's Word Speaks to Me"
Noon	Lunch
Afternoon	Free time, with some structured optional choices: group games (see references); tournaments; swimming; outings; etc.
5:30 p.m.	Dinner
7-9 p.m.	Evening session: "Who Am I? Self-Discovery"
9:30 p.m.	Free time

SUNDAY
9:30 a.m.-Noon	Morning session including break and worship: "God's People Speak to Me"
12:30 p.m.	Lunch and evaluation: most/least valuable activity for me; most/least valuable activity for our group in its spiritual development; changes I would suggest; other comments

WEDNESDAY
Leaders meeting to look over evaluations and reflect upon the strengths and weaknesses of the weekend

FRIDAY EVENING SESSION (1½ hours)

1. *Making handprints* (45 minutes): For this activity you'll need water-base printer's ink, a small rubber roller, a piece of hard plastic or linoleum approximately one foot square, sheets of colored construction paper and one handkerchief. All of these supplies are available from a paint or artist supply shop.

Have each person choose a sheet of construction paper and sign his name at the bottom. Then place a small amount of ink on the hard plastic or linoleum and smooth the ink to even thickness with the roller. Also roll the ink onto the palm until it covers the fingers and the palm evenly.

Crumple the handkerchief and place it under the colored paper. (The handkerchief helps lines in the palm to print clearly.)

Press the inked hand firmly on the paper with the palm directly over the crumpled handkerchief.

Put the handprints in visible places around the room.

2. Begin group singing while the handprinting is being finished.

3. *Fun 'n games:* Pick a partner, sit back-to-back and lock arms. On signal, everyone sits down. On signal, everyone stands. Repeat this exercise in groups of four. Then try groups of eight. How about having the entire group stand back-to-back, lock arms and sit down, then stand up?

4. *Who's here:* Try this exercise in circles of 8-12 people, or everyone if the group numbers 25 or smaller. The first person gives his or her first name, describes one favorite activity and acts out that activity: "I'm Sue and I like to swim." (She makes swimming motions.)

The next person introduces himself and reintroduces Sue: "My name is Bill and I ride motorcycles" (he acts as though he's riding a motorcycle), "and this is Sue who swims" (he makes swimming motions).

Go around the circle and have kids introduce themselves and all the people who've been introduced earlier, including the actions. Don't embarrass someone who forgets a name. Have fun, but be sensitive to those who are shy.

5. *Scramble awards time:* Report the winner of the "Traveling Scramble" game and award the crazy prize. You might want to read some of the more creative puzzle entries before placing all the puzzles on the walls with the handprints.

6. *My arrival, God's handiwork:* In groups of two or four, tell about the earliest birthday you can remember and a special gift or your most memorable birthday. In groups of eight, tell when the word "God" became more than just a word in your life. Point out that not everyone has experienced a personal relationship with God, and that it's okay to mention questions they have about God or issues they're struggling with.

7. *Minipresentation:* Have two volunteers read 2 Corinthians 5:17-18 and Jeremiah 1:4-9 aloud. Then say something like: "As we try to answer the question, 'Who am I?' we need to know what God wants for us. What does he think about us?

"We also need to look at ourselves—our interests, abilities, weaknesses.

"As we go about answering this question we also need to talk with other people. Hearing about our strengths and weaknesses from others often tells us things about ourselves that we overlook.

"Tonight we completed handprints. During the rest of the weekend feel free to write on someone's handprint qualities you appreciate in that person. Everything you write should be positive—no jokes or put-downs.

"Remember who's in your group of eight. We'll get back in these groups tomorrow."

SATURDAY MORNING SESSION (2 hours)

1. Group singing (10-15 minutes).

2. Have people get in the same groups they were in Friday evening. Then give each group a 200-piece puzzle without the picture of the puzzle. Challenge them to see how much they can assemble in five minutes. At the end of five minutes count the number of pieces each group has assembled.

Then give each group the picture of the puzzle and see how many pieces they can add to the puzzle in the next five minutes.

Possible discussion questions: In what ways is putting the puzzle together like or unlike putting my life together? In what ways is the puzzle like or unlike answering the question, "Who am I?" (10 minutes; allow an extra 10 minutes for total group interaction.)

3. *Studying God's finished picture:* Divide the following six sets of scriptures among the groups. Give the following directions: Take 15-20 minutes and

a. read the passages out loud in your group;

b. discuss what you think the passage says;

c. explain what you think the passage means in each of your lives today;

d. describe what the verse says we are in God's eyes.

The person whose birthday is closest to April 1 is the group's recorder and is responsible for reporting back to the entire group at the end of the study session. Use large sheets of newsprint to record answers.

The passages to be studied are: Group 1—Genesis 1:26-31; Group 2—Isaiah 43:1-3 and Colossians 3:5-17; Group 3—Luke 4:18-19 and Ephesians 5:15-16; Group 4—John 6:21-40 and 1 Thessalonians 4:3-5; Group 5—Ephesians 4:11-32; Group 6—Galatians 5:13-26.

Be sure to read through these passages ahead of time. You may need to help when different groups get stuck in their studies.

After each group of eight has finished discussing its set of verses, get the total group together and have the "reporters" report on what their verses meant to different group members.

4. *Mini-presentation* (5 minutes): Comment that we are to practice all of what we just studied in whatever we do. Provide an opportunity for young people to talk with you about making a commitment to Jesus Christ.

Close this portion of the session with prayer.

Take a 15-minute break. You might want to serve simple refreshments at this time.

SATURDAY MORNING SESSION CONTINUES

1. *Favorite things:* With kids in the same groups of eight as before, have each person share a song, poem, rotten tennis shoe—whatever they brought. If people forgot to bring their items, have them tell about their "favorite things." (10-15 minutes)

2. *Personal journal:* Have each person create a personal journal for the retreat, which can be as simple or as elaborate as individual creativity and available supplies will allow. Bring construction paper, laundry markers and old magazines to cut up. Have kids put their names on the front and back covers.

Introduce the journal as an important part of the self-discovery process. Indicate that it is to help each person begin putting down thoughts, feelings and decisions for future use. The journal's ground rules are simple: a.) What is written is strictly personal. No one is to read someone's journal unless he gets permission from the journal's owner. b.) No one will be forced to share what he's written. There will be opportunities for sharing what has been written, but each person is free to choose what to share and what not to share.

Hand out "Journal Reflection Sheets." (Produce these before the weekend, allowing ample space for each question.)

JOURNAL REFLECTION SHEET

1. List 10 things you love to do.

2. List 10 things you'd like to try sometime.

3. If I had my choice, I'd rather work with things or with people. *(Circle the number that best describes the way you see yourself.)*

Things 1 2 3 4 5 4 3 2 1 People

4. I enjoy working with my hands less than I enjoy thinking about problem-solving.

Working with hands   Problem solving
**   1 2 3 4 5 4 3 2 1**

5. Go back to questions 1 and 2. Rank the top five in each question.

6. List five things you don't like to do.

7. Put a check mark by those entries in questions 1 and 2 that might be related to a possible job or future career and list specific jobs. For example, if you "love kids," potential career areas could be child care, teaching, parenting, counseling, pediatrics, and so on.

8. List what you like and don't like about your parent(s) or job.

9. Write the name of one person you know who is working in a job you'd like to know more about.

Name: _____

Job: _____

10. Three things you like about yourself are:____

_____

Three things you don't like about yourself are:____

_____

11. List five jobs you'd consider. Give each a percentage of hand/problem solving and things/people.

12. If you could do anything for God and knew you couldn't fail, what would you do?

Before adjourning the morning session, ask people to:

a. finish their journal covers;

b. complete questions 1-4 during the afternoon (you may want to have your kids complete these questions before ending this session);

c. remind everyone to add positive comments to the handprints on the walls;

d. bring journals to the evening session;

e. come up with gags, skits and acts for the evening talent show.

SATURDAY EVENING SESSION (2 hours)

1. *Group singing.* During the singing have each person tear a name tag from a piece of construction paper that says something about him or her (a basketball, a roller skate, a TV, whatever).

2. Spend the first hour or so of this session putting on the talent show. Keep in mind that this event can be an important opportunity for people who haven't performed well in the small discussion groups.

3. *Self-discovery session.* Have everyone pair off and compare handprints, noting similarities and differences.

● Allow 15-20 minutes for the group to finish journal questions 5-11.

● In the original groups of eight, allow each person two minutes to talk about his or her feelings and thoughts about a future career choice.

● Spend a few minutes letting the entire group ask questions that came up in the smaller groups and add comments that might interest everyone.

● Place a small candle in the center of each small group and allow for a few minutes of silent reflection. You may want to read some scripture or have someone share a reflective song.

SUNDAY MORNING SESSION (2½ hours)

1. *Group singing* (10-15 minutes).

2. *Hearing God's words:* Ask volunteers in advance to read Psalm 139 and Luke 4:18-19 aloud to the group.

3. *Reports on needs and challenges:* In advance of the retreat, get a team of youth "reporters" to make presentations on specific needs in your community or area, in addition to global needs such as world hunger, threat of nuclear holocaust, refugees. (Examples of community needs are poverty areas, senior citizens and transportation and day-care.) If time permits you may also want to show the film "Tilt," a 20-minute animated film on global concerns. This film is available from CROP, Box 968, Elkhart, IN 46514.

4. Allow about 10 minutes for everyone to finish journal question 12.

5. Have two volunteers read John 14:12 and Ephesians 4:1-16 aloud.

6. *Speaking and hearing:* Ask the entire group to circulate among the handprints and add additional characteristics, strengths or qualities they have observed in the person.

7. Have each person find his or her own handprint and take it to the group of eight.

One person at a time hands his handprint to the person in the group whose first name begins with letter closest to G. That person reads everything that is written on the paper out loud. The group has an additional 30 seconds to write in other strengths and special qualities. Repeat the process until each person has heard what people wrote describing him.

8. *Happy birthday:* Say something like: "Whether or not you've made any decisions or commitments this weekend, you are invited to this birthday party. God offers us new birth each day and gives us the special gift of his Spirit to share with each other and the world." Have each person think of gifts he'd give to each person in his group of eight. The gifts can be material goods, skills or qualities. For instance, someone might give someone else the gift of patience to deal with a difficult life situation.

Go around the groups, with everyone focusing on one person at a time.

Sing "Happy Birthday" to "the new you" and have people point to someone as they sing. Sing the song a second time and have kids point to themselves.

9. Provide an opportunity for volunteers to tell about decisions they've made during the retreat. Encourage each person to complete the sentence, "One thing I want to do next is . . ."

10. *The gift of service:* Close with communion within the groups of eight in celebration of God's sacrificial love, and the new life he has given. (As an alternative ending, you could end the retreat by conducting a hand- or foot-washing ceremony similar to the one recorded in John 13.)

11. Close with a song.

RESOURCES

1. Game ideas for group recreation time: **The Best of Try This One; More . . . Try This One;** and **Try This One . . . Too**, Schultz, Group Books.

2. Songbooks: **Songs**, Songs and Creations, Box 559, San Anselmo, CA 94960.

3. Activities: **Recycle Catalogues 1 and 2**, Benson, Abingdon. **Values Clarification: A Handbook**, edited by Simon, Howe and Kirschenbaum, Hart. **Hard Times Catalog for Youth Ministry**, Benson, Group Books.

By J. Brent Bill

"By Our Love" has been used in a variety of settings—from a week-long senior high summer camp to a four Sunday evening intergenerational experience (with

"Smile, God loves you—and so do I." Those of us who work with Christian youth hear that expression frequently. Oftentimes it is echoed back and forth between members of the youth group. God is love. We are supposed to love him—and our neighbors. Yet I wonder how long it has been since we thrilled at the wonder of love. "Love" is so common in our circles and taken for granted.

"By Our Love" is a weekend to rethink and re-experience our ideas about love. It is a mix of the familiar (1 Corinthians 13) and the unfamiliar ("Barrington Bunny"). This use of the Bible and a modern Christian fable helps to open our eyes to the awesome fact that we are loved. This retreat also challenges youth by using discussion questions that are posed in the safety of small groups.

MATERIALS

Brought by leaders:
The Way of the Wolf by Martin Bell
"Barrington Bunny" film—United Methodist film library, E. Broad Street, Columbus, OH
projector and screen
songbooks (or songsheets) and guitars
"Bible Pair" game sheets and safety pins
"I.Q. Test" sheets and pencils
discussion question sheets for small group leaders

blank paper for session two
grapes
masking tape for "Horsey Back Tag"
popcorn and drinks
copies of "By Our Love" litany
fun films
sports equipment

Brought by teenagers:
pitch-in snack goodies
board games (Monopoly, Sorry, etc.)

---

participants aged 3 to 75). By arranging it to fit your needs it can be successful for you also.

PREPARATION

As with any activity, preparation is essential. Though the following retreat plan is detailed, it must be tailored to the needs of your youth group to be effective.

Try to get an approximate figure of youth who plan to attend. This can be done by taking a head count at a regular meeting. This rough

Love"

number will help you determine how many counselors are needed as well as the size of a retreat center. Ask your kids for their recommendations on possible counselors. Also be sure to ask people you feel would be good.

After you have the counselors, have a planning meeting. It would be wise to have youth representation at this meeting. This will avoid the "I know what my kids want and need" when you may not. It also helps them feel a part of the process and gives a sense of ownership on their part.

POSSIBLE SCHEDULE

FRIDAY EVENING

9:30 p.m.	Arrive
10 p.m.	Introductions and mixers
11 p.m.	Worship/Learning session 1: "By Our Love"
11:45 p.m.	Pitch-in of goodies brought by kids
12:30 a.m.	Bedtime

SATURDAY

7 a.m.	Wake-up
7:30 a.m.	Counselors' meeting
8 a.m.	Breakfast
8:45 a.m.	Worship/Learning session 1: "By Our Love—Toward Self"
10:15 a.m.	Outdoor games
11:15 a.m.	Free time
Noon	Lunch
1 p.m.	Worship/Learning session 3: "By Our Love—Toward Others"
2 p.m.	Free time
5:30 p.m.	Dinner
6:30 p.m.	Indoor games
7:30 p.m.	Worship/Learning session 4: "By Our Love—Toward God"
9 p.m.	Movies and popcorn
Midnight	Bedtime

SUNDAY

7 a.m.	Wake-up
7:30 a.m.	Counselors' meeting
8 a.m.	Breakfast
9 a.m.	Cabin cleanup
9:30 a.m.	Worship/Learning session 5: "By Our Love—As a Way of Life"
Noon	Lunch
1 p.m.	Departure

FRIDAY EVENING SESSION

Plan to arrive at the retreat site around 9:30. Even if it is a two-hour trip to the site, travelers won't have to leave until 7:30 p.m., allowing time to eat dinner with the family. Older counselors who have children and will be away from them for the weekend will appreciate this. Allow 30 minutes for latecomers and settling in.

If there are any new folks, guests or people who are unfamiliar with the leaders, have a time of introductions around 10 o'clock. After this, play the following mixers, or others that you would feel are more suitable to your group. I've used the ones listed with success.

1. **Bible Pairs**—Prepare sheets of paper with one-half of a Bible couple or event on it (e.g., Adam and Eve). Pin a name on everyone's back, without telling people "who" they are. They then have to find their match by reading the others' names and asking "yes" or "no" questions. Sample pairs are listed below:

Abraham and Sarah	Sermon on Mount and Beatitudes
Adam and Eve	Mary and Martha
Samson and Delilah	Mary and Joseph
Noah and The Ark	Cain and Abel
David and Goliath	Amos and Hosea
Daniel and Lion's Den	Easter and Resurrection
Jacob and Esau	Garden and Eden
Joseph and Coat of Many Colors	Angel and Gabriel
Moses and Ten Commandments	Isaac and Sacrifice
Joshua and Walls of Jericho	Jacob and Ladder
Prodigal Son and Fatted Calf	Ruth and Boaz
Zacchaeus and Sycamore Tree	Moses and Bullrushes
Matthew and Tax Gatherer	Luke and Physician
Jonah and Whale	Methuselah and 966 years old
Paul and Barnabas	Solomon and Wisdom
Peter and Rock	Wisemen and Star

2. **Upset the Fruit Basket**—Each person is assigned the name of one of four fruits—apples, bananas, oranges or grapes—so there are an equal number of each. Chairs are placed around the playing area in a circular shape, with one less chair than participants. The person starting the game stands in the middle of the playing area and calls one of the fruit. All people who are that fruit must change seats and the person in the middle tries to find a seat. Players *must* change seats. The game continues as people in the middle call out the names of fruit, attempting to find seats. Another call is "Upset the fruit basket," when everyone must find a new seat.

3. **Animal Farm**—Each person is given the name of one of four animals—cow, horse, chicken or pig—with an equal number in each

group. The lights are then turned off and the players begin making noises appropriate to their animal. The object is to locate the other animals in your group in the shortest amount of time.

4. **I.Q. Test**—This is to be done in animal groups. The group with the most correct answers gets to eat first.

1. If you went to bed at 8 a.m. and set the alarm to get up at 9 o'clock the next morning, how many hours of sleep would you get? _____

2. Does England have a Fourth of July? _____

3. Why can't a man living in Winston-Salem, North Carolina, be buried west of the Mississippi River? _____

_____

4. If you had a match and entered a room in which there were a kerosene lamp, an oil heater, and a wood-burning stove, which would you light first?

_____

5. Some months have 30 days, some have 31 days; how many months have 28 days? _____

6. A man builds a house with four sides to it and it is rectangular in shape. Each side has a southern exposure. A big bear comes wandering by. What color is the bear? _____

7. How far can a dog run into the woods? _____

_____

8. What four words appear on every denomination of U.S. coin? _____

_____

9. What is the minimum of baseball players on the field during any part of an inning in a regular game? _____ How many outs in an inning? __

10. I have in my hand two U.S. coins which total 55 cents in value. One is not a nickel. What are the two coins? _____

11. A farmer had 17 sheep; all but nine died. How many does he have left?

_____

12. Divide 30 by one-half and add 10. What is the answer? _____

_____

13. Take two apples from three apples and what do you have? _____

_____

14. An archeologist claimed he found some gold coins dated 46 B.C. Do you think he did? _____ Explain. _____

15. A woman gives a beggar 50 cents. The woman is the beggar's sister but the beggar is not the woman's brother. How come? _____

16. How many animals of each species did Moses take aboard the Ark with him? _____

17. Is it legal in North Carolina for a man to marry his widow's sister?

_____

18. What word in this test is mispelled? _____

19. From what animal do we get whale bones? _____

20. Where was Paul going on the road to Damascus? _____

_____

Answers:
1. *One hour*
2. *Yes*
3. *Because he's not dead*
4. *The match*
5. *They all do*
6. *White*
7. *Halfway. Then he's running out.*
8. *"United States of America" or "In God We Trust"*
9. *Ten—nine outfielders & a batter; six outs per inning.*
10. *50¢ and 5¢. One is not a nickel; one is.*
11. *Nine*
12. *Seventy*
13. *Two apples*
14. *No*
15. *They are sisters*
16. *None. Noah took them in.*
17. *No. He is dead.*
18. *Misspelled*
19. *Whale*
20. *Damascus*

215

At 11 p.m. have the group settle on the floor for a time of singing. The following songs, like the mixers, are suggestions.

> - "They'll Know We Are Christians by Our Love"
> - "Kumbaya"
> - "The Joy of the Lord Is My Strength"
> - "Pass It On"

After 10 to 15 minutes of singing, show the film "Barrington Bunny." When the movie is over, have the "animal groups" get back together, with a counselor acting as a discussion leader. The following questions are recommended. It is important that all groups use the same questions so as to insure continuity of overall focus.

> 1. In what way am I like Barrington Bunny?
> 2. What part of the film did I like best? Why?
> 3. What does the film say about love?

Allow 30 minutes for the film and discussion. At 11:40 have everyone come back together. Close this part of the evening by reading 1 Corinthians 13.

Snack time, a pitch-in of goodies brought by the kids, should go to about 12:30. Herd them off to bed at that time, realizing that it will be later before they actually enter the blissful state of slumber.

SATURDAY MORNING SESSION

Wake-up time is 7:00. At 7:30, while the kids are getting dressed and beautiful for the day, the counselors need to have a time of voicing concerns, direction and prayer. Breakfast is at 8:00.

At 8:45 have the group gather where you met the evening before. This morning's session title is "By Our Love—Toward Self." As with Friday evening, allow 10 to 15 minutes for singing. After the singing, read "Barrington Bunny," up through where the Silver Wolf tells Barrington that he is lucky to be a bunny.

Then break into "animal groups" and discuss the following questions:

> 1. Since Jesus said that we should love our neighbor as ourselves (Matthew 19:19) does this mean that we *have* to love ourselves before we can love others? How do we show love to ourselves?
> 2. Are there differences between loving yourself and being selfish? If so, what are they?
> 3. Say something you like about yourself.

The discussion time should take about 20 minutes.

When the discussions end, rejoin the larger group. Pin pieces of paper onto everyone's back. Then mill around, writing something nice about each other on the paper on their backs.

At the end of 10 minutes, assemble the group for a period of worship. Read Psalm 139:13-14 and 1 John 3:1-2. After reading the scripture, encourage the participants to reflect quietly on what has been read and the discussion questions. End with prayer. Total time of the morning session should be one hour and fifteen minutes.

Give the kids 15 minutes to read the papers on their backs and put on old clothes for a time of outdoor games.

At 10:15 have the group meet on a playing field. Get into "animal groups" and play the following games:

---

1. **Grape Toss**—Each team appoints a "tosser." The tosser gets a bag of grapes. The rest of the team makes a circle around the tosser, leaving a space of three feet. The tosser must go around the circle, tossing grapes in the open mouths of his team. The first team to have a grape in everyone's mouth wins.

2. **Horsey Back Tag**—Have the kids find their "Bible Pair" partner from the night before. Each team is made up of a horse and rider. The rider "mounts" the horse by jumping on the back of the horse with arms around the horse's neck. Each rider has a piece of masking tape placed on his/her back by the leader so that it is easily seen and reached. When the signal "Mount up!" is given, the riders mount their horses and attempt to round up the tape on the other riders' backs. The last rider left with tape on her/his back wins. Only the riders may take the tape off other riders. If a horse falls, then that horse and rider are out of the game.

3. **American Turkey**—The playing area for this game is 60 feet wide. All players line up on one "safety line". When the signal is given, they run across the field to the other "safety-line". Standing in the middle is one person who grabs a runner, holds him still while yelling "1-2-3-American Turkey." The rest of the players cross safely over. This continues back and forth until everyone is in the middle.

From the time the games end until lunch at noon, is free time—for the kids to rest and the adults to recuperate.

SATURDAY AFTERNOON SESSION

The next session is called "By Our Love—Toward Others" and meets at 1:00. As with the other meetings, open with singing.

Read "Barrington Bunny" from where Barrington is told that he is lucky to be a bunny through his giving of the gifts. Then get into the "animal groups" for discussion.

> 1. What are the ways that Barrington shows love to the animals in the forest?
> 2. How might we exclude individuals from feeling a part of our church family? Who needs to be shown love in our church and community? How?
> 3. How would you like others to show love to you?
> 4. Share a verbal compliment of love to the person on your right.

Conclude this segment by reading John 15:13-15 and having a time of silent prayer.

From now until dinner at 5:30 should be free time, allowing the young people to play their own games, do Bible studies or just visit. (See pp. 220-224 for creative Bible studies.) After dinner until 7:30 encourage board games and ping-pong, etc., for the teenagers while the counselors meet to review the day and pray.

At 7:30 once again bring the group together and sing, beginning the evening meeting: "By Our Love—Toward God."

Then read the entire story of "Barrington Bunny." Following the story, meet in discussion groups.

> 1. If all of us are Barrington Bunnies, then who is the Silver Wolf?
> 2. What new or fresh ideas about love have you learned from the story of Barrington Bunny?
> 3. In what ways have you felt like Barrington Bunny or other characters in this story?
> 4. What are some ways that you can show love toward God?

The scripture readings for this program are 1 John 5:1-3 and Matthew 22:37-40.

Following the evening program, have a time of relaxation, popping corn and showing films. Several cartoons and a feature film make for a lot of fun. Sleep time should be at midnight.

SUNDAY MORNING SESSION

Sunday morning begins the same as Saturday: 7:00—wake-up; 7:30—counselors meeting; and 8:00—breakfast. After breakfast until 9:30 have the kids clean up the retreat area and pack their belongings for travel home.

Come together at 9:30 for a time of singing and worship on the theme

"By Our Love—As a Way of Life."

After the singing, guide the group's thoughts along the lines of "living a life of love." The following points should be included in the talk:

1. Love is something we all want and need.
2. Love is a gift of God. We need only reach out and take it.
3. To truly love means to put the good of others first.
4. We are not perfect at loving. Love is a becoming—a process of growth. We all need practice.
5. Love needs to be our way of life.

At the end of the talk go to the small groups for the final time. While in the groups discuss the following questions:

1. Am I growing in my ability to love? How can I improve?
2. What does it mean to me to live the life of love?
3. How can I live a life of love at home? At school? Around people I don't like?

The talk should last 10 minutes, the discussions around 30. After these segments are completed, come together as a whole. Read 1 Corinthians 13, this time from a different version than was read Friday night. Following the scripture reading, conduct the group in a time where young people tell about their thoughts and feelings. Fifteen or so minutes is appropriate.

After the sharing, pass out copies of "By Our Love." Have the group form a circle and read the litany responsively. Then have everyone join hands and sing—a cappella preferably—"They'll Know We Are Christian by Our Love." End with prayer.

Lunch is scheduled for noon, with departure immediately following.

"By Our Love"

Leader: We are one in the Spirit, we are one in the Lord.

People: It is the Spirit bearing witness with our spirit that we are children of God. (Romans 8:16)

L: And we pray that all unity may one day be restored.

P: Behold, how good and pleasant it is when God's people dwell in unity. (Psalm 133:1)

L: We will walk with each other, we will walk hand in hand.

P: I will walk in the way of righteousness, in the paths of justice. (Proverbs 8:20)

L: And together we'll spread the news that God is in our land.

P: How beautiful are the feet of those who preach good news. (Romans 10:15)

L: We will work with each other, we will work side by side.

P: Commit your work to the Lord, and your plans will be established. (Proverbs 16:3)

L: And we'll guard each one's dignity and save each one's pride.

P: And whatever town or village you enter, find out who is worthy in it . . . (Matthew 10:11)

L: All praise to the father, from whom all things come.

P: I will give thanks to the Lord with my whole heart; I will tell of all thy wonderful deeds. (Psalm 9:2)

L: And all praise to Christ Jesus, his only son.

P: And all praise to the Spirit, who makes us one.

L: And they'll know we are Christians by our love, by our love.

P: Yes, they'll know we are Christians by our love.

BE MY VALENTINE

A Discovery Bible Study
By Dean Dammann

Objectives

1. That young people hear again the "Greatest Love."
2. That young people list the characteristics of love.
3. That young people write a prayer asking help in better loving Jesus, others and self.

Type the following instructions on a sheet of paper and give one to each person in your group.

Instructions

Form groups of five to seven persons. The person with the darkest eyes serves as group leader. Start with activity 1.

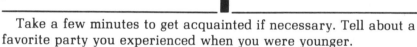

Take a few minutes to get acquainted if necessary. Tell about a favorite party you experienced when you were younger.

2

What is love? Webster's **New World Dictionary** lists the following definitions:

    a. A deep and tender feeling of affection for or attachment or devotion to a person or persons

    b. A strong, usually passionate, affection of one person for another, based in part on sexual attraction

    c. A strong liking for or interest in something

    d. A feeling of brotherhood and good will toward other people

    e. God's benevolent concern for mankind

    f. Man's devout attachment to God

Love has a different meaning for each of us. Which definition best defines the love you are most in tune with lately? Explain.

This retreat is an occasion to show our care for others through messages of love. A valentine is a message of love. The Bible is filled with such messages. Pretend that you are one of God's angels with the task of choosing valentine texts. The valentines will be sent by God to his family on earth. Read 1 John 4:7-21 to find appropriate valentine messages. List messages for three valentines: one you think would be appropriate for yourself and two others for friends or family members. Write the messages below.

[**Message to the leader:** *You might want to provide paper, colored laundry markers or crayons, magazines with colorful pictures, scissors, glue or tape and let your young people design their own valentines.]*

After everyone has chosen three valentine messages, take turns sharing them. Explain who they're for and why you chose them. Each person shares one before continuing to the second, and so on.

4

The last verse of 1 John 4 tells us to love others even as we love God. How are we to love? 1 Corinthians 13:4-8 identifies characteristics of love. Read 1 Corinthians 13:4-8 and choose some characteristics which apply to people you know. Choose at least two to rewrite or paraphrase as valentine messages. Write them out here: _____

After everyone has written two valentines, take time to share them with your group. Tell who would receive the valentines, explaining why.

5

If you were to receive a valentine, what would you want it to say? (Perhaps one of those shared in activity 4 would fit.) Share your selection with the group.

6

In Matthew 22:35-40 Jesus tells a questioner to love God. his neighbor, and himself. The word JOY can be used to remind us of the command to love—

Jesus
Others
Yourself

As you reflect on your love of Jesus, others and self, which has been most neglected? To close the Bible study, write a prayer asking for help in loving Jesus, Others and Yourself. Make it as specific as possible. When everyone has written a prayer, have a period of silence for each to pray that prayer silently. Close by praying together the Lord's Prayer.

THE STRAYING AND THE STRAIGHT

A Discovery Bible Study
By Dean Dammann

Objectives

That the good news of God's great love is made real for all participants. That participants can relate God's love to their times of straying. That participants repent of their "goodness and respectability" and reaffirm their dependence on Jesus Christ.

Instructions

Form groups of six to eight persons. The person with the darkest hair serves as group facilitator. Everyone in the group should have a copy of this study guide.

1. Take a few minutes to get acquainted. Share a good thing that happened to you during the past week.

2. Television and newspapers frequently carry stories of lost children. When these incidents occur a massive search usually occurs until the child is found. To explore how it feels to be lost or to have lost something do one of the following:

A. Recall a time in your life when you were lost. Make some written notes about the experience, including if you can, some of the feelings you experienced.

B. Recall a time when you lost something that was important to you. Make some written notes about the experience. Identify the feelings you experienced at the time.

3. Share your experience in your small group. Those who are sharing "A" above share first. Before those sharing "B" begin their sharing, talk about the common elements in the stories. Make a list of the feelings experienced. The "B" experiences should then be shared. Discover the common elements in the stories and make a listing of the feelings experienced.

4. Luke 15 has three stories about being lost—the lost sheep, the lost coin, and the lost son. The latter story is often referred to as the story of the prodigal son. Read the first two stories in verses 1-10. Why did Jesus tell the stories? Discuss in your group.

5. To dig deeper into the theme of this Bible study read quickly

Luke 15: 11-32. After you have read the story list below the attitudes and feelings you think were exhibited . . .

- by the lost son
- by the father about the lost son
- by the elder son
- by the father about the elder son

6. If you were to put yourself into the story of the lost son, where would you fit? On the continuum below indicate where you think you are right now.

"Strayed" **9 8 7 6 5 4 3 2 1** "Straight"
(lost son)   (elder son)

Share where you locate yourself and why with your group. If your meeting area allows, identify the continuum on the floor and then have each member of the group take a place physically to demonstrate his/her location. While standing have each share why he/she chose his/her particular location.

7. From the stories of Luke 15, it is clear that God celebrates when people are no longer lost. The stories also give some insights as to the response he expects from "sons." See verses 7 and 10. God expects us to _____

8. As people become more "straight" or respectable they lose sight of what God expects. Make a list of how Christians today fall into the traps of being straight, respectable, and pious even as the Pharisees and teachers of the Law identified in Luke 15:2 did. Example: criticizing those who don't attend church, Bible classes, etc.

9. Individually identify where you personally have strayed or flaunted your piety. Silently confess and pray for God's forgiveness.

10. Close by singing a song to celebrate God's forgiving love or by each sharing a sentence prayer beginning with the words, "I thank and praise God for . . ."

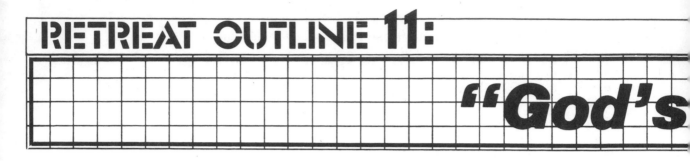

**By Jim Reeves,
Tim Johnson and
Deb Mechler**

**A retreat on being
a Christian and
living in today's
world.**

> **The theme:** God asks his children to dedicate their
> bodies to him.
>
> **Key verses:** Romans 12:1-2

GOALS

1. To know God calls us to be a living sacrifice for him.
2. To accept the responsibility of being a living sacrifice by
demonstrating a new attitude to God and others.

These goals were designed to help us get to the heart of the
issue of sexuality without overlooking some of the related issues.

PREPARATION

The retreat leadership met to discuss responsibilities for various portions of the retreat.

A suggestion for a pre-retreat session:

1. Find a cozy place for this pre-retreat session and invite all parents and youth to this meeting. The atmosphere should be conducive to discussion, i.e., movable chairs, soft lighting, comfortable surroundings.

2. When everyone arrives do some getting-acquainted activities. I would suggest doing one of the "Getting Acquainted" exercises found in the **Encyclopedia of Serendipity** by Lyman Coleman.

Some of your group's favorite songbooks

3. Introduce the retreat's theme and goals. Outline the entire retreat briefly and allow for questions.

4. If time permits, do part of the "Agree/Disagree" exercise (page 232) with this group, allowing the parents to participate in an activity that the kids will experience at the retreat.

5. Finish with refreshments.

MATERIALS, EQUIPMENT, FACILITIES

Many camps and conference grounds have these items on hand for you to use. But it is good to check with them beforehand.

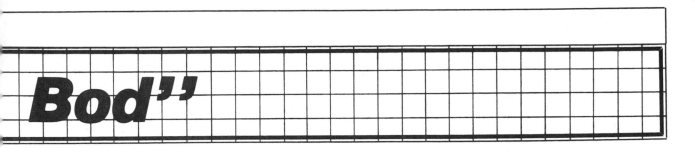

- Some of your group's favorite songbooks
- A 16mm movie projector
- Bring along some good, fun entertainment films.
- Copies of devotional booklets for group and personal use
- Tape player with cassettes of some selected top popular songs
- Bibles, dictionaries, pencils, paper
- Overhead projector with transparencies and pens (or butcher paper to put on the wall)
- Optional: a slide projector with enough blank slides for the whole group to have one

POSSIBLE SCHEDULE

FRIDAY EVENING

6:30 p.m.	Registration, settle in
7 p.m.	Meet for singing, get-acquainted activities
10 p.m.	Movies
12:30 a.m.	Lights out

SATURDAY

8 a.m.	Breakfast
8:45 a.m.	Quiet time
9:30 a.m.	"Pressures from the Outside"
Noon	Lunch
1 p.m.	Free time

3 p.m.	Organized recreation
5:30 p.m.	Supper
6:30 p.m.	Group singing
7 p.m.	"Pressures from the Inside"
10 p.m.	Talent show
12:30 a.m.	Lights out

SUNDAY

8 a.m.	Breakfast
8:30 a.m.	Quiet time
9 a.m.	"Question Box" (This is your chance to shoot questions at the adults.)
10:45 a.m.	Worship
Noon	Lunch

FRIDAY EVENING

1. If you go as a group make sure you leave the church in time to arrive at the camp site by 6:30 p.m. Unpack, give room assignments and let everyone settle in a little. Meet together as a group by 7 p.m.

Meet in a large comfortable room with movable chairs. Sit on the floor if you like. Sing some fast and fun songs to start things off. Mix crazy songs with spiritual songs.

2. 7:30 p.m.—Start with the group experience which comes from **Kiss Me** by Lyman Coleman, Serendipity House. The book suggests that you take six hours with this course. To cut it down to two hours use the following items from the table of contents: All of the "Getting Acquainted" session; "The Fire Drill" of the "History Giving" session only; the "Cars or Hats" activity from the "Affirmation" session. Finally, complete the "Scripture" portion of the "Goal Setting" session. The Serendipity exercises get everyone to think about being "God's Bod." Emphasize that the rest of the weekend will be geared to helping people look seriously at being all that God wants them to be. Then share the retreat goals and the key verse.

End this time in prayer. Give some free time after this event.

3. 10 p.m.—It's time for a movie marathon with some oldies but goodies. These could be a variety of comedies, mysteries, or dramas that the kids like. It is easy to find these types of films through the public library.

SATURDAY

1. 8 a.m.—Breakfast

2. 8:45—Small group devotions. We used the booklet **Quiet Time** from Inter-Varsity Press (Box F, Downers Grove, IL 60515).
We divided into groups of 10, with at least one counselor as discussion leader.

3. Everyone meets together for the general session at 9:30 a.m. We began by singing fun songs for 10 minutes or so. The leader then introduced the theme of the day by reading Romans 12:1-2 and saying something like this: "We are going to spend time looking at three different pressures we feel. We will move in round-robin fashion to different electives. Each elective covers the same subject all three times we rotate, so don't stay at the same elective twice. One subject is on 'The Effects of Music.' The second topic is on 'The Effects of TV and Media.' The third topic covers 'Peer Pressure.' Each elective is 40 minutes long. There'll be a five-minute break between electives. Let's break up our group into thirds and proceed."

If leaders are scarce for these sessions, teach the entire group all three sessions, one at a time.

If you use the elective approach, here is a suggested schedule:

9:30-9:40	Introduction
9:45-10:25	First round
10:30-11:10	Second round
11:15-11:55	Third round

The Effects of Music

Use the following outlines for this session.

"GETTING ROCKED WITHOUT GETTING STONED"

1. Put the following statements on the board or as graffiti around the room. Have the kids react to each one:
- Rock music has more suggestive lyrics than other forms of music (pop, country, opera).
- Some rock songs have important social messages.
- Rock music has an effect on how you behave.
- The beat in rock music in Satanic.
- Burning rock music records makes an effective statement to society.
- Christian rock is a good alternative to secular rock music.
- It is easier to commit sexual sin on a date when you're listening to sexy music together.

2. Have kids read the following passages and discuss how they apply to rock music: 2 Corinthians 10:5, 11:3, Philippians 4:8. (Two of these state that your mind can be led away from Christ. The question is whether or not rock music can have an effect on your mind.)

3. Pass out evaluation sheets and pencils. Play a secular rock song with suggestive lyrics and have each person evaluate it. Then discuss it. Do the same with a rock song that has meaningful/constructive lyrics. Then play a Christian rock song and evaluate it as well. Make the effort to bring a good stereo.

You may want to type the lyrics to the songs so your kids can read them as the song plays.

4. Tell about a few rock musicians who have gone from secular to Christian rock. (See Campus Life, January 1982.)

5. Read quotes from **Rock Reconsidered**, pages 70, 80-81, 131, 133.

6. Close in prayer.

"MUSIC EVALUATION SHEET"

Name of song: _____

Artist: _____

Quality of music (excluding lyrics)—Circle one: Terrible 1   2   3   4   Great 5

Message of the song (state briefly): _____

Quality of the message: Terrible 1   2   3   4   Great 5

Overall quality of the song: Terrible 1   2   3   4   Great 5

Is this song worth listening to? _____ Why or why not? _____

Other resources: **Rock Reconsidered**, Steve Lawhead, InterVarsity Press; **Rock**, Bob Larson, Tyndale Publishing House; **John's Guide to Music and Other Madness**, published monthly as a newsletter, 1580 Peachtree St., Atlanta, GA 30309.

Elective Two:
The Effect of TV and Media

This elective uses a film as a discussion starter. You have a choice of two: "TV and Thee" by Ken Anderson Films and "So Many Voices" by Gateway Films.

Follow up this film with discussion on its content.

"TV DISCUSSION GUIDE"

1. Where is your television set in your home? center of the room? in the basement? What does the location of your TV tell you about its importance to your family?

2. How many hours of TV do you watch each week?

3. What are your favorite shows? What makes them your favorites?

4. Philippians 4:8 is shown in some films printed over scenes of violence. What does this scripture say? Why does TV generally stay away from issues of right and wrong?

5. Have you ever turned a TV show off? If so, why?

6. How would your life be different if you didn't watch TV for 30 days?

7. What are guidelines for TV watching?

Elective Three:
Peer Pressure

Give a copy of the following "Peer Pressure or Support Group" sheet to each person. Take 10 minutes to conduct the interviews. Discuss the findings in groups of five.

"PEER PRESSURE OR SUPPORT GROUP"

1. What do you think is the biggest influence on students' actions in your school?

2. If Christians don't take a stand on your campus, why do you think they don't?

3. How would you define peer pressure?

4. Do parents experience peer pressure?

5. Is there a strong group pressure among Christians? Should there be?

Use a chalkboard or newsprint to tabulate the survey results. Explain that standards are important—a person needs to establish personal standards.

Tell everyone to divide the back of their survey sheets into three columns:

Physical Standards	Spiritual Standards	Social Standards

Have everyone read the following and paraphrase verses or parts of verses that fit into one of the three columns. The passages are Psalm 37:1-6; Proverbs 29:25; Romans 12:1-2; Hebrews 10:24-25; and 1 John 2:15-17. For example, the Proverbs passage can fit into the social and physical standards column.

Spend the last few minutes sharing some of the findings. Conclude with everyone vowing to actively support at least one other person in the group. End in prayer.

SATURDAY AFTERNOON

Spend most of this time for organized free time. If you need large group ideas, see chapter 19.

SATURDAY EVENING

1. We had dinner at 5:30 p.m., with free time afterward.
2. 6:30—Group singing and crazy games.
3. 7 p.m.—Start by saying: "We have discussed today the topic of 'Pressure': TV, music, friends. Tonight, we'll take a look at different types of pressure. Let's read Romans 12:1-2 again, this time as a group. We have another elective series, only they are 30 minutes in length. Choose two of the three to attend." The schedule looks like this:

7:15-7:45	First round
7:50-8:20	Second round
8:25-9:30	General session

The electives are:
1. Dating and relating to others.
2. Loving yourself.
3. Friendships and their effect on you.

Give directions on where to find each elective. Below is an agenda for each of the three electives. The general session follows.

——————— Elective One: ———————
Dating and Relating to Others

Have a copy of "Making Your Dating Life Count" for everyone. Hand it out and have all get into groups of three and work on this material for 20 minutes. Discuss everyone's findings.

"MAKING YOUR DATING LIFE COUNT"

Work through this exercise with two other people. Read Ecclesiastes 11:7—12:1.

1. Look up the word "perspective" in the dictionary and write down what it means. _____

2. How would you define "spiritual perspective"? _____
_____

3. Write Ecclesiastes 11:7-8 in your own words. _____
_____

4. How should you "live it up," according to verse 9? _____
_____

5. Does giving an "account to God for everything you do" scare you? Why?_____

6. How can you follow Ecclesiastes 12:1? _____
_____

7. Read 1 Peter 4:1-5. How should you act as a responsible person toward others according to this verse? _____
_____

How does this verse apply to dating? _____
_____

==== *Elective Two:* ====

Loving Yourself and Liking It

Hand out "Liking Yourself" sheets for everyone and have everyone complete it on their own.

"LIKING YOURSELF"

How do you feel about yourself? Who are You? What is your identity? Have you ever been aware of your "self" at any given time? This is called by another name: our self-concept. It is the image we have of ourselves, or our mental picture of ourselves. Three questions define who we are:

Who am I?
What am I?
Why am I?

Who am I: I am a male or female. I am _____ years old. This is my identity as a person.

What am I: I am a: housewife, househusband, business executive, blue-collar worker, student, or _____. This is my label.

Why am I: This is my reason for living or existing.

Our self-concept is usually built upon the way we have been answering these questions. It is our sense of being somebody. Let's go a step further and complete the section below. "I am _____" means I am this type of person and this is how I feel about myself.

I am _____
I am _____
I am _____
I am _____

Put a P by every positive statement.
Put an N by every negative statement.
Put FM if statement is true because another family member has said so.
Put F if statement is true because a friend has said so.
Put G if statement is true because God says so.
Put U if statement is true but is unconfirmed by anybody.

After all are finished, discuss their feelings. How important do they feel? How important does God feel they are? Comment that in God's eyes we are objects of great value to him. Follow this outline:

"In Christ" we have a godly self-image—
1. Objects of his great love
   John 3:16
   Romans 5:8
   Romans 8:1-4
2. Objects of great value to him
   Galatians 2:20
   1 Corinthians 6:19-20
   Ephesians 2:8-10

======= Elective Three: =======
Friendships and Their Effects on You

Get into groups of five. Everyone should get a "Friends" sheet to fill out on another person in the room. You could make sure that each person has a sheet filled out on him or her by writing in the names of these persons before handing out the sheets. Collect the sheets and give them back to the person that sheet describes. Discuss everyone's feelings. Point out how genuine support can build up a relationship and make it strong.

"FRIENDS"

Name:_____

What does this person remind you of and why?
a. color _____
b. flower _____
c. part of a car _____
d. animal _____

Why do you like this person? _____

What are this person's strong points? _____

Why is this person so interesting? _____

The General Session

Hand out the "Agree/Disagree" sheets. You may want to vary this sheet by selecting only those questions you feel comfortable with.

"AGREE/DISAGREE"

1. The two most important facts about us as human beings are . . .

Agree Disagree a. We were born with the mind and body of a human being.

Agree Disagree b. We are all sexual, all of our lives, each unique in his own way at any given moment.

2. Six features of human personality are . . .

True False a. God made man a rational being—a creature sharing intelligence.

True False b. God made man a creature of affect (the ability to share emotions).

True False c. God made man a creature who must obey God's every bidding.

True False d. God made man a creature with little understanding of values.

True False e. God made man with the ability to be conscious of himself.

True False f. God gave man a temporary spirit.

3. True False Intercourse is a language of the body.

4. True False Intimate self-disclosure at sexual intercourse invites self-disclosure at all other levels of personal existence.

5. True False I am really one person—my body and mind are one.

6. In God's mind, our bodies are . . .

(a) a temple   (c) flesh and blood   (e) good
(b) corrupted   (d) useful for his service

7. True False Jesus was sexless.

8. Agree Disagree "I desired all things, that I might enjoy life; God gave me life, that I might enjoy all things."

9. Sexual Fantasizing

Agree Disagree a. It is right.

Agree Disagree b. It is useful to relieve boredom.

Agree Disagree c. It puts us in a state of false euphoria and mindlessness.

10. True False Every man is a rock or an island—not needing help or support.

11. True False A man is the slave of whatever has mastered him.

12. True False Where your sexuality is, there will your heart be.

13. True False Sexuality is learned as we socialize and interact with others.

14. True False The way we think and feel about ourselves as bodies will always find expression in the way we think and feel about the world and about God.

15. Agree Disagree Human sexuality equals sex and sex equals genital sex acts.

Have everyone complete the questionnaire. Then put it on the overhead. Divide the room so that one side of the room is the "Agree" side and the other side is the "Disagree" side. Go down the list to point out the right answers. Occasionally stop and have everyone go to the side of the room which depicts their answer to the question. Discuss "why" they answered the statement the way they did. Spend 25 minutes on this part of the exercise.

Hand out the next sheet ("Sexuality") and divide the group into teams of five.

Assign to each group an area under the five headings and have them read the scripture verses mentioned. Provide groups with concordances and topical Bibles so they can find more information on that topic. The assignment is to paraphrase in their own words the meaning of sexuality as it applies to the specific area they are working on. Ask the teams to jot down questions they or their friends have in that area.

Sexuality is defined in broad terms as, "The whole person (thoughts, experiences, learnings, ideas, values and imaginings) as he or she relates to being male or female. It is the power to relate as a person."

After the groups have finished their task, have them share their results with the whole group. Recap what has been said and end in prayer.

SATURDAY EVENING

Use Saturday evening as a talent night or talent show. Do all sorts of crazy and fun stuff.

SUNDAY

After breakfast and devotions have everyone spend several minutes writing questions they would like to ask about the areas they dealt with on Saturday.

Then have a panel of sponsors and adults answer the questions which were submitted in writing.

We brought in some college students to conduct our worship service at 10:45 a.m. They used creative dramas and choral reading.

RESOURCES

Sexual Freedom, InterVarsity Press booklet.
Eros Defiled, John White, InterVarsity Press.
A Christian View of Youth and Sexuality, Steve Clapp, C-4 Resources.
The Dating Game, Herbert Miles, Zondervan.
Dare to Be Different, Fred Hartley, Revell.
Questions Teenagers Ask About Dating and Sex, Barry Wood, Revell.

"SEXUALITY"

Emotional
1 Corinthians 7:2-9
1 Thessalonians 4:3-8

Intellectual
Matthew 15:19-20
Romans 12:1-2

Social
Leviticus 18:20, 22

Spiritual
Ephesians 5:25-33

Physical
Psalm 139

RETREAT OUTLINE 12:

"I Can't See: Exper

By Joe Fowler

A young person's reflections on the feelings, frustrations and growth after 18 hours blindfolded.

All right now people, shut those beady little eyes of yours and imagine staying like that for 18 hours. Let me tell you, it's a real experience and I recommend anyone trying it.

Before the blindfolds went on, we all agreed to a contract, which essentially is a statement of the ground rules of the retreat. Then one by one, each of us lost all touch with our most indispensable sense—sight. It was the last daylight we would see until Saturday afternoon. Some of us were pretty bold in the beginning, until we learned that one wrong move could land somebody in the hospital.

"I felt awkward, clumsy and terribly dependent." Those immortal words of Ken Daniel say what a good many of us in the group felt.

Next on the agenda was getting from our church to the retreat site. This was an experience in itself. The members were completely dependent on the driver and each other's voices. It was a slow trip because we were traveling through mountains and it was extremely foggy. After what seemed a long time, we finally made it to the one room cabin in the Pocono Mountains.

The cabin's features were ideal for this retreat: one room with the kitchen area on the left, tables in the middle and an open area on the right. A fireplace was in the front wall with bathrooms on the opposite wall. The ceiling was high and above the bathrooms was a balcony for sleeping; it overlooked the rest of the cabin. Leading up to the balcony was a spiraling staircase.

The cabin's structure limited the extent people could pull out of sessions, although in the blind portion of the retreat it would have been next to impossible anyway. Everything that had to be done was just a short distance away, so it simplified movement.

GETTING ACCLIMATED

For a good number of people it was the first time they had been there. They were living in a place they had never seen, which I guess isn't really that awful, since blind people never see their surroundings either.

Then the advisors unloaded everything, which was an accomplishment in itself because 20 persons' clothes, sleeping bags and food is a lot of unloading for only a few advisors.

After settling in, we did some awakening exercises that involved doing some crazy things. At first I was a little reluctant to do them for fear of the

others watching me. But then I realized that everyone was in the same position, except for the advisors. Anyway, we were paired off with another person and we then had a personal discussion with that individual.

After that there was a short break in the schedule. Oh boy! That's free time! Big deal! We sat and sat and maybe once in a while someone actually spoke! It was really strange; you didn't know when to talk or really what to say. You were never sure if anyone was listening. Free time never went so slowly.

Then came the pizza. Oh, brother! That you should try. It's hot; it's greasy; it's slimy; and when you can't see, it's a mess! You're never sure if you're getting it in your mouth or on your lap. Since you usually don't say much when you're eating, it's like eating alone.

Did you ever have an affair with an orange? We did! We felt it, caressed it (top to bottom), moved it between our hands and rolled it on our faces. Peeling it with care, along with listening, feeling and smelling it, preceded tearing it apart, eating some and squeezing the rest all over our hands until they were good and sticky. In this experience we used all our senses but sight, and there really was no use for it.

Clean is a sensation you really don't fully appreciate until you are blind. We washed each other's hands with soap, water and salt, dried them and rubbed them in baby oil. After that treatment my hands actually tingled.

The last thing for the night was to experience a cup of water. Each of us was handed an empty cup and we were to realize its condition: empty, light and round. Our cup was then slowly filled with water. Listen . . . feel the weight change, and slowly drink it being aware of it moving down your body.

EASIER SAID THAN DONE

Bedtime! That's easier said than done. According to one advisor, it was a real dilly.

First we had to describe each sleeping bag and duffel bag to find out what belonged to whom. It never occurred to us to put identification on personal belongings. Once we got the gear to the person and the person up the circular steps to a cot, we thought we had it made. Oh, yeah! Judy HAD to go down and brush her teeth. Debbie HAD to go down and wash her face. And numerous other nightly chores in the bathroom too numerous to mention had to be done by almost all the other youth . . . use your imagination.

235

Now, waking up blind is really a hairy experience when you don't know what's coming off. But we all managed to figure out what was going on quickly. Judy and Debbie said what they felt: "As we undid our sleeping bags to prepare for bed, I had a feeling of fear to know that when I woke up in the morning it would still be dark for me."

Come 8 a.m.! It was time for a good hearty breakfast. Most of us were moaning about how the bandages itched. And they itched as long as we sat and thought about how much they itched.

After breakfast we went on one of the most "eye-opening" (ha!) experiences of the retreat: a blind walk in the forest. We broke off into groups, one leader for every five blindees. All six of us held hands and started out on our trip. While walking along I had a compelling fear that I was going to walk into a tree.

We then began to explore nature's wonders. Jean, our group leader, found different things and let each one of us try to figure out what they were. For instance, a mint leaf. We smelled, tasted, and felt it. And because of its distinctive flavor and smell, it wasn't too hard to figure out.

Judy had a good point: "Noises seemed a lot louder. Driving up in the car, the traffic and rain seemed louder. I heard things that I never took time to hear before." We walked for about one-half hour. In that half hour we became unbelievably closer to nature.

One of the final blind experiences was foot washing. We each went with a partner and washed one another's feet while a story about a similar situation with Jesus and his disciples was read to us.

SUGGESTIONS

What's that? You say you'd like to have a blind retreat like this in your group? Great! Let me offer a few suggestions. First, in planning our retreat we considered having half the group blind for half the retreat with the remainder of people partners of sight. Then we would switch roles for the rest of the retreat. We ruled this out because that would create a feeling of superiority among those with sight. This would put the participants on different levels.

With everyone blind, everyone was in the same position.

(continued)

VISION RESTORED

Now is the time for all good people to get rid of the blindfolds. Debbie and I sat face-to-face and slowly removed each other's blindfolds, keeping our eyes closed. Boy, did that hurt! We then counted three and opened our eyes for the first time in 18 hours, together. I imagined everything to be dull and dark. But, due to three large skylights, the room was bright. My initial sight was a flash of light that lasted for a fraction of a second. Then I saw Debbie, and for some unknown reason, I almost started to cry.

After our sight was restored, relationships and friendships seemed much more genuine and real. Here is a statement by Roger that might help you better understand what feelings came out of the retreat: "It's hard to say what made the experience such a high point for me as well as the other participants. I can only say that when we cut off the dependence of vision, the group members became quieter and less willing to do their own thing. They gradually began to support each other so that they could walk without falling. They centered their discussion on their feelings and 'observations' and almost no time on trying to impress each other with their physical, social, or intellectual abilities. In essence, the group freed themselves from the bondage of 'what will others think of me?' "

Now it's time for us to do some mind finding, soul searching or whatever you want to call it. One thing we got into was the love process, which is basically a good set of guidelines to follow when dealing with people. The five basic steps are: I see you, I hear you, I accept your right to be you, I need you and I love you. I'll end my explanation of it there because an entire chapter could be written on it.

We also did a values clarification, which is deciding in your own head what ideas or values held the highest priorities in your life and which ideas hold the least importance to you.

On Sunday, after breakfast, we had a celebration. To start, some sections of the number one best seller were read. Then we did "Live-Die Sheet," which is really fantastic. How it works: Each of us took a sheet of newsprint and wrote on it our name and two columns— "Live" and "Die." We all put them anywhere on the wall and began. Taking a marker, we went to each sheet and in the "Live" column wrote a good characteristic about that person that he should let live. In the "Die" column we wrote a bad point about the individual that we thought the person should consider doing something about. At the end we all took our own sheets and read them, and if inclined to do so, rapped with other people about them. I find this an excellent way of learning about yourself and is something you can refer back to later to see if you have changed in either column. It is also a way of restoring confidence in yourself and taking a good honest look at yourself and other people.

To close the celebration we did a love circle, which is quite an experience. Everyone stands in a circle. One by one each member stands in the middle of the circle. One by one, members go into the circle and greet that person in any non-verbal way. It sounds easy, but it's really risky when it comes to doing it. People are reluctant at first. It takes a lot of guts to walk out into the middle, and once you get there you get the feeling no one is going to greet you. But everything goes fine and you come out of it with a really great feeling.

For the rest of the retreat we had a cleanup, lunch and a quick evaluation of what we thought about the retreat. We loaded the cars up and headed for home. Like all retreats, going home, back to civilization, and school, and leaving this fantastic environment, was a real kick in the teeth.

The smaller the housing for holding the retreat, the better.

Use bandages with adhesive tape for blindfolds. They are not so easily removed. Otherwise the temptation to remove them might be too great. We did allow a rule that permitted a blindee to remove the blindfold if the situation became unbearable. The need, though, never came up. Keep in mind that in having a retreat, there is no right or wrong way. Use your good judgment and decide among your group what exactly is going to be done and what you are going to try to accomplish.

RETREAT OUTLINE 13:

"Handicaps and

By Mary Jo Davidson

An introduction to the world of the disabled.

People in our world suffer from the attitudes of others toward them. Yet there is no greater message in the life of Jesus Christ than the need to show God's love to *all* people in every situation. That love takes many forms, and with our disabled population we have missed one very important point. We have given our money, our time and our energy, but we have not given them what they want and need most—respect and a feeling of equality.

A lack of awareness of the problem and a lack of knowledge about disability are primary causes of the harmful attitudes we sometimes show toward those who are disabled. This retreat can be used with youth to help them look at this problem, see their attitudes, learn about disability and learn how to improve the quality of life of this important portion of our population.

POSSIBLE SCHEDULE

FRIDAY EVENING

7 p.m.	Departure from church
8 p.m.	Arrive at retreat site and settle in
8:30 p.m.	Session 1: "How Do I Feel About Disabled Persons?"
10 p.m.	Recreation or appropriate movie
11 p.m.	Free time
Midnight	Lights out

SATURDAY

7 a.m.	Rise and shine
7:30 a.m.	Devotions
8 a.m.	Breakfast
9 a.m.	Session 2: "What Is Rehabilitation?"
Noon	Lunch

1 p.m.	Session 3: "What Is It Like to Be Disabled?"
6 p.m.	Dinner in hotel banquet room
8 p.m.	Session 4: "How Do I Handicap People With Disabilities?"
10 p.m.	Recreation
11 p.m.	Free time
Midnight	Lights out

SUNDAY

8 a.m.	Rise and shine
8:30 a.m.	Devotions
9 a.m.	Worship service
10:30 a.m.	Brunch
11:30 a.m.	Departure

Disabilities"

LOCATION

Because of the activities involved in this retreat, the best site would probably be a city hotel or motel with meeting rooms rather than the secluded retreat facility that usually comes to mind when planning a retreat. (See "Growing Through Love," retreat outline #23 for hints on conducting a hotel retreat.)

To reduce the cost of holding the retreat in a hotel or similar facility, the Sunday activities could be eliminated by ending the retreat after the Saturday evening session.

The remainder of this retreat outline includes ideas for the four teaching-learning sessions only. Use the resources listed in chapter 19, for ideas on games, devotions and creative worship sessions. Invite interested young people to help you choose and implement those ideas. ideas.

SESSION 1: How Do I Feel About Disabled Persons?

Location: This session is held in a meeting room at your retreat site on Friday evening.

Objectives:
- To look at how we feel about those who are disabled.
- To look at how we react to disabled individuals and how we often treat them.
- To discover how able-bodied and disabled people are like, instead of different.

1. Hand out 3 x 5 cards and ask group members to write the first few thoughts that come to mind when they think of a person who is disabled or handicapped. Give them about five minutes. Then collect the cards and read them to the group. Summarize the main things you learned from this exercise and write them on a chalkboard or newsprint. Keep this for future reference.

2. Role play one or more of the following situations:

a. Two or three students are talking in the hall at school. A new student walks in the door with a parent and is looking for the office. They stop to ask directions. The boy speaks with an unusual voice and you notice hearing aids in both ears. How do you react to this situation? What are your thoughts about this new boy?

b. You are at a shopping mall and it is very crowded. You get behind a person who walks with crutches and has braces on both legs. He is walking slowly and you are in a hurry. How do you feel? What do you do?

c. You are with a group of friends on the first day back at school. A boy with cerebral palsy (walking with an uneven gait and one arm jerking continuously) approaches you and asks for directions to the gym. He is difficult to understand because of a speech defect. How do you react to him? How do your friends react to him?

d. You are having lunch with some friends and notice a person in a wheelchair at the next table. He has a device attached to his hand to help him eat by himself. He has finished eating and seems to be having some difficulty getting around the table to leave. What do you do?

e. You are walking down the street with a few friends and notice a girl with a white can walking in front of you. She makes a turn and comes to the wall of a building. She seems disoriented. What do you do? How do you feel?

After each role play discuss how each person in the situation may have felt. How did it feel to be disabled? How did you want other people to react to you? What are typical reactions to those who are different from us? Are we sensitive to their feelings, asking if and how we might help, instead of boldly assuming we know what is best for them?

Laughter may be a typical response to the role plays at first. If so, ask what the laughter says about our attitudes and reactions to those who are disabled?

3. List the ways in which those who have disabilities are just like you and me. When we meet others who have a noticeable handicap, our first reaction many times is to see how different they are from us. Actually, when we look closely, we can probably find many more ways we are alike than different. For example: We all have the need to be loved and accepted; we all need shelter; we all need food; we all want to be liked; we all want to have a good time; we all need clothing; we all want to look as nice as possible.

4. Discuss ways you can look beyond a person's disability and see a person with gifts, talents, expectations, disappointments, happiness and sadness—just like anyone else.

SESSION 2: What Is Rehabilitation?

Location: This session is held at a vocational rehabilitation agency in your community on Saturday morning. Details of the visit would, of

course, have been worked out with the agency administrators before the retreat. Be sure you have explained to the agency
representative exactly what you are trying to do during your
retreat and your purpose for visiting the facility.

Objectives:
- To learn about the facilities available to rehabilitate a person
who is disabled.
- To learn what life is like through the eyes of a person who is
disabled.
- To learn to interact with disabled people in a positive way.

During your visit to the rehabilitation agency try to have your group
discover what is being done to help disabled individuals attain their
highest level of functioning, adjust to their disability and eventually
find employment or some other meaningful activity in life.

Tour the facility and ask the agency representative to explain its
program to your group. Give your young people an opportunity to ask
questions.

Try to meet with disabled individuals who are clients of the rehabilitation agency. Let them share with your group what it is like to be
disabled. Before your visit to the agency you may want to have your
young people come up with some specific questions they would like to
ask the disabled persons. Some possible questions are:

1. How do you feel about having your disability? What are the disad-
vantages? What are the advantages?

2. What is the most difficult thing about having your disability?

3. Do you feel you are treated differently because you are disabled?
How?

4. What attitudes of others do you encounter most? Which do you
dislike? Which do you like? How do they make you feel?

5. What would you like to be able to do and can't because the proper
facilities are not available or because the attitudes of others prevent
you?

6. Do you like to have people help you?

7. How could I best help you if we were to go out to eat together?

8. What would you like for me to do if I find you having some difficulty in doing something (opening a door, getting into an elevator,
finding your way, maneuvering around something, etc.)?

SESSION 3: What Is It Like to Be Disabled?

Location: This session is held in a shopping mall in your community
on Saturday afternoon. Divide into small groups so as not to be
disruptive.

Objectives:
- To experience first-hand through simulation some of the dif-

ficulties disabled people encounter.

● To become aware of the way our world has been built for the convenience of able-bodied people, excluding our disabled population from many of the opportunities we take for granted.

1. Take turns using a wheelchair trying to get in and out of stores, go to a movie, get into a restroom, get a drink of water, get to the second floor of a store, etc.

2. Put ear plugs in several persons' ears and try to communicate with others in the group, clerks in the stores, go to a movie, etc.

3. Blindfold several of the people in the group. Have another person guide them in trying to find out prices of something you want to buy, take an elevator, find the restrooms, etc. You may want to also do this in a familiar setting to discover the difficulty of finding one's way around.

4. Supply a pair of crutches for several people to use in walking from one end of the mall to the other.

5. Now the person in the wheelchair also is unable to use his arms. Someone may need to push if the wheelchair is manual but that is the only thing the person is helped with. Try a variety of activities mentioned above.

There are many more examples you may use. Choose those which will be best for your group. A wheelchair or crutches may be available from a local rehabilitation agency if you explain your purpose or they can be rented.

After the simulation experiences, come together and discuss what you have learned. What was most difficult? How did others react to you? Were there any surprises? How did you feel?

SESSION 4: How Do I Handicap People With Disabilities?

Location: This session is held in a meeting rom at your retreat site on Saturday evening.

Objectives:
   ● To learn the difference between a disability and a handicap.
   ● To learn how we handicap others.
   ● To make a decision to act in the interest of disabled individuals, being sensitive to their feelings, wants, needs and rights.

1. Explain the difference between a disability and a handicap. A disability is the actual physical condition (loss of a leg, paralysis, blindness, etc.). That disability becomes a handicap when it keeps a person from doing something he or she needs or wants to do. All disabilities do not have to be handicaps. The sad thing is our attitudes toward disabled people handicap them more than their disability.

2. From the experiences you have had in the past few sessions, can you think of ways we might handicap a person with a disability? Some possible answers are:

a. By ignoring them, we keep them from enjoying regular interaction with others.

b. By discriminating against them, thinking they can't do things as well as able-bodied people, we keep them from enjoying feelings of accomplishment and working for a living.

c. By not making sure buildings are accessible, we keep them from taking care of certain businesses for themselves, enjoying some forms of entertainment, shopping for themselves, etc.

d. By continually doing for them, we keep them from meeting us on equal ground and enjoying relationships of equality.

e. By continually holding lower expectations of them, we keep them from attaining higher goals.

3. Repeat the first step from Session 1. Compare the answers. Have they changed? If so, how?

4. Divide the group into small groups of three or four people. Give each group a piece of paper on which to list at least three ways they can begin to act toward disabled individuals in a positive, sensitive way. Share them with the entire group.

RESOURCES

1. **Help for the Handicapped Child**, by Florence Weiner, McGraw Hill.

2. **Creating the Caring Congregation: Guidelines for Ministering with the Handicapped**, by Harold Wilke, Abingdon.

3. **Ethical Issues in Mental Retardation**, by David and Victoria Allen.

4. **New Life in the Neighborhood: How Persons with Retardation and Other Disabilities Can Help Make a Good Community Better**, by Robert and Martha Perske, Abingdon.

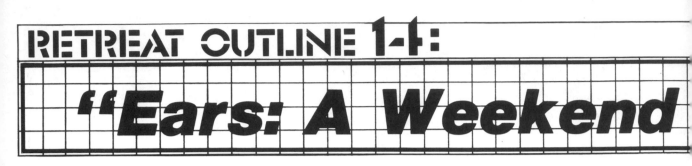

RETREAT OUTLINE 1-4:
"Ears: A Weekend

By Thom Schultz and John Shaw

A retreat for learning how to build up the skill of listening to each other.

Two of the most effective tools in your own personal Christian ministry are stuck on the sides of your head.

Listening is the primary tool used by psychologists and Christian counselors when dealing with people with various problems. Many burdens can be eased tremendously simply by "talking them out." But somebody has to listen.

Listening is also our primary way of getting to know a person. Sometimes we're really surprised to find out we like someone who, on first impression, really turned us off. All it takes is a little listening.

The "Ears" retreat is an unforgettable, high-impact experience in listening. Groups should be eager to benefit from this experience before ever making plans for the retreat. The retreat demands many hours of strict discipline—you will be unable to speak.

PLANNING

Before setting up the retreat, have at least one discussion on the importance of listening. Discuss problems often arising with friends, parents and teachers where a bit of listening by one or both sides would help a great deal. Then, discuss the idea of a weekend retreat where everyone must spend a certain block of time just listening. During the retreat, the group would be divided into dyads (pairs). One person would be free to talk, but the other would say absolutely nothing. At a certain point during the weekend, the listening-speaking roles for the dyads would be reversed.

Your group must really want to experience this type of retreat. It won't work if everybody sees it as a joke. This is not to say it won't be fun. There will be plenty of fun and funny moments.

After the group decides to do the retreat, select a site. The retreat works well in either a rural or urban environment.

SCHEDULE

FRIDAY NIGHT

After you arrive at your retreat site, break into a rousing mixer or game. Have fun and celebrate the weekend you're about to experience.

Then, determine the dyads. There are many ways to do this, so your

Listening Retreat"

group should decide which way is best for you. You may agree to number arbitrarily off by having someone pass out numbered slips of paper to everyone. Each slip would have a matching number, so all you need do is find the person with your number.

Another method involves a more personal approach. The group is given four or five minutes of silence to think about the partner each person would like to have for the rest of the weekend. You may decide to pick someone you'd really enjoy being with for the weekend. Or you may want to select somebody who you feel really needs to be listened to by someone. After the period of silence, walk to the person you've selected. Obviously, not all dyads will fall naturally into place, so you should have a second and third choice of a partner in mind. Remember, no one is required to reveal his reason for selecting the partner he did. This is not a popularity poll.

After the dyads are determined, agree who will be the 'A' partner and who will be the 'B' partner. Then hit the sack.

SATURDAY

Before breakfast, it should be announced that all 'A' people will be restricted from speaking from now until 3 p.m. Then proceed with breakfast. Mealtimes will be among the most meaningful experiences of the weekend. The talking partner will have to be aware of the silent partner's needs for sugar, more milk, etc. During breakfast, the 'B' people may feel tempted to ignore their silent partners and converse freely with other 'B' people. The common social phenomenon of shutting out naturally quiet individuals may become all too obvious.

After breakfast, each 'A' person is given a note pad and pencil. This will be available to them should they want to make notes about things 'B' will tell them.

Now, from about 9 to 10:30 a.m., each dyad should find a spot to talk and listen. The topic for 'B' will be your group. He should air feelings about what's right with your group, what's wrong with your group, what direction it's taking, and what kinds of things it should be doing in the coming year.

Then, from about 10:30 to noon, each dyad should remain together for some fun and games. Activity will depend on what's available at your retreat site. A dyad may engage in a game just for themselves, such as ping-pong, or several dyads may join for a team effort such as volleyball or tug-of-war. Several different types of activities should be offered.

Lunch will again be a very important part of the listening experience.

Then, from about 1 to 2:30 p.m., the dyads should again each find a place to talk and listen. This session will be the heaviest. The topic for 'B' this time will be himself. He should describe to 'A' who he is—not just what he is. His description of himself should go beyond, "I'm a junior at Lucille Ball High School." 'B' should share what sets him apart from every other person on Earth. He should also share his faith with 'A.' And, 'B' may also use this period as a "dumping time"—airing his gripes, problems, etc. Remember, 'A' must remain silent.

At 2:30 p.m. everyone should gather for some light refreshments. At this time, the leader announces the role reversal. From this time forward, 'B' is silent and 'A' may speak. (Be prepared for some loud vocalizations from the 'A' people—celebrating their voices.) Give a pencil and pad to all 'B' people.

From now until about 4:30, each dyad should again find a spot to talk and listen. The topic for this session will again be your group, covering the same feelings 'B' was invited to share during the morning session.

From 4:30 to 6 p.m., again engage in recreation, remaining in your dyads.

Then, experience dinner. With the roles reversed, you may notice some differences.

Follow dinner with some singing. Remember, only 'A' people may use their voices. The 'B' people may wish to become the rhythm section—clapping, stomping or dancing.

Then, from 7:30 to 9 p.m., each dyad should again find a spot to be alone. Now 'A' will share who he is with 'B.' And, like before the roles were reversed, this is also a time for sharing faith, gripes and problems. And, of course, 'B' may only listen, and take notes, if he wishes.

Now, at 9 p.m., everyone is free to talk again. Be prepared for more hollering.

At this point, the leader should outline the elements of effective communication and "active listening." Basically, this process involves a simple confirming of thought. When someone says something to you, as an active listener you should say what you interpret the other person to be saying. For example, if someone says, "I sure feel uncomfortable in this room," you might say "Do you mean it's too hot in here?"

Now, the dyads should again go off alone. But, this time, both people may speak. Be sure to take your note pads. Now is the time for feedback, telling your partner what you heard him or her saying throughout the day. Be sure to use the confirming process in this session. During this time, you'll really have an opportunity to use your active listening ministry skills with your partner, as you discuss each other's personalities, hopes, dreams, frustrations and problems. The notes in your note pad will help you remember what your partner said to you during the day.

Close the day with a group prayer.

SUNDAY

Enjoy breakfast where everyone may speak.

After breakfast, get your dyad together with another dyad. Discuss the value of the retreat. How did you feel? What did you learn? What was the most difficult part of the experience? Appoint one person in each foursome to report your feelings back to the total group.

Then, bring the entire group back together for celebration/worship. Give time to the recorders from each foursome to contribute feelings and hopes for your group for the coming year. Discuss the person of Christ as listener. Join in an agape meal.

FOLLOW-UP

Since this retreat is really a powerful one, you may want to reserve the next one or two group meetings for debriefing. Reserve a time during these meetings for your original dyads to get back together for a private talk. You may have some additional deep feelings that should be shared with your dyad partner.

RETREAT OUTLINE 15:

"Blessed are

By Edward McNulty

A retreat on peacemaking.

This retreat has several options to help your group to explore peacemaking both on the personal and the international level. The group will delve more deeply into the biblical concepts of Shalom than most have before. They will discover that scripture questions some assumptions they may have about violence, communication and patriotism. This should be a fun time but also an occasion for learning new skills for handling conflict and studying the issues of war and peace.

POSSIBLE SCHEDULE

FRIDAY EVENING

Arrive and unpack, either before or after supper

7:30-9 p.m.	Introduction of topic and Session 1
	30-45 minutes: Conflicts in Our World
	45-60 minutes: A film and discussion
9 p.m.	Break, possibly a short devotional service
10 p.m.	The Late Show: A feature film related to the topic

SATURDAY

7:30 a.m.	Arise
8 a.m.	Morning Watch (private devotions)
8:15 a.m.	Breakfast
9-10:30 a.m.	Session 2: The Bible and Peacemaking
10:30 a.m.	Break
11 a.m.-Noon	Session 3: Christ and Conflict
Noon	Lunch
1-6 p.m.	Free time. More mature groups will find plenty of material for an extra session.
6 p.m.	Supper
7-8:30 p.m.	Session 4: The Psychology and Ethics of Non-violence. Options: show films on Gandhi and Martin Luther King, Jr.
8:30-8:45 p.m.	Break
8:45-10 p.m.	Session 5: Preparation for Worship. Option: show slide-tape presentation "Study War No More"

SUNDAY

7:30 a.m.	Arise
8 a.m.	Breakfast
9-10 a.m.	Session 6: Peacemakers You Should Know
10-11 a.m.	Preparation for worship
11-noon	The group presents its own worship service on Shalom.

the Peacemakers"

BEFORE THE RETREAT

1. Carefully read the design, meet with other leaders and interested young people and choose from the options.

2. Round up the recommended supplies and equipment.

Supplies: Plenty of Bibles, Bible study aids, recommended books and pamphlets, paper, pencils, biographies of peacemakers, such as Francis of Assisi, William Penn, Martin Luther King, Jr., Gandhi, etc.

Equipment: Slide and 16mm film projectors, phonograph, tape player.

3. Order any audio-visuals to be used. When they arrive preview them and make arrangements for projectionist(s).

4. Duplicate any questions, quotes, rules or worship bulletins the group will need.

FRIDAY

Arrive, unpack and settle in. After supper gather together. This is a good time for group singing or warm-up games. Welcome everyone, go over housekeeping rules, introduce schedule and general topic.

Session 1: Conflicts In Our World

Option #1 Introduction

"As long as there are two humans, there will be conflicts. The problem is not just the conflict, but how to resolve it. Both are important. What are some conflicts in your own life, at home and school, locally, nationally and internationally?" (Either pass out paper for each member to write his or her own list or have the group call out conflicts as you print them on newsprint.)

A few conflicts the group might list:

Between parents and children: cleaning room, doing chores, what to wear, what to watch on TV, when to come home, choice of friends.

Between parents: how money is spent, where to live, friends, how to discipline children.

Between brothers and sisters: use of toys/possessions, bathroom schedule, chores, what to watch on TV.

At school: homework assignments, grades, classroom discipline, personality of teacher, dress code, morals and values of peers.

In community: zoning law, neighborhood or school integration, tax assessments, etc.

Nationally: management and labor, KKK and blacks, environmentalists and chemical companies, peacemakers and Pentagon and arms manufacturers.

Internationally: Russia versus United States, Israel versus Arabs, Irish Catholics versus Irish Protestants, Sikhs versus Hindus in India, Pakistan versus India over Kashmir, Red China versus Russia, Red China versus Taiwan, dictators versus guerillas, North versus South Korea, rich versus poor in many Latin American countries, whites versus blacks in South Africa and neighboring states.

How can the above conflicts be resolved (or are being resolved)?

Locally and personally: by shouting and arguing, divorce and separation, talking and reasoning things out, ignoring the problem, agreeing to disagree, "Cold War."

Nationally: by debates, letters to editors and congressmen, influencing and passing legislation, supporting candidates for political office, strikes and boycotts, joining movements and special groups (Common Cause, peace groups such as FOR and NAACP, Moral Majority), terrorism.

Internationally: by propaganda, raising the issue at the U.N., through diplomatic channels, special envoys and negotiators, building up arms, terrorism, breaking off diplomatic relations, embargoes and boycotts, secret attempts to undermine a nation's economy (such as our CIA uses), conventional war, nuclear war.

Option #2 Introduction

Have on hand stacks of old newspapers (mainly the front section) and news magazines. Divide the group into smaller groups of four or five. Let each person select a newspaper or magazine, read a story about conflict, and share it with members of the small groups. (Choosing and reading should take about 5-8 minutes, sharing it with each other another 8-10 minutes.)

After a suitable time, call the whole group to attention and ask the groups to share the types of conflicts they discovered. List these on a blackboard or newsprint.

After everyone has had a chance to report, go back over the list and ask how the conflicts are being resolved (or if they are). Write this down also: war, terrorism, negotiation, passing a new law, etc.

Options for the second part of the evening

Show one of the following films or slide-tape presentations (the source is given in the Resource section):

1. "Ground Zero at Bangor"—This excellent 28-minute film documents an anti-war protest in the Pacific Northwest. Both sides of the issue of building a nuclear submarine are presented. The chief protestor, a Lutheran campus pastor, gives the reasons for his becoming involved in a political issue. The study guide helps your group raise and look at the issues involved in the controversy over the arms buildup.

2. "The Myth of the Cowboy" is a slide-tape show requiring two screens and slide projectors and a tape player. The myth of the cowboy is the ideal of manhood that our culture, from Buffalo Bill's days to the present, holds up to our children. Images of the cowboy of the Old West, TV and movie heroes are projected and the violence, which they choose to resolve differences or combat evil, is examined and alternatives suggested.

3. Break for recreation and refreshments.

4. A Late Show (either a 16mm film or videotape) could be offered if you have enough funds. While this is of an entertainment nature, the subject of the film should relate to your theme. (I've seen too many retreats where the leaders just picked any old film to "keep the kids busy.") Consider the makeup of your group as you look through the film catalogs. Some of the films listed below are for more mature groups:

"All's Quiet on the Western Front" "Fail-Safe"
"The Americanization of Emily" "Gallipoli"
"Bridge on the River Kwai" "On the Beach"
"Catch 22" "Paths of Glory"
"Dr. Strangelove"

SATURDAY MORNING

If you use a "Morning Watch," give the group several of the passages relating to peace from Matthew 5. Ask them to be thinking, "How do I measure up?"

After breakfast and cleanup the group convenes again. The morning could be divided into two segments with a break in between.

Session 2: The Bible and Peacemaking

Have on hand Bibles, paper and pencils, Bible study aids: atlases, commentaries and dictionaries. Ask the members to get into the small groups they formed the night before. Tell them that they are going to study and discuss a Bible passage in depth. Point to and explain the various Bible study aids laid out on a table and the rules for using them (such as sharing, returning, etc.). Also mention the adult leaders who will offer help. They are to find answers for the following: What does the passage mean for the writer's day? for the church later on? for me today?

The passages: Isaiah 2:1-4 and Micah 4:1-4; Isaiah 11:1-9; Isaiah 65:17-25; Ezekiel 34:17-31; Matthew 5:1-6; 5:21-26; 5:38-48; 7:24-27.

Give the group at least 30 minutes to study and discuss their passages. Then call them back together to share their findings.

Session 3: Christ and Conflict

We've seen what Christ taught about relating to enemies in his Sermon on the Mount. For him this was no ivory tower theory or nice set of ethics to follow only if the other person would be nice too. It grew out of a deep understanding of God's Word and will for his life and ministry. We see this at the beginning of his ministry.

Have someone read Matthew 4:1-11. (This could be more interesting if three persons read it: one, the narrative; two, the words of the devil; three, the dialogue of Christ.)

Ask the group: What does it mean to worship the devil in context of this passage? What are the Jews longing for? How would many of them achieve their dream? To reinforce this point play ''Hosanna,'' ''Simon Zealotes,'' and ''Poor Jerusalem'' from the album ''Jesus Christ: Superstar.''

Ask: Did you notice any change in the crowd? What do they want Jesus to do? And Simon Zealotes? Who were the Zealots? What kind of ''power and glory'' is Simon seeking for Jesus? What is the meaning of Jesus' reply?

Divide into the same small groups again and let each choose one of the following passages that shed more light on Jesus' teaching about relationships and love:

1. Isaiah 53. This was part of Jesus' Bible. What style of leadership does it teach? Any similarity to Jesus? to the kind of lifestyle he commended to his followers? Compare that to the John Wayne or James Bond type of hero.

2. Jesus and the Centurion: Matthew 8:5-13. How did most Jews feel toward the Romans? Does this seem to bother Jesus?

3. Matthew 9:9-13 and Luke 19:1-10. How were tax collectors regarded? Why? What does Jesus do about them?

4. John 4:4-9 and Luke 10:30-37. What was the relationship between Jews and Samaritans? Did Jesus go along with this? What did he do about it?

5. Luke 19:41-44 and Matthew 26:49-52. What is the result of violence? How is this borne out in history? in Ireland and Palestine today?

6. Luke 23:33-47. How does Jesus react to his tormentors? What effect does this have on the thieves? on the Roman soldier? How would you feel if you had helped drive the nails into Jesus' flesh?

7. Acts 7:54—8:1. How does Stephen follow in the Lord's footsteps? What effect do you think this may have had on Saul? Could this have played a part in Saul's later conversion?

After 15-20 minutes, call the groups back together and have them report their findings. Overall, how does Christ handle conflict and hostility?

Conclude with a reading of Ephesians 2:11-18.

Afternoon recreation or option for extra session:

Show the short Gandhi and Hitler films as a study in contrasts of power. Assign materials on peacemakers and share reports on them. Ask groups to write a litany or other type of prayer on peacemaking.

Session 4: The Psychology and Ethics of Non-violence

What do you think of the admonition "never avenge yourselves"? What happens between warring groups and nations when they ignore this? How would Paul's statement in verse 20 be startling to an enemy? What do you think "heap burning coals upon his head" (RSV) means? Read this in several translations. The enemy expects you to react to him in the same way he treats you. When you refuse to do so, but return love for hostility, he is thrown off balance, confused. You've broken the agreement that the best way to settle differences is by violence. (The British confessed that they were baffled by Gandhi's tactics of non-violence, for *that* they could handle!) When the victim turns the other cheek and continues to reason with the opponent and to appeal to his better nature, he may get the other cheek slapped, and slapped again (Jesus warned us about a cross!). But the aggressor releases all sorts of confusing feelings, one of them being shame or guilt. The vicious cycle of vengeance is broken, and the possibility of reconciliation exists *as long as one person refuses to join in the self-perpetuating circle of hostility.* As Gandhi put it, "The hardest heart and the grossest ignorance must disappear before the rising sun of suffering without anger and without malice." Share the following "Ten Commandments of Fighting Fairly" with the group by listing them on newsprint or mimeographed sheet. Encourage discussion.

THE TEN COMMANDMENTS OF FIGHTING FAIRLY
(and non-violently)

1. Remember that you and your opponent are *both* human, and thus fallible. Either, or both, of you might be wrong, and thus should be open to new facts.

2. Gather your facts and state the reasons for your position as clearly as possible. Be grateful if your opponent leads you into a greater awareness of truth.

3. Never seek to humiliate your opponent. You are looking for truth, not victory. Thus, do not attack your opponent, but only facts or faulty argument.

4. Never dehumanize your opponent with labels and hostile names.

5. Beware of any note of superiority or patronizing air in your voice or body language as you present your case. The manner in which you face your opponent might be more important than your words and facts.

6. Look for the good in your opponent and his position. Try to find ways of appealing to the best in him, as well as in any onlookers. (Often sympathetic onlookers can, just by their presence, sway an opponent.)

continued

THE TEN COMMANDMENTS OF FIGHTING FAIRLY, continued

7. Absorb the hostility of your opponent in as cheerful a manner as possible. Never return insult for insult or blow for blow.

8. Use humor when possible, but it must be directed against yourself or the situation, not your opponent.

9. Keep praying for love, patience and courage. Use the prayer of St. Francis frequently in your devotions.

10. Practice the above in the little, everyday conflicts, and you will be ready if and when a major conflict arises. Keep in mind Matthew 5:10-11.

Session 5: Preparation for Worship

Tomorrow our worship service will include projects that you have created. Some possibilities: a peace banner, a litany or prayer(s) on peacemaking, a box collage on peace and war, skits or role plays on peacemaking, a choral presentation of a song, meditations on any of the peace scriptures.

1. Peace banners. This can be one large banner using symbols and words of love and peace. Bring along books and materials on symbols and banner making. Some groups have let individuals create small banners and then incorporated them into a large banner.

2. Writing litanies and prayers. Have on hand your church's worship/prayer book and other such materials to serve as models. Let volunteers look over materials (including biblical passages) and go to work.

3. Collages. Have boxes, old magazines, paste, poster paint/markers for volunteers to decorate. Paint large outlined peace symbols or words and fill them in with pictures. Stack the boxes up for a peace wall or into the shape of a cross. (Use a board to hold the boxes that form the transepts.) Make one side to symbolize our warfare, the other Christ's peace.

4. Skits. Think of situations of strife, big or small, real or fictional, and create ways that a Christian might resolve them.

5. Music. Bring multiple copies of folk hymnals with such songs as "Prayer of St. Francis" and "Let There Be Peace on Earth." Encourage youth to bring guitars and other instruments.

6. Meditations. Bring copies of "Alive Now" and other youth devotional materials for inspiration. Louis Fischer's "The Essential Gandhi" has good statements by Gandhi on non-violence that could be incorporated with scripture for a challenging meditation. You need not wait until Saturday night to begin these workshops. They could be described Friday and youth encouraged to start work during Saturday afternoon.

SUNDAY

Session 6: Peacemakers You Should Know

Option #1

Present reports, prepared by you or youth leaders on such peacemakers as Francis of Assisi, Mohandas Gandhi, Martin Luther King, Jr., the Berrigan brothers.

Option #2

Show the short films on Gandhi and Martin Luther King, Jr. Conclude with a challenge for participants to fulfill Christ's beatitude, "Blessed are the peacemakers, for they shall be called children of God."

Prepare for worship. Finish up or rehearse projects. Close with a creative worship service on Shalom.

RESOURCES

AUDIO-VISUALS

1. "Gandhi: A Profile in Power," 25 minutes, Learning Corporation of America, 1350 Avenue of Americas, New York, NY.

2. "Hitler: A Profile in Power," 26 minutes, Learning Corporation of America.

3. "Mahatma Gandhi: Soul Force," 25 minutes, Learning Corporation of America.

4. "I Have a Dream . . . The Life of Martin Luther King," 35 minutes, ROA Films, 1696 N. Astor St., Milwaukee, WI 53202.

5. "Ground Zero at Bangor," 28 minutes, Religious Broadcasting Commission, 356 Post-Intelligencer Bldg., 521 Wall St., Seattle, WA 98121.

6. "Myth of the Cowboy," and "Study War No More." Both require two slide projectors and tape player and are available from Visual Parables, c/o First Presbyterian Church, 49 So. Portage, Westfield, NY 14787.

PAMPHLETS

1. Fellowship of Reconciliation, Box 271, Nyack, NY 10960.

2. Institute for World Order, 1140 Ave. of Americas, New York, NY 10036.

3. SANE, 711 G St., SE, Washington, DC 20003.

4. World Peacemakers, 2852 Ontario Rd., NW, Washington, DC 20009.

5. Your denominational peace office or regional peace center will have many materials.

BOOKS

1. Bainton, Richard. **Christian Attitudes Toward War and Peace.** Nashville: Abingdon Press, 1960. Well-done historical survey.

2. Brown, Robert Macafee. **Making Peace in the Global Village.** New York: Westminster Press, 1981.

3. Easwaran, Eknath. **Gandhi, The Man.** Nilgiri Press, Box 477, Petaluma, CA 94953. A beautiful biography using quotes and photographs.

4. Gregg, Richard. **The Power of Non-violence.** One of the best of the analyses of non-violence.

5. Hersey, John. **Hiroshima.** New York: Bantam Books. A powerful description of the atom bombing of this Japanese city in 1945.

6. Miller, William Robert. **Non-violence: A Christian Interpretation.** New York: Schocken Books, 1960.

7. Shirer, William. **Gandhi: A Memoir.** New York: Washington Square Press, 1982. This excellent work is one of several now in print.

MAGAZINES

1. The Other Side, 300 W. Apsley St., Philadelphia, PA 19144. Lots of good information on social concerns from a Christian viewpoint.

2. Sojourners, 1309 L St., NW, Washington, DC 20005. A fine evangelical monthly on social issues; they offer a packet of materials on war and peace.

3. Cultural Information Service, P.O. Box 92, New York, NY 10156, publishes a helpful monthly review of films and literature. They offer a beautifully illustrated, 12-page "Gandhi" film discussion.

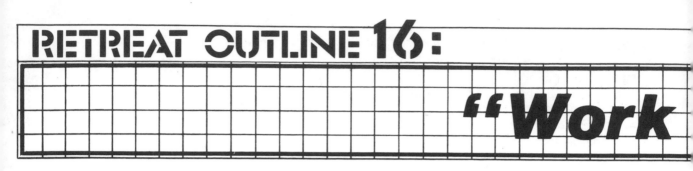

"Work

By Tony Danhelka and Gary Richardson

Your group can reach out to the needy.

Picture yourself at this unusual retreat. You're wearing the grubbiest clothes you own. Standing near the top of an 8-foot ladder, hammering drywall to ceiling joists, your hair loses that straight-from-the-stylist look. Beads of perspiration ski down your bangs and somersault off your nose.

Instead of listening to a superstar speaker tell how God can work through your life, you learn firsthand what it's like to rely on God to help you do things you thought you could never do—like working in the cold rain, doing carpentry or plumbing.

In addition to coming home with nostalgic memories and snapshots, you'll be leaving behind rock-solid, see-what-you've-done results. This retreat will go on helping people long after you've filed those Kodak keepsakes in a dresser drawer.

WORK TREKKIN'?

Work trekking is a project utilizing a group of young people from a church who decide to minister to people directly by freely giving their labor and love.

The idea of getting a bunch of friends together for painting projects and minor construction tasks isn't exactly new.

But work trekking takes the group project idea and adds a few unique wrinkles of its own. For instance, a work trek:

● discovers a needy and worthy project that generally is more than 10 miles from your church, but not more than 75 miles away.

● is a gift to the people who are the focus of the trek. The food, help, materials, lodging, even the soft drinks and bubble gum are provided by the church.

● generally combines a youth group project with the entire church helping in the planning and in raising the needed cash.

● is young people doing all the carpentry, plumbing, electrical and masonry work—with skilled adults helping out by giving verbal guidance.

● usually lasts one weekend, and at the most, one week of construction.

Trekkin' "

● is designed so work trekkers can return to the site for ministry-type follow-up experiences.

Okay, so you're sold on the work trekking concept. Your church leaders sound interested and your muscles are tingling from the thought of a new ministry challenge.

FIND THE PROJECT THAT'S RIGHT FOR YOU

Finding a project that's within 75 miles of your church will minimize transportation costs, make preparation visits possible and above all, allow a relationship for future ministries to develop.

In your search for potential projects, check for church camps needing repair. Also check with local government agencies for elderly or low-income people whose homes need repair. Many of the small people-helping organizations in your area may need a helping hand themselves.

Ask the local newspaper to publicize your search for projects. This stage of the planning process may take several months before you find just the right project for your group.

Factors to consider in choosing a work project: Can your church afford the needed materials? Do you have the youth power and the skilled adult help to complete the trek? Are there adequate facilities near the work site to house and feed all the trekkers?

THE INTRODUCTION VISIT

Once you've found what seems to be the right project, grab your leaders, cooking volunteers, construction experts and spend some time at the site. Don't forget to invite interested parents and any adults who want to come along. The earlier you can help the people in your church catch the vision of this special work trekking project, the better.

After getting acquainted and sharing the work trek concept with the persons at the work trek site, evaluate the work that needs to be done carefully. Start getting a mental picture of the necessary supplies. You'll also need to make arrangements for sleeping space, bathrooms, kitchen equipment, cafeteria, a meeting room and transportation.

257

Spend most of your time evaluating potential work trek sites. List every possible project: the jobs needed to be done, materials needed and number of workers required. A simple diagram of the work sites will help potential workers visualize the work to be done. Discuss the best possible weekend dates with the hosts.

PUBLICITY

Communicate the work trek vision to the entire church as early as you can. Announcements in the church bulletin, newsletters and on-the-spot announcements in church services are a must.

General interest articles can be written and mailed to everyone in the church.

As details of the work trek start firming up, share them with the church staff.

Plan an entire church service to share the work trek concept.

Since the work trek scene is relatively nearby, a publicity team can make a special trip to take photos for posters and bulletin boards. Super 8 movies can tell the whole story visually. Prepare a detailed mailing for everyone who's expressed an interest in the project—trekkers, skilled adults, parents, interested church members, friends. Include in the mailing a cover letter explaining the trek purpose, work site options, schedule of work trek activities, dates, what to bring and a challenge for personal ministry.

Local newspapers generally will be happy to run short articles on your upcoming plans, especially if you provide good quality black-and-white photos.

SKILLED HELP

Challenge all adults in your church to attend the work trek. But zero in on the trade-skilled people. Have your pastor help you chase down those special people. Then go to each person personally and share your trek vision.

ORGANIZE INTO TEAMS

Try to keep the teams balanced by age, sex and interest. Be impartial to sex roles. Guys and gals can—and should—work together as equals in work trekking.

It won't be possible to give every person his or her first choice of work sites. To help stay away from the SBAs (super bad attitudes), distribute the team list one week before the trek. Let the trekkers switch teams if they want to. Then two days before the trek, firm things up.

About a week before the trek, meet with everyone and discuss work sites, tasks and teams. Pray about last-minute difficulties and needs.

TRANSPORT MATERIALS TO THE WORK TREK SITE

During the last two weeks prior to the trek, place a large drop-off box near the entrance of the church.

One night before the trek, load the materials. Use a U-Haul trailer if you don't have a truck. Transport the materials to the site and arrange them at the different work areas. Use posters and signs to help guide teams to their proper work areas.

THE TREK

Begin with prayer. You'll be able to see the fruit of your careful planning and preparation—the excitement level will be high. You've planned for great results—you'll get them. The adult leaders and skilled adults should be servants: encouraging, motivating, trouble-shooting and getting extra tools, snacks, materials.

When teams get tired, they rest. When they want to talk, they talk.

After the work periods are over, a closing communion service can be a life-changing experience. Thank God for how specific people touched your life. It's good to name names and pray blessings for ministries accomplished.

COMING DOWN FROM THE TREK

Your first response upon returning home will probably be emotional. You'll be shocked at how much love could be generated through working together. The weekend gave meaning to your whole youth group experience.

Your second response may be depression. Life will be lonely without your friends working close to you.

Your third response may be guilt—"We should be doing this every weekend."

To keep yourself from crashing too badly, tell your church about your experiences and feelings. Meet with other trekkers about a week after the trek to talk about your feelings. Start talking about ideas for other ministries.

Picture yourself tired, worn-out and a little depressed. But you're more mature from experiencing God's work through you and your friends. It's worth the sore muscles.

RESOURCES

If you'd like more information on this brand of outreach ministry, contact Tony Danhelka at Riverwoods Christian Center, 35W701 Riverwoods Lane, St. Charles, IL 60174.

If you'd like to view a short, motivational film on work trekking, contact Inspiration Films, 7200 S. Central Ave., Box 249, LaGrange, IL 60525.

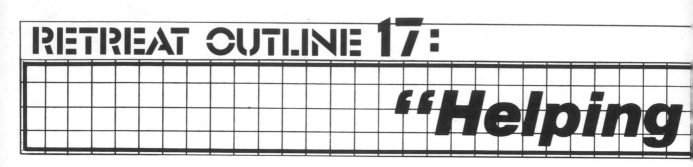

RETREAT OUTLINE 17:
"Helping

By Bill Ameiss

This retreat design is intended to help young people discover that they can help others, think through the kinds of help their friends need and practice ways in which they can help each other.

THE PEOPLE

Don't impose this retreat design on your young people. If you think the topic and direction are useful for your young people, share the idea with them. Let those young people help design the retreat's goals and purposes. If the young people don't become involved in setting the retreat goals, you may be wasting everyone's time. But if they meet needs and speak to concerns, get ready for an exciting time!

THE PLACE

Retreat sites vary greatly in what they offer and what they leave for you to do. This retreat design is intended for a place where meals are prepared by staff and not by the group itself. Should your retreat facility require time for cooking meals, setting tables, etc., adjustments can be made easily both before and after meals.

Get your retreat site booked as early as possible. Many good retreat sites are booked six months to a year in advance.

If a retreat center is too expensive, think of other options such as visiting a church in another town or someone's house. Many retreats have flourished with sleeping bags on gym mats for housing. Whatever you do, don't let the cost of a retreat center keep you from a valuable retreat experience.

PREPARATION

Weekend retreats help build good group relationships. At the same time they depend on good group interaction. Give some thought prior to the retreat (at least two meetings) with those committed to the retreat experience.

Use or adapt the following ideas for those optional meetings.

Goal setting—Share the retreat's goals and purposes with the entire group. Then pass out paper and pencils and have everyone answer the following questions: What are my reasons for attending this retreat? What's one thing I hope to gain from this retreat? What am I willing to do to make this a good experience for myself and for others in the group?

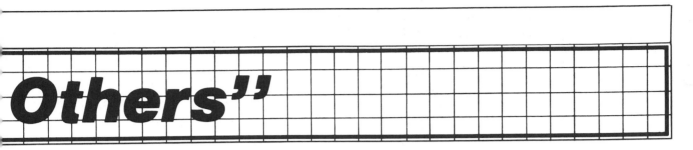

Others"

In groups of four to six, allow time for people to share their responses.

What really bugs me—The first retreat session calls for role plays on the topic, "What really bugs me about other people." Divide into groups of three or four and have each group secretly practice a two- to three-minute skit to be presented at the retreat.

Creative devotions teams—Divide volunteers into two teams. Challenge your devotion groups to use themes that deal with our helping, supporting, caring relationships. Among others, the teams might consider Luke 15:11-24; Luke 10:25-37; Galatians 6:1-2; John 13:4-9. Teams can use music, records, skits or readings to close the day's activities. Allow plenty of time for practice. You may want to help in the planning stages.

A "typical situation"—Try a fun activity that will help your group see a need for the retreat. Come up with a typical youth group activity. Then write on pieces of paper different roles to be acted out. For instance, the activity might be "deciding which group game to play." The goal is to come to a group consensus. Different roles can be "leader, wants to play volleyball," "leader, wants to play charades," "sad over lost lover," "angry with any leader," "doesn't like anything," "will agree to anything," and so on. After the activity has become totally frustrating, stop it and ask the different actors their feelings about themselves and the other actors.

Group Covenant— A retreat *covenant* (a promise between at least two persons) can be a meaningful commitment made by group members to each other. Have each retreater complete and sign the following covenant.

COVENANT

1. *We commit ourselves to treat each other as follows:*
2. *We will support and be responsible for each other by:*
3. *We expect our retreat leaders to:*
4. *We agree to handle any group behavior issues or concerns (such things as noise, sleeping times, drugs, alcohol, hassles/disagreements, and breaking the covenant) in the following way:*
5. *As a group on this retreat we want to accomplish: (list the group's goals)*

Signatures . . . .

A brief meeting prior to the retreat can reaffirm the covenant and firm up the details of meeting times, departure times, equipment to bring, etc.

POSSIBLE SCHEDULE

FRIDAY EVENING
5 p.m.—Meet at church to load and pack; final payments due
8 p.m.—Arrive at retreat center and get settled
8:30 p.m.—Games
9-10 p.m.—Session 1: "Honesty—The First Step in Helping"
10-10:15 p.m.—Devotion
10:15-Midnight—Night hike or free time
Midnight—Sack time

SATURDAY
8-8:30 a.m.—Breakfast
9-11 a.m.—Session 2: "What, Me Lost?"
11-Noon—Organized fun 'n games
Noon—Lunch
1:30-3:30 p.m.—Session 3: "Getting in Over Your Head"
3:30-5 p.m.—Fun 'n games
5:30 p.m.—Dinner
7-9:30 p.m.—Session 4: "Don't Just Stand There"
9:30-11 p.m.—Fun 'n games
11 p.m.—Live options: devotions and singing
Midnight—Sack time

SUNDAY
8-8:30 a.m.—Breakfast
9-11 a.m.—Session 5: Optional sessions
11-11:15 a.m.—Evaluation
11:15-Noon—Clean up, pack up, get ready to leave
Noon—Lunch and depart

FRIDAY EVENING SESSION (1½ hours)

You won't have time to complete all the options in this outline. Using key young people in your planning team, plan activities and studies that will best suit your group.

1. 8:30 p.m.—Begin with a crowdbreaker: "Spring Beauty Contest." Provide stacks of old newspapers (you'll need plenty), several pairs of scissors, rolls of Scotch tape and an abundance of straight pins.

Divide into groups of four or five persons each and make sure each group has the necessary supplies. You'll also need a separate room or corner where each group can work secretly.

Each group selects one person to be its entrant in the "beauty" contest. After deciding what person, place, thing or animal the entrant is to be, everyone goes to work—cutting, crumpling, bunching, rolling, piecing, pinning, taping.

Allow 15 minutes. Then call everybody together for a costume show and an awarding of prizes (a Barbie doll makeup set, a bottle of cheap perfume, a McDonald's gift certificate).

2. *Name tags*—Provide a large piece of construction paper, a straight pin and a laundry marker for each person. The object is to tear the construction paper into an animal that represents you. (Use a large piece of newsprint to show, step by step, what you mean.)

On one-half of the large name tag, have each person write two little-known facts about himself and then a lie. On the other half of the name tag, each person follows these directions: 1. Write a brief definition of help. 2. Jot down one reason people need help. 3. The kind of person I look for when I need help is . . . 4. When people come to me for help, it's usually because . . .

Allow enough time for everyone to complete each item.

Divide into small groups and have each person explain what his or her "animal" is. After guessing which statements are true and which one is the lie, each person shares answers to the sentences on helping. Encourage people to explain why they wrote what they did.

3. *What Really Bugs Me About Other People*—If you practiced the skits outlined earlier, put them on now.

4. *Forehead feelings*—Stick a large gum (or mailing) label to each person's forehead. Use a laundry marker to write a feeling on each one ("happy," "sad," "angry," "depressed," "love sick," "lonely," "dumped on," "happy-go-lucky," and so on). Have each person try to guess what feeling he has on his forehead by the way people act toward him. For instance, people would treat the person with the "happy" label as though he's happy. After the exercise, ask different people how they felt being treated the way they were.

5. *Bible study: "Honesty: The First Step in Helping"*—The following Bible study will work best when you use it as a worksheet which includes both the passage to be studied and the discussion questions.

Complete the Bible study in the small groups, with each person completing the response questions after reading the text. (Allow 30 minutes for this exercise.)

BIBLE STUDY—

"Honesty: The First Step in Helping"

A. "Logs and Specks": Read Matthew 7:1-5. Then answer the following questions.

B. My first reaction to "Logs and Specks" is: (Choose one.)
☐ Surprise! I never thought of my own weaknesses as "specks in the eye," not to mention "logs."
☐ Concern! I'm wondering if some folks see "logs" in my eyes, and I think they're just "specks."
☐ So what's new? Everybody has problems.
☐ Other:

C. One of my problems with "Logs and Specks" is: (Choose one.)
☐ I never really seem to spot any specks in others. I guess I'm just too trusting.
☐ You wouldn't believe the kinds of specks I see in others. Everyone is full of faults. It's unreal!
☐ It's hard to notice that log in my own eye, even when I strongly suspect there is one there.
☐ I don't look beyond the specks or logs sometimes but just tend to judge the person on what I see at first glance.
☐ Other:

D. The kind of specks I really find it easy to notice in people are: (Check any that apply.)
☐ People who are friendly in class but ignore you outside of class.
☐ People who act like they're too good for you.
☐ People who act like they're perfect, but then really foul up.
☐ Other:

E. To be perfectly honest, some of the logs in my life that I struggle with from time to time are . . .

F. Knowing I have logs to deal with makes me . . .

G. One thing Jesus is saying loud and clear to me through these words from Matthew is . . .

6. *Closing devotion.*

SATURDAY MORNING SESSION (2 hours)

1. *Wake up or lose your socks*—Tape off a circle on the floor that's large enough to seat the whole group. Everybody who sits in the circle is shoeless, but is wearing socks. On a "go" signal, the object is to col-

lect as many socks as possible. The people who lose their socks are out of the game (and the circle). They're also out of the game if any part of their body goes outside the circle. The last person in the circle wins.

2. *Group survey*—Hand out pencils and 3x5 cards, four cards to each person. Then ask the following questions (one answer for each card): a.) One thing that makes me angry is . . . b.) I really like it when people . . . c.) One thing the youth group can do to make me feel more accepted is . . . d.) One thing I'm struggling with right now is . . .

Collect the cards. Use one large strip of newsprint for each question and tabulate the answers while the groups are working through the following Bible study. Post the survey responses for everyone to see. You'll use some of the responses later in the retreat.

3. *Bible study: "What, Me Lost?"*—This is a good time to arrange new groups so that relationships are extended beyond just four to six people. Have the two persons from each group whose birthdays are closest to the retreat date switch groups. The rest of the group will remain intact. Have the group read Luke 15:1-7 together. Then hand out half-sheets of paper to each person and give the following items to share:

A. The part of this scripture that really spoke clearly to me was . . . (Allow participants time to jot down an answer, giving an illustration if necessary.)

B. Some of the ways people I know seem to get lost today are . . . (Again, give people time to write responses, giving examples where appropriate, such as—withdrawing from friends, getting angry over unsolved family problems, looking to drugs for help with problems, etc.)

C. I feel lost when . . .

D. Some people have been able to "find me" in my life and bring me back when I have been "lost." What they have usually done is . . . (Give people time to finish writing and additional time to share their responses in this small group. Instruct each group to close with prayer when finished.)

BIBLE STUDY— "What, Me Lost?"

---

4. *What's That?*—A first step in helping someone is being able to understand what he or she is trying to say. To get practice in listening, try this exercise: Divide into groups of three. Explain that you'll read a statement and each person will have up to three minutes to talk about it while the other two listen. The "talker" can either agree or disagree with the statement or add new thoughts.

The "listeners" are to try to understand the speaker's feelings and beliefs. They can ask questions to clarify what the speaker's saying, but may not comment or add thoughts. They also should keep eye contact with the speaker.

After everyone has expressed himself, ask the entire group to comment on how they felt and what principles of listening they learned.

Various listening topics are: (a) Guys are better than girls because . . . (b) Girls are better than guys because . . . (c) God guides our lives every second.

Use some of the responses to the group survey if you think they'll make adequate discussion topics.

SATURDAY AFTERNOON SESSION (2 hours)

1. *Amoeba Race*—Tie a long rope around each group that formed in the last session. Set up a course for the teams to run, perhaps to one end of the room, over an obstacle and back again. Race two teams at a time until you have a winner. To guard against crunched toes, all team members should remove their shoes.

2. *Over My Head*—Read Matthew 14:22-33. Assign roles and read the passage as a dramatic reading. The roles needed are: narrator, several disciples, Jesus, Peter.

3. After the dramatic reading, pass out sheets of paper and ask everyone to write the following items:

   a. One word that describes my feelings after hearing this story.

   b. The strongest truth I see coming out of this story is . . .

   c. Like Peter, I sometimes get in "over my head." When I do, it usually has to do with . . . (Possible examples are family hassles; someone of the opposite sex; making decisions; plans for the future.)

   d. Think of people whom you know who seem to be "in over their heads." What are some ways in which you might be able to reach out to them? (Again, provide adequate time for sharing, encouraging each group to close with prayer.)

4. *On the Spot*—This exercise is a story or situation that forces you to make a choice. It also gives everyone practice working through an important problem-solving process.

Talk through the following problem-solving steps before working through any "on the spot" situations.

Step 1:	Identify and clarify all aspects of the problem.
Step 2:	Try to identify what led to the problem.
Step 3:	Once you've identified the problem and its causes, look at its consequences.
Step 4:	What are potential solutions?
Step 5:	What's the best solution, based on the information you have?

Situation 1:

A new person is going to your school. She seems as though she'd make a good friend. But as you get to know this person you realize that her outgoing personality was a big front, that she's got the worst inferiority complex in the world. Today she stops you and says, "There's just no hope for me. I'm stuck with being me and I hate it." How would you respond?

Optional Topics:

Take various responses from the group survey question, "One thing I'm struggling with right now is . . ."

Situation 2:

There is a movie you've been wanting to see for some time but couldn't find anyone to go with you. Finally you decide to go alone because the movie is playing its last day. You're about to leave when the doorbell rings. There stands John, your best friend. He looks really upset. "I've got to talk to you now," he says in a whisper. "Things are bad at home. I don't know what to do." Just then the phone rings—it's another friend, Tom. "Hey, all right, you talked me into it! I'll pick you up in 15 minutes and we'll see that show!" What would you do?

SATURDAY EVENING SESSION (2½ hours)

1. *Teeth Teasing*—Have the entire group sit in a circle. The object is to never show your teeth. To speak, you pull your lips inward around your teeth to hide them.

One person starts by asking the person next to him, "Is Mrs. Mumble home?" The person responds, "I don't know; I'll have to ask my neighbor." This keeps going around the circle. When someone's teeth show, he's out.

Smiling is permitted provided the teeth don't show.

When asking or answering, contorting the facial muscles is okay to make the person next to you laugh.

The last one left is the winner.

2. *Conflict Is*—It's time to change two more members in each group. Have the youngest and oldest member of each group relocate. Then allow 15 minutes for each group to come up with a brief role play that illustrates a conflict people often face.

After the role plays, list different conflicts that group members have faced. Also refer to the group survey question, "One thing that really makes me angry is . . ."

3. *Bible Study: "Don't Just Stand There"*—Hand out copies of the following Bible study. When everyone is finished, begin the sharing in small groups.

BIBLE STUDY— "Don't Just Stand There"

A. Read 1 John 3:16-18.

B. Reading this text makes me feel . . . (Choose the best answer.)
- ☐ challenged to help as much as I possibly can.
- ☐ guilty! I don't really seem to be able to help a great deal.
- ☐ frustrated. I can do only so much!
- ☐ good. It is possible to help people from time to time.
- ☐ other:

C. The message that comes through the strongest to me is: (Select one.)
- ☐ Helping people means actions, not just nice words.
- ☐ It is easier to "talk" help than "do it."
- ☐ Helping people by actions is one way of showing your love for God.
- ☐ Our words about love for God have little meaning without actions of love toward people.

---

4. *Conflict time*—Discuss various ways of handling conflict when it arises in the group. (Denying that the problem exists, avoiding the problem, giving in to the other person, overpowering the other person, working through the problem.) List the different responses on newsprint.

Next, hand out sheets of paper and pencils and have everyone list three conflicts they have now or can remember having. Then have each person list what he or she thinks is his or her personal style of handling the conflict and what he'd like his personal style to be.

Take a couple conflicts from volunteers and have the small groups determine alternative ways of handling the conflict.

5. *Closing devotions.*

SUNDAY MORNING SESSION (2 hours)

Use one of the two optional sessions, depending on the needs and interests of your group.

Option 1: Create your own worship service. A particularly meaningful worship experience can be created by dividing the retreat group up into work groups to create an instant worship service. The following tasks are possible: (1) the worship setting—work on design, decorations, etc.; (2) music; (3) a message or sermon from the Word; (4) a celebration of communion—if this is appropriate for your group—or prayers.

Provide appropriate materials, particularly for the music and message teams. Let all of the groups know they have two hours in which to pull the worship service together and prepare it. You'll find a rewarding experience if you've never done it before.

Option 2: Helping, one more time. Meet once more in your small groups. Have volunteers in each group read the texts used in the four previous Bible studies: Matthew 7:1-5; Luke 15:1-7; Matthew 14:22-33, and 1 John 3:16-18.

After all the four sections of scripture are read, hand out a half-sheet of paper and share the following comments for individual response:

(1) The section of scripture that had the most impact on me was . . . The reason it had the impact was . . .

(2) One thing I learned about helping people was . . .

(3) One thing I discovered about being helped was . . .

(4) One thing that surprised me in these Bible studies was . . .

Allow time for everyone to finish writing responses. Then move into small groups of four to six for this last sharing. Allow ample time as the ability to share will have grown over the number of studies used. Again, ask each group to close with prayer. You might consider chain prayers, each person contributing, if your group is comfortable with that.

Evaluation: Provide a brief evaluation form which includes questions similar to the following:

---

(1) The best part of the retreat has been . . .

(2) The part I liked least about the weekend was . . .

(3) If we did another retreat next week . . .

(4) One thing I'll never forget about this weekend was . . .

Allow folks time to finish writing. Assure them that they need not put any names on their evaluation sheets. Read them carefully in reviewing the retreat.

The Bible studies used in this retreat appear in the study booklet **With a Little Help From My Friends** by Bill Ameiss, ©1980 by Concordia Publishing House. Used by permission.

RETREAT OUTLINE 18:

"Getting

By Wes Taylor

A retreat for teenagers and their parents

RETREAT PLANNING COMMITTEE MEETING

- Three youth, two parents, one youth counselor and youth director or minister
- Set goals for retreat, for example:
1. Help youth and parents understand each other's roles and concerns.
2. Understand the challenges of adolescence.
3. Help youth and parents communicate, share and listen.
4. Allow youth to share with other youth and parents with parents.
- Outline schedule for retreat

POSSIBLE SCHEDULE

FRIDAY EVENING

7 p.m.	Arrive at retreat center and get settled
8 p.m.	"All Together Now" (games and activities)
8:30 p.m.	Speaker and discussion groups: "What Does It Mean to Be Family?"
9:45 p.m.	Closing celebrations and family survey
10 p.m.	Games and crowdbreakers
11:30 p.m.	Lights out

SATURDAY

8 a.m.	Breakfast
9 a.m.	Games and singing
10 a.m.	Speaker and discussion groups: "Getting Along With Myself"
11:45 a.m.	Personal reflection
Noon	Lunch
1 p.m.	Crazy exercises
1:30 p.m.	Film and discussion: "Getting Along"
2:45 p.m.	Parent and youth panel: "Getting Along in the Home"
3:30 p.m.	Free time: games, activities, etc.
5 p.m.	Dinner
6 p.m.	Family Games
7 p.m.	"Sex, Rules, Behavior and Discipline"
9:45 p.m.	Together time: munchies, movies and much more
11:30 p.m.	Lights out

SUNDAY

8 a.m.	Breakfast
9 a.m.	Celebration: "Friendships and Family"
11 a.m.	Cleanup and pickup
Noon	Lunch and leave

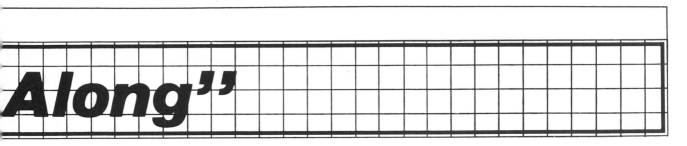
● Assign responsibilities, select menu, and secure resources

● Set rules for retreat—they should be agreed upon through discussion by planning committee

● Who will go? How will they be invited?

This retreat is for both youth and parents. Be certain that adequate time is scheduled so youth may share with youth and parents with parents.

FRIDAY

1. *All Together Now*—Use the resource list in chapter 19 for group game ideas.

2. *Family Picture*—Hand out sheets of paper and crayons and have people draw pictures of their families. Divide into groups of three or four and ask each person to explain his or her drawing to the group.

3. *Speaker and Discussion Groups*—Enlist the help of a qualified speaker to speak on the topic, "What Does It Mean to Be a Family?"

After the talk, divide into groups of six parents and six youth in each group. (Divide your group accordingly if you end up with an odd number of either group.) Begin by putting the parents in a circle with the kids sitting in another circle behind the parents. The parents do all the talking; the kids must remain silent and listen. After 10-15 minutes or so, switch and put the kids in the inner circle. They do all the talking while the parents listen.

4. *Closing Celebration*—Singing, telling stories, conducting a Bible study and using the enclosed prayer are a few ideas for this time period.

5. Have each person complete the following "Family Survey."

A Prayer to Be Used During the Retreat

(Give a copy to each participant.)

Lord, who am I?
Sometimes I really don't know.
And other times I really know me—who I am,
where I am going, what I want to do with my
life.

Sometimes I really like myself—other times I
can't stand to be with me. Why? What is it that
makes me one way one moment—and another
way the next moment?

Sometimes I really am confused about what I
believe. Other times I really know what it is I
believe. Sometimes I feel so hassled, I just want
to get away from people, but some of the time I
can hardly wait to see my friends, to be with my
family.

Lord, who am I?

Help me to know me. Help me to be able to
touch that inside me which is most me. Help me
to sort through all my doubts, fears, and hopes;
till I discover who I really am and how I fit into
my family. How I fit into your plans.

Thank you, Lord, for just listening. Thank you,
Lord, for caring about me. I know you love
me—and you are with me as I discover me more
fully. Amen.

FAMILY SURVEY

Directions: If the responses are not printed, please respond to the situations below as briefly as possible. If the responses are printed, please respond to the situation below by marking the answer which comes closest to your true feelings.

1. Of all the crisis situations which could (and do) occur in your family, the one you would have (have had) the most difficulty handling is: _____

    _____

    ____Death of a family member   ____Divorce
    ____Serious illness   ____Alcoholism or drug abuse in family
    ____Destruction of home by hurricane, flood, tornado

2. You have just received a phone call from your minister who informed you that your teenage daughter is at his house and is in trouble. All the way over to his house you try to anticipate what the trouble might be. Upon your arrival your miniuster informs you that he has bailed your daughter out of jail after she had been arrested for public drunkenness. Your immediate response is "Thank God it (she) wasn't (isn't): _____

    ____Worse   ____Injured   ____Pregnant   ____Drugs   ____Running away

3. How do you express the Christian faith with each other in your family? _____ _____

    _____

    _____

4. The television program you are watching is suddenly interrupted with the startling news that enemy nuclear bombs will be falling throughout the country within 30 minues. With less than 30 minutes to live, you reflect on your past life and decide the chief regret you have is:_____

    _____

    ____Not seeing my children grown
    ____That I did not accomplish what I wanted
    ____That I did not help others enough
    ____That I did not show enough love
    ____That I did not share Christ with enough people

5. Your teenager's steady date for the last six months has just terminated the relationship. Your teenager is really "down." What do you say in order to help him/her feel better: ____

    _____

    ____Want to talk?   ____Time will heal
    ____I love you.   ____Nothing
    ____It really hurts, doesn't it?

6. There are many forms of abuse which humans inflict on each other including various forms of physical, psychological, and spiritual abuse. Some forms are more serious than others, but we are all guilty of at least occasionally abusing those whom we love most. The most frequent way parents abuse children is: _____

    _____

    ____Spanking   ____Not listening
    ____Put-downs   ____Ignoring them
    ____Losing temper   ____Neglect
    ____Grounding   continued

7. The most frequent way children abuse parents is: _____
_____
_____Playing one against the other   _____Fighting with sibling(s)
_____Disregarding parent's values   _____Not talking with them
_____Disobedience   _____Running away

8. Parents often unjustly mistrust their teenage sons and daughters. The primary reason for this is: _____
_____
_____They were once teenagers, too.   _____Previous track record
_____Overprotectiveness   _____Lack of communication
_____Lack of confidence as parents

9. Describe your family in three sentences or less.

10. I get along best with my family when (describe the event or time): _____ _____

SATURDAY MORNING

1. *Games and Singing*—Use the resource list in chapter 19 for creative ideas. Be sure to choose activities and songs both parents and teenagers will enjoy.

2. *Speaker and Discussion Groups*—Find a dynamic person who's qualified to speak on the topic, "Getting Along With Myself."

Use the following information as the basis for discussion:

THE PSYCHOLOGY OF ADOLESCENCE

What looks like downright rebellion from teenagers is probably a normal task an adolescent performs in the process of becoming an adult.

Keith Olson, Christian clinical psychologist, said youth leaders need to understand adolescent behavior in order to properly minister to their group and individuals.

"Who am I?" Olson said the adolescent's primary psychological task is the search for self-identity, which has at least five characteristics.

1. *Self-ideal*—how a young person sees himself in the future. Long- and short-range goals are set. Some kids wish they could be like a certain person. Others aim for a mixture of values: honesty, courage, strong-willed, hard-working, generous, and so on.

2. *Self-concept*—how a young person presently perceives himself. Self-concept changes each day.

3. *Self-evaluation*—how the adolescent compares self-ideal and self-concept. The greater the distance between the two, the harder the struggle for self-identity.

4. *Self-valuation*—Even if the adolescent has a fairly accurate self-concept and realistic goals, he or she may not see the value of his life. Part of self-identity is a sense of being created by God and having a purpose in God's world.

5. *Self as the focus of power*—Adolescents become less and less dependent upon others as they leave childhood.

Common adolescent behaviors. As adolescents search for the answer to "who am I?" several common behaviors tend to manifest themselves. Olson outlined four of these.

1. *Preoccupation with body*—Most adolescents do not like their bodies. There is a fear of how one's rapidly changing frame will finally look in

continued

PSYCHOLOGY OF ADOLESCENCE

continued

adulthood. A few with well-proportioned bodies tend to focus most of their identity on it, all the time fearing others will discover little of value underneath the skin.

2. *Development of social relationships*—As adolescents break away from their families, they begin a surrogate family among peers. The pressures of peer groups are normal and intense as adolescents work at building friendships.

3. *Dramatic reactions*—Adolescents feel roller coaster emotions. As they discover more and more of themselves, however, emotions tend to stabilize.

4. *Dependence versus independence*—Usually called rebellion this is the struggle between dependence on parents and the development of independence. The adolescent constantly faces confusion whether to act as a child or as an adult. For example, a girl, 15, accepts a date with a man, 22. Her parents do not allow her to keep the date. She resents their "attack" on her independence and complains to her friends how rotten are her parents. Yet the dependent child within her is relieved that her parents saved her from a date she feared and didn't want to keep anyway. As the adolescent finds out more of his or her identity, responsible independent behavior eventually will evolve, an adult living without depending on parents.

3. *Personal Reflection Time*—Allow 15 minutes for everyone to find a quiet place and reflect on "Who am I?" and "How can I really be 'me' in my family?"

SATURDAY AFTERNOON

1. *Crazy Exercises*—Have a parent or teenager lead everyone in a few funny exercises. Aerobic exercises are usually fun to try in a large group. Or, have a laugh working out to one of the many "Christian" exercise records on the market.

2. *Film and Discussion*—Show the film "Run, Jimmy, Run." Plan a small group discussion period afterward. Encourage the parents and kids to meet in the same groups for this activity.

3. *Panel Discussion*—Ahead of time ask three youth and three adults to meet for a panel discussion. Questions you might want to ask:
How can you make things easier for your parents/kids to talk with you?

- How can parents/kids learn to listen?
- What things need to happen for parents and kids to trust each other better?
- What are creative ways to settle arguments?

Hand out slips of paper and pencils. Ask everyone to jot down questions they'd like to ask the panel and hand the papers to you. Screen the questions; read to the panel to answer.

4. *Free Time*—Plan structured activities, encourage parents and kids to spend this time together.

SATURDAY EVENING

1. *Family Games*—Consult the resource list in chapter 19 for ideas on games and activities families can play together.

274

2. Divide into teams of three with adults and young people on the same teams. Give each team one of the following situations to role play:

- Sibling rivalry
- Coming in too late
- Wanting the car
- Use of drugs
- Wanting more freedom

Each team is to plan its role play two ways: the situation where the conflict doesn't get resolved; the situation where the conflict gets resolved. Allow 10-15 minutes for the teams to plan their role plays. Then have each team show its two role plays to the entire group.

3. *Parental Authority*—Explore the use of parental authority by dividing into small groups and asking each person to answer the following open-ended sentences:

- I enjoy my parents when . . .
- I think that I am mature enough so may parents should . . .
- The most serious disagreement with my parents was . . .
- I wish they would understand that I am . . .

4. *Bible Discussion*—Read Ephesians 6:1-4 and answer the following questions:

- Why does the Bible hold parents responsible for providing guidance?
- Why are parents warned not to provoke anger in children?
- What kind of parental attitudes easily provoke anger in children?
- What decisions should be made jointly between parents and youth?
- What decisions should youth be allowed to make on their own?

5. *Bill of Rights*—Divide into teams of six to eight parents and young people in each group. The objective is to come up with a Bill of Rights for Youth and Parents.

A Bill of Rights might look something like this:

A BILL OF RIGHTS FOR YOUTH AND PARENTS

1. The right to be heard
2. The right to participate in family and individual decisions
3. The right to be loved and to love
4. The right to be yourself
5. The right to food and shelter
6. The right to safety
7. The right to be honest
8. The right to make a mistake
9. The right to your own things
10. The right to privacy

Have a representative read his or her team's Bill of Rights to the entire group. Then choose the top 10 listings to make a "Super Youth and Parent Bill of Rights."

SUNDAY

Use bits and pieces of the following worship session to create your own memorable retreat-ending service.

CELEBRATE: FRIENDSHIPS AND FAMILY

For Consideration

We are a Christian community. We are concerned for each other. We care. In this time and place we say to each other that we are here as friends in Christ. In a touch, a smile, a handshake, a song, or common bond, we will care for each other and be cared for by each other.

Saying Together

We gather to celebrate—
to worship the living God, and we gather
to get closer to each other human life
to encounter God
share our love with God and friend
get in touch with who we are and where we are going
to live more fully like Christ Jesus
to grow in faith, hope, and joy
and to be alive and new.

Singing   "Pass It On"—Kurt Kaiser

Listening   Ephesians 4:1-6

If we are to be more and more like Christ, then we need to take a closer look at ourselves

Confession

Lord,
We're uptight about so much these days.
   we wash our hands, our faces, our lives because we want to be clean.
But we're still uptight
   and we want to be free. Free to live and love and rejoice!
So Lord,
   make life holy,
Purify the obscenities that disturb us. Open us up to each other;
   intensify relationships; create conversations.
Help men and women talk more to one another,
   do more, cry and laugh more, care more together.
Help youth live out their full life
   with their senses open, that they may enter adult life fulfilled, freed.
Help adults complete their lives
   with purpose in what they do, freed of the weight of frustration.
Let us each be what we are intended to be;
   a part of your world, a part of our family, a lover and friend,

And let us seek the mystery in each other.
Give us awe and wonder.
Give us the freedom of the Christ
    who loves us all as brother and sister and who does everything we allow him
    to do to make us holy and glad.   Amen.

Silent Reflection and Meditation

Listening   "Could We Start Again" from "Jesus Christ, Superstar"

A New Community

Thomas Merton writes
    "Certain ones, very few are our close friends. Because we have more in com-
    mon with them, we are able to love them with a special selfless perfection,
    since we have more to share. They are inseparable from our own destiny, and
    therefore, our love for them is especially holy."

Share with two or three others what Merton's words mean for you.

Now share with one other person the meaning of these words in silence.

Passing the Peace
    "In the church's earliest manifestations, there was a keen appreciation of
    touch. Touch was the encounter through which love, commissioning,
    forgiveness, punishment, and communion were conveyed. Christ and his
    followers were sensitive to man's need for an incarnational dimension to the
    Word of God. The fact of God being fleshed out in Jesus Christ was not just
    something to be seen. Christ came not to give words about God. Through him
    the people could 'press the flesh' and know that God is good."
    —Dennis Benson

Pass the peace among each other.

A Deeper Look at Community (Relationships)

(Galatians 5: 13-15, 22-25)

To Consider
    "Community is more than contact; it is caring, compassion, concern, comfort-
    ing, creating, celebrating, conversing, communion and service. Community is
    always becoming—never complete. Two or more share life together, risking to
    show pain, loneliness, fears, angers; receiving understanding, support, en-
    couragement, and relationship. Community involves risking error for another's
    sake, losing oneself for a great cause, responding to a need for enhancing the
    qualitative character of human life. Thank God for community the making."
    —W. Stanley Smith, Jr.

Singing   "You've Got a Friend"—Carole King

A Closer Look at Friendship and Relationship

Prayer
    O Lord
    I need to learn—for you to teach me how to handle my relationships with peo-
    ple. Teach me the difference between being sensitive to the needs and desires
    of others, and the game we sometimes play with each other: between speak-
    ing the truth in love and meddling where I do not belong; between being bold,
    brace and strong, and acting pushy and bossy.

Help me to understand and practice the meaning of love—and remind me that it sometimes means gently admonishing someone else I care about, and at other times it means keeping my mouth shut.

Show me how to be flexible and adapt to the needs and circumstances of each person I meet and know. Help me to bend, to change, to listen, but not to go beyond my own beliefs and convictions.

I need to learn how to touch and not to grab, encourage, but not to put down and judge, to love and care but also to remember that my loving and caring touches many lives and some need me more. Help me to schedule my time, so that the deep commitments really get my energy and time.

Give me the sensitivity to know when someone needs to be alone, and when someone needs a friend.

Singing   "Give Me Your Hand" —Robert Blue

We Are Members of Christ's Community

Reading

Romans 12:1-5

Describe in your own words the meaning of community.

Listen

"The Meaning of Community" in *Alive Now*, Jan./Feb. 1980 by Henri Nouwen

A Litany for New Possibility

Leader: Let us pray for the virtues we would like to possess, the virtues that will bring new possibilities for human existence. Let us not be listless or unconcerned, never taking positions or getting involved with the world and the people around us.

Community: God, we would be alive— alive to the people around us, alive to our families, alive to the world and its concerns, alive to our own thoughts and feelings. God, we pray for life.

Leader: Let us not be frightened, anxious about everything we say or do, fearful that it may not be the "right" thing.

Community: Lord, we would be confident—confident in the truth you have revealed to us; confident in the love you have shown for us; confident in the new kinds of relationships you have granted to us. Lord, we pray for confidence.

Leader: But let us not be overbearing in our positions: never accepting the possibility that we might be wrong, always insisting that others must see and do things our way.

Community: God we would be open—open to new ideas, new insights, open to each other, open to a suggestion from parent or spouse. God, we pray for a spirit of openness.

Leader: Let us not give up before the end, turning away when things go wrong, dropping commitments before they have been brought to fulfillment in God's good time.

Community: Lord, we would be courageous—steadfast in our faith, dedicated to our commitment, strong in carrying out the promises we have made to live as your Son's disciples. Lord, we would be faithful. Amen.

Singing   "Peace, I Leave With You"—by Ray Repp

RESOURCES

BOOKS AND MAGAZINES

1. **Getting Along** by Charles Mueller (Augsburg Press, 1980). (Copy to each family; ask to read before.)
2. **Adolescence Is Not An Illness** by Bruce Narramore (Revell, 1980).
3. **Teenage Rebellion** by Truman Dollar and Grace Ketterman (Revell, 1979).
4. **Be A Better Parent** by Mary Kern (Westminster Press, 1979).
5. "Between Parent and Teen," **The Christian Home**, March 1982, p. 24.
6. **Teenage Sexuality: A Crisis and an Opportunity for the Church,** by Steve Clapp (C-4 Resources).
7. **Parents and Discipline** by Herbert Wagemaker (Westminster Press, 1980).
8. **Celebrate** by Wesley Taylor, 811 Center St., Oregon City, OR 97045.
9. "Responding to Changes in Family Life," in **Fellowship Times**, 201 8th Ave. S., Nashville, TN 37202 (spring 1982 issue).
10. **GROUP Magazine**, (November 1981) several articles on parents and the family.

FILMS AND OTHER MEDIA

1. **A Family Talks About Sex** (Mass Media, 2116 North Charles, Baltimore, MD 21218).
2. **A Fuzzy Tale** (Mass Media).
3. **Run, Jimmy, Run** (Family Films, 14622 Lanark, Panorama City, CA 91402).
4. **Image in a Bottle** (Family Films).
5. **In a Quiet Place** (Family Films).
6. **Focus on the Family** (cassettes) by James Dobson (Word, Box 1790, Waco, TX 76796).

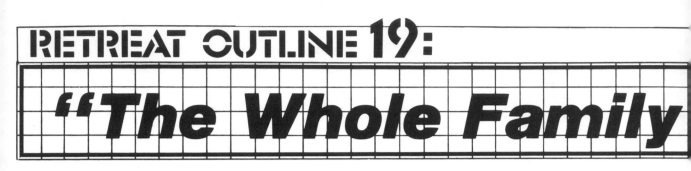

"The Whole Family

By Ruby Becher

Simple down-to-earth ideas for an intergenerational retreat.

Imagine your church's elderly, adults, young people, children and babies all spending a weekend together. Such a diverse group of people can have a memorable time together. I know; our church has put on intergenerational retreats for years. Here's how it works.

To be understood, accepted and loved is the need of everyone of all ages. From the time you leave home until you return, stress that everyone will sing, share, laugh, pray, play, worship and live together as one Christian family!

PREPARATION

1. Use simple language in everything you plan. Remember the broad age span you are working with.

2. A lodge with sleeping quarters, limited kitchen facilities and a meeting room serves best for this type of family retreat. A lake, woodland or mountain setting is desirable.

Reserve the same weekend every year, so the families can plan in advance.

3. You won't have everyone's complete attention, so learn to keep things moving in spite of interruptions. Strive for a relaxed atmosphere.

4. Take toys for the young and let the children play on the meeting-room floor during your sessions. They will entertain themselves.

5. Each family furnishes its own transportation to and from the retreat. Arrange transportation for attendees who don't drive. Everyone should arrive at camp Friday evening.

6. Each family packs sack lunches for the Friday supper and takes its own favorite cereal for breakfasts. Carry-in (potluck) meals are furnished by the families attending for Saturday noon, Saturday night and Sunday noon. Each family contributes its own specialties. Most of the food is prepared in advance, so little time is spent in the kitchen.

7. Everyone eats together.

8. We have a camping allowance in our church's general fund to help defray some of the retreat's expenses.

9. Use the element of surprise in the retreat. Only the camp director and pastor should know the complete weekend plans. That way there

are no preconceptions which can ruin the retreat before it starts.

10. Pick a theme early in the year and follow it in all your activities. We start planning the retreat a year in advance. We find we have a more relaxed retreat when everything is ready early.

11. Discover your members' talents and have them prepare to use them during a special part of the program.

12. Post a large cardboard clock on the meeting-room wall. Prepare signs to hang below which announce the time the next camp activity will begin.

IDEAS

Here are 11 ideas for you to use or adapt for your intergenerational retreat. Many of them are original, having been developed over the course of many retreats. Other ideas have been adapted from several sources, the chief one being **Ideas** books (available from Youth Specialties, 1224 Greenfield, El Cajon, CA 92021).

Idea #1: Build a Model of Your Church

This is a great craft that includes people of all ages. Shape and paint a large cardboard box to look like your church. Construct the roof so it can be opened. Make furniture for the altar area from construction paper. Cardboard strips spaced, set on end and taped to the sides of the box form the pews. Have bits of cloth, cotton, beads and colored pencils to use in making clothespin people.

Idea #2: Foot Puppets

Cut the back side out of a large cardboard box. Cut a window in the front side to look like a stage. Tape little strips of crepe paper or cloth to the top inside stage to make it look like a curtain. Puppets are made by painting faces on children's stockings and adding yarn hair. (This idea is found in Pack-O-Fun Magazine, 14 Main St., Park Ridge, IL 60068.)

Idea #3: Family Communion

Have each family meet together for communion. Adopt additional family members if there are people at the retreat without families. Give the fathers the elements of communion and the mothers a candle. Each family then finds a place around the camp area to share scripture and communion together. After about 15 minutes, all the families meet for a closing campfire service. The fathers can together light the campfire with their family's candle.

Idea #4: Balloon Togetherness

Blow up balloons of different sizes and shapes. Each person paints his or her portrait on a balloon. Hang the balloons together from the ceiling. Stress likeness to church families, all different yet all "tied" together.

Idea #5: Leafy Encouragement

Put a tree branch in a gallon jar using stones for support. Make leaves from colored construction paper with a string attached to the top of each. When a person thinks of something he is especially thankful for, he will write it on a leaf and hang it on the tree.

Idea #6: The Great Family Trade-off

Plan an afternoon where everyone switches families. The new families do something together—play games, go fishing or hiking. After the afternoon, the families meet together to answer questions such as these: Did your new family members treat you like your real family members? How was your new family different? What did you learn from this experience?

Idea #7: Hands Around the Room

Discover how big our world is: For every bit of kindness, or good deed that someone does for someone else during the retreat a drawing of their hands will be made on old newspapers, which are then pasted together to circle the room. The theme song will be "We've Got the Whole World in Our Hands."

Idea #8: The Prodigal Family

Prior to the reading of "The Prodigal Son," assign by card a character (father, young son, eldest son) to each person in the group. Read the story from Luke 15:11-32. Divide into three groups—all the fathers in one group, younger sons in another, and eldest sons in another. The discussion that follows should strengthen each other in their roles, talking over their feelings so they are prepared to meet with their families.

Each card contains a number at the bottom that indicates his family assignment. After the discussion groups, each family (father and his two sons) meets to role play the night after the feast at supper with the father, prodigal and eldest sons around the table. Each person responds as his "role" determines. After the family discussion, meet together with the whole group and discuss what happened.

Idea #9: The "Family" Game Show

The whole family plays group games. Divide into two teams: male and female. This keeps the pressure off the young and the older members, yet they are a part of the activities. Answers are group decisions and only one answer is accepted. The "battle of the sexes" makes for lively competition. Put a large chart on the wall to keep score. Use takeoffs from TV game shows, such as "I Guess" and "Password." Select your questions from the Bible.

Idea #10: The Family That Sits Together. . .

One game we enjoyed was having everyone sit in a circle on chairs. Ask questions about "how their day was lived." You might ask if they said "please, thank you," etc. If their answer is "yes," they move to the right. If their answer is "no," they stay where they are. It can be amusing to see four people trying to sit on the same chair.

Idea #11: Families Around the World

Arrange the room to resemble an airplane cabin with an aisle down the center for modeling costumes. Use crepe paper for seat belts and put a world map on the wall. The narrator speaks: "This is your pilot speaking. Good evening everyone and welcome aboard. It is a pleasure to be your guide, as we journey together around God's awesome world." (As you visit each country, mark it on the map with a smiling face sticker.)

Choose countries that interest you. Your local library has children's books which give interesting accounts.

Narrate a short sketch on the countries you visit and make them "come alive" as much as possible. Pause in different countries for displays of native costumes, dances, songs (recruit models, dancers and choirs ahead of time so they are prepared) and interesting notes on traditions and religion. Give souvenirs in some countries.

This can be a fun time that involves everyone at some point and also surprises everyone at other points (only the narrator knows all that will happen).

Arrive back to the United States and be greeted by Uncle Sam. Have a time of praise to God for his wonderful creation and prayer for peace on Earth.

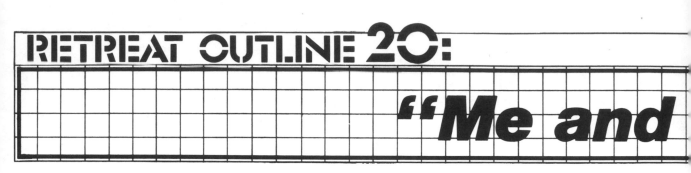

"Me and

by James Elsner

Learning what it means to be a responsible family member.

INTRODUCTION

The following program has seven sessions designed to help young people evaluate their present family roles and relationships. It also helps them think ahead to their future families.

The seven sessions allow a great deal of flexibility depending on time and space. As you prepare to lead these sessions, meet with a group of responsible youth.

1. Determine the retreat's setting and schedule.

2. Devotions, recreation and music are important! Who will lead games? Who will lead the devotions, worship and singing?

3. Ground rules make for a successful retreat. Establish these in this meeting.

4. Pray as a group that God will bless those who will be participating in the event.

POSSIBLE SCHEDULE

FRIDAY EVENING

6 p.m.	Leave from church
7-8 p.m.	Orientation and exploration: guidelines, camp and cabins
8-9:30 p.m.	Group building and devotions (Session 1)
9:30-10:30 p.m.	Snacks and games
Midnight	Lights out

SATURDAY MORNING

7 a.m.	Wake-up
8-9 a.m.	Breakfast
9-9:15 a.m.	Songs, devotions
9:15-9:45 a.m.	Group building, games (Session 2)
9:45-11 a.m.	Session 3
11 a.m.-Noon	Recreation
Noon-1 p.m.	Lunch

SATURDAY EVENING

1-3:30 p.m.	Music and games (Sessions 4 and 5)
3:30-5:30 p.m.	Recreation
5:30-7 p.m.	Supper and time for teams to work on worship
7-8:30 p.m.	Potpourri (Session 6)
9:30-10:30 p.m.	Games, snacks, singing
Midnight	Lights out

SUNDAY MORNING

7 a.m.	Wake-up
8-9 a.m.	Breakfast
9-10:30 a.m.	Meditation, goal setting, and worship (Session 7)
11-Noon	Recreation
Noon-1 p.m.	Lunch
1 p.m.	Cleanup and departure

My Family"

SESSION 1 (90 minutes)

Purpose: To build relationships among the group members.

Materials: Balloons, felt-tip markers, yarn, newsprint, masking tape.

Procedure:

1. *Songs*—Lead the group in several active, fun-type songs designed to create group interaction.

2. *Name Tags*—Give each person a balloon and the following instructions: With a felt-tip marker, write your name across the middle. At the end opposite the knot, list two things you're good at. On the middle (opposite your name), make a "life line" showing significant events.

Sample: Birth   School   Vacation   Junior High   Now

Near the knot, list three thoughts, feelings or expectations for the retreat. Tie a piece of yarn to the balloon and wear it around your neck.

3. *Partners*—Have each person choose someone of the same sex he or she doesn't know very well. He shares his name and two things about himself. Each partner completes the following: "The best thing that happened to me the first day of school (or other specific time) was . . ." Finally each shares his or her "life line."

4. *Teams of Four*—The two partners choose another pair of the opposite sex, preferably one they don't know very well. Each person then introduces his or her partner to the team of four telling the two things and one important event from the partner's "life line."

Have each person in the team of four complete and share one at a time the following:

● The best time of the day for me is . . .

● The first time I tried to swim (or drive) . . .

● If I knew I had only one week with my best friend, I would . . .

Finally, each person shares his or her thoughts, feelings or expectations for the retreat.

5. *Retreat Purpose* (5-10 minutes)—Explain to the group the purpose of the retreat. Emphasize the idea of being a family member back home in the large retreat group and in the team of four. Discuss briefly the responsibility one has to family members. Rules for the retreat may also be reviewed at this point.

6. *Team of Four Identity*—Give each team of four eight minutes to develop a poster, banner, flag, cheer, call, name or slogan to express itself. Then have each team of four share its "identity" with the large group.

7. *Devotion*—The focus of this devotion should be on thanking God for the people around us—those in families back home, those on the retreat, those in the team of four. Music and scripture should be used in this devotion.

SESSION 2 (30 minutes)

Purpose: Same as Session 1.

Materials: Tags with names of famous people, balloons, paper, pencils.

Procedure:

1. *Opening*—Begin with songs and a devotion restating the retreat's purpose.

2. *Partners*—Reform the pairs from Session 1. Have each person give his or her partner a 10-second greeting. Then reverse. Have each pair sit back to back. On a sheet of paper each should list the partner's:

- Color of eyes
- Color of shoes
- Color of hair
- Favorite magazine
- Favorite radio station

Have each pair face each other and share the results.

3. *Teams of Four*—Reconvene the teams of four and have each give its team "identity." Play one or two games designed to build group cooperation. Some possibilities from the **Encyclopedia of Serendipity** are: Charades (p. 51); One Frog (p. 54); Buzz (p. 54).

4. *Groups of Eight*—Form groups of eight by having two teams of four form a circle. Have each person introduce himself or herself by giving his middle name. Build the relationships in these groups by playing two games designed to foster group cooperation. Possibilities from the **Encyclopedia of Serendipity** are Imaginary Ball (p. 50) and Pass the Feetball (p. 55).

SESSION 3 (60 to 75 minutes)

Purpose: To provide scriptural input on family roles.

Materials: Handout #1, Bible, pencils, newsprint, markers.

Procedure:

1. *Songs*—Begin with songs that establish a mood for study and reflection.

2. *Introduction*—"We've spent quite a bit of time getting to know

each other better. Hopefully you feel part of a 'family' here on the retreat. But what about real families? We're going to begin our study of families by looking at God's order for them." Distribute handout #1 to each group of eight. Have participants on their own complete section A only.

3. *Sharing Section A*—Form four-plus-four sharing groups. Have four people sit back to back. Then have each of the four other people pair up with one of the four who are sitting. Share responses from handout #1 about "Father." Those sitting back to back remain seated. The other four move one person to the right. Share responses about "Mother." Rotate again. Share responses about "Daughter/Son." Rotate. Share responses about "Family."

4. *Girls and Boys Study*—Divide the group of eight into boys and girls. Girls complete Section B of handout #1 on "The Role of Women in the Home" by recording any biblical instructions given. Boys complete section B on "The Role of Men" by recording any biblical instructions given. When both groups have finished, reconvene the group of eight. Have the boys share "The Role of Men" with the girls. Have the girls share "The Role of Women." As a group, make a list of any new findings that were made about roles. Use newsprint and markers.

5. *Children in the Home*—In the group of eight, complete section C of handout #1. Again, record anything new that was learned.

6. *Large Group Sharing*—Have each group of eight report on their list of new things learned to the large group.

7. *Closing*—Use a devotion, prayer or song that fits the theme of this session.

SESSION 4 (60 to 75 minutes)

Purpose: To discuss typical family conflicts and ways to handle them.

Materials: Handout #2, Bible, pencils.

Procedure:

1. *Songs*—Open the session with appropriate singing. (Or, you may play a game to rebuild the groups of eight at this point.)

2. *Discovery Bible Study*—Reconvene the groups of eight. Have the groups select a leader to keep the discussion moving. Distribute copies

---

HANDOUT #1
Section A

Complete the following sentences:
  The perfect father is one who . . .
  The perfect mother is one who . . .
  The perfect daughter/son is one who . . .
  The perfect family is one in which . . .
(STOP! Wait for further instructions.)

Section B

**The role of men in relation to
  their wives:**
    Ephesians 5:21, 23, 25
    1 Peter 3:7
    Colossians 3:19, 21
  their children:
    Proverbs 22:6
    Proverbs 23:13-14
    2 Corinthians 12:14
    Ephesians 6:4
    Colossians 3:20
The role of women in the home:
    Ephesians 5:21, 22, 33
    1 Peter 3:1-2
    Colossians 3:18
    Proverbs 31:10-31 (If you can, read this from a Living Bible.)
(STOP! Wait for further instructions.)

Section C

What are some of the duties of children in the home? (Include any promises that are given.)
    Ephesians 6:1-3
    Colossians 3:20
    Mark 7:10
    Proverbs 23:22-25

of the study to each group. Allow 45 to 60 minutes for completion of the study.

HANDOUT #2
"Me and My Family"

1. The relationships among family members have been troubled ever since Cain killed Abel. What are some of the things that kept families in the Bible from getting along?

   Genesis 27:41 _____

   Genesis 37:11 _____

   Deuteronomy 21:18-21 _____

   Proverbs 21:19 _____

   Micah 7:6 _____

   Make two columns on the back of this sheet. Label them "A" and "B." In column "A" list some of the things that keep your family from getting along.

2. Read the letter below and then write a paragraph explaining how you would answer the father's questions. After the paragraphs have been written, share your answer with your small group.

   Dear Mr. Adams:

   I'm having a bit of trouble with my son. He never listens to me anymore. I ask or tell him to do something and he ignores me. The fact that I'm his father has no effect on him at all. I think he should respect me.

   If I had talked to my father the way that he talks to me, you know what I would have got. He would have whipped me with the razor strap until I forgot the words that I used. I don't know what's happening to these kids these days, but they just don't respect their elders anymore.

   I really think that my boy is a good boy. I don't want to beat on him like my dad did to me. How can I get him to listen to me? How can I gain his respect? How can I convince him that I love him and know what's best for him? I'll appreciate any help you can give me.

   Sincerely,
   Jim Anderson

3. Read Colossians 3:12-17. Discuss these verses, reflecting on what each verse has to say that might be helpful to parents and youth in getting along better.

4. On the back of this sheet in column "B," list some of the scriptural guides that you think might be helpful for your family in getting along better.

5. In your group, discuss what promise God gives to us in Proverbs 8:32 if we follow his guides.

6. Close the Bible study by each person speaking a short sentence prayer for his or her family.

SESSION 5 (50 to 60 minutes)

Purpose: Same as Session 4.

Materials: Handout #3, props as available.

Procedure:

1. *Role Play Planning*—Reconvene the teams of four. Have each team give their "Team Identity." Assign each team a "family conflict" situation. During this time, the team is to develop a five-minute role play on handling the given situation either the way it *really* happens or the way it should happen based on the scripture studied earlier.

2. *Role Play Presentations*—The presentations may be made at this point, later in the retreat, or in some other manner.

HANDOUT #3
"Family Conflicts"

SALLY:

Sally's parents have decided to go out of town for a weekend vacation. A conflict arises when a decision has to be made on where Sally, in junior high, should stay. Sally would prefer to stay with Jane, a friend whose mother is divorced and works the late shift. Sally's parents think she should stay with her older brother and his family.

   A. In your group, show how Sally's parents would approach her to stay with her brother and Sally's response as it would really happen.

   B. In your group, show how Sally's parents would approach her to stay with her brother and Sally's response as it would happen if guided by the scriptural principles discussed earlier.

GREG:

Greg, a new guy in the neighborhood, has been to Bill's house several times to shoot baskets. Bill's parents have objected to Greg as a friend for Bill because he is loud and rough with the basketball. When Dad got home from work one evening, he found the basketball hoop bent down and the net torn half-way off. Gloria, Bill's sister, told Dad that she had seen Greg shooting baskets about a half-hour earlier.

   A. In your group, show how you think Bill's parents would handle the situation and how Bill would respond as it would really happen.

   B. In your group, show how you think Bill's parents should handle the situation and how Bill should respond based on the scriptural guidelines discussed earlier.

PAULA:

Paula is a sophomore, a cheerleader and athlete, and has several dates because of her good looks. Carl, Paula's brother, is in eighth grade, is somewhat awkward, and plays second clarinet in the school band. Because of what seems to be their closeness in age, conflicts arise over household chores.

One evening while their parents are out, a disagreement arises over who will do the supper dishes (no dishwasher). During the argument, one of their mother's good vases is broken. Each child begins to blame the other.

   A. In your group, show what will happen when the parents arrive home and find the broken vase as it might really happen.

   B. In your group, show what will happen when the parents arrive home and find the broken vase as it might happen based on the scriptural principles studied earlier.

SESSION 6 (60 to 90 minutes)

Purpose: To discuss appropriate behaviors on dates.

Materials: Film: "Close Feelings" (Available through Insight Films, Paulist Productions, P.O. Box 1057, Pacific Palisades, CA 90272)
Projector and screen
Newsprint with discussion questions

Procedure:

1. *Songs*—Open the session with appropriate singing.

2. *Film and Discussion*—Introduce the film and the discussion process to the group. For discussion, form a circle with six chairs. Have five people sit in the circle while they watch a vignette from the film. Those in the circle discuss the questions from the newsprint. The remainder of the participants sit, watch and listen. They may join the discussion only when they sit in the unoccupied chair in the circle. When the discussion has run its course, change people in the circle and repeat the process.

3. *Closing*—Use a prayer seeking God's guidance so we live out our sexuality in a way pleasing to him.

NOTES ON "CLOSE FEELINGS"

This film has four vignettes, each dealing with a different aspect of our sexuality. Each vignette ends with a question and the discussion guide has several questions that can be used to focus on dating relationships. There are other films available that handle these same topics by acting as a catalyst for discussion. Find the right one for your group.

SESSION 7 (90 minutes)

Purposes: To establish personal goals for the next several months.
To close the retreat in a celebrative, worshipful manner.
To evaluate the retreat.

Materials: Handout #4, Bible, pencils, paper, envelopes.

Procedure:

1. *Meditation and Personal Covenant*—Distribute handout #4 to participants instructing them to complete the sheet in the time allotted. Allow them to find their own special setting for this.

2. *Songs*—Draw the group back together with songs. Collect the envelopes with the personal covenant as participants enter the worship area.

3. *Worship*—When all have gathered, conduct a celebrative worship. This event can (a) follow a liturgy prepared ahead of time; (b) be

led by retreat participants who have been assigned a song, skit, reading, etc.; or (c) be "led by the Spirit." Included in this event should be a message based on 1 Corinthians 13—the real heart of all our relationships.

4. *Evaluation*—After the worship has ended and in another setting, ask participants to complete an evaluation of the events.

HANDOUT #4
"Meditation and a Personal Covenant"*

1. Begin by praying for the Holy Spirit's guidance as you determine God's will for your life from this meditation on his Word.

2. Read Romans 12:1-3, 9-21. Read it several times until you are acquainted with its content. St. Paul here gives several things that a growing Christian "ought" to be and do.

3. First of all, write your reaction to "getting advice" on how you should be developing as a Christian. How do you feel, and how do you handle "being told what to do"?

4. Secondly, make a list of the different things Paul says a growing Christian should do. Write in the space provided here . . .

5. Now make this personal. Think about what you need to work on. Put Paul's "advice" in terms of your own relationships with parents, friends, brothers, sisters, pastors, teachers, lovers and any other of God's people with whom you live and work. Go over your list in 4 with each of several people in mind.

6. As you come to something that you need to work on, pray that God will give you the help you know you need. Talk to God as honestly and as sincerely as you would to any of your friends.

7. Write a letter to yourself on the attached sheet. Put down on paper some of the things you've just prayed about and want to work on during the next four months. When you have finished, put it in the envelope, seal it, address it to yourself, and turn it in as you enter the worship service. The letter will be mailed to you in four months. Only you and God know what is in it.

8. If you would like to spend more time by yourself, read Matthew 5 and 6.

---

*Adapted from **Resources For Youth Ministry 74.2**. Board of Youth Ministry, Lutheran Church—Missouri Synod, St. Louis, MO. Used with permission.

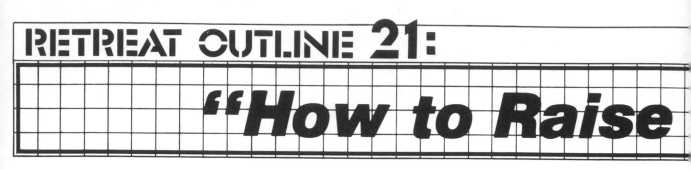

"How to Raise

By Jack Doorlag

A retreat to help young people understand and love their parents.

The theme of this retreat concerns the relationship of teenagers with their parents. As a result of participating in this retreat experience, young people will not only have at least four specific things they can do to intentionally strengthen their relationship with their parents but also will come home with a letter addressed to their parents.

PREPARATION

A two-hour planning session may be used to prepare for this retreat. It should involve the youth sponsors, some youth group leaders, interested parents, the pastor and Christian education or youth director. Whether or not a planning session is held, it is advisable to consult with all the sources just mentioned in preparation for this retreat.

Questions that should be discussed before this retreat is held, whether such discussion takes place on an informal basis or within a planning session, include:

1. Do our young people have a need to have a stronger relationship with their parents? In other words, is the proposed theme for this retreat relevant?

2. What words or phrases should we use to characterize the ideal, strong relationship between parents and their sons or daughters?

3. What two, three or four guidelines could we suggest to our young people for helping them build a stronger relationship with their parents? Is there any scripture that could be used to give support to these guidelines? What resources could we use to either introduce these guidelines or give credibility to them?

4. What activities might coincide with the retreat theme? What games?

5. Who will take responsibility for securing, organizing and presenting the "content" material for the retreat?

MATERIALS, EQUIPMENT, FACILITIES

The retreat which follows took place at a remote cabin located along

a river in a heavily wooded area. Materials that were taken along on this retreat included pencils, notebook paper, envelopes, love letters which sponsors secretly secured from parents of young people, a movie projector (with extra lamp), a movie screen, a take-up reel (don't forget this), lots of inner tubes for floating down the river, a heavy duty rope for tug of war, life jackets and plenty of food. Each young person attending the retreat was asked to bring one can of soup for "The Great Soup Phenomena" that was held Saturday noon. (Mix all soups together—tastes great!) They also brought something for a snack that they could share with the whole group (cookies, brownies, potato chips).

The films which were secured for this retreat came from TRAVARCA (Reformed Church in America, P.O. Box 247, Grandville, MI 49418). They are as follows: "Walk in Their Shoes," "Walls We Build," and "Walls and Windows."

Additional equipment and materials may be needed depending on what games and other activities are planned for this retreat.

POSSIBLE SCHEDULE

FRIDAY

2 p.m.	Leave church
3 p.m.	Arrive at retreat site
3-4 p.m.	Settle in, unpack, explore the area
4-5 p.m.	Icebreaker games (led by sponsors)
5-6 p.m.	Hot dog roast over campfire
6-7 p.m.	Film: "Walk in Their Shoes"
7-8:30 p.m.	Games (led by the retreat director)
8:30-9:30 p.m.	Quiet time, campfire discussion (led by the retreat director)
9:30 p.m.	Goodies by the campfire

SATURDAY

7:30 a.m.	Roll out of the sack
8-9 a.m.	Breakfast
9-10 a.m.	Film: "Walls We Build," quiet time, discussion
10-11 a.m.	Games (led by sponsors)
11-Noon	Free time
Noon	Lunch
1-5:30 p.m.	Tube down the river, tug-of-war, swimming

continued

293

POSSIBLE SCHEDULE, continued

5:30-6:30 p.m.	Dinner
6:30-8:30 p.m.	Capture the flag (led by youth group leaders)
8:30 p.m.	Quiet time, group discussion by campfire
9:30 p.m.	Toasted marshmallows by the campfire
10 p.m.	"Ask Your Pastor Anything Time"

SUNDAY

7:30 a.m.	Roll out of the sack
8 a.m.	Breakfast
8:30-9:45 a.m.	Clean up and pack up for home
9:45 a.m.	Worship—Film: "Walls and Windows"
10:15-10:45 a.m.	Writing a love letter
10:45 a.m.	Sharing and praying
11:15 a.m.	Leave for home
12:15 p.m.	Arrive at church

THE RETREAT

FRIDAY EVENING

1. You can find a number of ice breaker games in **Fun 'N Games** (Rice, Rydberg and Yaconelli), **Games and Parties for All Occasions** (James W. Kemmerer and Eva May Brickett) or **The New Pleasure Chest** (Helen and Larry Eisenberg).

2. Before showing the film "Walk in Their Shoes," introduce the theme as helping youth to discover specific ways to develop better and stronger relationships with their parents. As the first handout sheet for their retreat notebooks are handed out by the sponsors, the retreat director gives instructions for the young people to fill out the questions before them as they view the film.

3. The first handout sheet has the following instructions and questions:

a. Look for and write down three things that Stan and Shirley cannot understand about their parents.

b. What happens as a result in their home? in their relationships with Mom and Dad?

c. What helps Stan and Shirley to realize adult responsibility?

4. As answers to the questions are shared, try to relate to the young people that one way to have a stronger relationship with parents is to seek to understand them.

5. Before the young people begin their 25- to 30-minute quiet time, give your young people a second handout for their retreat notebook, instruct them to find a place where they will be by themselves, and inform them to come back to the campfire for discussion time after 30 minutes.

6. The second handout sheet has the following instructions and questions:

a. Pray for your parents right now.
   Thank God for them.
   If you can think of needs or problems they are facing right

now, pray to God on their behalf.

b. Pray for God's help as you study the Bible.

c. **1 Timothy 4:12**—"Don't let anyone think little of you because you are young. Be their ideal; let them follow the way you teach and live; be a *pattern* for them in your *love*, your *faith* and your clean thoughts."

1 John 3:18—"Little children, let us stop just saying we love people; let us *really* love them, and show it by our actions."

d. Questions for discussion:

● If we are to influence our parents, we must seek to understand them. This is one specific way we can show we love them. What pressures have your dad and mom experienced lately?

DAD
Is he facing problems at work?
Does he feel fulfilled in life?
Does he ever feel lonely?
Does he ever feel bored?
Has anyone hurt him deeply lately?
Are he and Mom getting along?
Does he feel good about his body?

MOM
Does she feel like her family appreciates her?
Is she under financial pressure?
Is it hard for her to work and be a mother at the same time?
Does she feel as though she is not needed?
Is she facing any changes in her life right now?
Has anyone hurt her deeply lately?
Is Dad giving her enough attention?

Do you think any of these pressures could affect their relationship with you? Why?

● Your parents need you. Think about the quote below and then write down how you would respond to the question:

"Your parents could be in great emotional pain at times and you may not even be aware of it. When they face deep emotional pressures, the last thing they need is to be hassled by you. They need your understanding and they need you. How does this make you feel?"

● What your dad needs from you is to know that you respect and value his counsel and advice. This shows him that you love him. Write down some questions you could ask your dad which could help him to share some of his opinions and thoughts concerning:

School

Friends

Future (work)

Selecting a marriage partner

Involvement in the church

● What your mother needs from you is respect and attention. Write down how you could compliment and thank her for:

Cooking meals

Washing your clothes

Keeping the house clean

Her appearance

● Paul, in 1 Timothy 4:12, writes that we should be a pattern for those older than ourselves in our faith. How can we be a pattern for our parents in our faith?

● How will seeking to understand our parents help us in raising good parents?

During the discussion time which follows quiet time, emphasize, at the appropriate moment, that youth can be a model and example to their parents by showing respect to their fathers and mothers. Spend considerable time listening to their responses.

SATURDAY

1. Before showing the film "Walls We Build," distribute the third handout for the retreat notebooks. That handout contains the following two questions:

a. As you watch this film write down what invisible walls exist between the parents and teenagers in the family visited.

b. What suggestions does the pastor in the film make to help members of that family break down those invisible walls?

2. Immediately following the film, distribute the fourth handout for the notebooks. This is another quiet time. Have the young people find a place by themselves for 25 minutes and follow instructions of quiet time given in the handout. The fourth handout sheet has the following instructions and questions:

a. Pray for your parents right now and that God will use this retreat to bring you and them into a closer, more loving relationship with each other.

b. Pray for your sponsors and retreat director as they lead this retreat.

c. Read the following verses of scripture:

Matthew 5:9—"Happy are those who strive for peace . . . they shall be called the sons of God."

Ephesians 2:14—"For Christ is our peace, who has made us both one, and has broken down the dividing wall of hostility."

d. In the film "Walls We Build," Cynthia makes the statement "What good is a family when it's a family of strangers?" What things lead to you feeling like a stranger in your own home? What can you do about it?

e. Christ wants us to follow his example (Ephesians 2:14) and be peacemakers in our homes. How can you be a peacemaker?

● Be aware of your parents' needs instead of looking for their faults and seeking to overemphasize how "awful" they are.

Read Matthew 7:3-5.

Read Philippians 2:3-4.

Your parents are (check one or more of the following):

☐ too strict?

☐ too overprotective?

☐ too old-fashioned?

☐ not understanding?

☐ set in their ways?

☐ unrealistic?

☐ insensitive to your needs?

☐ too busy?

☐ too nosy?

● Be willing and ready to forgive your parents.

Read Matthew 6:14-15, Ephesians 4:32, and 1 Corinthians 13:5. "Love does not take into account a wrong suffered."

Do you remember the last time your parents wronged you? What was your reaction?

What are your feelings about that incident right now? From the Bible passages above, how does God desire us to handle being wronged?

● Be willing to face injustices. There have been or there may be times when your parents will make accusations and decisions about you which are absolutely wrong. The real test of being a peacemaker is how we respond to the injustices others may inflict upon us.

Read 1 Peter 2:18-20. According to verse 18, are we to be respectful to only those authority figures who are good and loving? How does this make you feel?

According to verse 20, what attitude should we have when we have been wronged?

According to verse 20, what is God's response to our patience as we face injustice?

How will seeking to be a peacemaker help us in raising good parents?

3. After 25-30 minutes, bring the young people together in the same small discussion groups they were members of Friday night. Sponsors lead the discussion on the film and quiet time questions seeking to emphasize that still another way for students to have better and stronger relationships with their parents is to be aware of the invisible walls that often separate them from their parents, why these walls become built, and what they can do (e.g., forgive their parents and be willing to face injustices if need be to remove those walls).

4. Having lots of fun is important to any successful retreat, so the entire afternoon is devoted to having fun together.

5. Capture the flag is a game that provides lots of excitement especially in the dark.

6. Before distributing the fifth handout for the retreat notebooks, inform the young people that they will have 25-30 minutes by themselves for this quiet time.

7. The fifth handout sheet has the following instructions and questions:

a. Pray for your parents right now; ask God to guide you in this time alone with him.

b. Read Ephesians 6:1-3.

● According to verse 1, why should we obey our parents?

● According to verse 3, what are the benefits of obeying our parents?

c. Important to remember: God has given your parents certain abilities that will help us grow up and be the Christians God wants us to be. Some examples:

● They can see events, people and circumstances that will do us great harm. We may not believe it, but our parents have already experienced many of the situations we are now experiencing or will experience. They have made mistakes and learned lessons we can learn from, if only we give attention to their advice. They have insights concerning: jobs, friends, finances, dating, education, _____. See Proverbs 12:15. What does this say about following the advice of our parents?

● Parents can also see our strengths and weaknesses, especially attitudes which could hurt us unless we change. (Example: laziness, ungratefulness, temper, pride, rudeness, selfishness, sloppiness, or an unforgiving spirit.)

See Proverbs 3:11-12 and 15:31-32. How are we to respond to our parents' criticism and discipline? Are we to understand our parents' discipline as coming from God?

d. Questions for thinking: Have you ever used your friend as your parent? How would you do so?

e. Is there ever a time you should disobey your parents? (See Acts 5:28-29.) Does this give you any insight? Could you give examples of the principle stated by Peter?

f. How does obeying my parents reveal my commitment to Jesus Christ?

g. Now for the tough question: What does learning to obey my parents have to do with raising my parents?

8. After 25-30 minutes, have the young people gather in the same small groups they were members of before and have sponsors lead discussion by going through the questions asked. Throughout this discussion stress that still another way young people can have better and stronger relationships with their parents is to obey them.

9. One of the most meaningful features a retreat can have, no matter what the theme or purpose, is to provide an opportunity for the young people to ask their pastor anything they want. One way to facilitate this time is to have a fish bowl with paper and pencil so that a question can be asked anonymously. Make the fish bowl available Friday evening and inform the young people of its purpose. Be sure to emphasize that they can ask questions on any subject they desire. Of course, this requires having a pastor or retreat director who is willing to be vulnerable before young people of his church.

SUNDAY

1. Before the film "Walls and Windows" is shown as part of the worship service, the retreat director and/or sponsors should lead the youth group in a time of singing and prayer. Then, as sponsors distribute the sixth handout for their retreat notebooks, the retreat director introduces the fourth specific way they can have better and stronger relationships with their parents; i.e., communicate with them. The film, the retreat director goes on to say, speaks about communication. As the film is viewed, write down the answers that are given to the questions on the sixth handout.

a. Why do some people just talk and others really communicate?

b. What does listening have to do with talking?

c. Is communication possible between people who disagree?

d. It should be easy to talk to your parents. What makes it so hard?

2. Following the film, discuss the questions that have been shared, being sure to emphasize that communication involves listening. (Perhaps a listening-skills test could be given to see how well they listen.)

3. There are many ways to communicate with parents: by our actions, by talking with them, even by writing letters. After pointing this out to the young people, give the seventh handout for the retreat note-books. This handout instructs the young people to write a love letter to their parents. They are given paper, pencil and an envelope.

4. After 20 minutes have passed and they return to the prearranged meeting place, explain that the "mailman" delivered letters for them from their parents. Distribute the love letters to the young people which had been written earlier by their parents. Have them read their parents' letters and add a P.S. to their parents responding to what their parents had told them.

5. Before leaving the retreat site, spend time sharing and praying together about how God spoke to us at this retreat. Encourage each young person not only to give the letter to his or her parents but to communicate with them about the content of the letters.

6. Other things you can do: The eighth handout can be given to the young people to read on the way home. This handout has the following information:

a. Avoid raising your voice with your parents at any time—one sure way to start a real argument with misunderstandings and hurt feelings is to raise your voice during a discussion. See Proverbs 15:1.

b. Let God change your parents' minds: that's his job, not yours. It is often difficult when your parents refuse to give you permission to do something you really want to do. Take their answer as coming from God himself and go to him in prayer about the situation. As you know, God is very powerful and he can work to change your parents' minds anytime he wills it.

c. Astound your parents with the over-obeying method. It will help your parents know that you are maturing and can handle responsibilities on your own. The next time Dad asks you to wash the car, mow the lawn as well. Or, the next time Mom asks you to do the dishes, maybe clean up the living room as well. Not only will this blow your parents' minds, but, after a few attempts at this method (done sincerely by you, not as a way to manipulate your parents), you will begin to see it pay off!

d. Encourage your parents. Sometimes parents become confused and hesitant, too.

e. Set a good example for your parents by staying away from alcohol, cigarettes and drugs. Parents tend to copy the languages, styles and tastes of the young—it is the only reasonable substitute for finding the fountain of youth—so the example you set is very important.

continued

f. Be concerned about the outside activities of your parents. Insist that they bring their friends home so you can meet them. Be sure they get to bed at a reasonable hour, especially on weeknights. Wouldn't want them to burn themselves out, would you?

g. Carefully watch their activities in the home. The effects of television on adults is not the greatest these days. Daytime soap operas are much too strong for the average mother, and fathers may not be able to take all the violence and sex on nighttime shows, especially after a hard day's work.

h. Don't be too strict with your parents. Allow them to have some access to the telephone, the stereo or the car. Otherwise, they might get jealous and take it out on you.

i. Let them have their way sometimes, especially with the little things. If you show you are willing to give in some of the time, they are more likely to cooperate when it is some big deal you've got to have.

j. At least once each week, do something nice for your parents. The key is to do something before being asked. You will be surprised at the results!

k. Never, never, never do anything to betray their trust in you or make them question your honesty. When your parents lose faith in you and it is your fault, you have lost a whole bunch.

l. Love them as if you are loving Christ—your home will never be the same!

RETREAT FOLLOW-UP

At one of the first youth group meetings held in the fall, ask for "feedback" on the retreat. How many shared their letters with their parents? (Everyone in our group did.) What happened when your parents read the letters? Would you say your relationship with your parents is better and stronger than it was before the retreat? (Many felt it was.) What have you done to make the relationship stronger? (Many mentioned the ways presented at the retreat.)

Many parents have commented both to the sponsors and the pastor that they have noticed some positive differences in behavior in their sons and daughters since the retreat. All those who were involved in the planning and experience of the retreat believe it was the best one yet; one that's going to be hard to beat next year.

RETREAT OUTLINE 22:
"A Traveling

By Bruce Nichols

This retreat-on-wheels is a great change of pace for your group.

The theme for our four-day traveling retreat was "Getting to know you, God and the country around us better." Our goal was to build group unity and develop deeper relationships with God. Our retreat involved 17 people who traveled 1200 miles in four days using three cars.

The idea for this traveling retreat hatched during one of our youth group meetings when the kids had been reflecting on childhood vacations and family trips they had taken.

As plans for a traveling retreat began to develop, we learned that many in the group had already seen the areas we were considering traveling to. But they were excited about visiting these places again with their teenage friends.

PREPARATIONS

To generate interest we advertised the retreat in our church newsletter, talked about it at our regular youth meetings and placed a sign-up sheet on the bulletin board in our Christian education department.

We realized that not everyone would be interested in attending this kind of retreat. The youth and adults involved in the retreat would need to be willing to share themselves deeply with each other and with God. Our final roster of those planning to attend the retreat consisted of 12 youth, four adults willing to go along as sponsors, and one baby (the youth director's child).

We held a planning meeting for those who had decided to join our safari. At the meeting we formed three task forces to work out the details for the trip: transportation, program and food/equipment. We made certain that everyone attending the retreat (except the baby) was involved in the planning.

Transportation Task Force

The transportation task force found three people who were willing to furnish the cars for the trip and planned the itinerary. You may choose to use a bus or van if you have one available.

We chose to leave on a Thursday morning and return on Sunday afternoon. Since we were from Colorado, we decided to travel around our own state. For your retreat you could choose places of scenic or

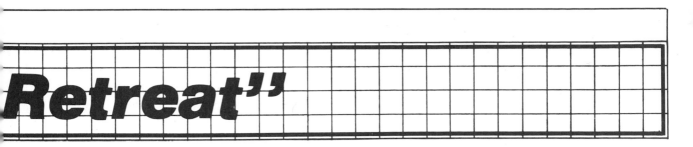

historic interest with a suitable camping or other lodging facility at hand every night. Logical locations to visit include state parks, national monuments, historic sites, the seashore, lakes, etc. Our schedule called for traveling approximately 300 miles each day—sometimes more, sometimes less—depending on where we were planning to spend the night.

Your travel task force should decide in advance what you want to see and do, the best routes to travel and where the group will spend each night. They should also check into admission fees and the necessity of reservations.

Program Task Force

The program task force planned our formal campsite activities and suggested "riding" activities.

Scripture passages they chose for us to study and discuss during the trip were: Matthew 6:19-24—"True Treasures," Romans 12:1-21—"Life and Love," Romans 13:8-14—"Authority," and 2 Timothy 2 and 3—"Faith."

A list of possible riding activities included discussing our scripture subjects, listening to good music or taped messages, playing counting games, guessing games (e.g. "Animal, Vegetable or Mineral"), singing songs, making signs with "good" messages to share with passing cars, writing in our journals (record thoughts, feelings, anything), praying, trying to be quiet for 25 (or whatever) miles, trying *not* to be quiet for 25 (or whatever) miles, and when all else failed, sleeping.

Some things to be aware of while traveling in cars are: be patient and respect others' needs; be alert for and accommodate car sickness and the need for rest stops; change seats and cars occasionally to relieve boredom and to give everyone a chance to become better acquainted with everyone else during the trip.

Food and Equipment Task Force

The food and equipment task force planned the menu for the trip and decided on the equipment that should and could be taken along. To hold the cost of the trip to a minimum, we camped out each night. A more affluent or resourceful group might choose other accommodations

303

if they wish—motels, churches, college dorms, etc. Since space was at a premium "traveling light" was important and each attendee was given a list of what he could bring along.

Our "community" equipment list consisted of four lightweight four-person tents, three camp stoves, three camp lanterns, three food coolers, three water jugs, one first-aid kit and cooking equipment (pans, etc.).

Each person was responsible for bringing a compact sleeping bag and one small suitcase or knapsack for personal items. Suggested personal items are casual clothes, raincoat or poncho, flashlight, Bible, small notebook, pen or pencil, towel, swimsuit (if appropriate), toilet items, jacket or sweater, plate, knife, fork, spoon, cup and extra cash for snacks. No hair dryers, makeup cases or radios were allowed.

Recreation equipment included a couple of Frisbees, a ball and compact games such as Uno. Make sure at least one person brings along a camera to record your great adventure for posterity and to use for publicizing future youth events.

The criteria for planning our meals was not "gourmet" but convenience. We planned to prepare the three breakfasts and three suppers ourselves and for lunch "dine" at fast-food restaurants to save time and avoid the bother of preparing that meal. To save space, we bought food during the trip for the meals we would be preparing ourselves. Camp meals were simple and consisted of such things as pancakes, eggs or cold cereal for the breakfasts and hot dogs, hamburgers, chili, etc. for the suppers.

POSSIBLE SCHEDULE

THURSDAY
Meet at church
Prayer circle of retreatants and parents before departing
Travel (stops for sightseeing and lunch)
Make camp at Great Sand Dunes National Monument*
Explore area
Supper (prepare, eat, clean up)*
Attend lecture by park rangers
Devotions
Collapse into bed

FRIDAY
Rise and shine

Quiet time for personal devotions
Breakfast (prepare, eat, clean up)*
Share from what we wrote in our journals on Thursday
Travel (stops for sightseeing and lunch)
Make camp at Mesa Verde National Monument*
Explore area
Supper (prepare, eat, clean up)*
Devotions (we had a foot-washing ceremony to demonstrate servanthood; singing; sharing and prayer)
Bedtime

continued

SCHEDULE, continued

SATURDAY

Rise and shine
Quiet time for personal devotions
Breakfast (prepare, eat, clean up)*
Travel (stops for sightseeing and lunch)
Make camp at Black Canyon of the Gunnison*
Explore area
Supper (pizza and pop; in our exploration we discovered a pizza place and no one felt like cooking)
Devotions (communion service, serving each other the bread and wine)
Bedtime

SUNDAY

Rise and shine
Quiet time for personal devotions
Breakfast (prepare, eat, clean up)*
Worship service (simple: read Luke 22:7-20, sing, share experiences and feelings from the trip, prayer)
Travel (stops for sightseeing and lunch)
Arrive home (greet long-lost friends and parents, lots of hugs)
Closing prayer

*Make sure everyone shares the chores so the same people don't get stuck with them every day.

EXPENSES

The cost of this kind of retreat will vary, of course, depending on such things as how far you travel, the kind of vehicles used, and how well you dine. Our trip (we split the expenses equally) cost about $20 per person.

RETREAT OUTLINE 23:

"Growing

By Doug Karl

A one-night retreat designed for a hotel.

PREPARATION

Begin preparation for the retreat five months in advance. Inform your young people that you are having a retreat but do not say where it is being held until one month before (to increase their anticipation of the event).

Inform your youth council of the intended retreat and ask them to provide any helpful input.

MATERIALS, EQUIPMENT, FACILITIES

Choose a site different from most retreat settings. We held our retreat at the Sheraton-Royal Hotel in Kansas City, Mo. God is just as able to speak at a hotel as he is in a rustic outdoor setting. Hotel facilities are perfect for a retreat in the middle of January: indoor pool, jacuzzi, health club, sauna, electronic game room, banquet and meeting room facilities.

Take the fullest advantage of the hotel's check-in and check-out times. Begin your retreat at noon on Friday and conclude at noon on Saturday. Select a Friday on which the kids are out of school to begin the retreat.

You may be able to exchange eating meals in the hotel for free use of the meeting rooms. (Sometimes this can be a substantial savings.) We had two meals—dinner and breakfast—served banquet-style at the hotel. This was the first time that some of the kids had ever been served by a tuxedo-dressed waiter or had a choice of three forks and two spoons to use.

Check out films and projector through your local library loan system. These may be films intended solely for entertainment.

Choose games and skits from various youth activity books. Role plays are always accepted with great enthusiasm.

We asked the special speaker for our retreat to speak on the following subjects: "How to Survive With Your Parents" and "Freedom

Through Love"

Through Christ." He related these topics to the retreat theme "Growing Through Love." It is sometimes good for the youth to hear someone besides the youth director.

Advertise your retreat in the monthly high school newsletter, church bulletin and announcements during Sunday school and Bible studies.

POSSIBLE SCHEDULE

FRIDAY

Noon—Leave church

12:45 p.m.—Arrive at hotel

1:15 p.m.—Group meeting

Allow time for check-in and processing. This is especially important if the hotel does not have all of your rooms ready when you arrive. The group meeting is a time to orient everyone to the hotel and communicate important information.

1:30 p.m.—Do it your way

During this time the kids can take advantage of the hotel facilities.

3:30 p.m.—"How to Survive With Your Parents"

Begin by singing some favorite gospel choruses, then have prayer and listen to your speaker. The speaker may begin with a crowd-breaker and a get-acquainted game. Our speaker began his talk by relating a personal experience which involved his parents' reaction to the following situation:

> *Your mother and father are missionaries to Africa. They are forced to come back to the United States after many years of service because your father develops a sudden illness. Within three months after their return your father dies. You are unable to attend the funeral because your are on tour with a professional singing group.*
>
> *A few weeks later your singing group is in your home town. You want to have everyone go to your house, have Mom wash clothes, fix meals, etc.*
>
> *Your mother says, "You can come, but I don't want your friends here." So you say, "If you don't want my friends, you don't want me!"*

Have different areas of the room sectioned off. Read the following questions and have the kids go to the place designated for how they feel toward a particular question.

What should the son have done?

a. Apologized to his mom but not gone home.

b. Taken his friends home anyway.

c. Apologized to his mom and gone home by himself.

d. Not gone home at all.

For example: If you feel he should have done "c" go to the back left corner of the room.

Speaker ideas: Use the word *P-A-R-E-N-T-S* in your talk. Take each letter and talk about what parents go through, why they do what they do, what their needs are, etc. Use your imagination to come up with your own set of words.

For example:

P—Patience

A—Allegiance

R—Responsibility

E—Enduring

N—Neat

T—Training

S—Spiritual leaders

5 p.m.—Group games

"Cut the Cake"—Pack flour into a big bowl and turn it upside down on a TV tray or baking sheet. It is a mold now; put a cherry on top. Everyone in a circle around the cake must cut off some part (large or small) of the cake and then the knife is passed around the circle. The more the cake is cut, the closer you get to the cherry in the center. Whoever cuts the cake, causing the cherry to "fall" has to pick it up with his teeth (with hands behind his back,) and eat the cherry.

"Moo Test"—This can be found in **More . . . Try This One** by Group Books.

"Light a Match"—This is good for getting to know people better. Each person lights a match and tells as much about himself as he can before the match burns down. The person who tells the most is the winner.

5:30 p.m.—Preparation for dinner

It is important to give the kids enough time between activities. If you do not, you'll always be frustrated because they are not on time.

6 p.m.—Dinner

Be sure to select something that the majority of your young people will like.

7:30 p.m.—After-Dinner Players (see following)

Select six kids to present the following sketch after dinner before the evening session.

It is fun to bill the "After-Dinner Players" as a special group, which they are.

"THE HISTORY CLASS"

SCENE: The classroom of a high school American History class.

CHARACTERS:

● Mr. Reed—A history teacher who is well-liked by most of his students. He is friendly but firm with the students.

● Clarence—A nice kid, but one who has unfortunately been labeled as the high school wimp. Because of the constant abuse, he is very insecure, walks slightly hunch-shouldered, with his head down. Don't overplay this character. Mold him after someone like him you might know in your high school.

● Danny, Patsy, Chip and Cathi—Should be portrayed as relatively normal high school students, with Chip and Danny being the main antagonists.

STAGING: Five chairs (or desks) should be placed onstage. (See diagram.)

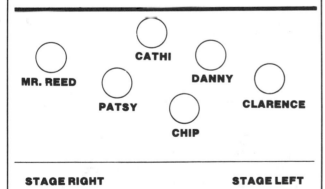

MR. REED
CATHI
PATSY
DANNY
CHIP
CLARENCE

STAGE RIGHT   **STAGE LEFT**

As lights come up, Danny and Patsy enter and are seated in appropriate seats.

PROPS: A stack of books, horn-rimmed glasses and a cardigan sweater for Clarence.

LIGHTING: Normal full stage lighting.

SPOTLIGHT FADES UP. DANNY AND PATSY ENTER CLASSROOM.

DANNY: Hey, wow, ol' Mr. Reed, our American history teacher ain't here yet.

PATSY: Yeah, you know, he's one of the few teachers I *like.*

DANNY: Yeah, me, too.

CHIP ENTERS.

CHIP: Hey, guys.

DANNY: Hey, Chip! *[GIVES HIM FIVE.]*

PATSY: Hey, aren't we discussing the movie "Roots" today?

CHIP: Yeah, Reed said the TV show was required viewing. I thought the reruns last week were pretty good.

CATHI ENTERS.

CATHI: Hi.

CHIP, DANNY and PATSY: Hi, Cathi.

CATHI: Did ya hear the latest? Some biology student left a partially dissected frog over on the heater.

CHIP and DANNY: Oh, gross.

PATSY: Cathi, please. I cry just hearing the names Bambi and Thumper, so just cool it.

CATHI: He kept hoppin' off the radiator and they kept puttin' him back up.

CHIP: Up? I'll tell ya what's comin' up . . . that linguini we had at lunch.

CATHI: They finally hit 'im on the head with a textbook . . .

WITH HAND OVER MOUTH AS IF GETTING SICK, CHIP GOES TO DOOR.

CHIP: *[AT DOOR]* Hey, guess who's comin'?

DANNY: Reed?

CHIP: No, good ol' brown nose.

CATHI, PATSY and DANNY: Clarence?

continued

PATSY: Yeah, crater face himself.

CLARENCE ENTERS.

DANNY: Trying to impress somebody with all those books, Clarence?

PATSY: No, all that acne. [LAUGHTER]

CHIP: Well, if you had a face that looked like somebody beat on it with a track shoe, you'd hide behind a stack of books, too.

CATHI: He's probably trying to impress the librarian.

DANNY: *[KNOCKING BOOKS OUT OF CLARENCE'S HAND.]* Ooooo, sorry, wimp.

GENERAL LAUGHTER AS CLARENCE KNEELS TO PICK UP BOOKS.

PATSY: How come you always walk all hunched over like that?

DANNY: He lives in the card catalog.

CATHI: Yeah, he and Dewey Decimal are good friends.

LAUGHTER. CLARENCE STANDS WITH BOOKS.

CHIP: *[LURCHING AT CLARENCE]* Actually he's all hunched over *[GRABBING CLARENCE BY LAPEL]* 'cause he's never sure when someone's gonna punch his lights out . . . Right, Clarence?

DANNY: Go park it somewhere else.

CLARENCE STARTS TO WALK TOWARD BACK OF CLASS.

CATHI: Don't harm Clarence, you might damage his briefcase.

PATSY: Or his violin case.

CHIP: Rumor has it that Clarence is gonna audition for the Lawrence Welk Show.

CATHI: Yeah, one look at them zits and the champagne lady's gonna pop her cork.

MR. REED ENTERS.

REED: All right, class . . . sorry I'm late.

CLASS TAKES SEATS.

REED: Now, today we're discussing the TV program "Roots" in the light of our recent studies of the Civil War period. How many of you saw the program? *[GENERAL AGREEMENT.]* Good, good, now what were some of the things we learned? *[HANDS IN AIR.]* Cathi?

CATHI: Well, for me it was hard to under-

stand how man can treat his fellow man so inhumanely.

HANDS.

REED: Chip?

DANNY: Yeah, they never broke him completely, but for the black man to have to fight for over one hundred years for freedom in a country that claims to be free, that's the real bummer.

GENERAL AGREEMENT.

CHIP: Yeah, ' cause when you come right down to it, none of us is any greater than anyone else. We're *all* equal.

THERE IS A PAUSE IN THE CONVERSATION. MR. REED APPROACHES THE CLASS, PUZZLED BY CLARENCE'S SILENCE.

REED: Clarence, you're kind of quiet today. Did you happen to see "Roots" last night?

CLARENCE: My . . . my parents weren't interested in watching it.

DANNY: *[SNICKERING]* Your parents prejudiced or something?

GENERAL SNICKERS.

CLARENCE: I . . . I think they're trying hard not to be. I mean, most of your parents aren't real supporters of blacks or minorities, either.

CATHI: Well, at least our parents let us watch "Roots."

CLARENCE: I watched it . . . I . . . I watched it alone, but I watched it.

CHIP: If he were my kid, I'd make him watch it alone, too.

GENERAL LAUGHTER.

REED: *[CALM BUT FIRM]* All right, class, cool it down.

CLARENCE: I . . . I was really touched by it.

GENERAL "OOOOO'S"

DANNY: Oh, Clarence, you're touched, period.

REED: And what did you learn from the program, Clarence?

CHIP: This oughta be a good one.

CLARENCE: I . . . I don't have any black friends.

DANNY: Or white ones.

CLARENCE: So, for me it's . . . it's difficult to learn everything there is to know about black people. "Roots" was a start, but it's still hard to come to grips with their despair and hope, victories and defeats by simply watching TV . . .

CATHI: Ooo, he's getting deep.

CLARENCE: I . . . I think it taught me to have compassion and to try harder.

PATSY: He could try all he wanted, but he'd never be my friend.

CLARENCE: And most of all, not to give up on myself or others.

CHIP: Talk about brownie points.

REED: Class, I'm wondering what you thought of this assignment.

GENERAL AGREEMENT BY CLASS.

CHIP: Great!

CATHI: The easiest history lesson ever.

DANNY: A cinch, let's have more.

REED: *[WITH SAD AWARENESS ON HIS FACE]* Good . . . Well, we've got that assembly today, so I'm letting you go early. You're dis-missed. *[THEY LEAVE. CHIP TURNS BACK.]*

CHIP: And, hey, wimp, do the school a favor and stay away from the student lounge. *[EXITS.]*

THERE IS A MOMENT OF SILENCE.

CLARENCE: *[TO REED]* They . . . they pick on me all the time but . . . I'm . . . I'm used to it.

REED: Are you?

CLARENCE: They don't mean any harm.

REED: Maybe, but does it make it any less painful? Look, I'm a history teacher, Clarence. I know real harm when I see it . . . The tragedy is they don't, not even when they see it on television.

CLARENCE: Over 120 million people saw "Roots." Do you think they really learned anything?

REED: *[LONG PAUSE]* I don't know . . . Do you?

LIGHTS FADE TO BLACK.

Reprinted by permission from **Jeremiah People Sketch Book**, Volume 5, ©1981 Continental Ministries. **Sketch Books** are available from Jeremiah People, Box 1996, Thousand Oaks, CA 91360.

After the skit the speaker began his session.

9 p.m.—Entertainment tonight

This time can be used in a variety of ways—skits, games, individual or group talent, or films. The variety is limited only by your imagination.

10:30 p.m.—Pool games

Make arrangements with the hotel manager ahead of time for permission to use the pool area after the normal 10 p.m. closing time. Managers are usually happy to assist you. Do not hesitate to ask for things. Have swimming races and other water events such as building pyramids in the water, chicken fights, water volleyball and water football using the ever-popular Nerf ball.

11:15 p.m.—Devotions

Devotional is taken from 1 Corinthians 13:1-7.

Assign the following questions to some of the kids ahead of time so they will be prepared to answer.

a. Give an example of someone being patient.

b. Give an example of someone being kind.

c. What type of situation would make you envious?

d. Give an example of someone being proud.

e. Give an example of someone being rude.

f. Give an example of someone being self-seeking.

g. Tell of a time when you were angry.

h. Tell of something that you think would be evil.

11:45 p.m.—In rooms

Be sure to give the kids enough time to finish their running around before they are to be in their rooms.

Midnight—Lights out, no leaving rooms!

This is the part of the retreat that is usually the most difficult to enforce. Do not tell the kids they have to be in bed or have the television turned off. They need to have some freedom within the restrictions. But, if they break the limits imposed, you as retreat director have every right to exercise your authority in whatever manner you see fit.

SATURDAY

7:30 a.m.—Wake-up call

It is a good idea to have the front desk give all of your rooms a wake-up call. This may not get the kids out of bed but at least you have alerted them to the fact that something is happening.

8:30 a.m.—Breakfast

9 a.m.—Morning devotions

If possible, have your pastor join you for breakfast and lead the morning devotions. Ask him to use Ephesians 4:15 as the text for his devotional.

9:15 a.m.—Group game

Use the pool area if it is open or get the group involved in some games and skits. Aerobic exercises are helpful in making sure everyone is awake.

9:45 a.m.—Do it your way

One final time to enjoy the hotel facilities.

11:30—Pack up and clean up

Noon—Check out and return to church

ADDITIONAL INFORMATION

When looking for a hotel do not let the big ones with the high rates scare you away. They are usually the ones that are most willing to work with you because they are accustomed to handling groups. For example, the hotel we stayed at had a normal room rate for four-person occupancy of $110 per night. We were able to get rooms with four-person occupancy for $45 per night.

Be sure to make reservations well in advance of your retreat (six to 12 months) because large hotels usually have a number of conventions throughout the year which could conflict with your only available date.

Things to keep in mind when having a retreat at a hotel:

1. Number one rule: Know where your youth are at all times. There are all sorts of people wandering the halls in hotels.

2. Remind your youth that they are in a public place with other people around. Running, yelling and throwing things aren't appropriate actions.

3. If you are in a large hotel complex it might be a good idea to provide your youth with a map of the facilities or take them on a walking tour.

4. In exchange for having your meals provided by the hotel you may be granted free use of the banquet/meeting room facilities. This can sometimes be a very substantial savings.

5. In order to reserve a block of hotel rooms and a meeting space it is best to schedule your retreat six to 12 months in advance.

6. In arranging a hotel retreat, the person to contact in the larger hotels is the sales manager. The director of catering is the person who will assist you in planning meals. He or she will also be in charge of scheduling your meeting room times.

7. Do not hesitate to ask for special arrangements or equipment such as piano, podium, chair setup, sound system, etc.

8. Request convention room rates, since they can be considerably cheaper. Work with your sales manager; he or she is there to assist you.

9. Call one week to three days before your arrival and ask that your rooms be ready when you arrive. If you do not, you may be forced into having everyone in one room to change into swimming suits until the remainder of your rooms are ready. This can be very frustrating and confusing. Be sure to talk to the manager when you call.

RETREAT OUTLINE 2-4:

"A Canoe

By Peggy Frey

A retreat to explore God's wonders in the outdoors.

You don't have to journey into the distant wilds to get the benefits from a canoe retreat. Our group experienced a tremendously successful canoe retreat at a nearby state forest that included a large lake and canoe rentals. We also used the lodge for housing and the trails for hiking.

This retreat helped our group learn to get along better with other group members. It's easy to be a Christian in Sunday school and church each week. But real life consists of living and working together with other people. This weekend gave each of us an opportunity to grow more in this way.

Here are checklists and outlines we used for our canoeing retreat. Use these as a basis in designing your own unique canoeing experience.

RETREAT GOALS

1. To grow closer in our relationship to God and one another
2. To gain a new appreciation of God's creation
3. To challenge young people with exploration and adventure

POSSIBLE SCHEDULE

FRIDAY EVENING

6:30 p.m.	Meet at church, load cars and trucks
8:30 p.m.	Assign sleeping quarters and set up tables and chairs for group dining
9 p.m.	Snacks (pizza and sodas)
9:45 p.m.	Crowdbreakers (See resource list in chapter 19.
10:30 p.m.	Explanation of rules
10:45 p.m.	Devotion (God's creation, the outdoors, our surroundings)
Midnight	Lights out

SATURDAY

5:40 a.m.	Watch sunrise
6:30 a.m.	Morning devotions (five-10 minutes by youth member—assign beforehand)
7:15 a.m.	Breakfast preparations for breakfast at 8 a.m.
8:30 a.m.	Breakfast cleanup; prepare food for lunch
10 a.m.	Canoe trip
Noon	Lunch on return from canoe trip
1 p.m.	Dinner preparations and cleanup
1:30 p.m.	Hike in Cook Forest to "Big

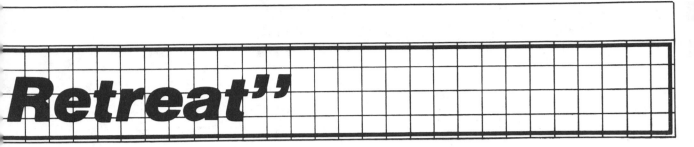

CHECKLISTS

PLANNING AND ORGANIZATION

____Write letters to agency requesting information of lodging, canoeing, etc.

____Write letters to various lodges to secure adequate accommodations for size of group

____Write letters to lodge for date, price and other available accommodations

____Mail deposit to reserve dates

____Telephone canoe livery to reserve canoes for group and let them know the time of the trip

____Send letters with all information (including registration form) to each youth group member and interested adults

____Complete menu for entire weekend

____Plan games, mixers and recreation

____Plan devotions and communion service

____Make lists for work crews for each meal and cleanup details

	Trees'' (group transported in back of pickup truck)
4 p.m.	Games
5:30 p.m.	Dinner and cleanup
6:30 p.m.	Campfire and stories (stories told by adult chaperone)
9:30 p.m.	Singing (indoors from books)
10 p.m.	Devotion: "The Wonder of God's Outdoors"
11 p.m.	Communion (group seated in circle with cross and candles in center; room darkened except for candlelight; bread passed around and piece broken off by each member followed by cup which bread is dipped in)

11:30 p.m.	Closing prayer
Midnight	Lights out
SUNDAY	
8 a.m.	Breakfast and cleanup
9 a.m.	Church service: group singing, solo, talk (led by youth volunteers), closing prayer
10 a.m.	Hike
Noon	Lunch and cleanup; prepare food for evening meal
1 p.m.	Biking and swimming
4:30 p.m.	Cookout at lodge
5:30 p.m.	Cleanup and load vehicles
6 p.m.	Depart

_____Secure adequate number of adult chaperones

_____Secure transportation (chaperones, vehicles and trucks)

_____Give each driver a map and directions

_____Assign youth members to cars for transportation

_____Hold regular weekly youth meeting at nearby lake with someone who owns a canoe to give some instructions

_____Give each youth member a copy of canoeing strategies and safety tips to read and study

_____Give each member opportunity to get in, row, and get out of canoe with help of instructor while on lake

_____Hold pre-retreat meeting with youth members at regular weekly meetings

_____Raise funds to pay for lodging, canoeing and food

THINGS NEEDED TO MAKE CANOE RETREAT EFFECTIVE

_____Woodsy setting in outdoors

_____Lodge large enough to accommodate size of group

_____Food for all meals and snacks

_____Games and all materials necessary for games (indoor games were prepared in case of rain)

_____Songbooks

_____Materials for worship service (we made a four-foot wooden cross with holes drilled in it for candles) to lay on floor for communion service, communion bread, juice, plate for bread and cup

_____Volleyball and net, frisbees

GETTING ALONG WITH THE WILDLIFE

The pesky mosquito abounds along waterways in the spring and can be bothersome enough to be classified as wildlife. Plenty of insect repellent should be carried and tents should be equipped with mosquito netting. Choose a campsite on an island or a point that can receive the benefit of any wind—this will also help discourage mosquitos.

Snakes may also be found around the water but they often disappear as soon as they know you are around. Care should be exercised on wilderness rivers to avoid an unpleasant accident. On rivers that receive a fair amount of canoe traffic, snakes do not seem to be much of a problem.

Complete your first-aid kit with the addition of Snakebite Freeze, which can be purchased at a pharmacy or ordered from Amerex Laboratories, Box 32827, San Antonio, TX 78216. This treatment does not require cutting and has been recommended by several outdoor magazines in the last few years.

Skunks and raccoons do not present a problem as much as an inconvenience. The enduring charms of the skunk come from the rear part, and the tail goes up before any real action begins. Skunks are inquisitive, so do not get excited if one wanders into camp. Let him have his way and he will wander out in his own good time.

Raccoons can open almost anything, so food should be wrapped and tied to a tree limb. Nothing is so surprising after your first night on the river as to find all your jars opened and their contents gone when you wake up for breakfast.

CANOE RETREATS AND SPIRITUAL THINGS

The rustic sounds and natural setting of the lake or river provide a beautiful environment for spiritual growth. In the wilderness of God's creation there will be frequent opportunities for in-depth conversations and the application of biblical principles to lifestyle and behavior.

The early morning hours might begin with a period of reflective meditation and prayer. A vow of silence might be effective during this time period. Some members of the group could keep a journal or diary to share with the group later.

Prior to the trip, Psalm 19:14 could be discussed in order to prepare for the morning quiet time. How do we meditate? What are acceptable meditations?

During each day's events, group members should focus on the conversation and behavior of the group. How are members of the group reacting to each other and to the situations that arise? Are you living out Christian principles, or have you removed Christian beliefs from daily life? Are group members practicing the servant role in their interactions? (See Mark 10:42-45 and John 13:3-15.) Do conversations begin with, "Let me help . . .," or do they start with, "Give me . . .," "Pass me . . .," "Carry my . . .," and "Get me . . ."

If an afternoon discussion period is planned it could focus on similarities between this canoe trip and life. How are stress situations on the trip like difficult times in our spiritual growth? Are there situations that can only be solved as we work together?

For a wide range of creative devotional experiences, different members could be assigned topics to present on the trip: Here are some ideas:

1. Musically talented members could be asked to write a song about the experiences and happenings along the way. This song could be presented the last night of the trip. Using a familiar chorus or tune the entire group could learn and sing "The Ballad of Our River Trip."

2. A River Jordan service could focus on crossing over some of the barriers of growth and life to better things. Spiritual crossing-over should be a central emphasis.

3. Creative river or lake parables could be built: "If Jesus did not have wheat fields, fig trees or mustard seeds, he might have picked up a . . . and said . . ."

4. Prayer exercises could focus on different elements of God's creation—sounds, sights, the wind, people, and so on.

5. Campfire share times give opportunities for group members to tell how they have been growing spiritually on the trip, some of the warm memories they will be taking home, and how their view of and relationship with God has changed as a result of this trip.

On the last day each member might find a meaningful symbol of the trip to take home. This might be a small piece of driftwood, shaped rock, or shell. In a future meeting members bring their symbols of the trip and share with the rest of the group the symbol's meaning. For instance, a rock might symbolize a promise or a covenant.

These symbols will remain meaningful for years to come.

INTERPERSONAL RELATIONSHIPS

In any activity where your group will spend long hours together in fun and work, there are bound to be some periods of tension. A canoe is operated by teamwork and does not float well when the occupants are feuding.

If the tension arises because the partners do not know how to steer the canoe, a little instruction will do a lot to help them restore harmony.

If the source of the tension arises from a personality, here's an opportunity to weld your group together. Campfire discussions and share times give people a chance to express their feelings and bring healing to your group.

DEVOTION: The Wonder of God's Outdoors

Begin by reading Psalm 19 (devotional talk used on Saturday evening).
Think of your surroundings.
Become aware of what's around you.
Become aware of what is going on around you.
Look for God in all of nature.
The world around us is full of mysteries and wonders.
Think about things we come in contact with daily:
   rocks, trees, wind, the solid earth we stand on, the world, sunlight on your back or hair, cool dampness of morning, raindrops, etc.
Contact . . . contact . . . .
Who are we?
What are we?
What is man that thou are mindful of him? (Psalm 8:4)
The Bible says, "The Lord God of Gods, He knows."
Did you know:
1. ● Every year a tree creates from scratch 99% of its living parts?
   ● A tree can lift or pump water up its trunk 150 feet an hour?
   ● A tree heaves a ton of water every day in full summer?
   ● A big elm in a single season can make as many as six million leaves, wholly, intricately, without budging an inch?
   ● There is a tree called Methuselah in California that is 4600 years old? Methuselah, a pine tree, has already been growing 16 centuries and was alive when King David wrote the Psalms.
2. For hundreds of years, man sailed the oceans, trying to find a way to reach a certain pinpoint of land. Yet, for thousands of years, birds have traveled from Arctic to Antarctic lands, landing at the same nesting sites year after year.
3. Man in an age of technology believes he's accomplished great engineering feats. Yet, small spiders are high-caliber engineers. Their webs hold many times their own weight. Spiders can lift

loads by dropping strands of moist web from an overhead limb to the object below by wetting it, letting it dry, shrinking as it dries and thus lifting an object.

4. There are millions of tons of water shifting around on this earth every day. The Bible says (Ecclesiastes 7) that all the rivers flow into the sea, yet the sea is not full. God has set its boundaries and it goes no further.

5. In the top inch of forest soil, an average of 1,356 living creatures are present in each square inch of soil.

Today, we were on the river. We can learn a lot from the river. For instance, a river:

- keeps its course
- lets nothing obstruct its pace
- is directed by God in its natural channel to the sea.

We, too, can be directed by God if we strive to be obedient and do what he wants us to. Mankind was born with a desire to be directed by a higher power.

Sometimes flooding occurs and rivers overflow their channels and become wild and unruly, eroding the earth and destroying whatever is in their pathway. Apart from God, our lives are unruly and headed for certain destruction.

A river spread too thin becomes a swamp that's still, stagnant and chokes out life around it. Our life becomes stagnant and dead without God.

Man can harness the river for useful purposes (sawmills, electrical power plants, gristmills). God can make us powerful vessels for his service if we give our life to him.

Rocks, ledges, trees, etc. cause the river to roll and swirl as it splashes over and around the obstacles it encounters. But the river remains intent on its goal of speeding toward the ocean. Trials, problems and testing experiences come into our lives, but as the river is intent on reaching its goal, so should we be intent on going on for God.

You might say, a river was born with the goal of reaching the ocean, but what about our goals? Do we have any? If so, what are they? Riches, popularity, power, prestige . . . were we too not born with a goal and purpose, to honor and glorify God by our very lives we live every day?

God wants to make that kind of life for us—if we'll let him. Man's original home in the garden of Eden was by a river. Man's eternal home in heaven will be beside a river.

I pray this night, young people, that you'll choose the life God has for you. If you've never met Jesus in a real and personal way, why not do it tonight? It can be the beginning of the greatest life you can have.

Wait a few minutes for their response, then proceed with instructions for communion and communion service. I allow flexibility in any service. If the kids aren't ready to listen and respond, you can always shift devotional times to another time.

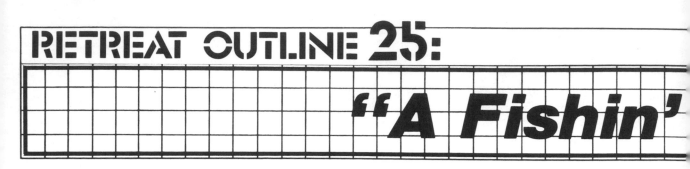

RETREAT OUTLINE 25:

"A Fishin'

By James Rhiver

Catch the fuller meaning of John 21 with this special interest retreat.

"A fishing retreat? What's that?" This question was asked many times as the publicity went out on this unique event in our group's schedule of activities.

Retreats have always been popular vehicles for Bible study in our group. And many of our members love to fish, so we planned a weekend combining fishing and Bible study.

Our fishing retreat was a big success—complete with campfire experiences, night fishing and fishing contests.

PLANNING THE RETREAT

Choosing the Bible study for the weekend was simple. In John 21, Jesus teaches some good lessons using fishing as a setting.

Here are some guidelines for planning a fishing retreat:

1. Find a location that provides some accommodations. We found a member who owned a clubhouse with running water, electricity, stove, etc. (Tents, etc., add adventure, but also more responsibility and planning.)

2. Check the necessity of having boats for fishing. (Be sure to check boating rules in the area.)

3. Be sure those "of age" have proper fishing permits.

4. Establish a "contract" with all participants: "We will have some Bible study time and much time to fish. If you don't like to fish, don't sign up!" (This latter statement is essential since many fishing areas offer little else to do.)

5. Limit the number of participants. We limited our group to ten, plus counselors. If you are fishing in a public area, most fishermen do not enjoy large groups around.

6. Make the cost minimal. With subsidy from the youth budget, we kept it to $5 per person. Your cost will be determined by distance, facilities, meals, etc. Bait is costly in some areas and is best supplied by the youth themselves.

7. Such a retreat requires that the leaders (or one of them) love to fish. (Sometimes only a fisherman understands the needs of other fishermen!)

Retreat"

8. Since a fisherman's cabin is not a room in the church, it may be better to make copies of the text rather than bring Bibles.

9. In our case, we had a communion service on Saturday evening. This is very meaningful to the community formed because it unites them in the body of Christ and offers a real chance for forgiveness that may be necessary when late hours and little sleep increase the level of irritation.

10. Prayer is essential. Anything with God's blessing is successful.

POSSIBLE SCHEDULE

FRIDAY

6 p.m.	Leave church
7:30 p.m.	Set up for weekend
8 p.m.	Evening fishin'
10 p.m.	Bible study, John 21:1-3
10:45 p.m.	Vespers
11 p.m.	Snacks, sleep, night fishin'

SATURDAY

5 a.m.	Breakfast
6 a.m.	Fishin'
9 a.m.	Doughnuts and Bible study, John 21:4-8
9:45 a.m.	Back to fishin'
Noon	Lunch
1 p.m.	Fishin'
5 p.m.	Supper and Bible study, John 21:9-14
6 p.m.	Fishin'
10 p.m.	Vespers with communion
11 p.m.	Sleep

SUNDAY

5 a.m.	Breakfast
6 a.m.	Fishin'
9 a.m.	Doughnuts and Bible study, John 21:15-19
10 a.m.	Fishin'
Noon	Lunch
1 p.m.	Cleanup
2 p.m.	Closing Bible study, John 21:20-25
3 p.m.	Leave for home

(Be flexible; biting fish do not read schedules.)

BIBLE STUDY ON
JOHN 21:1-3

*Purpose: to reflect on our relationship
to the resurrected Christ.*

1. Take time to share one exciting fishing trip or story.
2. Check your best reason for going fishing:
☐I love to clean fish.
☐I just like to compete with nature.
☐I like to get away from others sometimes.
☐I like the feeling of accomplishment.
☐I really don't know.
3. Read John 21:1-3 and check the best ending for this sentence: I feel the apostles wanted to go fishing because . . .
☐they were frustrated with the past events.
☐they were hungry and needed food.
☐they had nothing else to do.
☐they needed to "get away."
☐none of the above.
4. How would you have felt at this time if you had had the same experience (the death, resurrection, etc.)? (Check one.)
☐great   ☐wow!
☐confused   ☐who cares?

5. Using the same list, how do you feel about it as a Christian, today?

☐great   ☐wow!
☐confused   ☐who cares?

6. Close with a prayer about your relationship to the resurrected Christ.

BIBLE STUDY ON
JOHN 21:4-8

*Purpose: to recognize the resurrected
Christ as Lord of our lives.*

1. Have you ever had anyone tell you "how to fish"? Share your reaction to them.
2. Read John 21:4-8 and circle the answer you feel best answers this question: Why do you think the disciples did what Jesus told them to do?
a. They felt "commanded" to do it.
b. They wanted to prove this "intruder" wrong.

c. They figured early morning fishing was really better anyway.

3. If you had been one of the disciples, what would have been your reaction to this scene? (Circle one.)
   a. angry because you had been fooled
   b. eager, like Peter, to get to Jesus
   c. like the other disciples; take care of the most immediate concern: the fish

4. Where do you feel you would fit on the continuum when it comes to the Lord's guidance?

5. Sing together the hymn, "My God, My Father, Make Me Strong." Use guitar accompaniment or bring pretaped music.

BIBLE STUDY ON JOHN 21:9-14

Purpose: to find a relationship between the presence of Christ in communion and in our daily living.

1. Share a time when you ate with someone and enjoyed the meal because of the company.

2. What makes a meal a feast? (Circle one.)
   a. the food
   b. the people you're with
   c. the atmosphere (outdoors, fancy restaurant, etc.)

3. Read John 21:9-14. Check the statements that apply to both a communion celebration and a regular meal.
   ☐ fellowship with others
   ☐ presence of food
   ☐ forgiveness of sins
   ☐ presence of Christ
   ☐ bread, wine, the Word, forgiveness
   ☐ joy

4. Take time between now and the communion celebration this evening to meditate privately about your sins, your need for forgiveness,

323

| the assurance of the presence of Christ, and forgiveness through Christ.

BIBLE STUDY ON
JOHN 21:15-19

*Purpose: to become aware
of the "cost of discipleship."*

1. Check the word that best describes your feelings when someone tells you more than once to do something:
☐ put down
☐ angry
☐ bored
☐ important
☐ other
2. Read John 21:15-19.
3. Looking back to number 1, how do you think Peter felt?
4. Share how you would feel if your promise for being faithful would be crucifixion. (Check one.)
☐ scared
☐ happy
☐ disappointed
☐ doubtful
5. How do you react to your "cost of discipleship"?
☐ scared
☐ happy
☐ disappointed
☐ doubtful
6. Close with a prayer for strength in discipleship.

BIBLE STUDY ON
JOHN 21:20-25

*Purpose: to look at the purpose
for being a part of the church—
the body of Christ.*

1. Complete the following sentences:
a. If I could know something about my future, I would want to know...
b. When others are able to achieve more than I seem to, I feel...

2. Read John 21:20-25.

3. Looking at verses 20-22, check the reasons you feel Jesus answered Peter as he did.

☐He didn't want to offend Peter.

☐He was keeping John in the dark about his future.

☐He felt it was none of Peter's business.

☐He wanted Peter to be concerned about his own purpose in life.

☐He didn't know what would happen to John.

"Walkin' in

By Ben Sharpton

A creative retreat that uses a shoes and feet motif to help young people identify areas for spiritual growth.

All of us need to pull away from the ceaseless hassle of day-to-day life to reflect on our purpose and responsibilities as Christians. This retreat involves young people in the process of studying the basics of a Christ-centered lifestyle in an exciting and enjoyable way.

> **Goal:** To help young people and adults to examine their lives in a non-threatening atmosphere of acceptance to identify areas for spiritual growth and Christian commitment.

"Walkin' in the Light" contains three different "tracks" weaving throughout the entire weekend. These three complement and build upon one another to help bring about learning, involvement, and spiritual growth. The first track is that of fun. Activities have been designed into this retreat to make it a high-energy, enjoyable and exciting weekend that will be warmly remembered for years to come.

The second track incorporated within this special event is that of group building. As people establish relationships and break down the barriers that lie between them, sharing and support become easier and learning is enhanced. Special activities throughout the weekend help young people establish such vital relationships.

"Walkin' in the Light" helps participants share themselves (who they are and some of their history) with one another on Friday evening, affirm one another on Saturday, establish goals and identify areas of need on Saturday night, and celebrate together on Sunday morning.

The third track involves all participants in exercises which help them examine their lives and identify areas in which they need to grow spiritually. The content in this track has been divided into four segments which each correspond to one of the major group sessions. Your guest speaker, if you choose to have one, should focus his or her content around these same themes:

> **Session 1:** You Are Light! *(Self-worth)*
> **Session 2:** Walk a Mile in My Shoes *(Friendship and the perspective of others)*
> **Session 3:** Old Shoes Can Become New Shoes *(New Life in Christ)*
> **Session 4:** Shoelaces *(Tying it all together)*

the Light"

NOTE: Almost all of the activities in this weekend retreat package center around the theme, "Walkin' in the Light." Many of these activities incorporate either walking ideas (shoes, feet, etc.) or light ideas (candle-lighting service, light identification, etc).

POSSIBLE SCHEDULE

(Be sure to arrange this according to the needs of your group.)

FRIDAY

6 p.m.	Supper at camp
7:30 p.m.	Orientation session
9 p.m.	Session 1
11 p.m.	Midnight movie

SATURDAY

7:30 a.m.	Personal devotions
8 a.m.	Breakfast
9 a.m.	Session 2
11 a.m.	43rd Annual Walkin' in the Light Olympics

Noon	Lunch and free time
4:30 p.m.	Group time (optional)
6 p.m.	Supper/Path of Silence
7:30 p.m.	Session 3
10 p.m.	"Really Big Shoe"

SUNDAY

7:30 a.m.	Personal devotions
8 a.m.	Breakfast
9:30 a.m.	Session 4—Worship
11 a.m.	Pack
Noon	Lunch and departure

SCHEDULE

FRIDAY
7:30	Orientation
9:00	Session I
11:00	Midnight Movie

SATURDAY
7:30	Personal Devotions
8:00	Breakfast
9:00	Session II
11:00	43rd Annual Norman Park Olympics
12:00	Lunch
1:00	Bus departs for Reed Bingham State Park

Walkin in the Light

NOTE: A local quick-print shop can copy your retreat schedule for you on card stock which can be cut into small cards for everyone to carry with them during the weekend. This will help everyone be informed about upcoming activities and responsibilities.

BEFORE THE RETREAT

About three months (or more) before the anticipated date, form a Retreat Planning Team of youth and adults to oversee this special event. Give them all a brief overview of the retreat and share the ideas listed in this article. Rearrange the structure and rewrite the ideas so that it best meets the needs of your particular group.

Meet with your volunteer adults at least a week before the retreat to explain their roles and provide them with any information they may need. Be prepared for a barrage of phone calls during this week from parents and kids regarding last-minute details.

ONGOING ACTIVITIES

1. *Secret Partners:* Distribute cards to your group, each of which contains the name of one retreat participant (to spice up the retreat, have these cards cut in the shape of a shoeprint). The name that each person receives is his "secret foot buddy" for the weekend, and he should look for opportunities to secretly surprise his foot buddy during the weekend (make his bed, send flowers, arrange for someone else to give him a backrub, etc.). Decide if you want to reveal the identities of the foot buddies at the end of the retreat or keep them a secret.

2. *Stuffed Animal Give-Away:* Purchase a large stuffed animal ahead of time, and give it away at the end of the retreat to the young person who exhibited the most spirit and worked to make the retreat a success for everyone.

3. *Footnotes:* String a length of clothesline across your meeting room, with enough clothespins as you have participants for the weekend. Pin the name of each young person and adult to a different clothespin, and provide paper and pencils on which to write "footnotes." Anyone can write a note to anyone else on the retreat, but all notes must be positive in nature (no killer statements!), and authors may choose to remain anonymous. Classy footnotes can be printed ahead of time on multicolored paper.

ORIENTATION SESSION (1 hour)

1. Begin with a high-energy, action film like "Turned On" (available from Pyramid Films) to set the mood.

2. Lead the group in some group singing and crowdbreakers. A "One Foot Stand" is an activity in which everyone closes their eyes and holds one foot in their hand while balancing on the other foot. The person who holds that position the longest without opening his eyes gets a prize. "Foot Signing" is another crowdbreaker in which four or five people take off their shoes and try to get as many people to sign their foot within a certain time limit (2½ minutes). Be sure to distribute felt pens.

3. Take time to explain the schedule, introduce volunteer adults, explain the footnotes and secret partners, and display the stuffed animal that will be given away at the end of the weekend. Also, take time to state and explain any camp rules and the consequences for breaking any rules.

4. Play the "Anatomy Shuffle" game. Divide your group into pairs. After everyone has chosen a partner, instruct them to walk around the room among the other participants until you yell "stop." Then call out two body parts (foot-nose/elbow-arm/hand-armpit/etc.). They must find their partner, connect body parts (just one foot with one nose). Continue with more anatomy parts.

5. Form small groups for the weekend. These groups will be an integral part of the retreat activities. Begin by asking each participant to find a partner with whom they would like to participate in a small group during the weekend activities. (Adult leaders should not participate in this activity, but should choose a group after they have been formed.) These pairs should add their shoe sizes together, and then link up with another pair whose combined shoe size is six or more sizes larger or smaller than their own. This foursome then adds their shoe sizes together and joins with another foursome whose combined shoe size is three or more shoe sizes larger or smaller than their own combined shoe size. This group of eight will be their group for the weekend. Have adult counselors choose their groups, and assign each group a team name (patterned after a brand of shoe: Nike, Converse, Adidas, Buster Brown).

6. *Feet on the Rocks Game:* Instruct each team to sit in a circle and remove their shoes and socks. Give each group an ice cube, and explain that they are competing with the other teams to see who can pass their ice cube all the way around the circle using only their feet. After the first round, try for three laps, and even the five lap marathon.

7. Close this session by forming a large circle with each person resting their arms on the shoulders of the people standing next to them. Encourage them to get as much out of the weekend as they can and to try to make some new friends. Close in a brief prayer.

SESSION 1 (1½ hours)

"You Are Light!"

1. Begin with group singing and large group sharing. Have a brief time for people to share any needs they might have that the group could help fill (share toothpaste, borrow shampoo, etc.).

2. *Shoelace Sharing:* Divide into the groups of eight and give each group a shoelace. One at a time the members wrap that shoelace

around their finger, telling one thing about themselves each time they wrap the shoelace.

3. *Group Sharing:* One at a time, participants share their answers to the following questions (in their small groups):
- What is the earliest birthday you can remember?
- What is your favorite birthday?

4. *Shoe Search:* Everyone in the group sits with their feet pointing toward the center of the circle. Give them a chance to examine the different shoes in their group, and have each person pick one shoe that they feel seems most like them and why.

5. Bring the group back together into one large group and sing one song together or have a special number sung by one or more of your young people. After the song, have three different young people who have been contacted ahead of time read the following verses: Psalm 27:1, 1 Thessalonians 5:5 and Ephesians 5:8-10.

6. Introduce your guest speaker who should tell your young people that they are important, loved and special.

7. Close this session with a "Gift-Sharing Service." During the weeks before the retreat, contact the parents or close friends of each young person, and explain that you are asking them to secretly deliver a special gift for their son, daughter or friend. These gifts can be in the form of a note, poem, candy, etc., just as long as it expresses their love for the young person. Collect these gifts secretly and bring them along on the trip to be distributed at the close of this service.

Midnight Movie

Order a full-length motion picture from a national film distributor for viewing late Friday night. A quality film tends to calm everyone down and provide entertainment for those who are not ready for sleep.

SESSION 2 (1½ hours)

"Walk a Mile in My Shoes"

1. Begin with group singing and announcements. Your group may be a little sleepy, so be enthusiastic yourself. A crowdbreaker like a group backrub may help get things going. Instruct everyone to face one direction, reach and grasp the shoulders of the person in front of them and give them a backrub. After a few moments, have them all turn and face the opposite direction and give the person in front of them a quick backrub.

2. *Shoe Search 2:* Break into your small groups and have each team sit in a circle with their feet pointing inward. Each person picks a shoe that best describes the person on their left and right, and explains why

they picked that shoe ("This tennis shoe because you're athletic," "Those sandals because you like the beach," etc.).

3. *Group Sharing 2:* One at a time, have group members share their answers to the following questions with the rest of their group members:

> ● If you could spend a day as someone else (walking in their shoes) who would you pick?
> ● If you could have someone walk for a day in your shoes, who would you pick?
> ● If you were a successful shoe salesman, and could donate $10,000 to any charity, who would you give it to?

4. *Light Sharing:* Everyone thinks of a type of light (flashlight, spark, candle, spotlight, searchlight, etc.) that best describes the person sitting opposite them in their group and explains why they chose that item.

5. Bring everyone back together in one large group and sing a song or have a special number from one or more of your young people. After the song, have several young people read the following scripture verses as in Friday's session: John 3:19-20, John 12:35-36, 1 Peter 2:9, Philippians 2:14-16 and 1 John 1:5-7.

6. Introduce your special guest and have him or her share with your group about how they accept others (especially those different from themselves) and challenge them to reach out to new friends.

7. *Touch Service:* After the morning talk, close the session with a touch service. Ask everyone to close their eyes in meditation, and have half the group (those born in January through June) quietly walk around the room and touch those they wish to affirm friendship for, pray for, or simply to let them know someone cares. After a few moments, have the first group sit down and allow time for the second group to touch their friends.

43rd Annual Walkin' in the Light Olympics

Lead your group in some of the following non-skill games. Young people are divided into the same groups that they formed during the Orientation Session.

1. *Shoe Carry:* Each team divides into two groups and forms two lines facing each other about 50 feet apart. On the word "go," the first person takes his shoes off and runs to the other line carrying them in his hands. The first person in that line receives his shoes, removes his own, and carries both pairs to the next person waiting in the first line. This continues until all have gone, with the last person carrying the entire group's shoes.

2. *Broom Twirl Relay:* Each team lines up in single file at one end of the field. One broom for each team has been placed about 100 feet away on the ground. One at a time each team member runs to the broom, holds it to his chest and turns around ten times. When he returns to his group the next person can go. The first group to finish this exercise wins.

3. *Dragon:* Each team forms one line locking their arms around the person in front of them. Give each team a handkerchief which the last person in the line tucks into his pocket hanging out like a tail. On the word "go" each team tries to snatch other teams' dragons' tails. Only the first person in the line can use his hands.

4. See the **New Games Book, Fun and Games** or **Try This One** for other relays and games.

Group Time

This optional time is for each group to meet on their own. Time may be spent discussing what has been meaningful so far during the weekend, planning for the "Really Big Shoe" or in a "Shoe Box Sharing" in which everyone is given a 3 x 5 card to jot down any questions or problems they are facing. In this activity, these cards are collected in a shoe box, and one at a time drawn out and discussed.

Path of Silence

During the 1½ hours of this activity, no one is allowed to talk. All communication must be non-verbal. This should help your group try new forms of communication, and perhaps encourage them to spend some time in meditation.

SESSION 3 (1½ hours)

"Old Shoes Can Become New Shoes"

1. Begin this session with singing and large group sharing.

2. *Walkin' With God:* Divide into your small groups and have each member share with his group his answers to these questions:

> ● When did you first feel close to God?
> ● When have you felt closest to God?
> ● When have you felt farthest away from God?
> ● What would you like your relationship with God to be like?

3. Come back together in a large group, sing a song, and have various young people read these passages of scripture: John 1:4 and 9, Isaiah 49:6, John 8:12, Acts 9:3-6, and John 12:46.

4. Introduce your guest speaker again whose message should stress

what new life in Christ is like and how one becomes "born anew."

5. After the evening message, explain that each person is to go off by himself or herself for 20 minutes and spend time communicating with God (through prayer, Bible reading, contemplation, etc.). After the 20 minutes, come back together for a closing candle-lighting service.

6. As everyone begins arriving, pass out candles, and lead them in singing. Have a brief time for large group sharing, and then sing together an appropriate hymn while everyone lights their candles. Close in a brief prayer.

"Really Big Shoe" (1 hour)

This activity can be a fun talent night, skit night, or fashion show, with each team contributing a skit or two fashion outfits. Be sure to warn everyone well ahead of time so they can prepare their presentation.

SESSION 4 (1 hour)

"Shoelaces"

1. Devote a good deal of time to group singing. Some "community building" may have taken place, and singing together may prove to be special for your kids at this time. Announce any last-minute details regarding cleanup and departure. Pass out 3 × 5 cards and let everyone vote for the person with the most group spirit, and give away the stuffed animal.

2. Give each group a chance to share something with the large group (a skit, poem, thought, scripture verse, etc.) which they have planned in advance.

3. Give some time for individuals to share anything about God or the group in a large group setting.

4. *Important Steps:* Pass out scratch paper and ask each individual to jot down 15 to 20 important steps that must be taken in his lifetime. Divide into small groups and have everyone share three or four important steps they are facing now, or will be facing soon.

5. *Foot-Washing Service:* Read aloud John 13:4-9. Place a basin of warm water and a towel in the center of each small team. Ask the leaders of each group to pick someone in the group, take the basin to him, and wash both of his feet (after he has removed his shoes!). This person then takes the pan to another member of the group and washes his or her feet. Continue in this manner until everyone has had his or her feet washed.

6. Close this session with a song and prayer.

RESOURCES

Resources for Youth Ministry, Lutheran Church-Missouri Synod, 1333 S. Kirkwood Rd., St. Louis, MO 63122. Request issues 81.2, 81.3 and 81.4.

Badge-A-Minit, LaSalle, IL, (815) 224-2090.

Pyramid Films, Santa Monica, CA, (800) 421-2304.

Swank Motion Pictures, Houston, TX, (800) 421-2304.

Audio Brandon Films, (800) 241-3257.

Fun & Games, Rice, Rydberg, & Yaconelli, Zondervan.

New Games Book, edited by A. Fleugelman, Doubleday.

Songs, Songs and Creations, San Anselmo, CA 94960.

By Ben and Betsy Sharpton

Using Kermit and other Muppets for a junior high retreat on finding God's will.

Dreaming seems essential for a happy and creative life. Everyone needs to picture the ideal, if only to compare to reality. This retreat helps junior high youth to identify their dreams, mold them into goals and examine how they fit into God's plan—all with the help of those crazy creatures who have stolen our hearts, the Muppets.

PREPARATION

Work with your retreat committee to plan the activities for this event. If you work directly with youth in the planning process, be careful to avoid revealing the surprises built into this design. The counselor hide, late-night swim party/hayride and bonfire, and Muppet Movie are to be included without letting your young people know in advance. Such surprises add to the retreat's excitement.

POSSIBLE SCHEDULE

(NOTE: It is not necessary for young people to have copies of this schedule. Simply inform them of upcoming activities at the close of each meeting. This should add to the excitement.)

FRIDAY EVENING

5 p.m.	Meet at church to load and pack; final payments due; hand out name tags
6 p.m.	Muppet party
6:30 p.m.	Group singing and recreation

Session 1:

8 p.m.	"Scooter's Sharing Time"
9:30 p.m.	"The Muppet Movie"
11:30 p.m.	Sack time

SATURDAY

7:30 a.m.	Rise and shine (counselor hide)
8 a.m.	Breakfast

Session 2:

9 a.m.	"The Journey"
Noon	Lunch
1:30 p.m.	Muppet spectacular summer olympics
5:30 p.m.	Dinner
7:30 p.m.	Group worship service
9 p.m.	Pack and leave (or . . .)

(Option for a three day retreat:)

9:30 p.m.	"The Muppet Show"

SUNDAY

8 a.m.	Breakfast
9 a.m.	Worship service
11 a.m.	Pack and leave

Connection"

If you plan to use "The Muppet Movie," be sure to order in plenty of time. (Call Swank Motion Pictures, 1-800-325-3344, for information time and price.) Be sure to locate and gather all supplies prior to the retreat, especially items like the helium tank for the balloons in the worship service Saturday evening.

FRIDAY EVENING SESSION

Register everyone at the church before leaving. Hand out name tags to each person. (Customize each name tag with a picture of one of the Muppets. You can photocopy drawings of the Muppets [Kermit, Miss Piggy, Fozzie Bear, Scooter, etc.] and then attach these to the name tags. Coordinate the pictures so that everyone with the same character will stay in the same cabin or room. These cabin groups will also be discussion groups.)

6 p.m.—Muppet Party

Ask some of your counselors to decorate the meeting room in advance of this session. Use crepe paper, lights, posters of the Muppets, pictures to add to your atmosphere. Create a rainbow along one wall, the end of which is dipping into a large black pot or kettle. (This will be used later.) Consult a local bakery to create a special cake (with a rainbow design, a picture of Kermit, etc.) which you can share with everyone during the party. Have the song, "The Rainbow Connection" cued to play as the young people enter the room.

Gather your counselors and welcome the young people with cheers and applause as they enter the room. Share the special cake and punch and allow some time for informal visiting. Remind counselors that this short time offers an opportunity to help each young person understand that he or she is a special person.

6:30 p.m.—Group singing and recreation

Move directly into this activity (preferably in the same room).

1. *Spectacular Muppet Show Contest*—Hand a copy of the contest and a pencil to each person. The first person to complete *all* of the tasks in any order is the winner. (See next page.)

SPECTACULAR MUPPET SHOW CONTEST

Instructions: Complete the events below in any order you wish. You may not use the same people for more than one event.

1. Kermit: Find someone wearing green and introduce him to everyone standing around you—Kermit-the-Frog style. ("Ladies and gentlemen, let's give a big round of applause for that great television, movie and stage celebrity, ____(name)____. Yeaaaa!!") Have him initial here _____.

2. Miss Piggy: Have someone of the opposite sex tell you that you look lovely tonight and kiss your hand. Have him/her initial here _____.

3. Animal: Run up to anyone, jump up and down, screaming and hollering until he agrees to initial here _____.

4. Fozzie Bear: Get someone with brown eyes to listen as you say, "Wacka, Wacka, Wacka," and tell your favorite joke. He initials here _____.

5. Fozzie Bear 2: Get three others to sing, "Oh Beautiful for Spacious Skies" with you as loud as you can. One of them initials here _____.

6. Old Men: Look at one of the deer on the wall (or a unique feature of your meeting room) and tell one another that it's the most disgusting thing you've ever seen.

7. Muppet Show: Have someone listen as you shout, "Muppet Show" 10 times as fast as you can, without making a mistake. That person initials here _____.

8. Swedish Chef: Tell something to someone in the group in "Swedish." When he can understand you, he initials here _____.

9. Get six or more people together and do the "Two Bits" cheer for the Muppets. One of them initials here _____.

2. Divide participants into their appropriate teams according to name tags and direct the following games:

● *Relays*—With all the teams standing in a single-file line facing the leader, instruct young people to:
  ✔ line up in order according to birthdays
  ✔ line up according to height
  ✔ line up according to age (differs from birthdays)
  ✔ (others you may think of)
The team that finishes each task first wins.

● *Balloon Relay*—Teams line up in single file at one end of the room. Each person is given a balloon which he inflates and ties. When the signal is given, each person must run, one at a time, to the opposite end of the room, sit on the balloon and pop it. He then runs back to his team, tags the next player, and that player does the same. The first team to complete this activity wins.

●*Cyclops*—Each team chooses one person to be their team cyclops. Give each team old newspaper, masking tape, aluminum foil, etc., and instruct them to cover their individual completely, with the exception of one spot in the center of the face. When each team's cyclops is complete, he can tag other teams' members which removes them from the game. If any part of the cyclops' body begins to show, his teammates must stop and patch him up (a referee must approve the patch job). The team with the most members left after a given time is the winner.

For more games during the recreation time and Muppet spectacular summer olympics, see the following sources:

a. **The New Games Book,** edited by A. Fleugelman, Doubleday.
b. **Fun 'n Games,** Rice, Rydberg and Yaconelli, Zondervan.
c. **Try This One** and **More . . . Try This One,** Schultz, Group Books.
d. **Try This One . . . Too,** Sparks, Group Books.

3. Follow this recreation time with group singing and announcements. Introduce adult volunteers, explain camp rules and give time and place for the next activity. Be sure to explain the location of restrooms and meal times. (If your budget allows, purchase a Muppet doll—Kermit, Piggy, Fozzie, etc.—from a toy store and announce that this doll will be given to one of the young people in a drawing during the last session of the retreat.)

4. *Free time* (10 minutes).

8 p.m.—Session 1: Scooter's Sharing Time

This session is designed to help break the ice, to make sharing easier and to help your young people begin thinking about their dreams.

1. Give one 4 x 6 card to each young person as he or she arrives. Place a number of crayons or felt pens around the room. Read the following instructions, one at a time.

- In the middle of the card write your first and last name.
- Write any nickname you've ever had on the back of your card.
- In the upper right-hand corner of the card write your birthdate.
- In the upper middle of your card tell why you are here.
- In the upper left-hand corner of your card draw an animal that symbolizes who you are.
- Draw three hobbies that you have in the bottom middle of the card.
- To the right side of your name tell what you would need to do to improve any area of your life.
- In the lower right-hand corner draw your favorite possession.
- In the lower left-hand corner write the name of your favorite color in that color.

Break into your Muppet groups and ask each person to share his card with teammates. (Allow 30 minutes for sharing.) Collect cards after everyone has had a chance to share.

At this time explain Fozzie's "Warm Fuzzie" line. Explain that warm fuzzies are positive remarks or actions that we give one another that make us feel warm and accepted. Each person can jot down a warm fuzzie on the pieces of paper at any time to anyone present at the camp. These notes can only be positive, and may be anonymous if a young person prefers.

Secure each sharing card with a thumbtack to a wooden clothespin and attach to a piece of clothesline that has been hung prior to the meeting. The pieces of paper can be slipped under the clothespins. Be sure small pieces of paper and pencils are available throughout the retreat.

2. If you have access to a video cassette machine and television, show a brief segment of the "Muppet Show" to your group. Pick a segment with several characters in it, but don't make it too long. Perhaps the opening credits will suffice. If you can't get a video cassette recorder, name as many of the Muppets as you can. Divide into small groups and ask each individual to pick one of the Muppets that he can most identify with right now and why. (Allow time for all to share.)

3. Divide into small groups if you haven't already done so. Play the theme song "Rainbow Connection." Provide a copy of the words if possible. Use the following questions to help your discussion:

● Why do you think people dream so much?
● Do you feel the song is positive or cynical? Why?
● Who is included in the phrase "the lovers, the dreamers and me?"
● What feelings do you associate with dreams?

4. Now come together in a large group and hand out sheets of paper and pencils. Instruct your young people to take a few moments and think of their dreams. What ideals do they have in life? Have them jot them down without their names and then crumple the paper into a tiny wad. Pass out sheets of aluminum foil and wrap the crumpled paper in aluminum foil. Have each young person place his silver chunk in the pot at the end of the rainbow. Close this session in prayer and explain what and when the next activity will be.

9:30 p.m.—Muppet Movie

Show "The Muppet Movie" at this time. Provide popcorn and drinks and let the young people stretch out on the floor for viewing. If your budget is too tight for the movie, schedule a late-night swim party or hayride or bonfire, depending on the season.

SATURDAY MORNING

7:30 a.m.—Counselor Hide

For a little added excitement, wake all of your counselors first. They quietly dress and then sneak off into the woods to find a hiding place. After everyone has had a chance to hide, wake the young people, telling them that their leaders are missing and that everyone must find them before breakfast will be served. When a counselor is found, he must report immediately to the dining hall. This will wake your group up and get them ready for a day of excitement.

9 a.m.—Session 2: The Journey

This segment of the retreat is a set of brief seminars or learning centers which the young people will share in their small groups. Before the session, have the room decorated with cardboard road signs on top of several long poles. Beneath each sign, participants in their Muppet teams (the original small groups) will huddle for that seminar. Seminar guides and signs are given below. Allow about 30 minutes for each group for each seminar.

1. **Fear** ("Stop" sign)

List things that can cause fear. Mark a line through items that are totally unreasonable. Place a check by any items that deal with spiritual matters. Circle the top five fears faced by young people today. Read Matthew 10:26-31. What reassuring words does this share? How can being afraid help motivate a person to overcome his fears? If you have time, discuss each item and ask for volunteers to share ways that each fear can be overcome or avoided.

2. **Killer Statements** ("Road narrows" sign)

Discuss the latest situation comedy on television. Often such shows will contain a lot of critical statements. Ask if anyone can recall any of these put-downs. Share ways in which killer statements can hurt both the giver and the receiver. Read together Matthew 7:1, Romans 14:1-4, and Luke 6:41-42. What do these verses say about put downs? What is a Christian response to killer statements?

3. **Loneliness** ("One way" sign)

Pass out 3 x 5 cards and pencils and have each person complete the following sentence: "Loneliness is . . . " Answers can be serious or funny. Collect these cards and read the answers to your group.

Ask for volunteers to recall the loneliest time in their lives. Read together Luke 22:39-46. How do you think Jesus felt?

Why? What advice would you have given him? Read Psalm 56:3, 11 and John 14:26-27. Explain what these passages say about loneliness. In groups of three or four, write letters to a friend who has expressed his loneliness to you. What will you tell him?

4. Gossip ("Dead end" sign)
Begin by playing the game of Gossip:

Everyone sits in a circle and the leader whispers a meaningless phrase to the person on his right, who whispers the same phrase to the person on his right and so on until everyone in the circle has heard it. Ask the last person to repeat the phrase aloud. Note how much it differs from the original. Play one or two more times.

Ask the group to define gossip. Is it still gossip if the content of the conversation is true? If confidentiality is assured, is it still gossip? Read James 3:2-9, Galatians 5:22-23, and 2 Timothy 3:1-4. What do these verses say about gossip? What is the best way to handle a situation in which someone offers to tell you some juicy gossip? What is the best way to handle a situation in which someone gossips about you?

5. Add any other road-sign seminars that you think would be important to your group.

SATURDAY EVENING SESSION
7:30 p.m.—Group worship service

(Before the young people arrive, arrange the rainbow and pot of gold from Friday night's session into a worship setting at the front of the room.)

Begin with group singing. (Add special music by some of your young people if possible.) Hand the aluminum chunks in the kettle to each young person. After opening and reading them, ask for volunteers to share any meaningful dreams on their sheets.

Divide into Muppet teams again and go around the circle sharing your answers to these questions:

- Share anything you have learned this weekend.
- God's involvement in my life at this time is most like:
  - ► *Kermit*—the emcee and general leader
  - ► *Scooter*—the head stage hand
  - ► *Fozzie*—a stand up comedian
  - ► *Two Old Men*—sitting back in the balcony
  - ► *Miss Piggy*—flirting
  - ► *Other?* _____
- Using the same comparisons, I would like for my relationship with God to be like . . .

● I think God is _____ (very, semi, casually, not at all) interested in my dreams. Why?

Come back together in one group and have someone read Psalm 139: 1-18 and John 15:5-10. In a *brief* talk, explain that God is love and is extremely concerned about our lives, our dreams and goals. He wishes to be a part of our entire life: spiritual, physical, emotional and social. Explain that dreams can become goals when one chooses to commit himself to them and states them in specific, concrete and measurable terms.

Hand out the goal-setting sheets and pencils and have each young person complete his worksheet.

For a special closing, obtain a canister of helium (see a local welding shop) and some balloons. Give each young person a helium-filled balloon, string and tape and have him attach his folded work-sheet to the balloon. Step outside in a clearing and form a large circle. Have several young people share a prayer thanking God for his love and concern and then sing a meaningful song. On the final verse, everyone releases their balloons and goals into the air (symbolically to God).

KERMIT THE FROG'S GOAL-SETTING WORKSHEET

State your dream: _____
_____

What steps must you take for this dream to come true?
1. _____
2. _____
3. _____

State your dream in specific, measurable words:
_____

Pray silently that God will guide you in this goal, or lead you into something better suited for your life. Trust him.

Optional

To stretch this retreat into three days, include a talent show ("The Muppet Show") for late Saturday night. If one of your participants can do an impersonation of Kermit, let him emcee.

On Sunday morning, close with a large group worship service. Give each Muppet team one of the following responsibilities which they will share during this service:

Scooter	Give the morning message in any medium you choose. (You'll need to provide plenty of guidelines.)
Fozzie	Find and share some meaningful scripture.
Miss Piggy	Write and share your own affirmation of faith.
Rolf the Dog	Write and share a litany of praise.
Old Men	Lead the group in an opening and closing prayer.
Kermit	Pick and lead three songs for the group to sing.

Be sure to pass out these responsibilities well ahead of time. Choose a suitable order and have each group share their work during the worship service.

RETREAT OUTLINE 28:

"Clownin'"

By Walter Mees, Jr.

An introduction to worship through clowning.

The purpose of this retreat is to foster in the young people a greater appreciation for the joy of the Christian life, as they explore their feelings in light of scripture accounts of Bible people's feelings and what caused them. A special feature of the retreat is the introduction to worship through clowning.

POSSIBLE SCHEDULE

FRIDAY EVENING

9 p.m.	Arrive at retreat site
9:30 p.m.	Get-acquainted session
	● Welcome
	● Singing
	● Name game
	● Retreat theme presented
10:30 p.m.	Snack time
11:30 p.m.	Lights out

SATURDAY MORNING

7:30 a.m.	Rise and shine
8 a.m.	Breakfast
9 a.m.	Morning session
	● Wake-up exercise
	● Study/discussion time
	● Movie: "White Rock Blues"
	● Study/discussion time
Noon	Lunch

SATURDAY AFTERNOON

1-4 p.m.	Recreation
4 p.m.	Afternoon session
	● Explain concept of clowning
	● Movie: "Mark of the Clown"
5:30 p.m.	Dinner

SATURDAY EVENING

6:30 p.m.	Evening session
	● Explanation of clown worship
	● Workshop to prepare materials and scripts
	● Assign worship service responsibilities
9:30 p.m.	Snack time and games
11:30 p.m.	Lights out

SUNDAY MORNING

8 a.m.	Rise and shine
8:30 a.m.	Breakfast
9 a.m.	Clowns dress and apply make-up
9:30 a.m.	Worship service
Noon	Lunch
1 p.m.	Departure

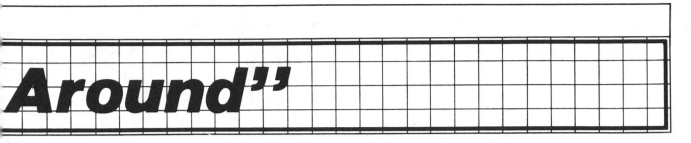

Around"

PREPARATION

Unless you are already familiar with the technique of clown worship, it will be necessary for you to become familiar with this powerful medium. View the film "Mark of the Clown," attend performances by mime troupes, watch old silent movies or those of Marcel Marceau. Take a look at the resource listing at the end of this retreat outline. While silent communication is not difficult, it is quite different from speaking. Clowning emphasizes expressions and uses body language. It is fun, but requires learning.

You will need at least three program leaders whose general duties are "worship leader," "study leader" and "manager." Also choose a meeting room that feels slightly crowded (i.e., not too large).

MATERIALS

Newsprint, markers, pencils, paper, Bibles, name tags, 3 x 5 cards (10 each), one yard of string each, an instant-print camera, film, joyful posters, films ("The Mark of the Clown," "White Rock Blues"), cocoa supplies, projector, screen, extension cord, volleyball.

The Retreat

FRIDAY EVENING

Though you may have to travel a long way to the retreat site, a Friday evening session is necessary to prepare the group for the weekend by creating a group feeling.

1. Have everyone sit on the floor in a circle. The "manager" or "worship leader" introduces himself, welcomes everyone and leads 15 minutes of singing.

2. Name game. Go around the circle and have each person say his or her own name after saying the names of all those who have gone before. It is helpful to have leaders spaced around the circle, and to end with a leader who gets all the names right. If more than one church is present, have each person tell which church he's from. Alternatively, have each person tell "Why I came on this retreat." An ambitious group might try to remember this information along with each name.

CLOWNIN' AROUND

3. The worship leader presents the retreat theme by using John 15:1-11, particularly verse 11: "These things I have spoken to you, that my joy may be in you, and that your joy may be full." End with prayer.

4. Cocoa and cookies precede lights out.

SATURDAY MORNING (3 hours)

1. Wake-up exercise. Pair the young people off, giving each of them a yard-long piece of string. Have them make slip knots in each end and fasten them to their wrists (like handcuffs) with the "chain" parts of their handcuffs crossed. Once they are attached, invite them to try to separate themselves without removing the "cuffs." (Clue: grasp "chain" in middle. Slip your doubled "chain" through either partner's cuff from the back. Open the doubled chain to form a loop. Pass your partner's hand through the loop. Pull. You will be free unless you have twisted the chain.) While it is unlikely that any couple will release themselves, it is good to release one pair at a time, allowing them to share the "secret" with others.

2. Number the group to obtain as many groups of four to five as you need. Introduce the "study leader," who leads the morning session. The study leader hands out paper and pencils and asks each person to write answers to these questions: "What makes me sad?" "What scares me?" "What depresses me?"

3. Each group shares answers and picks its favorites to write on newsprint with a marker. They also choose a spokesperson.

4. Each group shares its newsprint with the whole group. The study leader draws out connections between feelings and causes.

5. The study leader hands out colored 3 x 5 cards and scripture assignments (i.e., blues read Genesis 3; yellows read "David and Bathsheba" [2 Samuel 11:2-5]; pinks read "Peter's denial of Jesus" [Matthew 26:69-75]; whites read "Judas' betrayal of Jesus" [Matthew 26:47-50]).

Tell the groups to "Write on the card examples of fear, sadness, disappointment in the story, along with the *cause*. Share your findings with your small group. Report back interesting ones to the whole group for discussion about such feelings and their causes."

6. Watch "White Rock Blues" and discuss the cause(s) for the main character's depression and what the movie tried to each about it.

7. Reassemble the groups of four to give and ask "What makes you happy or joyful?" Process in 2, 3, and 4 is repeated.

8. Again hand out cards and assign such passages as Psalm 51; 1 Peter 1:3-9; The Raising of Jairus' Daughter (Matthew 9:18, 23-25); The Wedding at Cana (John 2:1-11). Repeat the procedure in point 5, looking for joy and its causes. The study leader sums up the learning during this session.

SATURDAY AFTERNOON SESSION

This period from after lunch until 4 p.m. is devoted solely to recreation such as hiking, swimming, volleyball, softball. The only restriction is on unacceptable behavior, but it is wise to organize options for most of the group to do. Impress upon the young people the 4 p.m. regathering time.

1. At 4 p.m., allow for cooling off, etc., by introducing the concept of clowning and showing: Then see and discuss the film "Mark of the Clown." You might even precede the film with a short skit in which you appear in makeup and costume.

SATURDAY EVENING SESSION (3 hours)

The general purpose of this session is to explain clown worship and to plan for Sunday's worship service. The evening is generally divided between a presentation by the "worship leader" and a workshop period to prepare materials and scripts. The worship service is divided into as many parts as you decide. The worship leader explains these as he or she introduces the idea of clown worship during a 1- to 1½-hour presentation. Possible parts and descriptions follow:

CLOWN WORSHIP

Invocation: *"We worship a triune God—that is, a God who has revealed himself to us in three persons."*

Three boxes can be decorated to present the persons of Father, Son and Holy Spirit together with their characteristic roles: creator, redeemer, faith-giver, for example. The back side of all three boxes could be constructed so they make up the number "1" when held together. At least three clowns are needed to present the concept of invocation. (Remember, clowns don't talk!)

"Because we all have sinned, Jesus died to take away that sin. Therefore, we regularly and often confess our sinfulness and know that we are forgiven."

A group of clowns might pantomime a theft, for instance, with a change of heart followed by a request for forgiveness which is granted. The clowns should creatively show that forgiveness is granted for the sake of Christ's sacrifice rather than out of the goodness of the one injured.

Scripture: A lesson may be read here, preferably one which can be acted out. The good Samaritan, the stilling of the storm, and the prodigal son are a few of many that lend themselves to this form.

Sermon: One of our clowns used his gift of drawing to relate to us in complete silence the message of God as vine and ourselves as drawing our life from him. You could also develop an activity that uses a long rope as the vine and includes everyone as branches.   continued

---

CLOWN WORSHIP, continued

Communion: Different religious traditions can do different things with this element of the worship service. One approach is to lead the group one-at-a-time to different places around the meeting site, especially if it's out of the city, for a period of silence under a tree, beside a stream, etc. In this sense, communion is with God—the creator of what we experience there. You may have other ideas.

Offering: This is an important aspect of clown worship, because it is a tradition to reverse the regular pattern and have the "minister" offer something to the people. Balloons symbolize joy, nuts or grapes make good reminders of the vine/branches theme of the sermon.

Praise: Finally, the silence stricture may be removed for singing favorite songs of praise.

The presentation of the clown worship ideas is followed by a planning period during which each group is assigned a particular portion of the service. Each group plans its own strategy for conducting its part of the service. End the evening with a couple tiring games, a time of singing and sharing, cocoa and cookies and lights out.

SUNDAY MORNING SESSION (2 hours)

After breakfast, schedule time for clowns to dress and make up using the same "clown white" that is used by mimes and sold at suppliers of stage makeup. You'll also need a few sets of color sticks, all of which are quite inexpensive. Start with a layer of good skin lotion before appying anything else. The makeup comes off with cold cream and plenty of tissues, soap and water. Those who aren't clowns will prepare the worship areas as well as their part of the service. There's always some last-minute planning to do.

When the clowns are all ready (don't rush this, but allow time for the kids to get "into" it), have the service begin with fanfares and falderal and maybe even a parade! Record the service with an instant-print camera. The flashes will simply add to the circus-like atmosphere that is a necessary part of clown worship.

When the service is over, have a photo session to memorialize each clown's face and costume. This was a highlight of our experience, as well as seeing those pictures and sharing them with families back home.

Surprisingly, by the time makeup is off and props and decorations for the service are put away, it's time to have lunch, pack up and go home.

We did our evaluation the next time the group got together. The girls were unhappy about the food; the boys were thrilled with it. Everyone wanted more volleyball next time. Some said they liked the Bible study best, but everyone loved the worship service.

RESOURCES

1. Funny Farm Clowns, Inc., Route 2, Butler, GA 31006.

2. Clowns of America, 1633 Dyre Street, Philadelphia, PA 19124.

3. **Be a Clown** filmstrip, Contemporary Drama Service, Box 457, Downers Grove, IL 60515.

4. **Getting Started in Clown Ministry,** by Tim Kehl, Office of Communication Education, 1525 McGavock St., Nashville, TN 37203.

5. Floyd Shaffer films: **The Mark of the Clown, A Clown is Born** and **That's Life,** from Mass Media Ministries, 2116 N. Charles Street, Baltimore, MD 21218.

6. **The Complete Youth Ministries Handbook,** by J. David Stone, Abingdon.

7. **The Complete Floyd Shaffer Clown Ministry Workshop Kit,** produced by Dennis Benson, P.O. Box 12811, Pittsburgh, PA 15241.

8. Holy Fools, P.O. Box 1828, Springfield, IL 62705.

By Edward McNulty

This retreat equips the video generation with tools to probe the bad stuff—and good stuff—on TV.

Most retreats include rules banning TV sets and radios. Here is a retreat, however, in which a TV set is an important part of the program. "TV or Not TV?" provides a series of experiences which help the participants probe the medium which probably takes up much of their leisure time. The TV world of values and role models will be compared to the scriptures so that the young person can be better equipped to choose the good of TV and be on guard against the evil. This should be a fun retreat, and yet one for relating the ancient gospel to an important aspect of contemporary life.

ADVANCE PREPARATION

1. All leaders should thoroughly read over this design and select those portions which they decide to use. (Hopefully, a retreat committee including several of the youth will decide on this.)

2. Choose option one (page 352) or two (page 353). For option one arrange to have one or more TV sets. Check with the camp management about TV reception in the area. Few camps are equipped with outside antennas, so if the reception is not good enough for the "rabbit ears" kind, you will have to pretape all TV segments and bring a VideoCassette Recorder with you.

If you choose option two, be sure to rent the film "Television: The Enchanted Mirror" or the multimedia show "Television: Wasteland or Wonderland?" (The addresses of all resource companies and publishers are listed at the end of this outline.)

3. Bring a 16mm film projector and a screen. If you order the multimedia production, you'll need three Kodak carousel slide projectors and a tape player. (But not necessarily three screens, as you could tack or tape up a couple of sheets on the wall.)

4. Choose and order any of the other films described in this outline.

5. Order for each leader a copy of the books: **TV: Friend or Foe?; Television: A Guide For Christians;** and **When TV Becomes a Member of the Family.** The second book has numerous projects and group ideas, so you might want to order a number of copies at the special group rate.

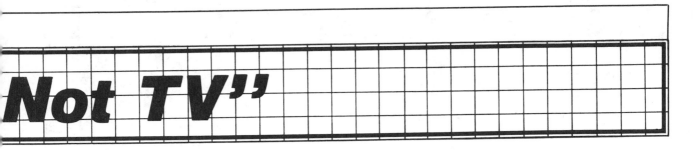

6. Bring extra Bibles, newsprint and felt-tip markers, paper and pencils.

7. Prepare and bring copies of the "TV Profile." This should look like:

MY TV VIEWING PROFILE

TIME	Sun.	Mon.	Tues.	Wed.	Thurs.	Fri.	Sat.
7 a.m.							
8							
9							
10							
11							
12							
1 p.m.							
2							
3							
4							
5							
6							
7							
8							
9							
10							
11							
12							
1-7 a.m.							

POSSIBLE SCHEDULE

FRIDAY EVENING

Arrive and eat supper

7:30-9 p.m.   Session 1: "The Televi-
Free time; possibly a late
Time"

9-?   Free time. Possibly a late
show presenting one of
the TV movies

SATURDAY

8 a.m.   Breakfast and Morning
Watch (Select scriptures
dealing with values.)

9-10 a.m.   Session 2: "Kids, TV and
Role Models"

10-noon   Free or study time
Noon   Lunch
1:30-3:30 p.m.   Session 3: "TV Advertising and Gospel Values"

3:30-5:30 p.m.   Free or study time
5:30-7 p.m.   Supper and clean up
7-9 p.m.   Session 4: "A Closer
Look at TV Formats and
the Gospel"

9-?   Free time; preparation
for the presentations of

TV skits; preparation for
Sunday worship (ask
youth to participate);
show one of the rented
TV films listed at the end
of this outline

SUNDAY

8 a.m.   Breakfast and Morning
Watch

9-10 a.m.   Session 5: Tie together
loose ends from other
sessions, summarize
what has been learned,
show one of the TV
films.

10-11 a.m.   "A TV Worship Service"
11-Noon   Clean and pack up
Noon   Lunch and leave for
home

Note: Some groups will find that they can
cover only part of the suggested material in
the suggested time span. Feel free to extend any of the sessions.

FRIDAY EVENING SESSION:
"The Television Experience and My Time"

1. Give a brief overview of the weekend's theme and activities. This
should be designed to arouse the group's enthusiasm as well as to give
information.

2. Ask: "Do you have any idea how much time you spend watching
TV? We're going to try to get a better idea of this. Take one of the TV
Viewing Profiles now being passed out and fill it in with a small check
for each hour of the day that you watched TV last week. If last week
wasn't typical for you, select another week. Then go back and write in
the initials of the name of the program that you watched at each time.
If you can't remember, use these 'TV' Guides to help jog your
memory." (NOTE: You might want to work through this exercise before

going on the retreat. If so, one of the leaders can tabulate the sheets ahead of time and now give a summary of the group's TV Profile.)

3. "Were you surprised at how much time you spent watching TV? Most people are. Surveys indicate that the typical family watches TV from 4 to 8 hours a day. The higher figure is almost always true when children live in the household. Where do you fall within this range?

"What other activities do you enjoy? Also list other activities for which you have no choice (school, chores)." (Give five minutes so that each person can write down his or her list on the Profile Sheet. Ask them also to estimate how much time they spent each day or week at the activities.) Have the members share their lists. Write the activities down on a sheet of newsprint. Included will probably be:

- Eating
- Reading
- Talking with friends
- Listening to records/radio
- Sports activities
- Playing games
- Hobbies
- Sleeping
- School
- School clubs/activities
- Chores
- Job
- Church
- Private devotions/Bible study
- Community service

"Which of these activities would you rank among your top five favorites? Which takes up the most time? Which do you have any real choice in? This can give you an idea of where your priorities are."

5. "Let's compare the TV experience with some other activities so that we can see what is unique about each. Where and when do you usually watch TV? With whom? How is watching TV different from:

- Reading a book?" (Reading: more private, intimate than TV since the author can include the characters' thoughts; uses your imagination more since words are just clues as to what a person or the setting looks like; more choice, a whole library full, than of TV programs; novels are more complex and longer than TV stories.)
- Going to a movie?" (Movie: You have to go outside the home; pay; more imposing images due to huge size of screen; more profanity and sex; theater is completely darkened so that your attention is forced to the front; yet, the audience reaction is important, such as the comments and cheering in some films.)
- Listening to radio/record player?" (You can do other things such as homework; better sound, especially with headphones or the stereo volume up; wide selection of music that you choose; you imagine the performer or dream up your own images to go with the music.)
- Going to a concert or play?" (You have to order tickets well in advance; go out of the house; the communal aspect is important, especially at a rock concert.)

6. If you have a TV set along, begin by saying something like: "Okay, we've been talking *about* TV for some time now. Let's watch just a few minutes of it to refresh our minds and get us thinking more about it. We're going to flip around the dial to see what's on tonight." Turn the set on and watch whatever is on for a couple of minutes; then do the same with the other channels. (Ignore the groans or plea for "just one minute more!") If reception is poor at your camp, record a few minutes of TV on your VCR and play it back at this time. Or, show the multimedia production: "Television: Wasteland or Wonderland?"

7. What types of TV programs are offered? List these on newsprint:

✔ Adventure/action shows	✔ Sports
✔ Police/detective	✔ TV films
✔ Hollywood feature films	✔ Educational shows
✔ Cartoons	✔ Musical variety shows
✔ Game and quiz shows	✔ Talk shows
✔ Situation comedies	✔ Commercials
✔ Live coverage of events	✔ Concerts
✔ News and documentaries	✔ Religious shows
✔ Miniseries, TV "novels"	

Which are your favorite kinds of shows? Which do you think contribute most to your understanding of life and the world? Which are a waste?

SATURDAY MORNING SESSION (Option 1):
"Kids, TV and Role Models"

1. Say something like "We want to take you back a few years to your childhood. Can you remember ever not having TV? What were your favorite shows when you were little?"

Turn on your TV set and watch one of the cartoon shows. Or play a prerecorded videotape of one. Some questions for discussion:

a. What is the story about? Is the plot typical of the entire series? Does this cartoon look familiar?

b. Who are the main characters? What are they like? Are they believable? If they're superheroes, do they have any human weaknesses? are they all good, never tempted to use their super powers for themselves? Are the villains entirely evil? What do you think the heroes or villains do in their leisure time?

c. Is evil always depicted as something "out there," always in the bad guys? What does the program say is the best way to fight evil? Is any alternative to violence ever suggested? Compare this to Matthew 26:52 or Romans 12:14-21.

d. Is the world as simple as this show suggests? Do you think children should grow up watching such shows without talking them over with adults? Did your parents ever watch such shows with you and talk about them?

e. What are some other children's shows that are on Saturday mornings? What are they like?

f. What do the commercials tell children about what is important in life? How do the ads match the format of the shows? Will the children have to unlearn any of the things which they are taught on Saturdays?

(Option 2:)

1. Show and discuss the 16mm film "Television: The Enchanted Mirror." Use the excellent discussion guide that comes with the film, working in some of the above questions.

2. *TV Role Models for Children and Youth:* Divide into groups of three or four. Let each of the groups pick a male or female TV character. (You could require that half of the groups choose a female.) Each small group should describe its character: what he/she looks like; how the character relates to people, reacts to crises and deals with conflicts; what he/she believes in. What does this character suggest an ideal man or woman should be like? Compare this to the qualities that Jesus suggests will be found among his people in Matthew 5:1-13.

3. *Role models from specific characters:* What do the following suggest an ideal man or woman should be? Use characters from shows on on TV. Compare them: (fill in blanks with current TV characters).

_____	_____
_____	_____
_____	_____
_____	_____
_____	_____

4. How do women come across in TV advertising compared with men? Who usually has the problem? Who usually enters with the solution? Is this really much different from the Popeye & Olive Oil stories?

SATURDAY AFTERNOON SESSION:
"TV Advertising and Gospel Values"

Option 1: Watch several TV ads. (Tune in at the beginning of a half-hour period to be sure to catch several). Or play back the five to ten minutes of prerecorded spots. Proceed with the questions below.

Option 2: Show one of the films:
"The 30-Second Dream," a 15-minute analysis of TV ads;
"Kids For Sale," a hard-hitting attack on TV ads from Action For Children's Television; 22 minutes; "TV Commercials," about 10

minutes of various TV spots.

Use the discussion guides that come with the films and work in some of the following questions.

●What does the ad man use to capture your attention? (Camera techniques, color, animation, stars, a story, humor, music, etc.)

●What problem is shown? What promise is made to the viewers?

●List some of the products that you have bought because of TV ads. Did the product live up to the ad's claims? Why or why not?

●List the following dreams/values on newsprint. Have the group add the products that promise to fulfill that dream/need:

►Popularity	►Success	►Sex appeal
►Love	►Self-esteem	►Security
►Health	►Adventure	►Good times
►Nutrition	_____	

How many of the previous dreams/values are Christian values?

1. In groups of three or four rewrite the Beatitudes (Matthew 5:1-12) as Madison Avenue's values. After 10-15 minutes let each group share its version with the others. Some examples to get started:

Blessed are the bold ones who wear Johnny Carson suits, for they shall inherit the best jobs and girls.

Blessed are those who wear designer jeans, for they shall be considered cute and in the know.

Blessed are you when you are persecuted by pain, for Anacin and Bufferin shall deliver you.

2. See chapter 17 of **TV: Friend or Foe?** and chapter four of **Television: A Guide For Christians** for additional ideas and suggestions. The latter has enough ideas and projects for an entire retreat on advertising.

SATURDAY EVENING SESSION:
"A Closer Look at TV Formats and the Gospel"

1. If yours is a large group, let the members sign up on a first-come, first-served basis to discuss one of the following TV program formats. Keep the groups evenly divided by limiting the number allowed in each group. Two groups could discuss the same topic.

    a. Situation comedies
    b. Adventure shows
    c. Sports
    d. Soap operas

2. The assignment for each group is twofold: Talk over the TV for-

mat using specific shows the group has seen. Below are some suggested questions and ideas for each format. Then each group should work up a skit using a Bible story or gospel idea/value as it might come across in that format on TV. Some ideas are suggested, but don't let them limit the groups' imagination.

3. Suggestions and ideas for the TV formats:

a. Situation comedies

● Describe the main characters of several popular sitcoms. What are they like? How do they relate to others? In a manipulative way (like Lucy in "I Love Lucy"), or in a caring way (like Hawkeye in "M*A*S*H")?

● Is the humor in the quirkiness of the characters or in the situation? Are we laughing at or with the person? What's the difference? (You might compare Bill Cosby's humor with Don Rickles'.)

● Is the plot believable? That is, have you come away saying, "That's happened to me," or "I know someone like that!"

● What are the proper roles of men and women as suggested by the show? What does the show say is important in life?

See pages 74-78 of **Television: A Guide For Christians** for a script of an "All in the Family" version of Luke 18:9-14.

b. Adventure shows

● Describe the characters. What are they like, and how do they relate to others? What does the series say a man or woman should be and do?

● What is the conflict? How is it resolved with violence or deceit?

● Does the show shed any light on a human/social problem? Does it oversimplify it or suggest an easy answer?

● Is the hero the kind of person you want to become or have for a friend? How would he or she fit in with Jesus' disciples?

Possible story ideas: Rewrite the story of David and Goliath as an episode from a current popular adventure series. Other good stories: The Parable of the Good Samaritan and the Parable of the Prodigal Son.

c. Sports

● What is the chief aim or point of the sport? What skills do the players need? How much cooperation is needed between them?

● How much does violence or the threat of injury add to the public's interest in the game? in football? hockey? auto racing? Do the cameras and announcers frequently go back to recap a particularly violent moment? Why?

● How important is winning to your enjoyment of the game? How do we regard losers? How was the cross a sign of losing in the Roman Empire? Was Jesus a winner or a loser according to Roman and Jewish standards? Those of our own culture?

Develop a game for the other groups to play with a baseball format. Make up questions based on the Bible for the "pitcher" to throw at those "at bat." A missed question is a strike, etc. One member of your group serves as "pitcher," a couple of others can serve as sports announcers and make comments on the performance and reputation of the various players. Don't announce it ahead of time, but declare at the end that the winners, in true Christian spirit, get to wait on the tables at the next meal or perform some other service for the others.

d. Soap operas

- Are all soap operas on in the daytime?
- What makes a soap opera different from a regular drama? (Overemphasis upon suffering and conniving, a pessimistic viewpoint.)
- Describe some of the characters in popular soap operas. What are they like? How do they relate to others?
- Are the plots and solutions believable?

Some story possibilities: Adam and Eve (See Genesis 2, 3 & 4); David and Bathsheba (see pages 22-26 of **Television: A Guide For Christians** for a script from "The Loves of David") or the story of Ruth. What elements in the Bible would have to be exaggerated to fit the soap opera format? Any left out?

Schedule a time for each group to share its masterpiece, perhaps late in the evening or during the next session. If you have a videocassette recorder (it should be easy to borrow a camera also), videotape the skits, show them to the group, and back home to others also.

SUNDAY MORNING SESSION

This is a catch-up time for groups that didn't finish everything during a previous session, or that want to probe more deeply into some of the material in the three books.

Help the group summarize what has been learned. Some summary questions:

- What are some good points about TV?
- What are some problems or bad points about it?
- How can we use TV as responsible Christians?

Paul Borgman's **TV: Friend or Foe?** has some helpful points if you want to make a closing statement.

WORSHIP/CELEBRATION

Prelude—Play a recording of "God Save the People" or "We Beseech Thee" from "Godspell."

Call to Worship—Read Isaiah 55:1. (Could be read responsively.)

Hymn of Praise—"This Is My Father's World"

Call to Confession—Isaiah 55:2

Write a confession based on our too casual acceptance of TV's false values; or use the "Visual Litany of Confession" from Visual Parables, a 5-minute, 16mm reel of TV spots with a prayer and response for each spot.

Assurance of God's Pardon—Isaiah 55:3 and John 3:16

A Song Response of Thanksgiving

The Scriptures—Could be some from the above sessions.

Meditation—Leader's comments or interaction with the congregation on TV and Isaiah 55:1-3, or TV values and the Beatitudes, or show the excellent film "TV & Thee." (There's even a beautiful litany at the conclusion of the film.)

Closing Hymn of Commitment

Pass the Peace

RESOURCES

BOOKS:

TV: Friend or Foe? available from David C. Cook Publishing Company, 850 North Grove Avenue, Elgin, IL 60120 or any religious bookstore.

Television: A Guide For Christians, available only from Visual Parables, c/o First Presbyterian Church, 49 S. Portage, Westfield, NY 14787.

When TV Becomes a Member of the Family, available at many Catholic bookstores or from Visual Parables.

FILMS:

(The following three films are available from Mass Media Ministries, 2116 N. Charles St., Baltimore, MD 21218.)

"Kids For Sale." 22 minutes.

"The 30-Second Dream," 15 minutes.

"Television: The Enchanted Mirror," 28 minutes.

"TV & Thee," 22 minutes, from Christian film distributors in major cities, or directly from Gospel Films, Box 455, Muskegon, MI 49443.

"TV Commercials," 10 minutes, "A TV Litany of Confession," 5 minutes, and the multimedia kit, "Television: Wasteland or Wonderland," all from Visual Parables.

RETREAT OUTLINE 30:

"A Rock 'n

By Galen Schwarz

Whether you plan a weekend retreat or an overnight lock-in, here are ideas on incorporating a study of lyrics into your activities.

One of the most beneficial retreats we have offered our young people used current records and albums as the medium to present biblical truths. Most kids are more familiar with rock groups than they are with the Bible. The use of lyrics as a teaching tool meets the young person's interest and gets him or her to apply the Bible's content to life situations.

THE PLANNING PROCESS

1. Have each person who plans to attend the retreat bring his or her favorite record or album to you at least one month before the retreat.

2. Many albums have the words to the songs printed on the jacket cover or on a sheet inside the jacket. If the lyrics are not available, someone, preferably a young person will need to listen to each record until the words can be written down. (Each participant should have a copy of the words at the retreat.)

3. As a group, listen to the albums at least twice, or until you can decide on one song per album, if possible, that you find appealing, and that you think may have theological merit. To have merit, a song must present a biblical truth or must stand in opposition to a biblical truth. The merit in this case would be the manner in which the song compares to or contradicts scripture.

DETERMINING THEOLOGICAL MERIT

This part is the most fun and the most challenging.

1. With a copy of the words in front of you, underline significant words that are found in the song's lyrics.

Example: A song may contain phrases like:
- Lonely world
- Everlasting dream
- Everlasting love
- Everlasting love will never die
- Give me what I hunger for
- I was yours before the stars were born

2. On a sheet of paper list these words or word combinations in the left-hand column. Now turn to your concordance and look up these words, jotting down a few Bible passages that make reference to or use the same words as the lyrics.

For the particular song, your work sheet may look something like this:

1. Lonely world	**1.** (Since there is no reference to "lonely" in **Young's Analytical Concordance**, try to word associate. I chose "alone." You may choose "world" in addition to or instead of "alone." The passages the concordance revealed were: Psalm 102; Isaiah 14; Matthew 14; John 6; John 8.

2. Everlasting love
   Hosea uses "loving kindness" as a means of translating the Hebrew word for everlasting love.

3. Everlasting dream

4. Love that will never die (eternity)

5. Give me what I hunger for

6. I was yours before the stars were born

2. Deuteronomy 32 (everlasting arms); Psalm 100 (everlasting mercy); Jeremiah 31 (everlasting love).
   Hosea 2

3. Daniel 2
   Joel 2

4. (try your own)

   _____

5. Matthew 5

   _____

6. John 1

   _____

In cases where the words do not specifically apply, or if the above process does not yield any significant words or Bible references, use this alternate method:

ALTERNATE METHOD OF DISCOVERING BIBLE REFERENCES

After listening to the music a number of times, think of concepts or themes that the song describes. A work sheet for lyrics of this nature might look like this:

1. "Standing by myself"
   (identity)
   (separation from parents and friends)
   (pleasing other people)
   (doing things your own way)
   What themes could you think of from the phrase "standing by myself"?

1. Christ in the Garden of Gethsemane
   The temptations of Christ
   Christ leaving the crowds
   Peter's rejection of Christ
   Judas' denial of Christ
   What Bible stories come to mind?

Now that the lyrics have been found and the biblical stories or passages discovered, you are ready to fill in your lesson plan with discussion, activities or a movie.

With both large and small groups, the times we have used music to present the grace of God in Jesus Christ have been some of the most joyful for both the young people and myself.

"Use Your Talents

By Ben and Betsy Sharpton

This retreat gives members of your group a chance to put their interests, talents and abilities to work in preparing a creative worship service.

This retreat is designed to give the young people in your group opportunities to share their faith using different talents and abilities. The final product of the event will be a worship service (shared during the final session of the retreat, or perhaps with your entire congregation after you return home) created and presented by two or more teams utilizing specific talents or methods. However, these teams may choose to continue to function throughout the year, providing your group and your church with new methods of worship and study, and giving your kids continuing opportunities to express their faith.

A great deal of flexibility has been incorporated into this retreat design to allow your planning group to choose the central worship theme as well as the specific teams to be offered. Take time to adapt or add to any suggestions that would better suit your particular group. This retreat could even be repeated at the beginning of each year (early fall) to organize your group and to help your young people begin to establish new relationships.

BEFORE THE RETREAT

At least two months prior to your retreat weekend use the following study in one of your regular group meetings. This material will guide your planning committee in its preparations, as well as begin to prepare your young people for service.

YOU ARE GIFTED

Goal: To lead your young people to understand that they have been blessed with certain talents and abilities, and to encourage them to use their abilities in outreach and worship.

1. If group singing is a part of your regular activities, choose songs dealing with serving and helping ("One in the Spirit," "Try a Little Kindness," "Look All Around You," etc.).

2. Verbal Rorshach: Explain to your group that you are going to say several words, one at a time, and they are to vote (thumbs up or thumbs down) as to how they "feel" when they hear these words. Ask for volunteers to share why they voted as they did after each vote. Use these words:

Jesus	Work	Happiness	Slave	President	Helper
Love	Peace	Servant	Great	Leader	Talent

3. Pass out copies of the following personal "Gift-giving" survey. Ask each person to complete the survey. After everyone has finished, ask for volunteers to share anything they have learned.

THE PERSONAL, ANONYMOUS HANDY-DANDY GIFT-GIVING SURVEY

Approximately how much money a month do you spend on . . .

food

entertainment _____

clothes _____

transportation _____

savings _____

Christian giving _____

Approximately how many hours each week do you spend . . .

sleeping _____

eating _____

in school/work _____

on the phone _____

goofing off _____

praying, worshiping, serving, etc. _____

"Do not store for yourself treasures on earth, where moth and rust destroy, and where thieves break in and steal. But store up for yourselves treasures in heaven where moth and rust do not destroy and where thieves do not break in and steal. For where your treasure is, there your heart will be also."—Jesus (Matthew 6:19-21)

4. Write the following items on a blackboard or newsprint. Together instruct your group to rank order these abilities as to their importance to the church (most important gets a ranking of "1").

____Preaching	____Working miracles
____Serving others	____Prophecy
____Teaching	____Speaking in strange languages
____Encouraging	____Showing kindness
____Wisdom	____Faith

Now, read together 1 Corinthians 12:14-31. Use these questions to help your group dig deeper into this passage:

(a) What does this passage say about the process of ranking different abilities?
(b) Do verses 28-30 contradict verses 14-27?
(c) Sum up the entire passage in one sentence.
(d) In what ways do we "rank" different abilities in the church today?

PERSONAL CONTRACT

THE BODY OF CHRIST: The church is made up of people who have committed their lives to Jesus Christ and willingly share their time, talents and resources in ministry to one another as directed by the Holy Spirit.

I, _____, understand the above concept and dedicate the following talents, which I feel I have, to be used in ministry to my church and community.

(Check [✔] boxes in which you have interest or skill. Place a star [★] in boxes in which you are willing to dedicate some time and energy right now.)

ABILITY	INTEREST	SKILL	ABILITY	INTEREST	SKILL
Musical Talents:			Mime	☐	☐
Instrumental_____	☐	☐	Other_____	☐	☐
Singing in youth choir	☐	☐	Creative Writing:		
Singing in quartets, trios, etc.	☐	☐	Writing plays, skits, etc.	☐	☐
Leading singing	☐	☐	Writing newspaper publicity	☐	☐
Operating sound system	☐	☐	Articles for youth newsletter	☐	☐
Interpretive dance and movement	☐	☐	Articles for church newsletter	☐	☐
Other_____	☐	☐	Other_____	☐	☐
Media:			General Helps:		
Slide photography	☐	☐	Setting up tables and chairs	☐	☐
Creating multimedia shows	☐	☐	Cleaning up after events	☐	☐
Operating audio-visual equipment	☐	☐	Preparing refreshments	☐	☐
Film developing	☐	☐	Typing	☐	☐
Other_____	☐	☐	Telephoning	☐	☐
Creative Dramatics:			Other_____	☐	☐
Acting in skits, plays, etc.	☐	☐	Worship:		
Behind-the-scenes work (lighting, directing, building sets, etc.)	☐	☐	Light candles	☐	☐
Puppetry	☐	☐	Usher	☐	☐
Clowning	☐	☐	Read scripture	☐	☐
			Speak	☐	☐
			Other_____	☐	☐

Having identified the above abilities which I feel I possess, I also offer my availability to be used by God as he leads me.

_____   _____
Signed   Witnessed

5. With everyone sitting in a circle (larger groups should divide their circles into smaller groups of six to 10 each), have everyone share some example of how they have seen or could envision the person sitting on their right serving God.

6. Hand out copies of the Personal Contracts, and give each person time to fill his or hers out. Close the meeting with a group song (or perhaps with a special solo, like "I am Your Servant" by Larry Norman) and allow anyone who would like to follow through on their commitment to place their contract in the center of the group.

PLANNING SESSION

Soon after this group meeting, call a planning session with your retreat committee. Study the retreat design, and adapt any ideas presented here to better meet the specific needs of your group. Compile the findings of the Personal Contracts, and decide which teams you will wish to incorporate in your retreat. Brainstorm together and come up with some potential leaders of each team. Assign different young people the task of approaching each of the leaders. It would be advisable for you to send them a letter of explanation as well.

Next, work together to select a worship theme. Below you will find some suggestions. Add any others that might appeal to your group. Select just one theme for all the groups to utilize during the weekend.

RETREAT THEMES

Love
One in the Spirit
Friendship
Joy
God's World

SCRIPTURE

1 Corinthians 13	John 13:34-35
1 John 4:7-21	1 Thessalonians 2:17-20
Matthew 5:43-48	Psalm 33:1-9
Ephesians 4:1-16	Psalm 96
Galatians 6:1-2	Psalm 97:1-6
1 John 4:7-21	Genesis 1-3
John 15:9-15	John 1:1-5
Romans 15:1-7	

POSSIBLE TALENT TEAMS

Multimedia	Uses slide shows, videotape, motion picture, lights, etc.
Drama	Performs skits and plays, writes some of their materials.
Clowns/Mime	Visits hospitals, nursing homes, performs skits, etc.
Puppetry	Puppets sing, act out skits, etc.
Banner Making	Creates banners, mobiles, stained glass, etc.
Interpretive Dance	Uses dance and sign language to act out message of scripture or song.
Magic	Presents illusions and magic to illustrate Christian message.
Ensemble/Choir	Chooses music and rehearses for worship.
Newsletter	Publicizes events, writes articles, etc. During retreat, may publish three or four issues to highlight daily activities and team events.

Note: You may chose to offer two or more seminar groups for young people to choose from during the retreat since some people may not be ready to serve on a team.

After you have selected your theme, your talent teams and possible leaders, pick a retreat site. Be sure to choose one that will serve your needs well. For instance, if your theme is "God's World," you may want access to beautiful nature scenes for your multimedia group. However, if you are using slide shows, you will want to choose a location close enough to a big city to have your slides processed in five hours. (Check this out in advance.) Large cities also afford record and music shops, theatrical stores for makeup and props, quick-printing facilities, etc. In fact, you might choose to have your retreat at a downtown motel or hotel, using their convention rooms as meeting rooms, and the restaurant as your dining room.

THE RETREAT

FRIDAY NIGHT—Session 1

Begin the retreat with group singing and loosening-up activities. Plan total group recreation to use up excess energy and get your group to interact together. Explain the schedule, location of rooms and facilities, rules, etc. Finally, break into teams (which young people signed up for previously as they registered) and work through the following exercises in each team.

1. One at a time, have people in your team share their name and their present mood as if it were a weather report (fair, partly cloudy, etc.), and their all-time favorite movie.

2. Next, go around the circle in your team and have each person describe himself or herself as a body of water (river, ocean, stream, etc.).

3. Look together at the worship theme and scripture verses for the retreat. Ask the question: "What would you want to tell others about that subject and scripture?" Write one sentence that sums up your team's thoughts on the subject.

4. Brainstorm together and list on newsprint as many ideas as you can for sharing your thoughts through your team's medium. Include possible songs, settings, scenes, background, special effects, dialogue, etc. Try every possibility.

5. Begin to narrow down your choice of ideas. Pick one song to portray, or one skit to perform, or two or three banners to create. Combine any ideas that would fit together. Be careful not to try to overdo it. You can always go back and add to your production, but trying to do too many slide shows or skits or dances can only discourage you. Ask for volunteers to be responsible for wrapping up your script (if you have one). A multimedia script will include the words to scripture or a song that you wish to portray. Jot down any pictures that might best portray each particular line. Be sure to utilize the slides you brought with you. A drama, clown and puppetry script will include any words or actions to be delivered plus any significant movements to be portrayed. An interpretive dance script will contain the words to the song you are using, and specific movements jotted above each line.

Ask for volunteers to perform special necessary tasks for your portion of the worship service (take pictures of a sunrise, clean up the props, set out the makeup, interview others on the retreat with a tape recorder, etc.).

6. Finally, choose two representatives from your team to meet as members of a coordinating committee. This committee (two from each team) will meet following each team meeting to discuss what each team is doing, how far along they are on their project, what specific needs they expect, etc. This is vital to keep conflicts from arising between the teams. Remember, this isn't competition, but communion!

7. Close together in prayer. Have everyone join hands, and ask for volunteers to share a sentence about the retreat, their hopes and the specific project your team will share in worship on Sunday.

SATURDAY MORNING—Session 2

Since your group will probably still be half asleep, be sure to incorporate exciting, eye-opening crowdbreakers and "movin' around" songs. Share any pertinent announcements and ask the representatives from each team to share their team's plans. Break into your teams again and work through these exercises in each team:

1. Ask your group to share their answers to each of the following questions. However, they must not tell the truth on one of the questions. The group must try to guess which question was the one lied about.

　　a. If you could visit any country in the world, which would you visit?

　　b. If you could donate $10,000 to any charity, which would you pick?

　　c. If you could be famous for anything throughout the world, what would you want to be famous for?

　　d. What is your favorite pastime right now?

2. Have everyone share around the circle, and describe the person on his or her left as a color. (Example: "bright yellow because he is so happy" or "deep blue because her thoughts are so deep".)

3. Study together Ephesians 4:11-16. As a group, answer these questions:

　　a. Who is it that has given gifts? (see vss. 7-8)

　　b. Why were gifts given? (vss. 12-13)

　　c. What does the phrase, "speaking the truth in love" mean to you? (vs. 15)

　　d. How does vs. 16 relate to the experience that is taking place on this retreat?

　　e. If you were to describe the person on your right as a part of the body (hand, ear, eye, foot, etc.), which would you choose to describe him or her?

4. Pray together for a few minutes, asking God to guide you as you prepare for your part in the worship service. Review the decisions made in Friday night's meeting. If any scripts were to be prepared, read over them, changing them where necessary. Spend a good deal of time in practice or in the field (multimedia). Finally, decide what supplies you might need from town. (Note: Members of your multimedia team may choose to go downtown also to get some quick shots of city life.) Give your order to your team representatives who will pass them on in the coordinating meeting.

SPECIAL SUPPLY LIST

Each team will want to bring the following supplies.

MULTIMEDIA
Old 35mm slides
Cameras
Film
Slide projector(s)
Tape recorder
Magazines
Contact paper

DRAMA
Skits and plays
Props and costumes
Lights
Makeup

CLOWNS/MIME
Makeup
Costumes
Props
Clown/mime plays
Pictures of clowns
Clown/mime films ("Mark of
the Clown," "The Box," etc.)

PUPPETRY
Puppets
Puppet-making supplies
Puppet stage
Puppet plays

Muppet videotape
Tape recorder

BANNER MAKING
Old banners
Burlap
Scraps of felt
Scissors
Glue

INTERPRETIVE DANCE
Tape recorder
Costumes

MAGIC
Magic books
Props
Costumes

MUSIC ENSEMBLE/CHOIR
Sheet music
Instruments
Tape recorder

NEWSLETTER
Newspaper articles (GROUP Mag-
azine's "The World Times")
Paper/pencils
Artwork
Small mimeo machine

SATURDAY AFTERNOON—Recreation, Free Time, Practice

Organize a formal time of recreation during the afternoon to keep the entire group mingling together. If some of your young people are really getting into their particular projects, they may want the extra time to practice or prepare. Be flexible enough to allow this if it is necessary, but encourage whole group interaction as well.

During the afternoon activities, have one or more of your adults travel to town for supplies (film developing, makeup, props, paint, felt, etc.). Try not to burden him or her with "retreat requests" (volleyball, food, sleeping bags, etc.)

Give your kids plenty of free time for recreation, relaxation and getting to know one another as well as to practice and prepare their portion of the worship service.

Note: Since some of your teams might be finishing their plans sooner than others, provide some activities that individuals can enjoy. Another seminar, a planned hike through the woods, arts and crafts, even minicourses in the other team activities might prove to be fun and meaningful.

SATURDAY NIGHT—Session 3

Lead the group in some large group activities, like singing and recreation, to help maintain a large group perspective. Call on the team representatives to share any updates on their team's activities. Share any last-minute announcements that might be pertinent. Give everyone a chance to share anything with the group (something they've learned, a new thought, a scripture verse, etc.). Then, break into your small groups for their final formal meeting. Use these steps in each group.

1. Begin your team time with a group hug. Have everyone stand in a circle with their arms on the shoulders of the people next to them. Very slowly, have everyone step toward the center and squeeze together.

2. Review what has been accomplished thus far. Talk about the portion of the worship service that your group will be responsible for. Is your team's talent one that could be utilized year-round in worship and outreach? What suggestions would your group offer that could help the group leaders continue to offer such a team? Would your kids be willing to commit the time and energy to see their team continued?

3. Read together Matthew 25:14-30. Ask for volunteers to share how they would tell this parable using their team's specific talent (multimedia, drama, whatever). Brainstorm together to find ways that this group could invest the talents they have been using during this weekend in service to God. (Note "Talents" in this specific passage refer to money. The meaning is interchangeable only in English.)

4. Read the article from Sojourners magazine entitled, "The Career of Horville Sash." Read also Matthew 23:11-12. Specifically, what does it mean to serve others? Give examples.

5. Close this time with a foot-washing service. Read together John

13:4-9. Take a bowl of warm water and a towel and place them in the center of your team. After a brief prayer of thanks for the opportunity of serving, the leader places the bowl at the feet of one of the young people. After removing his or her shoes, he washes his feet in the bowl and dries them with the towel. That person then goes to another member of the group to wash his or her feet until all have washed and been washed. Close with a prayer.

SUNDAY—The Celebration

The worship coordination committee should have met often enough to adequately plan the worship session. Have them insert hymns, solos, prayers and readings where appropriate. During the worship service, each group presents their portion of the worship service only when it is their turn in the schedule. Otherwise, all are members of the congregation and should worship together. At the close of the service, or shortly afterward, bring the coordinating committee together for a brief time of evaluation and goal setting. Discuss the feasibility of continuing the teams, and the amount of commitment it will take. Close in prayer.

RESOURCES:

MULTIMEDIA
1. **The Youth Group How-to Book,** Group Books.
2. **Ideas** #7, 8, 9, 11, 12. Youth Specialties, El Cajon, CA.
3. **Multimedia in the Church,** John Knox Press.
4. **Creative Tape Recording for Audio-Visual Education,** Tribune-Republic Publishing Co., Greeley, Colorado.
5. **Celebration, Festival, and Kaleidoscope,** Serendipity House.

CLOWNS/MIME
1. **The Youth Group How-to Book,** Group Books.
2. **The Floyd Shaffer Clown Kit,** Contemporary Drama Service, Downers Grove, IL.
3. **The Complete Youth Ministries Handbook,** Abingdon Press.
4. **Catching the Rainbow,** Abingdon Press.

DRAMA
1. **Ideas** #21, 22, 23, Youth Specialties, El Cajon, CA.
2. Contemporary Drama Service, Downers Grove, IL.
3. **The Playbook for Christian Theater,** Young Calvinist Federation, Grand Rapids, MI.
4. **Discussion Starters for Youth Groups,** Series 1-3, Judson Press.

PUPPETRY
1. **The Youth Group How-to Book,** Group Books.

2. **Fellowship of Christian Puppeteers,** 16 Albro Ave., Troy, NY 12180.

INTERPRETIVE DANCE

1. **Look Up and Live**, Macalester Park Publishing Co.

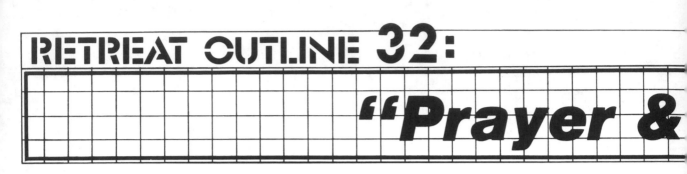

RETREAT OUTLINE 32:

"Prayer &

By Gwyn Baker

An opportunity for college students to retreat from their special kinds of hassles.

INTRODUCTION

The purpose of this retreat was to give college youth a chance to get away from campus to be refreshed outdoors, play and be challenged with spiritual content. This was also planned as an outreach for our college ministry core group

We have a core group (12-14 people) which is responsible for planning the program for our district churches' weekly college ministry. In planning this retreat, I first recruited a master of ceremonies/recreation leader and a speaker. We discovered that the more people we can get involved with separate details, the more time we as leaders have to spend one-on-one with the youth.

This retreat is an annual event for our district youth and friends, planned especially to minister to those youth who have come up through our youth programs.

The date for the retreat is usually set after Easter but not too far into the spring quarter. The retreat location was our district church camp, which has cabins, dining hall, chapel and recreation facilities.

We let college youth committees be in charge of planning the menu

POSSIBLE SCHEDULE

FRIDAY EVENING

5-6:30 p.m.	Check in and get settled in cabins
7 p.m.	Supper
8-10 p.m.	Session 1
10-11 p.m.	Get-acquainted fun
11 p.m.	Refreshments

SATURDAY

8:30 a.m.	Breakfast
9-9:45 a.m.	Quiet personal reflection
9:45-Noon	Session 2
Noon	Lunch

1-5 p.m.	Free time: canoeing, hiking, volleyball, basketball, studying (?), sleeping, etc.
5-6 p.m.	Supper
7-9 p.m.	Session 3
9-10 p.m.	Recreation and refreshments
10:30 p.m.	Vespers

SUNDAY

8 a.m.	Rise and shine
8:30 a.m.	Breakfast
9-10 a.m.	Personal reflection, cleanup
10 a.m.	Worship and communion

Solitude"

and setting up KP rosters. This was the first time we let the college students do their own cooking and dishwashing, but by doing so we cut the cost of the retreat in half. This also served as a good get-acquainted activity, plus the students felt more responsible for the weekend. More students were able to come because of the lower cost.

We mailed publicity during the first part of the quarter to ministers of our local churches and individual youth.

MATERIALS

Overhead projector/transparencies and screen
Question sheets for each person
Schedule sheets
Pencils
Songbooks
Communion elements
Book table (from area bookstore) on prayer and devotion
Baby sitter (if needed to encourage speaker to bring his or her family)
Name tags and pins
Laundry markers

FRIDAY EVENING

When the youth arrived one of the college youth registered them and gave each person a schedule and map of the facility. Leaders from the core group were assigned to different cabins to serve as hosts and hostesses. Creative name tags were ready for each person.

Supper was the first opportunity for everyone to meet together. The master of ceremonies welcomed everyone and created a warm tone. He directed table games with the purpose of having everyone get acquainted.

Cleaning up, washing dishes and going over the weekend's schedule were helped along with a song or two.

Session 1

We began with active, fun singing and kept the first night very light because most participants were tired.

PRAYER & SOLITUDE

Our speaker began his session by handing out questions for the youth to answer individually. This got people involved personally in the topic.

The preparatory questions used were:

1. If you had to list three or four essential elements for the development of the spiritual life, what would they be?

2. Which word best describes your Christian lifestyle: *distracted* or *directed*? Why?

3. Read the story of Mary and Martha in Luke 10:38-42. With which sister can you best identify? Why?

4. If you hear the term "desert experience" used, does this evoke a positive or negative image for you? Why?

5. One writer has called busyness a "demon." In what sense is he right? In what sense is he wrong?

The teaching was centered on "busyness" using Luke 10:38-42. The speaker set an overall tone and where we would be going in content.

After the teaching session the group was divided into small discussion groups. It is important to get youth with people they don't know or don't know well. These small groups were one key to the retreat's success, because youth need to express their thoughts.

The small group discussion questions were:

1. Discuss how "busyness" has become a 20th-century god. Relate this to your life goals.

2. Describe some concrete ways you can escape the compulsion of busyness, even in your academic setting.

3. Is it wrong to be busy?

4. Which of these presents the greatest problem to the development of your spiritual life?
   a. lack of time
   b. distractions—inward or outward
   c. demands
   d. consistency
   e. discipline

Recreation helped get the group working together. We used a Western theme to do creative team games. Refreshments were served.

SATURDAY
Session 2

Time after breakfast was set aside to deal with Matthew 4:1-11. Input was similar to the night before but on the subject of solitude.

Before the teaching session the following preparatory questions were answered individually:

1. How would you define solitude?
2. Why did Jesus need solitude?

> **3.** Why is solitude such a rare commodity in Christian life today?
> **4.** Why do you think the Holy Spirit led Jesus into the desert?

After the teaching session we discussed the following questions in small groups:

> **1.** Take a few minutes to sketch out how you will build solitude into your life.
> **2.** Share your "strategy" with your group as well as the peculiar struggles you will face in your setting.

The speaker challenged each youth to spend one hour in solitude during the afternoon.

Saturday afternoon was free time, but a few optional activities, such as Frisbee and softball, were structured just by stating a time.

Session 3

The night input session was evaluation of the "solitude experience" and learning about silence and listening.

Preparatory questions used were:

> **1.** What is silence?
> **2.** In what sense is silence a *spiritual* discipline?
> **3.** What relationship, if any, do you see between silence and prayer?
> **4.** What makes silence such a difficult discipline in our world?
> **5.** Describe your level of feeling *most* of the time when you pray—restless? relaxed? hurried? distracted? others

Discussion questions for small groups were:

> **1.** Talk about the time you spent today in solitude, silence and prayer. What was easy about it? Hard? Did you have more inner or outer distractions?
> **2.** What mark did this "desert experience" leave upon you?
> **3.** How did prayer "fit" into your solitude and silence?
> **4.** Share the most significant learning experience of this structured solitude.
> **5.** Do you have a "spiritual director"? Discuss the concept. Will you make it a goal to *be* one or to *find* one on your campus?

Recreation the second night was less structured because the group was more comfortable together. The vesper service was cancelled because everyone seemed to have had enough sharing in small groups. Be flexible to the needs of the group.

SUNDAY

The worship service tied together all we had learned plus added a beautiful creative outdoor communion and time for commitment.

"Who's Got

By Denise Turner

A retreat using the book of Ephesians to help your kids discover God's will for their lives.

Do your church youth retreats turn into celebrations of recreation with a few table blessings tossed in for good measure? Do the members of your youth group always leave home "just as they are" and come back "just as they were?" If so, maybe it's time to try something new. With a few good ideas and a lot of prayer, a youth retreat can work some wonders for your church. I know, because my church recently sponsored a retreat that resulted in decisions that had more to do with a call to commitment than with a crackling campfire. The theme of this retreat is "God Has a Secret."

POSSIBLE SCHEDULE

FRIDAY EVENING

6 p.m.	Let's Get Going (Prepare to leave; explain rules, etc.)
8:30 p.m.	The Search Begins
10 p.m.	Popcorn Break (guys cook it.)
11:30 p.m.	Cabin Confab
Midnight	Zzzzzz

SATURDAY

7:30 a.m.	Up and At 'Em
8 a.m.	Breakfast
9 a.m.	Think Time
9:30 a.m.	Clue #1: The Secret is Clear
10:30 a.m.	Clue #2: Discovering a New You
Noon	Lunch
1:30 p.m.	Canoe Trip or Softball Game or Jumbo Olympics
5:30 p.m.	Dinner
7 p.m.	Talent Time (Show to be based on small group activities of the morning)
8:30 p.m.	Movie Time
10 p.m.	Movie Talk-back
10:30 p.m.	Build the World's Largest Hot Fudge Sundae
11:30 p.m.	Pray-lude
Midnight	Zzzzzz

SUNDAY

7:30 a.m.	Up and At 'Em
8 a.m.	Breakfast
9 a.m.	Think Time
9:30 a.m.	Let's Celebrate
10 a.m.	Clue #3: The Secret at Work
11 p.m.	Famous Last Words (Communion can be included here if desired.)
Noon	Lunch and Homeward Bound

a Secret?"

In the Bible, "mystery" refers to a previously hidden truth that has been divinely revealed, yet still contains a supernatural element in spite of the revelation. The mystery referred to in this passage is that God's kingdom is being built not just from the Jewish nation, but from all mankind.

This retreat is built around the idea that God is letting his people in on secrets of living in today's world. The retreat time is spent searching for the ways God can become real in each person's life.

Since everyone loves a secret, build mystery-style clues and teasers into all of your "God Has a Secret" publicity. "Find a clue to God's secret in Ephesians 4:22-24," you might say. "Then come to the retreat and find out how to find a truly new you."

DETAILS

Rules about lights-out time, off-limits areas, etc. should be set by the planning committee and explained to the young people before they leave the church. Of course, a few silly rules could be read first: "Rule #1—During the weekend, each senior high must be accompanied by at least two junior highs in order to go into the bathroom; Rule #2—Junior highs will not be allowed to go into the bathroom during the weekend."

Think Times are private devotional moments built into each morning. Bible passages should be chosen for these times and question sheets given to each young person (or printed in a retreat program booklet). The purpose is to get each young person to apply Bible passages to his or her life. For example, the first Think Time might center around Colossians 1:15-20, which fits in well with the retreat's theme. First, instruct each young person to find a quiet place, read the passage and list five things the passage reveals about Jesus Christ. Then, have each youth jot down, next to each of the five things, one time when he has seen that aspect of Jesus at work in his life.

The following morning, Think Time could center around Colossians

3:12-17. On the study sheet, certain words from the passage would be listed: "kindness, patience, humility, helpfulness, forgiveness." Each young person would think of at least one time in his life when he exhibited each quality—one time when he was humble, helpful, etc.

The *Cabin Confab/Pray-lude* times should also be planned ahead. A youth or adult leader could be assigned to each cabin, and he or she should be prepared with questions/songs/prayer activities. The first night's confab, for instance, could involve asking each young person to share one new thing he or she learned during the day. Then, everyone could take turns offering sentence prayers of thanks to God for good things that happened throughout the first day of the retreat. (Give the young people examples . . . "Thank you that the bus didn't break down again, God.")

On the second night, the pray-lude could begin with a discussion of that morning's devotional time. Encourage each young person to talk about something he wrote down on his paper that day. Ask the young people if they had any trouble coming up with examples of Jesus at work in their lives. Then pray together about discovering more about Jesus and about each other during the remainder of the retreat.

Additional good ideas for Think Times and Confab/Pray-ludes can be found in Dennis Benson's **Hard Times Catalog for Youth Ministry** (Group) or **Recycle Catalogues** (Abingdon).

The Search Begins is an introduction to the weekend. This is the time for "getting-to-know-you" games. (Have each person tell his first name and favorite toy as a child, for example.) You might also include time for each young person to graph his spiritual life: Using graph paper, instruct each young person to start with the year zero and draw a graph by thinking of all the things that have affected him spiritually through the years. Camp experiences, church activities and times of making commitments to Christ are all possibilities. The lines will go up and down, of course, and will provide some interesting and revealing pictures for study. Ask the young people to look closely at their own graphs and remember why they grew spiritually, or didn't grow, at certain points. Then discuss how Christians can help each other reach higher on their spiritual graphs.

Next, the retreat speaker/leader could discuss the book of Ephesians, the fact that God is disclosing a mystery to his people, and ways to begin the search. If there is a small, dusty room or basement somewhere nearby, take the retreaters there and ask them to close their eyes and imagine they are in jail as the first two chapters of Paul's prison epistle is read. Take along lots of Bibles, pencils and paper, and ask each young person to choose a key verse, something that has meaning for him, to write on a piece of note paper and carry with him throughout the weekend. (Remind the retreaters to pull out their verses and read them periodically.)

Then ask, "What is Paul saying in these two chapters that still applies to us today?" Have everyone read Ephesians 2:1-10 silently and rewrite that passage in his or her own words. Take turns reading and discussing the original passages that result.

Clue #1: The Secret Is Clear is a study of Ephesians 3. Ask someone who reads with authority to read this chapter aloud. Instruct the young people to think of two words or phrases in the passage that really hit home for them. Then ask for volunteers to share and explain their phrases.

Next, ask the following discussion questions:

1. Can you put God's secret plan into your own words?
2. Why was the plan kept secret?
3. Why did Christ come to earth?
4. Where do we, as God's children, fit into this secret plan?

If time permits, you could set up a role play in which a Christian tries to explain God's "secret" to the average "man on the street."

Clue #2: Discovering a New You centers around Ephesians 4 and 5—and upon finding out "who I want to be and how I can apply God's will to my life." Divide the young people into interest groups. (Assign an adult leader to each one if possible.) They would then spend the morning delving into personally chosen creative activities. Here are options you could offer . . .

1. Song Writing: This group composes an original song, possibly using a well-known tune. You could ask them to stay within the retreat theme if desired.

2. Reader's Theater: This group writes and practices a short drama or acts out a Bible parable such as the Parable of the Tenants (Matthew 21) or the Parable of the Unforgiving Servant (Matthew 18).

3. Nature Hike: Offer this group scriptures about nature. (Try Psalm 65 and Matthew 6.) Ask them to gather things that symbolize both the newness and oldness of life. They should also be ready to explain how each discovery could be applied to their own lives. Aspiring artists might want to sketch scenes that have special meaning for them.

4. "Banster" Making: Since making real banners can be expensive, this group designs poster banners ("bansters") using poster board backgrounds and felt scraps, construction paper, leaves, wood and other available materials.

continued

5. *Photo Scavenger Hunt:* Polaroid cameras are used to snap candid shots of other interest groups or some special glimpses of nature. Group members give titles to each photograph.

6. *Interpretive Dance:* Christian music could be interpreted through simple movements devised by the young people themselves. Bring along a record or two to use for this purpose or a tape and recorder. ("In Christ There is No East or West" is a good song to interpret.)

Jumbo Olympics time could include bubble-gum blowing and peanut-butter-and-jelly sandwich eating contests and also piggyback or three-legged races. This could be held indoors in case of rain.

For *Movie Time,* consider renting a secular movie the kids are excited about. (There are good ones available through the mail.) Then stage an in-depth talk-back session in which you explore ideas represented in the movie and values and emotions portrayed. Ask the young people what the actors were trying to say, and ask them what the Bible says about some of the events that took place in the movie.

Let's Celebrate is a time for singing and for sharing different things that each person experienced during the weekend. Bring along songbooks and a guitar, if possible.

Clue #3: The Secret at Work is a study of Ephesians 6—accepting the reality of "Jesus in you" and then putting on the armor of God. First, read verses 1-4 and ask each retreater to write a private letter ("Dear Mom and/or Dad," perhaps) explaining one problem the young person faces at home. (Assure your young people that no one will peek at their letters.) Encourage everyone to describe the problem in depth—what caused it, who is involved, etc.—and to try to come up with at least one solution to it (or positive result that might come out of it). Next, have someone read verses 10-24 and ask the group to brainstorm different ways someone can become a stronger Christian. They could vote on one or two of these to discuss more fully if time allows.

Closing thoughts *(Famous Last Words)* could center around talking about different ways to live in the world and still be true to God's teachings in the book of Ephesians. Encourage the retreaters to think of people they know who are good examples of this. Ask them why these people are able to do such a good job of living the Christian life. Then, instruct the young people to think of times during the past month when they were true to one of the teachings in Ephesians—and to think of the roadblocks that often stand in the way when they really want to make the right choices. Ask the young people to jot down notes listing negative attitudes or actions that clutter their lives and then throw the pieces of paper into a fire or wastebasket, thus symbolizing the end of each attitude or action. End with prayer time.

EXTRA TIPS

It seems to help to alternate fun activities with creative study times. For example, a knee beauty contest (with the upper three-fourths torso behind a screen) could be preceded by a TV IQ session (in which the young people rate their favorite TV programs according to Christian criteria). For a little extra zing, the kids could even act out their favorite commercials during the TV discussion.

Never underestimate the value of retreat evaluation and follow-up. There are lots of interesting ways to evaluate and use a retreat. One way is to ask each participant to write answers to pertinent questions. (What are you missing at home this weekend? What would you be doing back home right now? Why did you come to this retreat?) Collect the papers, and return them to their owners at the end of the weekend so you can add more questions. (What have you learned from the retreat? Will it make any difference in the way you relate to the people around you? Were your expectations realized? Why or why not?) Collect the papers once again and mail them to the young people about six weeks later. You might be surprised at the results you observe in the meantime.

RETREAT OUTLINE 3-4:

"The Last

By Edward McNulty

This retreat, combining a study of the film "Oh God!" the rock musical "Jesus Christ: Superstar" and the Bible can help your youth gain a fresh understanding of the gospel.

BEFORE THE RETREAT

A month or more before the retreat order the film "Oh God!" If you have access to a videotape player, order the film from local videotape dealers that rent tape versions of films. A videotape will be far less expensive than the 16mm film format. Check the address list at the end of this retreat for distributors.

Arrange for the following equipment:

● Videotape player. A member of your church, perhaps a businessman or an auto dealer, probably has one.

● Or, a 16mm film projector. If you don't own one, check with your library.

● If you use a Charlie Chaplin film, order it through your library.

● A record player and a copy of the Bill Cosby album containing "Noah." Other comedy albums that might prove useful.

● A stack of Bibles and folk hymnals.

● Paper, pencils, laundry markers and newsprint.

● Some of the books listed in the resource section at the end of this retreat for a browsing table.

PREPARING THE GROUP MEMBERS

● Ask your young people to think about the following: In drama there are two major categories: tragedy and comedy. Is the story of Jesus Christ tragedy or comedy? Give reasons for your answer.

● Ask them to listen, at home or at a youth meeting, to recordings of "Godspell" and "Jesus Christ: Superstar."

BACKGROUND FOR THE LEADERS

Does God laugh? Is the story of Jesus Christ a comedy or a tragedy? Such questions would not have occurred to our Puritan ancestors. Running the universe is too serious a business. God might laugh, as asserted in Psalm 2, but only in derision over the defeat of his enemies. God would never laugh in the sense of chuckling over a good joke. Such questions are just too frivolous for a serious Christian. Not so, claim a number of modern theologians. Faith and laughter—Charlie Chaplin and Christ—have much more in common than most people think. As

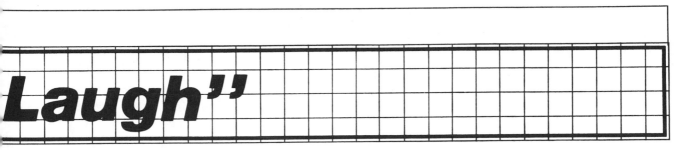

Laugh"

we'll see, the gospel of Jesus Christ can even be called "The Good News Comedy."

A lot of people were upset when in 1964 the film "Parable" opened at the New York World Fair's Protestant Pavilion. This film featured a white-faced mime portraying Christ in a circus setting. The film wasn't very funny, but it was profoundly moving—and upsetting to those who could not cope with the very unorthodox setting. Since then, "Parable" has become the most widely used short film in the church.

A few years after "Parable," the rock opera "Godspell" burst onto the scene, packing in the crowds on Broadway, then the movie theaters, and now often in school auditoriums as well. "Godspell" is funny, as a clown-Christ leads his band of disciples through their dance and pantomime routines interpreting the gospel of Matthew. Again, some Christians have been upset by this unorthodox depiction of the gospel.

In 1977, "Oh God!" shook some Christians as if it were an irreverent attack on God. Instead of being sacrilegious, "Oh God!" was a fresh approach to an understanding of faith, and a probe of the old question, not *look* like George Burns, but he might deliver a similar message—one that official custodians of the church might miss.
that official custodians of the church might miss.

Although it was definitely not a Christian film, "Oh God!" did have parallels with scriptural themes, especially in the way that faith was portrayed.

Actually, comedy is intrinsic to the very nature of the biblical message: the good news that God cares so much for his created world that he has invaded it in the form of his Son. This is a reversal, as noted earlier, of the usual viewpoint. Many think that the story of Jesus, for instance, is a tragedy, since the Crucifixion is such an important part of the story. Andrew Lloyd Webber and Timothy Rice did when they wrote the rock opera "Jesus Christ: Superstar." Many Christians were upset because the work ends with the soft musical piece entitled "John 19:41" rather than with a loud, celebrative affirmation of the Resurrection. The authors, not believers themselves, stated that they wanted people to draw their own conclusions as to whether Jesus was actually raised from the dead or not. Hence, the quiet, meditative ending.

This is a fair reply, if the authors are to avoid any phony facade of faith. Their view of the story of Jesus is a tragic one, the story of a good Jewish boy gone wrong. It is told from the standpoint of Judas who accusingly demands of Jesus, "Why'd you let things get so out of hand?" "Superstar" has much to offer us in dramatic intensity, in understanding Jesus' human side: his sufferings, temptations, frustrations and disappointments. But "Superstar" cannot fully satisfy the Christian because it is unbelief searching for, but not finding, a Resurrection faith.

"Godspell," on the other hand, supplies us with the Resurrection. And thus its whole viewpoint and tone is different from "Superstar." Jesus did not let "things get out of hand," as can be seen by his testimony before Pilate (John 19:10-11):

> *Pilate therefore said to him, "You will not speak to me? Do you not know that I have the power to release you and power to crucify you?" Jesus answered him, "You would have no power over me unless it has been given you from above . . ."*

Pilate caves in to the priests' and mob's threats and blood lust. Once the carpenter is dead, they think he is out of the way and they can rest easy. They have had the last laugh on the upstart who challenged their authority. Not so, however, as the old saying goes, "He who laughs last, laughs best." Jesus rises from the grave. Death and sin have done their worst, but he emerges alive, more powerful than before, for his Resurrection rekindles the faith of the women, of Peter and the other disciples. Soon the church, the new body of Christ, is spreading throughout the world in joy and love.

A tragedy is a dramatic story that ends sadly. The hero, and often a good part of the cast, ends up dead or defeated through a fatal flaw in character. For Macbeth it is his lust for power. For Oedipus Rex it is the fates or the gods.

A comedy is a story with a good ending. "All's well that ends well," in Shakespeare's words. The story may not be funny at first sight, but it affirms that, despite tragic elements, life is good and there are rewards for those who love and strive for integrity. Ol' Charlie Chaplin gets into all kinds of scrapes, almost never gets the girl, but in the end he picks himself up from where he has fallen, dusts himself off, adjusts his derby, and waddles/dances off down the road. For him, life is a waltz among slippery and dangerous banana peels, but always with the possibility of the good overcoming the bad.

The young people who participate in "The Last Laugh" retreat should be able to approach the story of Christ from this fresh perspective. Thus the Resurrection, Christ's and ours, takes on a new dimension. They will see it not as some event way off in the dim past or in some future beyond our death or the end of time. Young people will see the Resurrection as full of insights that are helpful for living now, enabling us to laugh and rejoice despite the "crucifixions" of the everyday world.

THE RETREAT

FRIDAY EVENING SESSION

1. After settling in, gather the group together and go over such chores as rules, assigning responsibilities and introducing the schedule.

2. In just a few sentences summarize the material on "The Last Laugh." Then discuss:

● What kinds of humor can you think of? (Satire, sarcasm [Don Rickles' put-downs and ethnic jokes], slapstick comedy, life situations that evoke laughter [Bill Cosby's stories of his family].)

● What makes you laugh? Any idea why? (Among the answers of "why" should be: the gap between our pretensions and reality.)

● What do you think the difference is between tragedy and comedy?

Write the responses on a large sheet of newsprint.

3. Play "Name That Character." Tape or pin on a volunteer's back the name of a TV comedy character. The person stands in the middle of the circle and tries to guess from non-verbal clues who the character is. The person is allowed to ask questions which are answered with a shake of the head *yes* or *no*. If unsuccessful after a minute, the person can be given such verbal clues as the character's favorite expression or an imitation of his/her voice. Go around until everyone has guessed his character.

4. Gather together again and discuss the characters.

● Why are they funny? How true to life are they? Do you feel like that character at times? Does the character ever shed any light on faith and life?

5. Show the Charlie Chaplin film. (If possible, show "The Tramp.") Afterward discuss such questions as:

● Why is Charlie funny? Why has "the Little Tramp" appealed to us over the years? (The little guy versus the big guy or a cruel, hard world is a universal theme.)

● Do you see any sign of a "little resurrection" in the film? That is, any hope for a better world? (The way Charlie rebounds from disappointment at the end of the film [especially in "The Tramp"].)"

6. Secure four volunteers to read the parts of the Klunker Family episode from the book **Television: A Guide for Christians**, chapter six. Give each volunteer a copy of the book so that the cast can get together for a brief rehearsal.

SATURDAY MORNING SESSION

1. Sum up briefly Friday evening's discussion. Then point out that there is humor in the Bible. It has to be searched for, since centuries of piety and super-soberness have covered it up. Divide the participants into groups of four to six.

2. Hand out cards with the following scriptures and comments written on them. The groups should discuss the passages and think up various ways they could be interpreted: role play, cartoon, mime, etc.

a. **Numbers 22:1-35—"Balaam and His Ass."**
Who are the Moabites and why are they trying to hire Balaam? What did the Hebrews think of the curse of a sorcerer? Which "character" in the story sees the true situation? Why would the Hebrew storyteller tell this story with a lot of glee?

b. **Isaiah 44:9-20—"A Put-down of Idolatry."**
What kind of humor is this? It was meant to be read aloud: with what kind of voice inflection? Note verse 19. What was probably the historical setting of the Hebrews (captives of whom?)? How is this humor similar to that of the captive East Europeans today?

c. **Matthew 6:2-4—"Blowing Your Own Horn."**
Close your eyes and picture this or draw a cartoon.
Matthew 6:5-7—"Show-Off Prayers."
The group could compose the kind of prayer Jesus is putting down. What kind of humor is this?

d. **Matthew 6:16—"Look-At-Me Saints."**
Try on the various dismal faces of the super-pious.
Matthew 7:1-5—"Speck Removing in a Log Jam."
Draw a cartoon or act this out.

e. **Matthew 15:12-14—"Blind Guides."**
A good slapstick skit? Who would appreciate Jesus' story? Who would not?

f. **Matthew 19:23-24—"Needling the Rich."**
Picture the scene in your mind. Draw a cartoon or act it out to see how ridiculous this is. A form of exaggeration? Your pastor may be able to explain how some scholars miss the point of Jesus' exaggeration and try to "explain" the needle. Again, who among Jesus' hearers would *not* appreciate the story?

g. **Matthew 18:21-35—"Pay Up!"**
How could this be an old-fashioned "meller-drama"?

3. Circulate around the groups to see if any need help. Some will because so many are unaccustomed to this way of looking at the scriptures.

4. After 30-45 minutes, call the groups back together. Give each

group 3-4 minutes to read the passage to everyone and to present its findings, including any creative interpretations. If a group has had trouble finding any humor in the passage, ask the others to see if they can help. Also let the larger group ask questions.

SATURDAY AFTERNOON SESSION

1. Call the group together and outline what happens next. Tell them they will soon divide into groups about twice the size of those of the morning. They will choose one of the passages of scripture listed on the newsprint, discuss it and plan a skit or other creative interpretation based on the passage. This will be shared with the rest of the participants as part of the creative worship service on Sunday. Be sure everyone has a Bible and pencil and paper.

2. As examples of creativity:

a. Play the "Noah" skit by Bill Cosby.

b. Have your four volunteers read the Arnie Klunker skit based on the story of The Pharisee and the Tax Collector (from chapter six of **Television: A Guide For Christians**).

3. Dismiss the groups, instructing them to choose a discussion leader. (A quick method of choosing: whoever has a birthday closest to April Fools Day.) Circulate to see how the groups are faring and offer suggestions if any are bogged down.

4. The passages to be assigned:

a. **Genesis 3—"Passing the Buck."**

How must the pair have appeared to God, cowering in the bushes and trying to hide their nakedness? Could either accept responsibility for the act? How is verse 20 a touch of grace, a sign that this story with tragic elements is basically a comedy?

b. **Genesis 18:1-15 and 21:1-7—"The Birth of Laughter."**

Why does Sarah laugh? How would similar news be received at your local senior citizens center?

c. **Genesis 25:19-26—"The Birth of the Grabber."**

Picture the scene inside the womb. Do you think the Hebrew storyteller took this literally? Or, was he trying to make a point about the kind of person Jacob was "right from the start"?

d. **Genesis 27—"Jacob, Momma's Boy and Cheat."**

This is a Bible hero? How does the story illustrate God's grace?

e. **Genesis 28—"Jacob, the Bargainer With God."**

Does his prayer sound familiar? How do we put strings on our piety and obedience? What is his view of God?

f. **Genesis 29:1-30—"Jacob, the Fall Guy."**

Why did the storyteller recite this story with great glee? How do Jacob and Laban "deserve" each other? What finally happens to Jacob? Does he change?

g. **The Book of Jonah—"Jonah the Prophet, Good Ol' Lovable Jonah."**

What is Jonah's attitude toward Ninevah? Why? What does his fleeing tell of his view of God? What is the real message of Jonah?

SATURDAY EVENING SESSION

1. Allow some time for the groups to work on their creative projects.

2. Call them together to watch "Oh God!" Questions for discussion after the film:

a. Was John Denver a likely candidate for a prophet? Why or why not? How is his reaction similar to Moses' or Jeremiah's call? See Exodus 3 and 4; Jeremiah 1:4-10.

b. How is Mary's Magnificat (Luke 1:46-55) similar to what happened to John and the panel of theologians, and to his encounter with the "evangelist"?

c. John has trouble accepting God on God's terms. How do we often expect him to "look" or act like we think or want? In what ways did God surprise the people of the Old and New Testament times? (e.g., where did the wise men go first to find the newborn King?)

d. The prophets and ultimately the King of Prophets, Jesus, learned that when God calls us there is a cross involved. (See Matthew 10:38 and 16:24.) What is John's "cross" in the film? How is this similar to Matthew 5:10-16?

e. How did the scene in the judge's chambers show that the filmmakers understood the biblical concept of "faith"? Is faith something that can be proven and thus captured on audio or videotape? (Note: the Crucifixion was witnessed by believers and nonbelievers, but what about the Resurrection?) To whom did Jesus appear? List them. Are any of his enemies in that list? Why not?

f. " 'Oh God!' is a biblical film but not a Christian one." React to that statement. Why is it not a Christian film? What is the view of God that is taught? How does this film help us to understand our faith better?

SUNDAY MORNING SESSION

1. "Sunday school" consists of listening to brief excerpts from "Jesus Christ: Superstar" and "Godspell." As time permits, play a few songs from each, being sure to include the very last cuts from each album.

a. Compare the two endings. Which rock opera is a tragedy and which a comedy? How do the endings bear this out?

b. Read 1 Corinthians 1:18-25. Why is the cross "folly" to most people, including Judas in "Superstar"? (See the title song.) What is it that made "the foolishness of God" wiser than men? How does the

Resurrection make that awful Friday *"Good Friday"*?

2. Present an informal worship service. See the one at the end of chapter six of **Television: A Guide For Christians** for one possible liturgy using comedy. Arrange the scripture-based skits in biblical order. Use the actual Bible passage for the scripture lessons. Some possible songs: "Lord of the Dance," "Joyful, Joyful We Adore Thee," and other lively music. See Norman Habel's excellent book **Interrobang** for some delightfully suitable litanies and prayers. Whatever form you come up with or songs you choose, the element of Resurrection, of our being able to thumb our nose at sin and death because of the good news of Christ should definitely come through, enabling us indeed to laugh last, and thus best.

RESOURCES

FILMS

- "Oh God!"—available on videotape from your local videotape dealer.
- "Oh God!" is also available in 16mm film format from Swank Films. They have several regional offices. The headquarters is: 201 S. Jefferson Ave., St. Louis, MO 63103.

BOOKS

- **Television: A Guide For Christians** is available from Visual Parables, c/o First Presbyterian Church, 49 S. Portage St., Westfield, NY 14787. This book could be the basis for some exciting experiences with TV and the gospel. Ask for bulk rate prices (more than five).

OTHER BOOKS FOR THE LEADER

- **The Feast of Fools**, by Harvey Cox, Harvard University Press.
- **The Mad Morality**, or the **Ten Commandments Revisited**, by Vernard Eller, Abingdon Press.
- **God, Man and Archie Bunker**, by Spencer March, available from: Resource Ministries, 3027 S.W. Turner Rd., West Linn, OR 97068.
- **The Gospel According to Peanuts**, by Robert Short, John Knox Press.
- **For God's Sake, Laugh!**, by Melvin Vos, John Knox Press.

CONTRIBUTORS

Bill Ameiss
Gwyn Baker
Ruby Becher
J. Brent Bill
Jerry Christensen
John D. Cooke
Dean Dammann
Tony Danhelka
Mary Jo Davidson
Jack Doorlag
Mike Eastman
James Elsner
Joe Fowler
Peggy Frey
Foch Fuller
Bob Good
Jan Hancock
Kent Hummel
Tim Johnson
Doug Karl
Larry Keefauver
Paula Keeton
Mark Lawrence
Renee Lofgren
Edward McNulty

Deb Mechler
Walter Mees, Jr.
Catherine Mumaw
Virgil Nelson
Brian Newcombe
Bruce Nichols
Susan Norman
David Olshine
Keith Olson
Jim Reeves
James Rhiver
Gary Richardson
Thom Schultz
Galen Schwarz
John Shaw
Rickey Short
Ben Sharpton
Betsy Sharpton
Charles Stewart
Wesley Taylor
Denise Turner
Marilyn Voran
David Wiebe
Bill Wolfe
Frank Zolvinski

Other Youth Ministry Resources From GROUP Magazine and Group Books:

GROUP MAGAZINE

The most complete youth ministry leadership periodical. Each issue features practical ideas, youth ministry philosophy, ministry management tips and personal growth and enrichment. $18.50 per year (8 issues).

GROUP BOOKS

HARD TIMES CATALOG FOR YOUTH MINISTRY, by Marilyn and Dennis Benson. Hundreds of low-cost and no-cost ideas for programs, projects, meetings and activities. $14.95.

THE BASIC ENCYCLOPEDIA FOR YOUTH MINISTRY, by Dennis Benson and Bill Wolfe. Answers, ideas, encouragement, and inspiration for 230 youth ministry questions and problems. A handy reference. Hardbound. $15.95.

THE YOUTH GROUP HOW-TO BOOK. Detailed instructions and models for 66 practical projects and programs to help you build a better group. $14.95.

COUNSELING TEENAGERS, by Dr. G. Keith Olson. The authoritative, complete and practical reference for understanding and helping today's adolescents. $19.95.

THE YOUTH GROUP MEETING GUIDE, by Richard W. Bimler. This resource provides years of inspiration, ideas and programs for the most common youth group activity—the meeting. $11.95.

THE BEST OF TRY THIS ONE. A fun collection of games, crowd breakers and programs from GROUP Magazine's "Try This One" section. $5.95.

MORE . . . TRY THIS ONE. A bonanza of youth group ideas—crowd breakers, stunts, games, discussions and fund raisers. $5.95.

TRY THIS ONE . . . TOO. The newest in this popular series. Scores of creative youth ministry ideas. $5.95.

Available at Christian bookstores or directly from the publisher: Orders Dept., Group Books, P.O. Box 481, Loveland, CO 80539. Enclose $2 for postage and handling with each order from the publisher.

RETREAT RECORDS
(Use these pages for retreat notes, evaluation, record-keeping, etc.)

RETREAT RECORDS

RETREAT RECORDS

RETREAT RECORDS

RETREAT RECORDS

RETREAT RECORDS

RETREAT RECORDS

RETREAT RECORDS

70612

RETREAT RECORDS